THE CENTENNIAL YEARS

OTHER BOOKS BY FRED A. SHANNON

The Organization and Administration of the Union Army, 1861–1865

The Farmer's Last Frontier: Agriculture, 1860–1897

American Farmers' Movements

America's Economic Growth

THE
CENTENNIAL
YEARS

A Political and Economic History of
America from the Late 1870s
to the Early 1890s
by

FRED A. SHANNON

edited by

ROBERT HUHN JONES

☆

Garden City, New York
DOUBLEDAY & COMPANY, INC.
1967

Library of Congress Catalog Card Number 67–12857

First Edition

PICTURE CREDITS

1. From *Harper's Weekly*, Aug. 11, 1877
2. From *Harper's Weekly*, Aug. 11, 1877
3. From *Harper's Weekly*, July 12, 1884
4. By permission of Marvin W. Schlegel and the Archives Publishing Company of Pennsylvania, Yardley, Pennsylvania
5. From *The Pinkertons* by Richard Wilmer Rowan
6. From *Harper's Weekly*, July 1, 1876
7. From *Harper's Weekly*, July 1, 1876
8. From *Harper's Weekly*, July 15, 1876
9. From *Harper's Weekly*, July 15, 1876
11. From *Harper's Weekly*, July 17, 1880
12. From *Harper's Weekly*, July 10, 1880
15. From *Harper's Weekly*, June 14, 1884
16. From *Harper's Weekly*, Aug. 2, 1884
17. From *Harper's Weekly*, June 14, 1884
18. From *Harper's Weekly*, June 30, 1888
20. From *Harper's Weekly*, July 19, 1884
21. From *Harper's Weekly*, June 23, 1888
22. From *Harper's Weekly*, Jan. 20, 1877
23. From *Harper's Weekly*, Jan. 20, 1877
30. By permission of Malcolm S. Forbes and the Forbes Magazine Company
46. From *Harper's Weekly*, April 10, 1886
49. From *Frank Leslie's Illustrated Newspaper*, May 15, 1886
50. From *Frank Leslie's Illustrated Newspaper*, July 31, 1886
51. From *Harper's Weekly*, Oct. 23, 1886
52. From H. W. Schotter, *Growth and Development of the Pennsylvania Railroad Company;* Allen, Lane and Scott, 1927
53. From *Frank Leslie's Illustrated Newspaper*, May 15, 1886
54. From *Frank Leslie's Illustrated Newspaper*

PREFACE

THIS is Professor Fred A. Shannon's book, and since it would not be proper to dedicate his own work to him, it was decided to establish, with the proceeds of this volume, a scholarship in American history for graduate students at the University of Illinois. The publication of this work and the establishment of the scholarship has been undertaken on behalf of the graduate students whose Ph.D. was supervised by Shannon, in order that they may leave tangible evidence of their gratitude and friendship for the "old man."

Students chose to work with Professor Shannon, sometimes with trepidation, because they knew that if they could survive his biting criticisms and penetrating scholastic demands they would emerge better scholars and men for the experience. Nearly all who chose to do so found that underneath a crusty outer shell there dwelt a very warm and friendly man who took genuine interest in their intellectual development. Professor Frederick W. Kohlmeyer, formerly editor of *Agricultural History*, said of Shannon's approach to life: "[He] possessed . . . a sense of wit, an earthy sense of humor, and a keen intelligence. He relished controversy; . . . he was convinced that nothing would do more to stimulate historical scholarship than a good academic fracas. . . ."[1] And many a "fracas" he had. Friendly ones, such as the running series of good-natured insults that enlivened his meetings with the late Professor William B. Hesseltine of Wisconsin, and others, not so friendly, such as that with the late Professor Walter P. Webb of Texas.

Shannon was born on Lincoln's birthday, 1893, at Sedalia, Missouri, the son of Scotch-Irish frontier farmers. His father, a young tenant farmer when Fred was born, had been a miner, sawyer, section hand on the railroad, and had learned telegraphy. In August, 1893, the Shannons moved to Clay City, Indiana, seeking better fortunes. But in the depression years of the 1890s life proved anything but happy for the family, which found it a desperate struggle merely to survive. Young Fred grew up in a hard and shabby environment that left him with few childish illusions. "He once said, retrospective of the ways of small rural towns, that if . . . God made the country and man the city, then the devil made the small town, and the devil took pains to fashion the job perfectly."[2]

When the family moved to Memphis, Tennessee, in 1903, his father obtained employment in a sawmill, where young Fred worked—for five cents an hour! He watched a workman disemboweled by a spinning saw, and learned that the widow received no compensation from the firm. In 1905 the family returned to Indiana, residing at Brazil, where Fred continued his education both in the schoolroom and in life. He worked at many part-time jobs: on nearby farms, at a bakery, and in a canning factory, where, at fourteen, he earned ten cents an hour. Earnings from a paper route saw him through high school. Upon graduation in 1910 he worked in a glass factory and later on a dry farm in Kansas. In the fall of 1910 he entered Indiana State Teachers College, and upon graduation became an elementary-school teacher. At about the same time he married Edna May Jones. Thereafter, he became a high-school principal, and then, in 1919, equipped with an M.A. from Indiana University, he "became the history department" of tiny Iowa Wesleyan College.

While at Iowa Wesleyan, he worked on his Ph.D. under the late Arthur Schlesinger at the University of Iowa, receiving that degree in 1924. Not far apart in age, Schlesinger and his pupil became good friends. Shannon's experience at Iowa Wesleyan greatly broadened his knowledge of history, because, as he once remarked, he had to read widely in order to teach ancient, medieval, European, and American history. He went to Iowa State Teachers College in 1924 as Assistant Professor of History. In 1926 Shannon accepted appointment to the history faculty of Kansas State College. While there, he published his monumental doctoral dissertation, the two-volume *The Organization and Administration of the Union Army, 1861–1865* (Cleveland: The Arthur H. Clark Co., 1928), for which he won the Justin Winsor Prize, and, a year later, the Pulitzer Prize in history. The first edition of his American economic history text, now called *America's Economic Growth*, and published by Macmillan, appeared in 1934.

In 1939 Shannon went to Williams College as Visiting Professor of Economic History, and the next year to the University of Illinois, where he remained until he retired in 1961. He loved to spend his summers teaching on other campuses, often making a vacation of it for his family. Columbia, Cornell, Harvard, Missouri, Ohio State, Stanford, West Virginia, and Wisconsin all provided this kind of opportunity for him. While at Illinois in 1940, the Social Science Research Council devoted its *Bulletin* No. 46 to Shannon's *An Appraisal of Walter Prescott Webb's The Great Plains*, which was described by some as "an assault on" Webb's work. It was a painstaking dissection, in accurate but none too gentle terms, that led to verbal battles between them. Shannon once observed that he was paid for the critique, and gave the S.S.R.C. its money's worth. If he violently disagreed with Webb, he never fostered the impression that he thought ill of him as a man or as a teacher.

In 1945 Shannon published *The Farmer's Last Frontier: Agriculture, 1860–1897*, as volume five of the Rinehart Economic History of the United States, certainly an outstanding volume in a generally good series. This book reflected Shannon's abiding interest in and firsthand knowledge of American agriculture. Two journal articles, "The Homestead Act and the Labor Surplus" (*American Historical Review*, LXI, 1936) and "A Post-Mortem on the Labor Safety-Valve Theory" (*Agricultural History*, XIX, 1945), helped to bury the notion that the frontier or the farm served to absorb discontented urban laborers. In another small book, which this writer helped to put together, called *American Farmers' Movements* (Princeton, New Jersey: D. Van Nostrand Company, 1957) Shannon included the American Indians as American farmers. His interest in the Civil War did not wane, however, for in 1947 he had published *The Civil War Letters of Sergeant Onley Andruss* (Urbana: University of Illinois Press, 1947).

The death of his wife, almost exactly ten years before his own, was a very real shock to him. In visits to his home in Urbana, where he lived alone, did his own cooking, washing, and cleaning, one often felt that Mrs. Shannon was present in spirit. Conversation nearly always turned back to her, even at dinners he gave for his graduate students. In 1955, while returning from a visit with relatives in California, as he told it, his auto struck a mountain goat and he struck the steering wheel. He emerged with a set of beautiful black eyes coincident with the opening of the fall semester. It was not long before he apparently suffered a series of minor strokes, which left him partially paralyzed. At first, he insisted on meeting his classes and rejected the idea of hospitalization. He was proud of his illness-free record, and remarked: "If I should fall down in class, just prop me up and I will continue." With the aid of Professor Frederick C. Dietz and other members of the history department, and with the prodding of his son, Fred, a physician in Wickenburg, Arizona, Shannon was grudgingly hospitalized. To aid in his recovery, he went to the warm climate of Arizona and spent the remainder of the year there. Although he was not supposed to work, he kept his assistants busy (by long distance) researching and checking out this present volume. Apparently a large portion of it was composed at that time.

In 1956 he returned to his office in Lincoln Hall, continued to work on this manuscript, and began on another. He told Professor Dietz that his illness had been a good thing, "because it warned him that he must really get down to work to finish what he needed to." He had in mind a history of American agriculture, and subsequently work on the present volume languished, a contract was mutually terminated, and he threw himself into his new venture. Frequently he worked until dawn, sometimes flat on his back on the cot in his study, much to the chagrin of his assistants, who found it most difficult to decipher the scrawled instructions he wrote to them in that position. He would catch a few hours' sleep, and return to the campus for his customary nine o'clock class.

His retirement in 1961 neither slowed his work nor ended
his teaching. When stricken with his fatal illness he was visiting professor at the University of South Carolina, and had
contracted for the same work at Texas the following semester,
where, interestingly enough, he would have joined his old
antagonist, Webb, who once had remarked that "if anybody
ever sets up a Pulitzer Prize for criticism, [Shannon] will
have a good claim to several *ex post facto* awards."[3] Those
whose books had been critically reviewed by Shannon, or
who had suffered from his barbs at historical-society meetings, could sympathize with Webb.

Basically, Shannon appeared to be an unreconstructed
Populist, a fact explained, perhaps, by the circumstances of
his youth. His attitudes toward farmers, businessmen, and
public officials, in short his philosophy of life, certainly suggests the connection. He felt that his early association with
the raw side of life was decidedly advantageous, and he was
especially sympathetic to those students who had grown up
in middle-class urban environments and who he believed
knew little of life as it really was. Hence he seldom missed
an opportunity, in story or anecdote, to acquaint them with
the facts of life. In a graveside ceremony, Professor Dietz
said that Shannon's "greatness lies in his goodness as a man.
He loathed oppression and stupidity with an angry hatred
and he had the fiery courage to cry out against it wherever
he found it, whether it was the unfeeling cruelty of the lords
of the world in dropping the atom bomb on Hiroshima or
the silly regulation of an overbearing bureaucrat which in-
terfered with his getting from the library a book which he
needed in his work."[4]

Early in 1952, asked to take part in a discussion concerning
the "Contributions of History and the Social Sciences to the
Curriculum in American Civilization," he began with these
words:

> To a hard-bitten old historian, who once taught in a
> department of economics, who in a varied career has
> taught government and geography, who once sat
> through a course in philosophy and two or three in
> psychology, and who has observed the antics of the

sociologists from the sidelines, it is nothing short of amazing that anybody should ever ask what can be the contributions of history and social sciences to a course in
American civilization. The only answer that he can give
is that, obviously, they must be the core of the whole
piece of fruit, the leaven of the lump, or the meat and
pepper in the salmagundi. Let others furnish the pickled
herring, oil, vinegar, and onions.[5]

After denouncing elementary- and high-school education because nobody thought of American civilization as a course
until these schools "fell under the control of zealots dedicated
to the idea that the public schools flourish for the sole purpose
of giving children practical instruction in brushing their teeth
. . . doing folk dances, supporting the parent teacher association, giving pupils gold stars . . . and perhaps just incidentally giving them a semester's course in general science
and another in the social studies," he continued, declaring
that under the circumstances, the place for a course in
American civilization would be the college student's first
semester. Such a course would not include as much history,
economics, geography, and political science as he would like,
"but it could easily contain far more of each than . . . the
brain of a freshman ordinarily contains."

Such a course would also act as a preparatory course for
students in the liberal arts, and as a useful survey course for
students in engineering, home economics, and the like. In an
earlier day, college students wouldn't have needed to study
American civilization, whatever their deficiencies in their
basic precollege education, because, he said, they would have
had a "fair chance to familiarize themselves with those subjects." However, this was before colleges required students
to take physical education, R.O.T.C. or other military drill, or
courses in rhetoric (or mathematics) that were primarily
remedial in nature. "It was before anybody ever dreamed
that the time would come when a person could get a Ph.D.
in physical education or home economics," and as a result,
"liberal education is being crowded off the boards in colleges
as well as in preparatory schools." So, Shannon concluded, he

had to take a stand for American civilization "before the offer of even that much is snatched away."

In arriving at a definition of civilization, Shannon agreed with one proposed by the cartoonist ["the eminent anthropologist"] V. T. Hamlin, whose creature "the poet laureate Foozy of ancient Moo" put it this way: "'Bout all that amounts to, as I can see / Is th' herd instinct developed to a high degree!'" Or, Shannon continued, "civilization is what any people at any time call by that name when describing their own cultural attainment." Choosing examples from history, and openly admitting taking them to fit his thesis, he stated that "civilization is the power to destroy, and that nation is the most civilized which can carry on the work of destruction with the most effectiveness. Today the outstanding contenders for supremacy are the U.S. and the U.S.S.R. A few years hence the aspirants for the heavyweight title may well be the termites and the buzzards." Evidence for this point of view Shannon found in the popular conception "that great nations are the ones capable of conquering weaker ones." Again, he used examples from history to support his thesis, concluding, "For centuries Switzerland has been a peaceable, neutral, relatively prosperous and highly cultured aggregation of contented peoples, but it has no standing at all as a world *power*. Hence, it scarcely figures at all in any discussion of civilization."

Shannon next made a case for the synonymous use of the terms civilization and power, which naturally led to the use of war as a contribution to civilization. He admitted that "if incessant warfare alone is to be considered the mark of civilization, then we would have to grant that savages have probably been more civilized than the great powers," which would be "damaging to the national ego." They betrayed their low cultural status, however, by being exceedingly efficient in their warfare, holding human life "as cheaply as the peoples of any great power today, but they were satisfied with the destruction of life alone." Civilized nations learned to use their "intelligence and ingenuity to devise new and more expensive ways to extinguish this life in warfare." They proceeded to destroy not only the fighting man's life, but nations as well, thus raising the costs of war astronomically. In so doing, civilized nations stimulated industry, kept unemployment at a minimum, and boosted their economy. "But suppose that, in spite of all efforts to keep peace from breaking out, the calamity should befall." No problem, really. Enact universal military training, continue preparing for war, thus keeping the factories running, the labor surplus absorbed, and the people undersupplied just enough to make them belligerent! With luck, war would return. Since the soldiers had been trained to fight the last previous war, and the military supplies were those that proved most efficient in the last war, when the next war comes it means the retraining of the army and the scrapping of stores as obsolete, which will be all to the good, "for it will double or more than double the cost of the new war and therefore create doubled prosperity."

Shannon admitted that much of his discussion of civilization had been pointed toward conclusions that he did not necessarily hold, but it did represent "what seems to be the most popular judgment on the matter" and therefore worthy of attention. It appeared as if this side of civilization was so distasteful and inhuman that Shannon hoped those who heard him would consider its implications and weigh carefully their own reactions to the world they lived in lest they make the civilization of their generation a part of the cynical round he visualized for them. Education, he implied, in a course of American civilization or in general, had some very serious business to attend to.

The questions of civilization and culture absorbed more than a little of Shannon's attention. His presidential address to the Mississippi Valley Historical Association in 1954 was entitled "Culture and Agriculture in America."[6] After discussing rural and urban culture, he went on to observe that "if there has been little culture among farmers, and perhaps no more among the plutocracy of the cities, maybe it is time to hint that a broad diffusion of culture throughout the population of the world or any of its areas has never existed." Although a great deal has been written of the culture of China and India, both ancient and modern, "nobody has

ever demonstrated that this culture was ever shared by more
than one person in a thousand, either in the city or the country." So poverty-stricken were the masses, so involved were
they with misery and famine, "that culture was not even a
thing they heard about." And so it has continued to the
present. Neither city nor countryside in America could claim
a monopoly on culture. "Maybe the *Arkansaw Traveler*,
played on a fiddle or a 'French harp' at a backwoods 'hoe-
down,' is not to be compared with a symphony orchestra
playing the Brahms *Rhapsody*, but the old-time fiddler was
at least on a par with the heavyweight 'ivory bender' pound-
ing out *Sally in My Alley* in a tenderloin honky-tonk." Not all
country music was confined to the fiddler or the "'hillbillies'
sounding their *A* by blowing . . . across the orifice of an
empty 'moonshine' jug. The tender care given the old parlor
organ by many a pioneer farmer's wife, in the long transit
over rough roads to a new home, is an indication of a yearn-
ing for music of some sort, even in the absence of proficiency."

In concluding this address, Shannon pointed to the disap-
pearing barriers between rural and urban areas in America,
which have blurred the lines of separate cultural development
of the areas, and the labor-saving devices that have increased
the leisure of both the farmer and the city laborer, which increase their chances for "cultural uplift." Shannon does not
say that these factors mean, or will mean, a greater diffusion
of culture today than at any time in the past. Although he
did not say so in his paper, he doubted that it did. But he
couldn't resist a stab at the urbanite who assumed that all
culture was urban. His address, he said, "was designed to
answer the assumptions of the urban elite who, assuring
themselves that any culture different from their own is not
deserving of the name, smugly inquire: 'Rural culture,' did
you say? Don't you mean 'agriculture'?"

Shannon's career would be incompletely noted if one
failed to observe that, alongside his teaching, writing, speaking, and other activities, he raised a family of four. Included
were his son Fred, whom he delivered at birth before a
doctor could arrive, and three daughters, Lucille, Mary, and

Marjory. A kind father, he was proud of his children and spoke of them often. In addition, he was something like a father to the fourteen young men he shepherded to the Ph.D. degree. He exercised an important influence on the lives of all of them, but that does not mean that all shared his philosophy of life, nor did he expect them to. Though exacting and painfully critical of his students' efforts, he would, after the final oral examination, smile at the nervous but successful candidate, extend his hand, offer his congratulations, and remark, "Doctor, you may call me Fred." Suddenly, it all seemed worthwhile. In addition to the Ph.D.'s (whose names, last known affiliations, and dissertation titles follow the Preface), many of whom have been active in scholarly publishing as Shannon hoped, there were the usual number of Masters candidates, graduate assistants, and other students who felt the Shannon touch at one time or another in his forty-three years of college teaching.

On behalf of all these persons, this volume is produced. Some of the chapters were distilled from as many as four separate Shannon drafts, others from only one rough draft. Occasionally it was necessary, for the sake of style, to delete material or relegate it to the footnotes, or to change the wording, but every attempt has been made to keep it Shannon's book in Shannon's style, and to preserve his organization and points of view throughout. As the title implies, it is intended as an economic and political history of America, spanning roughly the period from the Centennial of the Republic in 1876–77 to approximately the four hundredth anniversary of Columbus' voyage in 1892. The variance from this period is minor. Because it is an economic and political history, the reader will find very little diplomatic or social history in these pages.

Of the bibliography, Shannon acknowledged in an early draft that manuscripts were valuable for the composition of monographs in any field of history, but "the writer of a general treatise must be humble enough to admit that the printed record, at least for the late nineteenth century, is so complete that he need not delve into such a mine of information unless he wishes to show an excess of erudition. . . . In the follow-

ing up of obscure points, there was some use of newspapers"
which he cited in the footnotes but felt it unnecessary to
repeat in the bibliography. The editor has tampered somewhat with the bibliography in an attempt to bring it up to
date. On this score, the editor is indebted to Professors Roy
V. Scott and Harvey Wish, who were of material assistance.
Professors Roy A. Rauschenberg, Helen Reinhart, and Allen
M. Wakstein, along with Robert H. Jones, assisted in the
preparation of the original drafts back in the 1950s.

This edition could not have been produced without the
cooperation of the late Fred Shannon, M.D. (also a noted
herpetologist), who located his father's manuscript and encouraged its editing and publication, and two of Shannon's
daughters, Mrs. Mary Sommer of California, and Mrs. Marjory King of Urbana, who also gave their encouragement
and aid in untangling legal problems. The patience of Mrs.
Kay Scheuer, Doubleday editor, is hereby also recognized, as
is the time and talent of my wife, Estelle, who typed and
helped to proof the entire manuscript.

ROBERT HUHN JONES
Western Reserve University
April, 1966

o   o   o   o

Shannon's fourteen Ph.D.'s, their locations, and their dissertation topics follow. The variety of topics suggests the range
of Shannon's interest. In alphabetical order: Richard Bar-
dolph, head of the Department of History of the Woman's
College of the University of North Carolina, "Agriculture
Education in Illinois to 1870: The Press" (1944); James G.
Burrow, professor at Middle Tennessee State College, "The
Social Politics of the American Medical Association, 1900–
1954" (1956); Theodore L. Carlson, professor of economics
at Western Michigan University, "The History of Land Occupation, Utilization, and Tenure in the Illinois Military Tract
to 1900" (1947); Guy J. Gibson, professor at Wisconsin State
College, Stevens Point, "Lincoln and the Union League Movement" (1957); Robert H. Jones, professor at Western Reserve

University, "A History of the Military Department of the Northwest During the Civil War, 1862–1865" (1957); John B. McCann, deceased, "New Deal Farm Production Controls, 1933–36" (1950); Frederick A. Palmer, professor at American International University, "Westerners at Home: Comments of French and British Travelers on Life in the West, 1800–1840" (1949); David E. Robbins, chairman of the Social Studies Division at Roberts Wesleyan College, "The Congressional Career of William R. Morrison" (1962); Howard L. Scamehorn, professor at the University of Colorado, "The Formative Period of Aviation in Illinois, 1890–1919" (1956); Roy V. Scott, professor at Mississippi State University, "Agrarian Organizations in Illinois, 1880–1896" (1957); Elwin W. Sigmund, professor at Wisconsin State College, Stevens Point, "Federal Laws Concerning Railroad Labor Disputes: A Legislative and Legal History, 1877–1934" (1961); Robert A. Smith, professor at Mankato State College, "The Technologies and Working Conditions of Colonial Free Laborers" (1950); Marvin Wachman, president of Lincoln University, "The History of the Social-Democratic Party of Milwaukee, 1897–1910" (1942); and Allen M. Wakstein, professor at Boston College, "The Open Shop Movement, 1919–1933" (1961).

Contents

ILLUSTRATIONS

Republican Politicians: Roscoe Conkling, Shelby M. Cullom, Alonzo B. Cornell, John Sherman

Merchants of Note: Frank W. Woolworth, Marshall Field, John Wanamaker

Prominent Capitalists and Their Associates: W. H. Vanderbilt, Thomas A. Edison, Leland Stanford, Cyrus W. Field, Chauncey M. Depew, William B. Allison

Labor Leaders: Terrence V. Powderly, Uriah S. Stephens, Peter J. McGuire, Samuel Gompers

Strike Leaders: Joseph R. Buchanan, Peter M. Arthur, Frank P. Sargent, Martin Irons

Railroad Presidents: Jay Gould, Charles E. Perkins

[FOLLOWING PAGE 242]

Artist's Conception of the Haymarket Bombing

The Anarchist Trials: Chicago's New Rogue's Gallery System for Identification of Criminals

Advocates of Violence in Labor Disputes: Theodore Roosevelt, Thomas A. Scott

The Less Fortunate: Execution of the Men Convicted in the Haymarket Bombing

The Chicago Anarchist-Labor Troubles: The Week Following May 3, 1886

The Condemned Chicago Anarchists: Samuel Fielden, Michael Schwab, August Spies, Adolph Fischer, George Engel, Oscar Neebe, Louis Lingg, Albert R. Parsons

Their Executioners: Judge Joseph E. Gary, John Bonfield

THE CENTENNIAL YEARS

Chapter I

THE NATION'S CENTENNIAL

THE year 1877 marked the beginning or the ending of no spectacularly important event in American history. The inauguration of Rutherford B. Hayes as President gave disgruntled Democrats a chance to jeer about the man who was "serving Samuel J. Tilden's term," and the ensuing administration added to the earlier bitterness between Republican factions. But before the century closed both the President and his administration were becoming difficult to remember. The Forty-fifth Congress, convening in the same year, would be virtually unidentifiable except for the Bland-Allison Silver Purchase Act of 1878, which solved no problem and satisfied nobody. Tumultuous strikes on the railroads called attention to the relatively ineffective organization of labor at a time when business strode rapidly toward consolidation, but the strikes contributed little to the growth of labor unionism. The Granger decisions maintained the doctrine of state supremacy in an era when that assurance was already slipping, for within a dozen years the court effectually reversed itself. The removal of military protection from the carpetbag governments of the last two reconstructed states represented merely the last clod on the grave of an earlier promise to make the freedmen of the South the political and civil equals of their former masters. This delayed afterthought, called the "end of Reconstruction," has arbitrarily caused the year 1877 to be frequently selected as a division point between American epochs. For most practical purposes even Reconstruction had suffered defeat before that date, whereas the process of making white supremacy unassailable was to continue for many years afterward.

In 1877, however, the American people had some reason to be feeling exuberant. The Republic had just completed its first century of independence, thus disproving any suppositions that the new experiment could not endure. Though the issue had sometimes been in doubt, the country had survived even a huge civil war and now it showed that it could not be redivided by a "stolen election." The first century ended in 1876 with a world's fair at Philadelphia called the Centennial Exhibition. Fair visitors learned of the material, artistic, and cultural advance not only of the United States but, through the exhibits of many foreign countries, of much of the world. As the second century of the Republic dawned, Americans were in a better position than usual to take stock of their own advance against the background of global developments. And, as the depression of the seventies ended, Americans looked ahead with confidence.

In 1890 the country entered the first year of the second century of its experience with the federal Constitution. On April 25, 1890, President Benjamin Harrison approved an act of Congress "to provide for celebrating the four hundredth anniversary of the discovery of America by Christopher Columbus, by holding an international exhibition of arts, industries, manufactures, and the products of the soil, mine, and sea in the City of Chicago, in the State of Illinois."[1] This act launched the World's Columbian Exposition of 1893, which focused attention on the changes wrought by a century. But national progress since the Centennial Exposition was striking in itself.

A sufficiently exercised imagination might draw a seemingly close parallel between the several problems of the early Republic and those of a century later. Whether or not any similarity in public issues was authentic or factitious, it is certain that the United States of the 1880s differed so from the same country of the 1780s that any extended analogy of the two eras breaks down. The nation's area had multiplied by three and a half and the population by sixteen. The states north of the Ohio River by 1890 experienced the most amazing numerical growth, with over a fifth of the nation's 63,000,-000 inhabitants living on not quite a twelfth of the country's total area. Two-fifths of the people lived on one-seventh of the American land area in the Atlantic states. The four groups of Central states had 46 per cent of the total area but 54 per cent of the people. New England, with the smallest area of any of the sections, had, next to the Pacific and Mountain states, also the least population, about a fourteenth of the total.[2] In 1880 the median point of population was about sixteen miles west of Springfield, Ohio, and it did not cross the line into Indiana until some twenty years later. The theoretical *center* of population in 1890 was near Columbus, Indiana.[3]

Perceptive observers noticed that the rate of population growth began to slacken. Between 1790 and 1860 the numbers had almost exactly doubled every twenty-three years. In fact, the same rate seems to have prevailed, at least approximately, ever since 1650.[4] But it took thirty years for the figure of 1860 to double, and it was not until 1934 that there was another repetition.[5] It was also clear that there was a growing tendency for an increasingly large portion of the population to reach a mature age. Probably because of a high rate of infant mortality, the median age of white males in 1790 was 15.9 years, but a century later it was 22.9. At most counts the median age of males ran slightly above that of females and the age of whites above that of colored peoples.[6] Another indication of a greater maturity of age in the population was the continuing growth of life expectancy at birth. This was 35 years in 1789 and 44 in 1890. The greatest saving of life occurred before the age of twenty, and the life expectation of fifteen years after sixty was in 1890 about the same as in 1789 or in 1945. While more people, year by year, were growing to maturity, to middle age, and to old age, the extreme of old age remained about stationary.[7]

Through the decades the population had also been getting paler. By the first census nearly a fifth of the people belonged to other races than white, Negroes accounting for all but a very few. The eleventh census showed that the colored portion had diminished to an eighth, again mostly Negroes. Nine-tenths of the Negroes in 1890 were in the Southern states, as they had been for a century. A quarter of a million Indians, a little over 100,000 Chinese, and some 2000 Japanese comprised nearly all of the others.[8]

From 1870 to 1890 one person in seven was of foreign birth. The ratio had been slightly higher in 1860 and it was not to become noticeably lower until after 1920.[9] These aliens were fairly well distributed over the country except for the South. In the other sections they averaged about a quarter of the total population in 1890; another quarter were native white people of foreign parentage; and only half were Americans of the third generation or longer. On the other hand, in North Carolina only one person in 435 was an immigrant and one in 222 was native born of immigrant parents.[10]

In 1880 nearly 93 per cent of the foreign-born population were from northwestern Europe, from Germany, and from Canada. Nearly 2,000,000 of the 6,680,000 total came from Germany alone, and almost an equal number were from Ireland, while Canada was not far behind, and those from the Scandinavian countries approached 500,000. But an increase in entries from central, southern, and eastern Europe was becoming noticeable, though the total immigrant population from those areas was as yet only 4.2 per cent of the numbers from all sources. Then, in 1890, regardless of an increase of nearly 2,000,000 Germans, Scandinavians, British, and Canadians, the central, southern, and eastern European element more than doubled its ratio among the 9,249,560 foreign-born residents in America.[11] This trend was to grow.

Although the immigrants of the new type came from countries where educational opportunities for the common man were almost nonexistent, America continued to gain in its fight against illiteracy. Low educational attainments in the South, and particularly among the freedmen, adversely affected the national picture. Illiteracy among all people ten years or more of age was 16.97 per cent in 1880 and 13.34 per cent in 1890. The rates in terms of per cent for native whites in the same years were 8.75 and 6.23, among foreign-born whites 12 and 13, and among colored peoples 70 and 56.76. As far as comparison can be made, the native-white rate in the United States ranked favorably with the declarations for the advanced countries of western Europe.[12]

The greatest gains were among the Negroes, but the new

immigrant problem gave cause for anxiety. The American schools would have to redouble their efforts if they were to abolish illiteracy except for the feeble-minded. Even among native whites the opportunity for improvement was patent, especially in the South where the educational revival of the 1830s had made only slight headway. Whereas, in 1870, over three-quarters of children of school age in the North were enrolled in the public schools, in the South the fraction was less than a third. The Southern figure virtually doubled in the next score of years and reached a point not far below the average for the nation. But in 1890 the average school year in the South was only about 90 days as compared with 134 days for the country at large, including the South. Expenditures for schools and wages of teachers in the South were correspondingly low.[13]

A part of the spirit of the times is shown in the substantial effort to improve schools and bring education to more people. In the entire United States in 1870 the number of children of ages five to seventeen enrolled in the public schools was 57 per cent of all. In 1880 the figure was 65.5 per cent and in 1890 it was 68.6 per cent.[14] Another striking feature was the growth of public high-school enrollments and the relative decline of private academies in the work of secondary education. Between 1876 and 1890 the enrollment in public high schools grew from 23,000 to 203,000 while that in private institutions increased only from 74,000 to 95,000. The greater achievements were to come in the next two or three decades, before the watering down of the curriculums began to negate the importance of numerical growth.[15]

A significant phase of the educational revival was the increasing attention paid to teacher training. The normal school, taking its name from the French *école normale,* achieved prominence through the pioneer work of James Gordon Carter (1795–1849). Normal schools controlled by the states and by many counties and municipalities became rather common in the 1870s, and many others were private. Often, the distinction between a private normal school and an academy was very hazy. By 1890 there were 135 public normal schools with nearly 27,000 students and 43 private ones with about 8000 total enrollment. But reclassification in 1893–94 multiplied the private schools to 238, with 28,000 students.[16]

All these figures represent earnest effort more than solid achievement. Many of the students on enrollment had little more than an elementary-school education and some had less than that. Furthermore, a good share of the students were simply taking the opportunity of attending a school close at hand, with no serious intention of becoming teachers. Also, many of the normal schools were county or local affairs with no assurance of permanence to guarantee substantial achievement. In general their purpose was to teach a trade and to elevate teaching above the primitive level of pupils reciting back to the teachers lessons memorized from a textbook, the teacher keeping just a jump ahead of the pupils. Prospective teachers received intensive training in the subject matter they were later to present to their own classes, with special stress on teaching methods.

Teachers colleges began to appear in the 1880s, the one associated with Columbia University being in full swing by 1888. Periodical teachers institutes also achieved prominence. Local institutes were often valuable study centers, but the state institutes were too often burdened with a depressing amount of "inspirational" lectures of the claptrap variety later to be associated with the names of Elbert Hubbard and Russell Conwell. But even the worst of the offerings were no doubt of some value to teachers, many of whom had not progressed in their own education beyond the equivalent of the eighth year in the graded schools.[17] The licensing of teachers for some years yet to come was still largely subject to the whim of the county superintendent, who himself might or might not be a grade-school graduate.

The business interests of the country also had a stake in the expansion of education, particularly at the high-school level. If the schools would take over the training of young people in commercial and business courses, business itself could procure typists, accountants, draftsmen, commercial artists, and other specialized personnel prepared for their work at public expense and at a great saving to employers.

Some American educationists, as exemplified in the National Education Association, joined in a cordial understanding with business by injecting utilitarian subjects into the curriculums, and also by indoctrinating students with the economic theory of *laissez faire*. Prominent educationists backed the magnates of business and industry in their battles against agrarian and industrial unrest in the 1870s and 1880s. Speakers before the N.E.A. repeatedly assailed the methods used by various groups seeking redress of grievances and advocating social reforms, the Populists being an especial target, the Pullman strike of 1894 another. The superintendent of schools of New Bedford, Massachusetts, said in 1877 that "the born leaders from among the poor, if they be not tempered by culture, become the ignorant demagogues whose leadership is anarchy," and in 1885 a delegate from New Orleans told the N.E.A. that "the high school education detects and exposes the fallacies of socialism; the poor learn that they have an interest in respecting the property of the rich. . . ."[18] It may be doubted that such arguments added any real strength to the secondary-school movement, and there is no convincing evidence that the bulk of the American people concerned themselves greatly about the relatively unobtrusive movements in education.

Similarly, it seems doubtful that most Americans were excited about what was going on in the churches, where really significant changes were under way. In 1890 just about an even third of the 63,000,000 people belonged to or were claimed as communicants of the more than 140 religious organizations. Two out of each three members were Protestants, and most of the rest were Catholics, Jews being relatively few outside the greater urban centers. But the figures of communicants are not very important. Jews counted only heads of families, Catholics included all adherents whether active or not, while many Protestant bodies listed only persons who had formally joined the church. Millions of Americans had some more or less vague preference for a particular religious faith, or at least a half-formed notion about heaven and hell, but were willing to take their chances.[19]

The prevalence of healthy sectarianism resulted in far more

denominations than there were easily distinguishable divisive doctrines. For example, there were seventeen different brands of Methodists, thirteen of Baptists, and twelve of Presbyterians. H. K. Carroll, the census analyst, remembered the difference between two branches of the Reformed Presbyterians by noting that the official publication of one had a pink cover while that of the other had a blue cover. Classifying three of the Baptist organizations as "regular," he observed that the old designations of verbs might appropriately be used in describing the Baptist splinter groups as "Regular, Irregular, Redundant, and Defective." The old Plymouth Brethren, rejecting the place name in their title, divided into groups known as Brethren I, II, III, and IV,[20] and in later years added a V and VI. But some of the excessive splitting was based on language and place of origin of the adherents. For example, there were Danish, Norwegian, Swedish, German, and English Lutherans with little if any doctrinal differences. Furthermore, racial segregation resulted in separate organizations for white and black in the same denomination, and several churches were still divided into Northern and Southern branches, dating from the prewar years.

There was a wide range in the whole list of sectarian bodies between those of a nonevangelical, liberal tradition and others with fundamentalist belief and far-flung missionary activity. Also, the period was rife with new sects. The decline of revivalism among the larger denominations encouraged the rise of new groups hoping to preserve the personal and enthusiastic religion of earlier years. The "holiness" issue also began to disturb the churches, especially the Methodist denominations, as elements within them attempted to restore John Wesley's emphasis on Christian perfection. When the church leaders showed little sympathy, the dissatisfied elements began to establish holiness and pentecostal groups until by 1926 they numbered at least twenty-five.[21] The Salvation Army invaded the United States from England in 1879, making its appeal to the submerged classes that had been largely ignored by the "respectable" churches. A year earlier, Charles Taze Russell at Pittsburgh, by an eclectic choice of Hebrew prophecy and esoteric arithmetical computations, arrived at the revelation that the "Millennial Age" had arrived in 1874; that in 1914 this would be succeeded by social revolution, turmoil, chaos, and the resurrection of the dead; and that the true millennium would follow. The Russellites, through their International Bible Students' Association and its publication, the *Watchtower,* gained many converts.

Theosophy got a start in 1875 under the sponsorship of Elena Petrovna Blavatsky and Henry Steel Olcott. The exposure of many of Mrs. Blavatsky's miracles as frauds seems not to have harmed the movement, which at the time of her death in 1891 claimed 100,000 adherents in all parts of the world. It was also in 1875 that Mary Baker Eddy published the first edition of her system in *Science and Health,* and four years later she established "The First Church of Christ, Scientist" in Boston. By 1890 there were 250 Christian Science practitioners. Spiritualism continued to provide the desired excitement for those who sought contact with the invisible worlds, reaching new heights under the activities of Margaret Fox and her sisters Leah and Catherine. The movement seemed to suffer no serious setback in 1888 by the confession of the sisters (later retracted) that the whole system was a fraud and deception.[22]

The growth of religious organizations by multiplying and dividing was not the only phenomenon of the age. There were also profound and far-reaching changes within the churches. The frontier influence, which still colored much of the religious thinking, poorly equipped the churches for their responsibilities in a rising industrial society. As the increase in national wealth and its concentration in the hands of a few created new problems, a division of spirit in the churches held back the development of a united religious sentiment powerful enough to cope effectively with the challenge of the new order. The rapid growth of the cities involved accelerated congestion of people in the slums, and the churches were slow to realize that they had any responsibilities in such areas. The rising tide of immigration resulted in large foreign-language settlements that tended to maintain their Old World way of life and to resist assimilation into the American pattern. For lack of much effort at understanding, there was a tendency among church leaders to deplore what they considered immorality and irreligion among the aliens, and to shun them rather than offer a helping hand.

Other factors adversely affected the prestige of the churches in meeting the problems of industrial society. The influence of rationalism was increasingly discrediting the voice of authoritarian religion, while the textual study of the Bible led a growing number of scholars to modify their views of its accuracy and divine origin. James Freeman Clarke's *Ten Great Religions,* first published in 1871, had by 1892 gone through thirty editions.[23] This work of a devout American clergyman convinced masses of people that the great moral precepts and spiritual uplift wrought through the ages were not the monopoly of a single religious system. Fundamentalists inveighed against this concept as a blow delivered below the belt against their foreign missionary effort. Charles Darwin's *Origin of Species* (1859) aroused controversy mainly among scientists until the publication of his *Descent of Man* (1871) brought the implication home to the disciples of the Book of Genesis. Darwin's concept of man's ancestor as "a hairy quadruped, furnished with a tail and pointed ears, probably arboreal in habits"[24] was exceedingly offensive to persons accepting the idea of man's creation in the image of God. Yet, an increasing number became conditioned to the shock as most of the leading scientists accepted all or large parts of the Darwinian doctrine. The squabbles and heresy trials against ministers who accepted the scientific point of view had not entirely abated by 1890,[25] and there was to be a brief revival of name-calling a generation later.

The assault on orthodox positions by evolutionists probably caused less consternation than the inroads of Biblical criticism. This was nothing new, going back at least to Martin Luther, Thomas Hobbes, and Baruch Spinoza in the sixteenth and seventeenth centuries. David F. Strauss and others had continued the movement in the 1830s and 1840s, but it did not become a highly controversial matter in America until the second half of the nineteenth century. In 1892 Charles A. Briggs, a professor in the Union Theological Seminary, could write that "the Higher Criticism has advanced steadily since the time of Astruc [Jean, 1684–1766] and Eichorn [J. G., 1752–1827]. It has made no retreats. Its career has had a series of victories for more than a century." For his publication, Briggs secured prompt suspension from the Presbyterian ministry. The Seminary then severed its Presbyterian connections and Briggs became an Episcopal clergyman.[26]

Another trend was known as secularism, encouraged by the enormous increase in church wealth. As people began to believe that the heavenly riches they once sang about were attainable on earth, there were fewer shipments of treasure above and a greater concentration on acquiring earthly fortunes. For new pillars, the church began depending on men of wealth. The assumption of religious leadership by businessmen brought an emphasis on organization, system, and efficiency in church operations. Industrial consolidations found their counterparts in some of the churches in the multiplication of boards and connectional officials.[27] The influence of secularism, combined with the impact of alien religious traditions, challenged the lingering features of puritanical conduct and thought. Many Lutherans and Catholics from Germany offended the religious conscience of numerous Americans by an insistence on keeping the "Continental Sunday" in all of its gaiety. Blue laws still prevailed in several states, banning all obvious amusements or labor except the most essential. In 1885 South Carolina and Vermont still had laws requiring church attendance, and in Pennsylvania one neglected penalty for nonattendance was sitting in the stocks. But not all of the efforts of the Department of Sabbath Observance in the Woman's Christian Temperance Union, the American Sabbath Union, the Sunday League of America, and the International Sabbath Association could keep these blue laws alive. Abolition or relaxation of such legislation occurred all the way from California to Massachusetts before 1890, but the insistence of organized labor on a weekly day of rest had some countervailing influence.[28]

Though the prohibition movement had support from many religious bodies, they did not offer an official united resistance to the liquor business. In 1876 the Episcopalians took a stand for temperance but would not indorse total abstinence. The

Presbyterians and Congregationalists warmed up to the subject a little more enthusiastically in the early 1890s. On the other hand, it seems certain that Protestant organizations in general led in the movement of nonsectarian united fronts for the regulation, limitation, and abolition of the liquor traffic.[29]

More vital and important at the time was the rise of the "social gospel." As the industrial revolution congested the population of the cities, as the millions of poor immigrants poured in to add squalor to the slums, and as the gulf widened between wealth and poverty, increasing numbers of Protestant clergymen began to feel that they were losing out in the race with Catholics and Jews in taking care of the poor, and decided that something must be done about it. The Congregational ministers Lyman Abbott and Washington Gladden were joined by others in agitating for the application of church effort to the ameliorating of current social injustices.

Out of this movement grew the institutional church, especially among Congregational, Episcopal, Baptist, and Methodist groups, while the Presbyterians were least interested of the major religious bodies.[30] The care that these churches gave to newly arrived immigrants and to organized philanthropic and educational efforts among the poor people in their localities greatly increased membership in the active organizations.[31] But, as the American novelist Winston Churchill was to show, institutionalized churches without deep social reform proved to be not only futile, but a mockery of the real needs of the day.[32]

In these years of budding educational advance and religious ferment, increasing numbers of the people also were becoming aware of socioeconomic maladjustments and of reform movements aimed at their amelioration. Emerging from a generation of sectional strife and hatred comparable to the intolerance and cruelty of childhood and adolescence, the nation found itself coming into a young adulthood that was overshadowed by problems of business and society that were not to be solved simply by the application of salves and dosing with placebos. In many cases excisions and deep purgings were needed, but the harsh methods of the medicine men of the day, in dealing with bodily ailments, were disregarded by the dominant social reformers, who sought mainly to hide the running sores of the commonwealth by covering them with court plaster and tape.

Chapter II

THE UNDOING OF RECONSTRUCTION

T O THE freedmen of the South the decade following Reconstruction contained little of promise. The trend was
toward a return to the antebellum status of political, economic, civil, and social subordination to a master class. In the
first dozen years after the Civil War the dominant faction of
Congress had used the Negroes and their votes to support
a national program of benevolent aid to the rising business
interests of the North, and by 1877 this assistance seemed no
longer to be essential. The wartime tariff rates had become
an established part of protectionist policy; federal and state
governments had given the railroad builders over 286,000
square miles of land, nearly a tenth of all the land in the
United States;[1] and the Fourteenth Amendment was coming
to be understood as a guarantee to corporations against laws
interfering with their "life, liberty, or property." Even though
Hayes had been elected President by a dubious process and
by the narrowest possible margin, even though the House of
Representatives had been captured by the Democrats, it
seemed that these business gains were safe against any future
Democratic assault and that the bulk of the Republicans had
grown complacent about the conservative transformation of
their party. Southern support of conservative policy was no
longer of prime importance, carpetbag governments upheld
by federal military power had become an embarrassment,
and Negro votes could now be ignored. So, in 1877, "home
rule" came back to the last three of the reconstructed states.

But "home rule" meant government by the same kind of
masters that had dominated politics and economic and social
life before the war. The personnel had changed somewhat,
but the spirit was almost identical.[2] Southern white people
rallied to the support of their wartime military men and in

1876 sent forty-nine of them to Congress. In succeeding elections several of the Southern states sent delegations to Washington composed almost wholly of veterans.[3] The "Bourbon" Democrats were rising to power and, whether representatives of the old planter and yeoman farmer classes or of the newer industrial interests,[4] they were dedicated to the restoration of white supremacy.[5]

During Reconstruction, the restriction of Negro suffrage had been partially achieved by force, intimidation, and fraud. The Bourbons added legislation to the list. The federal courts and Congress prepared the way for permanent disfranchisement. Court decisions on cases arising in South Carolina in 1871 and in Kentucky in 1874 refused punishment of persons molesting Negroes on their own premises, established the doctrine that the Fifteenth Amendment did not confer the right of suffrage on anyone, and left it up to the election officials to deny ballots for any other reason than race, color, or previous condition of servitude.[6] In 1881 federal jurisdiction receded still further when an Indiana court held it was legal to prevent a citizen from voting at a state election, by violence or otherwise.[7] Finally, when a mob physically abused some Negroes they took away from policemen in Tennessee, the United States Supreme Court in 1883 held that this was the action of individuals, and not of the state. It was up to the state government alone to give relief.[8] Negroes found it almost impossible to prove that they were beaten or intimidated simply because of their race and their desire to vote, or that the state itself, by its indifference, denied them the suffrage.

On June 18, 1878, Hayes, in order not to kill army appropriations, signed a bill containing a rider that effectually ended the employment of troops to police elections.[9] The use of federal deputy-marshals and supervisors was still possible, but after 1877 this power lapsed into disuse and, before long, Washington officials ceased to press the issue. Thereafter, the state governments did about as they pleased, and the burden of proof fell on the Negro to show that there was discrimination. Legislatures used numerous effective means to achieve disfranchisement. Most common were centralization of control over election boards, gerrymandering, a poll-tax requirement for voting, complex laws for registration and polling, and educational qualifications.[10] Intimidation and violence added zest to the system.

North Carolina most effectively applied the device of centralization. The legislature selected all justices of the peace, who in turn chose the boards of county commissioners, which next appointed the election officials. This practice facilitated control by the more conservative elements of the population. Elsewhere, legislatures devised numerous adaptations of the gerrymander, the most conspicuous example being the "shoestring district" of Mississippi. The counties in the delta, from the Tennessee line to the Gulf, an area about three hundred miles long and averaging something like twenty miles in width, had the densest Negro population in the state. By putting all of these counties in one district, the legislature allowed the Negroes to control one seat in Congress and rendered them an ineffective minority in all the rest of the state.[11]

Because a poll-tax requirement for voting barred the more impecunious white men as well as the Negroes, it was not used in many of the states in the earlier years. In order to get the white vote out, the Democrats often had to bribe the poorer men by paying the tax for them, while Northern Republicans sometimes did a like service for the Negroes. Because of this and other annoyances, in 1882 and for a few years afterward, Virginia abandoned the poll-tax device. On the other hand, Arkansas successfully used this method, almost to the exclusion of all others. Tennessee had repealed such a plan in 1873, but returned to it in 1890. Georgia, under the provisions of her early state constitution, had never been without such a safeguard except during the Reconstruction years.[12]

Though in theory whites and Negroes suffered alike, it was plainly evident that it was the Negroes who lost nearly all of the votes. Senator Alfred Holt Colquitt of Georgia virtually admitted this fact in 1887: "Then consider that in Georgia no one is allowed to vote who has not paid his taxes, it matters not what is the color of his skin. The defaulters for taxes among our colored population are numerous, and the number is becoming greater year by year."[13] He did not go on to explain that it mattered little whether the Negro paid his tax or not, for even with a receipt he was not assured of a vote. Some petty offense could always be conjured up against a recalcitrant Negro, whereupon an obliging deputy sheriff could run him out of the county shortly before an election, thus disfranchising him since the receipt was valid only in the precinct where the tax was paid. Or a circus might visit the town before election day and accept poll-tax receipts as admission, resulting in a large attendance at the circus and a small showing of Negroes at the polls.[14]

The use of complex registration and election laws prevailed in several of the states, and at one time or another in all of them. But it was in South Carolina that the Negro was most adroitly relieved of the franchise by ingenious exploitation of his ignorance and illiteracy. By an Act of 1882 a complicated system of eight or more ballot boxes came into use. There was a separate ballot and box for each of eight groups of candidates, all the way from county officials to governor, representative in Congress, and presidential electors. Each individual local question also had a designated ballot and box.[15] This practice became almost completely effective because of the Negro's usual inability to read. Though, after coaching, he might memorize the location of the various boxes, he could not be sure that their relative positions had not been shuffled before his final lesson. Ballots and boxes were labeled, and the election officials were permitted to read the titles on request, but otherwise it was illegal to speak to the voter or to deposit his ballot for him. Many white electors also were illiterate, but there were ways to make the voting process easier for them.

Again, the polling places were often set at points far distant from the most densely populated Negro communities, making it necessary for the prospective voter to travel several miles to deposit his ballots. At rivers, the ferries would be out of use for repairs. Confusion, crowding, and fighting near the polls sometimes diverted attention until the closing time. Occasionally the voting place was changed without notice to the Negro; again, he was informed of a change that had never taken place.[16] Frauds of a more palpable nature were common. These included the use of boxes with false bottoms, multiple voting by trusted henchmen, meddling with the accounts and the registration books, and the stuffing of ballot boxes with tissue ballots. This was before the day of the Australian secret voting system, and each political party printed and distributed its own ballots in any size or texture it desired. The voter marked his ballots before going to the polls, and sometimes under the supervision of party workers who also accompanied him to the voting place to make sure that bought merchandise was delivered according to the terms of the contract. Trusted voters received one large, heavy-paper ballot and several miniature tissue-paper ballots to be folded inside the large one, thus simplifying the process of voting early and often. When the counting began there would be more ballots than registered voters, whereupon a blindfolded man would withdraw the surplus number from the box, and the clumsiest fingers could easily distinguish between heavy paper and tissue. A Senate investigating committee disclosed that, in the election of 1878, at one polling place there were 620 names on the voting list and 1163 ballots in the box. When the surplus was removed there were 464 tissue and 156 heavy ballots left to count.[17]

The educational qualification did not make its entry until 1890, when Mississippi wrote it into her constitution. The complex features of that doctrine became a model for other states. It required of each elector a two-year residence in the state and one year in the precinct. By February 1 in an election year he had to pay all taxes, including a poll tax of two dollars a year for the two previous years. He was also supposed to register at least four months before the election, this registration being denied unless he was "able to read any section of the constitution of this State; or . . . be able to understand the same when read to him, or give a reasonable interpretation thereof."[18] Thus it became possible, instead of asking a literate Negro to read the constitution, to insist that he give an interpretation and to reject even the most erudite exposition as fallacious. But if the officials wanted the vote of any illiterate man, his declaration that he understood would suffice. The embarrassment produced by this dual application of the law led in 1895 to the adoption of the "grandfather clause," putting any ignoramus on the permanent registration list if he or his father or his grandfather were allowed to vote in the state before 1867 or would have been allowed to if they had lived there. Benjamin R. Tillman boasted for the South Carolinians: "We stuffed the ballot boxes. We shot them. We are not ashamed of it. With that system—force, tissue ballots, etc.—we got tired ourselves. So we had a constitutional convention, and we eliminated . . . all the colored people whom we could under the Fourteenth and Fifteenth Amendments."[19]

Congress acquiesced in this flouting of the Constitution since neither then nor in later generations did it pass any legislation putting in force that part of the Fourteenth Amendment stipulating that, whenever any state deprived adult male citizens of the vote for any other reason than rebellion or proved crime, its representation in Congress should be reduced in the proportion that the disfranchised element bore to the total number of adult male citizens in the state. Illiteracy and the lack of a poll-tax receipt were not crimes; yet, before the end of the century, not only the Negroes, but the bulk of the white people as well, lost the suffrage through this subterfuge. In 1888 the average vote for a member of Congress in five Southern states was less than 8000, while in five Northern states it was over 36,000. Kansas, with a vote three times that of South Carolina, had only as many representatives. Colquitt was correct, as far as he went, in saying that the small vote in Georgia was "because there was no such opposition as to call out the vote," but he failed to suggest that the lack of opposition was caused by the disfranchisement of that element of the population which might have restored a bipartisan South. In the Forty-first Congress (1869–71), there were forty-four Republican representatives and twenty Republican senators from the South. Of course, this was at a time when many of the white men had not yet received amnesty. But the later restoration of suffrage to former rebels cannot alone explain the fact that in the Fifty-first Congress (1889–91), there were only three Republican representatives from the South, and not even one senator, or the other fact that the Southern legislatures became almost unanimously white. Mississippi, because its local gerrymandering followed the pattern of the "shoestring district," was an exception, having six Negroes in the lower house in 1890.[20]

The policy of disfranchisement was accompanied by a cumulation of devices to limit the civil and social status of the colored population, and the virtual nullification of the Civil Rights Act of 1875 by the United States Supreme Court in 1883[21] facilitated the action. In the early years after the war many public eating places in Mississippi still served both races in the same room, although at separate tables, and black and white mixed freely at the bar. As in antebellum days, it was not deemed that separate graveyards were needed to prevent miscegenation of the dead. Segregation on railroad trains extended only to first-class cars, and as late as 1877 even this restriction did not exist in South Carolina.

But the animosities generated during Reconstruction expressed themselves during the Bourbon ascendancy in a flood of segregation laws. Friction was greatest where the economic status of the two races was closest. The white man could be made a little more docile and contented with his lot if led to believe that he held a social advantage over the Negro. As Vann Woodward says: "It took a lot of ritual and Jim Crow to bolster the creed of white supremacy in the bosom of a white man working for a black man's wages."[22] As the two races met at the mines and wharves, and in the cotton fields, the demand for measures of discrimination became increasingly insistent, and legislation followed. The laws applied to almost any place where the two races might otherwise mingle indoors, from schools, theaters, restaurants, hotels, and churches to waiting rooms and trains. Separate first-class accommodations on trains came to Tennessee by act of 1881, although as yet there was no segregation in second-class coaches. Legislatures passed various similar laws in Florida (1887), Mississippi (1888), Texas (1889), Louisiana (1890), and in Alabama, Arkansas, Kentucky, and Georgia

in 1891. The Mississippi act was the first to establish segregation in waiting rooms at the depots, and the Georgia law
extended the principle to streetcars. Enforcement was rigid
as the movement got into full swing.[23]

Sometimes the results were fairly ludicrous, as at a ram-
shackle Chesapeake Bay steamship waiting room at York-
town, where the only heat on a wintry day came from a
rusty old stove in a big arch sawed out of the race-line parti-
tion, the rough benches on one side of the stove occupied by
white men and like benches on the other side by Negroes,
each shivering in the enjoyment of separate but equal accommodations.[24] But accommodations were not even approximately equal in many cases, as in a later bus station in Vinita,
Oklahoma, where the three rest rooms were labeled "White
Ladies," "White Men," and "Colored People." At other places
in the same state there were rest stops, privately owned, that
did not admit Negroes at all, and there were not even any
bushes in the vicinity.[25]

The spirit that subjugated the Negro race socially and
politically was, naturally, one that produced violence and
bloodshed. After 1882, when statistics are first available for
lynching, the number shows a rapid increase.[26] If the charge
of rape could be conjured up in association with a Negro's
crime or misdemeanor, death at the hands of a mob was just
as certain as its immunity from prosecution afterward. Resort
to lynching established a fear among the Negroes which no
legal action could achieve. The race problem, however, does
not fully explain the rising tide of violence. The South set a
record in the 1880s almost without parallel anywhere in
Christendom. Although the statistics for homicides are far
from complete, South Carolina reported almost three times as
many in 1890 as the six New England states with a population more than four times as great. In the same year, Massachusetts, with "cities and slums and unassimilated immigrants
. . . had only 16 homicides as compared with 65 in Virginia,
69 in North Carolina, 88 in Kentucky, 92 in Georgia, and
115 in Tennessee." Italy, with perhaps the highest homicide
rate in Euope, had fewer convicted murderers in 1890 than
the South Central states with a third less population.[27]

Hip-pocket law was a leading arbiter of disputes between 1870 and 1915. Not many subjects were too trivial to invoke its use. Many deaths resulted over imagined slights to women, but the spreading of a lie, or disrespect to kinfolks, even disputes over dogs and saddle horses, or whether chickens would eat beans, brought daily battles. From the Kentucky mountains, where in the later 1880s lawless mobs terrorized several counties and prevented the opening of the courts, and throughout the entire cotton belt, there was a code of honor higher than the law.[28] Prevailing economic, social, or religious standards appear to have excluded no class from extralegal processes. The efforts to maintain the color line may have set the practice in motion, but it certainly did not stop there. Accounts of bloody engagements among planters, lawyers, doctors, railroad presidents, editors, and preachers appear in the newspapers of the era. Though dueling was on the wane, shooting on sight seems to have been just as effective.

General lawlessness and the quasi-legal method of dealing with the Negroes had their counterpart in the repudiation or scaling down of state debts. The Fourteenth Amendment had outlawed the war debts, but prewar obligations, and those piled up, often fraudulently, by the Reconstruction governments, awaited settlement at a time when the Southern states in their impoverished condition were in no mood to assume the task. Repudiation started during Reconstruction in Louisiana and the Carolinas, but the general "readjustment" awaited the return of the Bourbons. Mississippi in 1875, Georgia in 1877, and Arkansas in 1884 adopted constitutional amendments to settle the problem. Florida eased out of its responsibility for certain railroad bond issues by court decisions in the late 1870s. Alabama in 1876, the Carolinas in 1879, Louisiana in 1882, and Tennessee in 1883, after a series of abortive efforts at compromise, repudiated many bond issues by legislation. Mississippi's repudiation was of prewar debts of forty years' standing, and did not involve Reconstruction obligations. Virginia, after years of litigation, controversial legislation, and compromise, in 1892 finally reached a settlement satisfactory both to the state and to the bondholders and therefore not classed as repudiation. The disputed portion of the Texas debt was too small to call for action. Aside from Mississippi, Virginia, and Texas, repudiation totaling over $116,000,000 occurred in the other eight states of the former Confederacy. This ranged from $4,000,000 in Florida to more than $29,000,000 in North Carolina. Arkansas, Florida, and Georgia relied on simple repudiation with no frills; Tennessee, on a general scaling-down process. Alabama, Louisiana, and the Carolinas used a combination of the two methods, while Alabama, Louisiana, and North Carolina also defaulted interest on the scaled-down debt.[29]

The readjustment program met heavy opposition before adoption in Virginia, Tennessee, Arkansas, and Louisiana, where strong factions lined up to guard the credit of the states. In 1880 a split over the issue among the Democrats of Tennessee placed the Republicans temporarily in power, and a like schism appeared to be imminent in Arkansas before the readjusters succeeded. The settlement in Louisiana was a compromise between the rural repudiationists and a combination of powerful newspapers and bondholding companies that fought all scaling-down efforts. Perhaps the hardest battle was in Virginia. Against extreme odds, the readjusters began in 1879 to take over the government from the "funders," and won their first battle in 1882, only to recede in the compromise of a decade later.[30] The arguments of the readjusters, that the repudiated bonds were fraudulently issued in the first place, would seem more candid if it were not that, in the zeal to relieve the taxpayers, honest debts of both pre- and postwar issue went into a common limbo with the rest.

Other conditions in the South indicated further that corrupt financial dealings were not a monopoly of the hated carpetbaggers. After the restoration of home rule, many of the new political leaders could have put to shame the penny-ante scalawags and their Reconstruction graft. The disposal of the public domain furnishes a good example. After the Homestead Act was applied to the South in 1866, Southern members of Congress, almost to a man, fought the measure until ten years later they secured its repeal over a bitter opposition led by William S. Holman of Indiana. The opposition to restricted entry was based on the feeble contention that the remaining public land was not fit for homesteads.[31]

In the squandering of the public domain that followed, the Federal Land Office received ample direction from Southern men. Between 1881 and 1888 hordes of capitalists and lumbermen flocked to the South to share in the spoils. In the wave of excitement the Illinois Central Railroad ran special trains from Chicago, carrying eager speculators to Mississippi and Louisiana where the biggest sales were concentrated. Forty-one groups and individuals from the North purchased some 1,370,000 acres of federal land in Louisiana and nine from the South bought 262,000 acres. Thirty-two Northern groups secured 889,000 acres of such land in Mississippi and eleven Southern groups obtained 134,000 acres there. Seven Northerners got 122,000 acres in Alabama, seven more procured 114,000 acres in Arkansas, and six bought 64,000 acres in Florida. James D. Lacey of Grand Rapids, Michigan, probably excelled them all in purchasing for himself and his associates over 107,000 acres in Louisiana and Mississippi, their entire holding of timberlands being 5,000,000 acres, mostly in the South. Speculators also procured large holdings from the land-grant railroads and from the states. In 1860 the federal public domain in the five states just named amounted to 47,700,000 acres, but this had dwindled to about 14,400,000 acres by 1890. Though a sizable portion of the public domain still remained in the South, the best timber, mineral, and arable land had gone into speculative holdings.[32]

While the ultimate responsibility for the raids just mentioned lay with the federal Land Office, the Southern states themselves were not outdone in this grim policy of plunder. In 1881 the Florida legislature sold 4,000,000 acres to a Philadelphia syndicate headed by Hamilton Disston. The price was twenty-five cents an acre, and the deal went through under circumstances as shady as ever covered the activities of the carpetbaggers. The state of Texas, while in the hands of home-rule politicians, in two or three years fraudulently sold 700,000 acres of its land.[33]

The long-prevailing concept of probity among public officials in the redeemed South may be expressed in the words of Holland Thompson: "There was little scandal anywhere. No governments in American history have been conducted with more economy and more fidelity than the governments of the Southern states during the first years after the Reconstruction period."[34] Certainly the Southerners had great faith in their Bourbon leaders. The idea prevailed that military heroes who had so recently defended their soil would be equally courageous in civil affairs. The increasing dominance of the one-party system and its control by a ring generally prevented the spread of publicity concerning malfeasance in office until it was too late to be of help. Yet cases did come to light. The scandals associated with the Colquitt administration in Georgia were the first disclosed. The comptroller general and the state treasurer resigned after impeachment and were joined by the commissioner of agriculture following an investigation of their activities which began in 1879. Yet Colquitt was re-elected in 1880. In Tennessee, Marshall T. Polk, nephew and adopted son of James K. Polk and state treasurer after 1877, disappeared in January, 1883, after embezzling over $400,000 of public funds. Once apprehended he was sentenced to twenty years in prison and a fine about equal to the treasury deficit. Within three weeks of the Polk exposure, the highly regarded state treasurer of Alabama, Isaac H. Vincent, disappeared leaving a default of some $233,000. He escaped to Mexico and progress in his apprehension was apparently hindered by fear of his knowledge of the guilt of others. Ultimately he received a fifteen-year sentence.[35]

These were not isolated cases of defalcation. Early in 1883, it was disclosed that Thomas J. Churchill, elected governor of Arkansas in 1880, had in an earlier term as treasurer defaulted to the extent of over $80,000. He attributed the deficit to faulty bookkeeping, which explanation received general acceptance. William E. Woodruff, who succeeded Churchill as treasurer in 1880, left a shortage of more than $138,000 ten years later. James W. ("Uncle Dick") Tate, the respected state treasurer for Kentucky for ten consecutive terms, disappeared in 1888, short to the extent of $229,000 in his accounts. William L. Hemingway, treasurer of Mississippi, received a sentence of five years for the embezzlement of over $315,000. The greatest fraud, however, occurred in Louisiana. Information leaked out about 1889 that Major E. A. Burke, the state treasurer, had robbed the state of $1,777,000, in addition to some accrued interest, by means of bond frauds. At the time of exposure, he was in London and soon went to Honduras to enjoy the benefits of his loot. The discovery of bonds in his bank box reduced the state's loss to $793,000, but Burke successfully eluded Louisiana courts.[36] Along the border of the South, in 1890 the people of Maryland found that their own treasurer had stolen $100,000 of state funds.[37]

The size and number of these embezzlements seem enormous when compared with the meager support given by the "redeemer" governments to cultural and social agencies of the states. School systems and other public institutions felt the strain of poverty, and petty government officials received inadequate pay. Although the Southern people did not seem to feel the outrage they had formerly vented on the carpetbaggers, they learned that their pockets were just as empty when the pickpockets were their own neighbors.

Political corruption also loomed up in the convict-leasing system so widely adopted in the Southern states. This practice had existed in Kentucky and Louisiana in antebellum days, and it spread to all of the rest of the former Confederacy and to West Virginia, Maryland, and Missouri by 1877. The motives for adopting the system were numerous and some of them were plausible, but the main effect, probably anticipated, was to bring common labor in competition with unpaid prisoners and thus beat down wages in general. Furthermore, strategically placed politicians found in the practice a most satisfactory way to augment their personal fortunes. Georgia's Civil War governor, then Senator Joseph E. Brown, procured a twenty-year lease on the labor of three hundred strong men for exploitation in his Dade coal mines, paying the state about eight cents a day for each. Senator John B. Gordon, the gallant Confederate soldier who, as lieutenant general, led the last charge at Appomattox, was also associated with a company that got a similar lease. Colonel Arthur S. Colyar, general council for the Tennessee Coal and Iron Company, leased Tennessee's prisoners for $101,000. Robert McKee, well acquainted with the inside of Alabama's politics, declared that the state warden, John H. Bankhead, in a few years grew rich, though his annual wage was only $2000.[38] Alabama then rewarded Bankhead with a seat in Congress from 1887 to 1907, and three of his sons and grandsons succeeded him in Congress, unstained by the iniquity of the ancestor.[39]

Alabama's revival of the leasing system came less than a decade after its abolition in 1882 because of excessive cruelty inflicted on the prisoners by the lessees. The revived system contained a few attempted reforms, but subleasing was still possible with the consent of the warden and the governor.[40] Subleasing also prevailed in Mississippi, Louisiana, and Arkansas. In Mississippi nearly all leases after 1880 went to the highest bidder. Until 1883, Texas gave complete control of convicts to lessees. The profitableness of the practice taxed the ingenuity of legislatures to devise more skillful penal laws for ensnaring a greater supply of convicts. Thus, Mississippi adopted the "pig law" which between 1874 and 1877 increased the penal population of the state from 272 to 1072. Within fourteen months after the repeal of the pig law in 1887 the number of prisoners dropped from 966 to 484. Under this law the theft of property in excess of ten dollars, or of swine or cattle irrespective of value, was grand larceny, subjecting the offender to a possible five-year penitentiary sentence.[41]

The leasing system provided business enterprise with a supply of laborers made to work under the most oppressive conditions, and at a trivial payment to the state. Newspapers of the day occasionally described the wretched working conditions, but the evils continued. From the point of view of the employers of such labor, one of the main advantages was that the system acted as an effective check on strikes by free men. Colyar of the Tennessee Coal and Iron Company almost boasted of this fact: "For some years after we began the convict labor system we found that we were right in calculating that free laborers would be loath to enter upon strikes when they saw that the company was amply provided with convict labor. I don't mind saying that for years the company found this an effective check to be held over the heads of free laborers."[42] This statement was recorded in 1892, before Colyar could know that the existing guerrilla warfare between striking miners and the state militia in the Coal Creek region of the eastern part of Tennessee was soon to result in the abolition of the contract system in that state.

The depressing effect of prison labor on the wages of free men was not the worst feature of the new economic structure. As Southern industries developed, the demand for additional laborers would far outstrip the convict supply and the resulting frictions would result in a gradual abandonment of the unfair practices. But the South, with its new industrialization, was still predominantly an agricultural section, and the conditions of farm laborers were not so easily to be improved. In fact, the tenant, sharecropper, and credit system, developed in 1877 and extended thereafter, did much to restore the absolute control of planters over labor gangs and at a cost less than that of owning slaves. Bare subsistence costs no more for a free man than for a slave, and the planter did not have capital tied up in the free laborer. Slaves had to be fed even during slack periods of work, but the free man could be laid off to "root hog or die" during the unproductive winter months.[43]

The plantations of the South still existed, and the average size of landownerships was on the increase, but the system of management had undergone significant changes. The owners in many cases were not of the same families that had been in control before the war, and more often than in earlier decades the owners did not live on the land. Though early in 1865 the freedmen had some reason for hope that the federal government was to give each family forty acres, by 1880 it was seen that very few of the new landowners were Negroes. In Georgia, only about one Negro in a hundred owned land and, though the black race still constituted about half of the total population, what acres they possessed had less than 2 per cent of the total value of all land in the state. The situation

was about the same in Mississippi, while Tennessee, Alabama, and Louisiana reported very few colored owners. The
bulk of the Negroes, and whites as well, were still engaged in
farm work, but merely as tenants, croppers, or hired laborers,
and the percentages were on the increase. In 1880 a little under 45 per cent of the operating units were farmed by tenants and croppers, but by 1890 the percentage had grown to
nearly 54. In the latter year in the entire Confederacy approximately four-tenths of the farms were worked in this way,
the percentages ranging from 23.6 in Florida to 55.3 in South
Carolina.[44] Furthermore, by the end of the century six-tenths
of the 4,400,000 wage laborers on American farms were in
the South Atlantic and South Central states. Then and in 1890
a third of all agricultural wage workers were Negroes and
nearly all of these were in the South. Three-eighths of the
Negro workers were women and girls. Of the 663,000 female
wage laborers of all races in the United States in 1900, all but
19,000 were in the South, and three-quarters of the number
were Negroes.[45] A further analysis of the data shows that
before the end of the century there were about as many white
as black wage laborers in Southern agriculture (about 1,400,-
000 of each). These persons, if adult males and paying for
their board out of their wages, received in 1890 from $14 to
$16 a month (sometimes less than $10) while the average in
the North Central states was $23 and in the North Atlantic
states $25.[46]

Also, by 1900 there were some 150,000 whites and 233,000
Negroes listed as cash tenants, besides 402,000 white and
229,000 Negro sharecroppers. In earlier years the percentage
of Negroes among the tenants and croppers was much larger.
Unlike tenants, the sharecropper had no lease on the land.
Just before plowing time in the spring he was hired to grow
a crop of cotton or perhaps tobacco on a patch of land, the
acreage of which depended on the number of able workers in
the family who could be relied on at the season of heaviest
demand. A family with several cotton pickers would be allotted
more acres than a smaller family. Every task was under the
direction and inspection of the owner or his agent. There were
landlords who encouraged some crop diversification, but most

of them demanded that the cotton cropper grow nothing but cotton. After the gathering of the crop the landlord took possession, evaluated it, deducted from the cropper's share any debts owed to the landlord, and if anything was left paid the rest to the cropper. Shares varied from time to time and from place to place, but the customary arrangement was one third of the crop for rental of the land, a third for the labor of the worker, and the other third for the work of horses or mules, the use of implements, seed, fertilizer if any, and other sundry items of farming expense. Most often, the worker supplied nothing but his labor and therefore got credit for only a third of the crop. He was not even assured of the use of the house during the winter months before he could be hired anew.

In the more fertile parts of the South, where this system flourished most, the more energetic of the croppers might well have saved up enough of their earnings to have bought their own land, had not the practice met so much discouragement. Some of them succeeded in spite of the obstacles, though never any large proportion. But, as the system worked out, very few of the workers ever managed to save anything at all. The main reason for this was the crop-lien credit system that grew and flourished alongside the new type of labor control. Before 1877, the country merchant had taken the place of the prewar factors for extending credit to farm operators. Tenants, sharecroppers, small independent landowners, and sometimes the planters themselves depended on these storekeepers for credit. But in time, either the storekeeper took over the plantation or the planter bought out the storekeeper, and thus the landlord and the merchant became one.

In areas where small landlords working their own land predominated, a village store might pursue a like practice of extending credit for supplies during the growing and harvesting season. Under these circumstances, the landlord-merchant would supply groceries and other needs to the tenants and croppers, charging the costs to the workers' share of the crop. When hired, the cropper gave bond for usually not more than $100 to the storekeeper, his crop being the security, and this sum was the limit of what he would be furnished during that crop year. Under the excuse of risks involved, this store bill included the raising of prices anywhere from 10 to 200 per cent above what was charged to cash customers in regions where the credit system did not prevail. These rates were the extremes; most often the charge was between 40 and 110 per cent. In 1880, when corn brought $0.75 a bushel in cash stores in South Carolina, the price to credit customers was $1.25 and sometimes more. This meant at least 100 per cent profit on the wholesale price the merchant had paid. But here an interesting question arises. Was the laborer actually a credit customer? He earned each week's supplies before he obtained them. He received no week's wages. He got no interest at the end of the year for withheld wages, but out of his share of the crop he paid enormous interest on his "furnish," which he had already paid for with his labor. The answer to this enigma is that the law was on the side of the landlord-merchant.

Whatever the price of cotton, it seemed that the laborer's debt for provisions either balanced or exceeded the value of his share of the crop. Consequently, not only was he perennially short of money, even to pay his poll tax so he could vote, but he was also bound to his job and was immobile. If in debt to the store at the close of a crop year, he was bound by law to sign a contract for another year's labor in the hopeless effort to pay off the obligation. This was nothing less than peonage and could continue as long as the worker seemed to be a desirable asset to the employer. While thus bound to the soil and the job, the cropper had to abide by the employer's orders that cotton alone should be the crop, regardless as to how much this absence of rotation robbed the soil of fertility. The one-crop system, in consequence, spread throughout the staple-production areas. Perhaps Thomas D. Clark is correct in discounting the assumption that the inedibility of cotton accounted to a great extent for its rise as the one crop of the cotton belt.[47] But cotton above all other crops afforded the best security for the merchant. Poor transportation facilities and bad roads made the extensive production of more perishable goods hazardous. Even corn was not a satisfactory commodity to ship for great distances except under the most favorable conditions. For one reason or another, therefore, the laborer was forced to grow cotton regardless of his own impoverishment or that of the soil. If he grew corn and hogs for his own consumption he would buy less pork and meal from the plantation store, so it was the practice of some of the storekeepers to lessen the cropper's credit to the extent of his truck-patch output. The cropper, therefore, could not supplement his income by raising some of his food, so he rarely continued in the practice. So little corn was grown in the cotton belt by 1900 that cattle sometimes did not recognize it as feed and would nose an ear of corn out of the pile of cottonseed hulls and trample it underfoot.

From midsummer until early January was the cotton-picking season, during which time the cropper's family picked the field over and over again, carrying each sack as picked to the landlord's gin. Rarely did the laborer try to lay aside a little of his own share to sell independently. On mere suspicion of such an endeavor the landlord-merchant would get a court order for the seizure of the entire crop, the cost of the procedure coming out of the laborer's annual store credit. This system led to plentiful and ingenious abuse. Books could be kept so that at the end of the year the efficient laborer would always be in debt and, consequently, compelled to sign a new contract for the succeeding year. On the other hand, the books could balance nicely for the unwanted cropper, who then could be denied another contract. This practice positively encouraged shiftlessness on the part of the worker. If efficient, he made himself a peon; if slipshod in his husbandry, he could get out of debt and try his fortune elsewhere. Clark maintains that the merchants' books were generally kept accurately and that errors were as likely to be against the interest of the store as against the worker, and this contention is supported by the studies of others.[48] But bookkeepers do not take account of twelve-ounce pounds and rigged peck measures. It may also be presumed that the more orderly books were the ones preserved for the observation of posterity. The bookkeepers themselves, when in a convivial mood, have described the shrewder tricks, and novelized ac-

THE UNDOING OF RECONSTRUCTION

counts written by Southerners, such as Thomas Sigismund Stribling, are most revealing.[49]

The illiterate cropper was wholly at the mercy of the book-keeper, who could read an account at a speed unintelligible even to the most enlightened of people. After the books were balanced so that the store bill exactly equaled the cropper's share of the cotton and the cropper then remembered a bale that he had not yet hauled in, it was possible for the book-keeper to find two pages of the ledger stuck together, so that a recapitulation of the debt would again exactly cover the extra bale. As the cropper's morale was broken, his resistance to injustice was largely overcome. As Jacqueline Bull has said: "Sometimes the customer of the store was too timid to ask how his account stood. It was often considered a reflection on the integrity of the landlord or merchant for a tenant to keep his own accounts."[50] The landlord-merchant developed through the years a most paternalistic and unapproachable manner. On an economic basis he rose above his neighbors and felt removed from the lower castes. The more ulterior his motives the greater were his chances of success. As another southerner has written of the merchant: "Thousands would attempt it and fail; hundreds of others would barely hang on. But let a man have a firm eye for the till; let him have it in him to remember always that the price of senti-mental weakness was disaster, to return a quiet no to the client who was hopelessly involved, not to flinch from the ulti-mate necessity . . . of stripping a father of ten children of his last year of corn—and his prospects of growing rich were bright."[51] A cropper, even if bold enough, courted disaster by engaging in the objectionable practice of insisting on his rights.

Yet, as W. J. Cash said, not many of the planter-merchants became rich. There were crop failures; laborers ran off when their work was most needed; the constant planting of a single crop wore out the soil until it was almost worthless, and fertilizer was too costly for the coffers to stand the strain. The planter as well as the cropper was often in debt. Perhaps most of the planters did not consciously rob the workers, and the continuously unbalanced accounts of many show that "the bed of the patriarch was not always an easy one." The lien holder even robbed himself when he kept the cropper's credit limited to food consisting almost wholly of salt pork fat, corn meal, and an occasional jug of molasses—fuel alone and very little muscle-building food with an adequate vitamin content. Persons living on such food throughout the year, except for some greens in the spring of the year, soon became lank, potbellied, and pellagrous. They did not have enough energy to do their best work even when they were not discouraged by the bookkeeping system from wanting to exert effort. So the landlord himself suffered by cause of the diminishing returns of agriculture, and the agricultural South as a whole became poverty-stricken. In a portion of South Carolina in 1880 the average yearly credit of a family was only $77, which represented the entire cost of living of a family at prices probably at least half again those charged by cash stores. The families actually were living on about $50 worth of goods for the year. This is not the way to build general prosperity.

Although no figures are available by decades, Alex Arnett concludes that probably between 80 and 90 per cent of proprietors, tenants, and sharecroppers, black and white alike, gradually fell at least partially under the crop-lien system. Matthew B. Hammond, writing in 1897, declared that 90 per cent of the planters and workers of both races were ensnared by the system in Alabama and believed that about three-quarters of the planters and laborers were involved throughout the cotton belt. The lien system was also quite extensive in the tobacco regions, black and white workers being about equally involved.[52] In 1893 a Senate committee received testimony that 90 per cent or more of the cotton growers in certain regions were insolvent. Involved planters testified that they too had agreements with merchants to raise too much cotton and were denied the right to grow their own food. Many an independent farmer, especially of the small landowning group, was becoming so deeply indebted that he lost his farm to the merchant and became a tenant on his ancestral acres. This was a factor in the recruiting of Farmers' Alliance members in the 1880s and of the Populist party in the 1890s. As overproduction of cotton increased, its price de-

clined. This called for more overproduction and still lower
prices until credit got so low that the cycle dragged near to a
halt at starvation's verge. The price of land got so low and
the soil so thin that merchants were loath to advance credit
on land mortgages, which helps to explain why mortgages
were so few in the South as compared with the more prosperous areas of the Northeast and the North Central states. It
was the black-soil, rich-soil areas of the South that had the
largest numbers of tenants and sharecroppers, and it was there
that this impoverishment went on most consistently. Small, independent farmers in the upland and hill areas, which
planters in the past had shunned, prospered in comparison
with the black-belt farmers, and mainly because they were
relatively free of the crop-lien credit system.

Word constantly came out of the South that labor was paid
badly because it was inefficient and shiftless, but the reverse
of this view is more likely to be the correct one. Slaves had
been inefficient because of the knowledge that regardless of
how hard they worked they would get only their daily subsistence in payment. Sharecroppers and tenants were perhaps
even more inefficient than slaves because they did not even
get adequate sustenance. Sometimes actual peonage existed.
A planter needing additional field hands could get an obliging
deputy sheriff to arrest a bunch of hangers-on around a back-
alley crap game in town and get them fined possibly thirty
dollars or sent to the chain gang for six months. The planter
then would offer to pay the fine so as to release the impecunious loafer from the chain-gang horror. The culprit would be
promised that he could pay off the planter at a seemingly fair
rate of pay. But in practice the board and room charged
against the victim was just enough more than the daily wage
to keep him forever in debt and at labor as long as he was
wanted. Release came with death or total disability. Violence
or attempted escape resulted in unexplained disappearances.
Buzzards circled down into the swamps while the deputy
sheriffs went out to arrest some men caught stepping on the
grass of the courthouse lawn, or spitting on the sidewalk. A
practice of this sort was ended in Georgia as late as January

12, 1942, when the Supreme Court of the United States nullified a state law that had legalized the system.[53]

Thus, after the restoration of home rule, the South had undone Reconstruction. The Confederacy had, in a military way, lost the Civil War. It had fumed and fretted under the system of Reconstruction and the excesses of carpetbag governments and military policing. Then, with the restoration of the old leaders to power, it had disfranchised the Negroes and ultimately the bulk of the poor white people as well; it had repudiated the carpetbag debts as well as many honest debts; it had engaged in its own style of carpetbag corruption and chicanery; and it had restored economically unfree labor. Not all of the results were beneficial, even to the master class.

Chapter III

HAYES AND PARTY DISSENSIONS

ONLY gradually did Northern politicians, of the group that had long flourished on the agitation of a punitive Reconstruction program, give up the struggle. The "waving of the bloody shirt" and the admonition to Union veterans to "vote as you shot" were not entirely abandoned as useless in vote-getting until the election of 1888 made evident to all but the politically deaf and blind voters that politics was becoming the handmaiden of economic interests. From 1877 onward, it became increasingly more evident that political developments depended on economic motivation, though it was far from demonstrable that the voters always knew what was for their economic betterment.

Just as the Electoral Commission was reaching its final vote on the seating of Rutherford B. Hayes as President, the Supreme Court of the United States handed down its fundamental decision in the Granger cases,[1] a significant step along the road to governmental regulation of the economy. At the same time, the Knights of Labor were beginning to reveal their strength, and before the close of the year the secret Trainmen's Union was to inaugurate the first great railroad strikes. By 1878, the Standard Oil Company had effected a strong pool in its march toward monopoly of the petroleum business, and state and federal investigation of its activities began. In the same year came the Bland-Allison Act for the reinfusion of silver into the United States currency. Also, in 1878 a Socialist Labor party took definite form, and in the following year Henry George, with his *Progress and Poverty*, led the long series of writers in protest against the inequities of the existing economic order and its leaders.

As compared with these developments and manifestations, the administration of Hayes was somewhat short of spectacu-

lar. As the agitation over the restoration of Bourbon rule subsided, there was in the North a residue of feeling that reform
in national politics should go on further after the exposure of
rascals in the Grant administration. Samuel J. Tilden had run
for the Presidency in 1876 as a reform candidate, and it was
felt that the somewhat colorless Hayes would at least not
hamper reform movements. But Hayes was not in a position
to accomplish much except to keep his promise to remove
the military from the last two carpetbag states, to offer some
opposition to a Democratic House and an almost evenly divided Senate in their determination to repeal the whole set of
Reconstruction election laws, and to make some tentative efforts to clean up the civil service. In each of these lines of
endeavor he made enemies within his own party. When he
accepted the nomination he had pledged himself not to run
for a second term,[2] and by 1880 his re-election seemed to be
an impossibility anyway.

Hayes, who spent half of the preceding ten years as govern-
nor of Ohio, had been relatively detached from national politics and was not closely connected with administrative factions. He had played a rather inconspicuous part in the
campaign of 1876, and had resigned himself to the completion of his gubernatorial work at Columbus if the Electoral
Commission wavered by one vote toward Tilden. True to the
prevailing Victorian principles, the inauguration did not take
place until March 5 (the fourth being on Sunday) but he had
privately taken the oath of office prior to the expiration of
Grant's term. Unbound by factional ties, innocent of more
than a few elaborate promises, illustriously obscure, and
"negatively honest," he was in a position to hoe his own row
or to be a safe tool in the hands of the party managers who
had maneuvered him through the Electoral Commission.

Yet, little more than a month of the administration had
passed before the new President's actions had begun to split
the factions already existing in the Republican party into sects
that by 1880 were known as "Stalwarts" and "Half-Breeds."
It was Senator James G. Blaine of Maine who coined the
term "Stalwart Republicanism" to describe the members of
the Senate who opposed Hayes in his policy of terminating

military rule in the South.[3] But Blaine's feud with Roscoe
Conkling of New York kept the "Plumed Knight" out of the
Senate oligarchy headed by Conkling, James Donald (Don)
Cameron of Pennsylvania, and John A. Logan of Illinois. So
Blaine became the leader of the Half-Breeds, in open opposition to the oligarchy, though Blaine was as conservative
and self-seeking as any of the Old Guard.[4] It was Conkling
who drew the distinction between Stalwart and Half-Breed,
the latter including all who opposed him, and Blaine was the
most outspoken of the opponents. Conkling fought his major
battles in the New York arena of politics and patronage, but
the state factions did not remain isolated from the national
scene, and some of the fiercest skirmishes raged in Washington.[5] Until nearly the end of the administration, the fight in
the nation's capital was not so much between Stalwart and
Half-Breed as between Senate leaders of both factions and
Hayes. It centered on the President's refusal to let the oligarchy name the members of the cabinet, his withdrawal of
troops from the South, and the civil service question. It was
this latter issue that dragged on into the presidential campaign of 1880 and which clearly divided the Republicans
into mutually hostile camps.

When Hayes refused to give Blaine, Cameron, and Conkling the privilege of naming favored politicians to cabinet
posts, their sponsors considered this a grievous slight, for their
status as state leaders depended on their control of the patronage. Surely, this political upstart from Ohio could not be
serious in his quixotic promise of civil service reform.[6] But
Hayes generally remained firm, both as to cabinet appointments and minor offices, though his proposal to make Joseph
E. Johnston Secretary of War, in fulfillment of a promise to
bring a former secessionist into the official family, gave way
before vehement protest.[7] The Senate then accepted a minor
Confederate army officer, David M. Key of Tennessee, as
Postmaster-General. But James N. Tyner of Indiana, the preceding head of that department, retained as first assistant in
control of minor appointments, tended to cancel any efforts
toward civil service reform in the Post Office Department.
Carl Schurz of Missouri as Secretary of the Interior was as

offensive to straight party men as Tyner was to the civil service reformers. He had played the cuckoo role in too many political nests. Simon Cameron of Pennsylvania resigned from the Senate and secured the election of his son Don to his seat in protest against the failure to secure a cabinet appointment for himself. William M. Evarts of New York, as Secretary of State, had the political disadvantage of never having been a member of the Senate.[8] The Senate's Old Guard could not block these appointments, but, in resentment, could interfere with other presidential plans.

In withdrawing military support from carpetbag governments, and in recognizing the Democrats F. T. Nicholls and Wade Hampton as governors of Louisiana and South Carolina (April 9 and 10), Hayes was simply keeping his foremost campaign promise, and there was little that Republican politicians could do about it.[9] On the other hand, significant restrictions on the spoils system could be accomplished only with Congressional aid. In view of the fact that the Republican platform of 1876 had called for reforms in the civil service, Hayes certainly had reason to expect his own party's members of Congress to support him. For that matter, as early as 1871 President Ulysses S. Grant had received authority to draw up regulations for appointments, define the duties of the officials, and establish rules of conduct,[10] but the failure of Congress to renew appropriations in 1873 effectively vetoed the efforts of the civil service board from which George W. Curtis had already resigned, and the spoilsmen's practices remained thoroughly unimpeded.[11]

In accepting the nomination, Hayes clearly indicated that, after the withdrawal of troops from the South, the main object of his administration would be the restoration of the civil service to the efficient conduct of governmental tasks instead of maintaining it to fulfill the party obligations of members of Congress. The offices, he said, "have become not merely rewards for party service, but rewards for service to party leaders." The effect was to destroy "the independence of the separate departments of the Government"; to encourage extravagance, incapacity, and dishonesty; and to impair strict accountability to superiors. Furthermore, the spoils system "obstructs the prompt removal and sure punishment of the unworthy; in every way it degrades the civil service and the character of the Government." Civil servants should have tenure subject only to the maintenance of good character and satisfactory performance of duties. "If elected, I shall conduct the administration of the Government upon these principles, and all constitutional powers vested in the Executive will be employed to establish this reform."[12]

Any effort of Hayes or the reformers of his party to effect his promised "thorough, radical, and complete" reform faced strong opposition from the regular party organizations, the professional politicians, the political machines, and the party press of Republicans and Democrats alike. The unwillingness of party leaders to surrender their control of patronage soon led to open conflict between Hayes and the most powerful leaders of his party in Congress. Neither party, either in the House or the Senate, gave him support for remedial legislation.[13] Outside of Congress there was considerable help, and on May 16, 1877, a group headed by Henry W. Bellows, noted as the founder and president of the United States Sanitary Commission, and Dorman B. Eaton, president from 1873 to 1875 of Grant's Civil Service Commission, formed the New York Civil Service Reform Association.[14]

Even without supporting legislation, Hayes found some things he could do. At the first meeting of the cabinet, he asked Evarts and Schurz to draw up rules to govern appointments in the various executive departments. Schurz immediately set about cleaning up the Department of the Interior. John Sherman, of Ohio, also set to work on the Treasury Department by appointing a commission headed by John Jay to investigate the management of the New York customhouse. The commission was presumably impartial, having no plan for the dismissal of any officials then in charge, but quite soon it began making suggestions in that direction. In a series of six reports the Jay Commission revealed numerous examples of ignorance, incompetence, carelessness, and fraud on the part of customhouse employees. As a consequence, returns to the treasury in proportion to revenue collected were far less for the port of New York than for similar service in

England. Nothing short of a thoroughgoing reform and reorganization, said the commission, would improve matters.[15]

After reading a preliminary report of May 26, Hayes wrote to Sherman, saying that he agreed with the recommendations.[16] The public generally expressed approval and commendation. Politicians and the partisan press found the decree intolerable. If the President's views should prevail, the party would be ruined, and the country would fall into chaos without Republican leadership. Nevertheless the executive attack on the New York customhouse continued. It soon became evident that reforms could not be effective as long as Chester A. Arthur remained collector and Alonzo B. Cornell naval officer, so on October 19, 1877, the President and cabinet agreed to nominate the elder Theodore Roosevelt and LeBaron Bradford Prince, both of New York, to replace Arthur and Cornell, and Edwin Atkins Merritt of the same state for the position of surveyor, and to send these names to the Senate for confirmation, which he did, ineffectively, on October 28.[17] This action violated Conkling's senatorial prerogative concerning appointments in New York, thus further injuring his feelings while he was already fretting over the order of June 22.[18]

In a message to Congress on December 3, 1877, Hayes called for legislation to make his program effective. Then again he presented the names of Roosevelt, Prince, and Merritt, thus bringing Conkling and his followers into open conflict.[19] Conkling, swayed both by personal and party motives, aware that "courtesy of the Senate" demanded that no persons be given offices in New York without his own approval and nomination, delayed action on the nominations as long as possible. Ultimately, the Senate turned down Roosevelt and Prince, while confirming Merritt.[20] Thus, the first round of the fight seemed to go to Conkling and the reactionaries, but Hayes had only to wait for the adjournment of Congress to remove Arthur. This occurred on July 11, 1878. Roosevelt having died in the meantime, Hayes elevated Merritt to the post of collector, gave Silas W. Burt the position previously held by Cornell, and made Charles K. Graham surveyor, all subject to Senate approval when it should reconvene.[21]

The reform element of the Republican party deemed essential the removal of Arthur and Cornell, regardless of the fact that Arthur was the darling of Conkling and Cornell was chairman of both the New York and the national Republican committees, but Hayes had based the dismissals on the wrong grounds. He had acted simply for the reason that the service demanded the replacement of the existing officers. The reformers felt that the President should have stated specifically that the removal of Arthur and Cornell was because they were agents of the spoils system.[22]

When the Senate convened for the short session, late in 1878, Conkling renewed his battle to retain control of the patronage in New York. This time, however, he faced an accomplished fact. New officials, sympathetic with the President's reform views, now held the offices of collector, naval officer, and surveyor in the customhouse. Consequently, delaying tactics were of no further avail; Conkling had to win outright rejection of the nominations.[23] However, on February 3, 1879, the Senate approved the nominations of Merritt, Burt, and Graham, in spite of a bitter effort of Conkling and the Stalwarts to prevent the action. The victory probably belonged more to John Sherman than to Hayes, for the Secretary of the Treasury exerted his influence on several of the senators and even threatened to resign his cabinet post if approval of the nominations failed.[24] Though the Senate reluctantly acquiesced, this was the only instance in which Hayes won either the cooperation or approval of that body for his reform measures.

During the remainder of the term, Hayes could not fulfill any more of his pre-election promises. Much of the failure resulted from his attempts to work through the agency of traditional organizations.[25] Yet, near the close of the administration, some of the professional reformers were ready to admit that the President had achieved as much as he could and that further efforts at that time were useless. But he ended his term generally unpopular with that group for accomplishing too little,[26] and equally out of favor with the politicians of his own party for doing too much.[27]

Contemporary views were not generous and, before the assassination of President James A. Garfield, the general public was ready to laugh in enjoyment when the political wheel horses referred to the "snivel" service reformers. This general apathy is revealed in an incident in Chicago in 1880 when a reform lecturer "widely advertised an address on the Civil Service and what must be done to make it an effective arm of government. Eight curious people turned out to hear him."[28] Perhaps the most useful thing accomplished by Hayes was to prepare the way for the achievements of Arthur's administration. One contribution in this direction, aside from the Senate battle, was the appointment by Hayes of Dorman B. Eaton to study and report on the British civil service,[29] thus providing a guide for Congress when the time for action came. Meanwhile the nomination of Cornell for governor of New York and of Arthur for Vice-President was a complete repudiation of the whole Hayes administration.

It was not for lack of more serious issues that politicians worked up such a lather over the civil service, but sometimes it is much more convenient to thump the tubs over minor affairs so as to divert public attention from needed reforms of greater magnitude. Changes in the existing order are likely to violate vested interests, and in 1878 election or re-election to Congress depended on keeping happy those persons most likely to furnish ample campaign funds. In fact, the state platforms of the Republicans, Democrats, and Greenbackers[30] in 1878 were loaded with demands on issues big and little, the more inconsequential the problem the more definite the proposed cure. Foremost among the planks of Republicans and Democrats were charges of election frauds in 1876, contentions over the administration's Southern policy, rebel war claims, and the "bloody shirt." After the tariff juggling of 1872 and 1875, that issue was not prominent in 1878, but various state platforms took a theoretical stand with no great degree of agreement within the parties. The evanescent Greenbackers and the newly organized and ineffective Socialist Labor party were quite definite in their labor demands. But Democrats and Republicans also made indulgent comments on such matters as Chinese immigration, prison contract labor, lien laws to protect wages, strikes and violence, hours of labor, safety legislation, and just rewards for labor. The Greenbackers added demands for a postal-savings system, a federal labor bureau, and equal pay for equal work of men and women.

Likewise, some state platforms of the major parties dwelt with more or less wisdom on the problems of the public lands, railroad land grants, railroad regulations, internal improvements, the regulation of corporations, hostility to monopolies, economy and honesty in government, the civil service, a graduated income tax, equalization of taxes so as to catch bondholders and corporations, a limitation on the federal courts, the size of the standing army, and even temperance and prohibition. At least one Prohibition party platform demanded woman suffrage.[31] Then there was the monetary question valiantly advanced by Greenbackers, under whatever party names they operated in the various states, and to a lesser degree among Democrats and Republicans. Despite the strong Greenback vote in 1878, this issue was not a decisive one.

It was only to be expected that in 1878 Democrats and Republicans should refight the election of 1876. In preparation for the campaign the Democratic House of Representatives, on May 17, 1878, appointed the Potter Committee (chaired by Clarkson Nott Potter of New York), which promptly showed to its own satisfaction that Tilden had been robbed of the Presidency. Then, on October 7, 1878, too late for an effective Democratic reply before the election, the *New York Times* began publishing the "cipher dispatches." During the dispute over the election of 1876, these telegrams had been sent by Republican and Democratic wheel horses alike to various Southern election officials, offering bribes to influence the seating of Hayes or Tilden electors. The telegraph company had turned these dispatches over to the Republicans, who destroyed those bearing on their own activities and published those that might throw a shadow on the integrity of Tilden. It has generally been conceded that there was guilt on both sides, but that neither Hayes nor Tilden knew anything about what was being done. The destruction of the Republican dispatches in itself arouses an ominous suspicion.[32]

The Democratic state platforms generally declared that Tilden had been defrauded. That of Illinois called the seating of Hayes "the monster political crime of the age—a crime against free government and the elective franchise." Others, more moderate, like those of Missouri, Nevada, and Ohio, accepted the results of the election as official, but asked for further investigation. The Pennsylvania platform also urged examination into the records but was so cautious as to add: "But we oppose any attack upon the President's title as dangerous to our institutions."[33] Some of the Republican platforms defended Hayes's title, while others ignored the charges. That of Alabama denounced the Potter Committee, while Connecticut assailed the Democratic accusations as "seditious," and Vermont called them heretical.[34] Indiana used the word "anarchy," and judged that the Democrats were merely trying to cover up their own intimidation of Southern voters, and the Oregon platform spoke of the Democratic attempt to steal the electoral vote. South Carolina Republicans were particularly vehement, charging the Democrats with "frauds, violence, and intimidation," with "assassinations and murders . . . preceding that election," with "violent seizure of the State government after that election," and with a succeeding process of intimidation in some counties, "whereby the Republicans are actually prohibited from meeting and organizing."[35]

The South Carolina complaint points up the reaction against Hayes's policy of Southern conciliation, a matter considered in nearly every one of the Republican and Democratic state platforms. The Democrats often congratulated the country on the restoration of home rule, seeing this as a defeat of traditional Republican policy. The Democratic platform in Alabama was unique in open affirmation of white supremacy. Though promising "protection to all the colored people," it declared that the continued welfare of the state required "the union of the great governing race—the white

people of the land." Connecticut Democrats were content to
call for "a cessation of sectional hostility" and to oppose those
persons seeking to "keep alive animosities between different
sections. . . ." The Illinois Democrats firmly approved "the
final settlement of the questions resulting from the late civil
war upon the principles of local self-government so long supported by the Democratic party. . . ." On the other hand,
the Republicans were divided on the support of their own
President. Some of their platforms contained implied criticism of the Southern policy while others, notably those of
Massachusetts, Minnesota, Ohio, Vermont, and Wisconsin,
showed warm approval.[36]

The infrequency of unguarded endorsement of Hayes in
Republican state platforms suggests a widespread skepticism
within the party, an attitude that was reflected in the statements of some of the leaders. The loss of control of the House
of Representatives and the consequent failure of Garfield to
achieve the speakership in October, 1877, they laid to
Hayes's Southern policy. On top of this, his civil service efforts further reduced his Republican support. Wendell Phil-
lips and William Lloyd Garrison attacked the Southern policy,
and Conkling dolefully complained that "the Government is
rapidly passing absolutely into the hands of those who sought
to destroy it."[37] William E. Chandler roundly denounced
the Southern policy, publishing his letters on the subject in
pamphlet form early in 1878. Suggestive of the influence of
Conkling, the New York Republican platform contained no
endorsement of Hayes, but demanded "full and unintimi-
dated elections in the South" and "equal rights and liberty"
for all. Pennsylvania Republicans also omitted commendation
of Hayes and took a strong stand for the fruits of Southern
reconstruction.[38] Connecticut, Iowa, Kansas, Michigan, Nebraska, Nevada, and New Hampshire were also among the
Northern states whose Republican platforms, either ex-
pressly or implicitly, criticized the President for his Southern
policy, including failure to protect the Negro vote.[39] As
might have been expected, the Southern Republicans were
the least appreciative of all in their attitude toward Hayes.
The Alabama and North Carolina platforms were plaintive on

the subject, and the Tennessee convention flatly refused to pass a resolution declaring that ". . . we cordially endorse the Administration of President Hayes."[40] The Greenback platforms were uniformly silent on the question. Also, they shied away from comments on the "bloody shirt" argument, fearing to lend support to either of their stronger rivals. But the Illinois Republicans referred to the Democrats as "rebels and their sympathizers" and deplored their "lack of honor and patriotism," while William Lloyd Garrison acclaimed the "bloody shirt" by saying: *In hoc signo vinces.*"[41]

Though the Republican state platforms generally endorsed protective tariffs and the Democrats favored free trade, there were many degrees of difference within the parties. Thus, contrary to the traditional party stand, the Iowa Republicans declared for "a wisely adjusted tariff for revenue," while the Pennsylvania Democrats, as could be expected in that state, declared that the lowered rates of the Act of 1872 "struck a fatal blow at the industries and labor" of that commonwealth.[42] The Greenbackers, following an opportunistic trend, disagreed as much as any on this issue.

The appeal for labor votes was an important element in many of the platforms. Thirteen Greenback statements demanded the abolition of prison contract labor, the Massachusetts declaration being especially specific. Illinois and Kansas Democrats were equally direct, as were also the Alabama and Tennessee Republicans,[43] while the Socialist Labor party really meant it. Five Greenback, two Democratic, and two Republican platforms blazed a new trail by demanding legislation insuring labor the first lien on employers' assets.[44] The general reaction of the parties to the strikes of 1877 was reflected in a condemnation of violence and occasional references to arbitration, and suggestions of resort to the ballot,[45] the latter being a particularly naïve idea. The Greenbackers were unique in proposing postal-savings banks and a federal bureau of labor, but both the Democrats and Republicans of New Hampshire joined them in suggestions for limited hours of labor. A few platforms of all parties called for safety legislation, and the Missouri Democrats asked for laws "to secure to each man . . . the just rewards of his own labor,"[46] whatever that may have meant.

Planks dealing with public land policy were frequently combined with the question of federal aid to or regulation of railroads, or both, and with little regard to party lines. Here, the Greenbackers took the most advanced stand, eighteen of their platforms advocating federal disposal of lands to settlers only. Delaware, Ohio, Massachusetts, and New Jersey joined Connecticut in being strictly realistic in their approach. Realizing that free farms were only a will-o'-the-wisp to persons really needing the land, the platforms of these states recommended government aid to finance the ventures. The Nevada Republicans, in a state where homesteading was almost an impossibility anyway, also took this stand. On the other hand, the Oregon Republicans would have the government sell land to the people and give the proceeds to the railroads, while the Pennsylvanians would reserve lands for the people, without further assistance,[47] thus giving little hope to the dispossessed of the country. The Democrats of Connecticut, Nevada, Ohio, and Pennsylvania took a like stand. Quite obviously, the safety-valve myth was riding high.

Several of the platforms of both major parties expressed opposition to land grants to railroads, but certain Southern and Western states advocated a continuation of the old policy, specifically, aid to the Southern Pacific and the Texas and Pacific railroads as advocated by Alabama Republicans and Arkansas and Louisiana Democrats. A far different plea came from the Missouri Greenbackers, who favored a railroad from St. Louis to San Francisco, built, owned, and controlled by the government. Oregon Republicans and Democrats as well called for federal aid for private enterprise.[48] In a like manner, demands for federal regulation of railroads occurred in some of the platforms of all three parties, while Greenbackers and a few of the Democratic platforms also condemned monopolies, the Minnesota Democrats proscribing "monopolies of all kinds."[49]

It was almost inevitable that the monetary situation should receive unusual attention in this campaign. The bottom of the business cycle following the Panic of 1873 had just been reached, but none could yet affirm that conditions would not become still worse. In the six years there had been over 47,-000 bankruptcies involving losses in excess of $1,200,000,000. Commodity prices in 1878 and 1879 were at the lowest point since the Civil War, and for farm products the prices were considerably below the general level.[50] For example, cotton at ten cents a pound was bringing only half the price of 1872. Wheat, corn, barley, oats, rye, hogs, and cattle also had reached bottom.[51] Unemployment was still near its three million peak. Since 1873, there had been rumblings against the demonetization of silver, and the discontent had increased with the adoption of the Resumption Act in 1875. The substitution of national bank notes for greenbacks was gall and wormwood to debtors, who next saw the volume of national bank notes declining as the government redeemed the bonds that secured the notes. The volume of currency was shrinking, and prices were falling in a corresponding degree, while debts remained at their earlier level. This led to new demands for free coinage of silver and for a green-back currency system. The organ of the National, or Green-back, party announced to its readers that only with a green-back currency could people sleep easy, knowing that business failures could not affect its value.[52]

It was easy to demonstrate that the per capita of circulating money had declined from $31.18 in 1865 to less than $19.00 when Congress passed the Resumption Act, and the coinage of gold in succeeding years could not correct the situation. Furthermore, the Greenbackers and other reinflationists were not greatly impressed by the passage of the Bland-Allison Act over Hayes's veto on February 28, 1878, or by the measure of May 31, 1878, stopping the retirement of greenbacks under the Resumption Act. The former fell far short of free and unlimited coinage of silver and the latter was something like locking the stable after all but one crippled pony had been stolen.[53] The appeal of Greenbackism to thousands of Democrats and Republicans caused the major parties to do some hedging on the question in their platforms in all parts of the country. The call for stable greenbacks in place of the national bank notes, whose volume was usually in reverse size to the demand, found a place in Democratic platforms even in the Northeastern states. The Republicans added a tinge of color to their monetary record by proclaiming in their campaign textbook that their party was the "FATHER, FRIEND, AND GUARDIAN OF THE REPUBLICAN GREENBACK."[54] Nevertheless, the continuing business depression, labor unrest, and the resumption and silver policies contributed to bring the Greenback vote up from about 83,000 in 1876 to over 1,000,000 in 1878. This vote was not a mere aberration of the wild and woolly West or of a resurgent South. The largest vote, 124,000, was in Iowa, followed in order by 110,000 in Massachusetts, 96,000 in Pennsylvania, and 80,000 in New York.[55]

The larger Greenback votes resulted from fusion with other political parties or factions. In Massachusetts, the Greenbackers supported Benjamin F. Butler, who was running for governor with Democratic support as well. In New York State, outside the metropolis, there was fusion with the Labor Reform party, while in Pennsylvania the union was with the Workingmen's party. In seven of the eight Congressional districts of Wisconsin the Greenbackers had candidates, three of them being supported also by the Democrats. In Iowa, there was an effective combination with the Democrats in two districts, which elected Edward H. Gillespie and James B. Weaver to Congress. In Illinois, Adlai E. Stevenson, a Democratic candidate for Congress, owed his election in part to the Greenbackers. No Greenbacker was elected to Congress without such fusion, but thereby the party secured fourteen representatives in Congress: three from Pennsylvania; two each from Illinois, Iowa, and Maine; and one each from Missouri, Indiana, Texas, Alabama, and North Carolina.[56] While the Greenbackers were jubilant about these results, Hayes likewise felt that the election returns were gratifying, referring to what he called "the crushing defeat of Butler" in Massachusetts, and calling it "one of the best events that has happened since the war."[57]

Hayes needed what comfort he could get from the election of a Republican as governor of Massachusetts, for there could be no gratification over the Congressional races. But the Democrats also had reason to ponder the returns in the House of Representatives. In the election of 1876 the results had been 156 Democrats and 136 Republicans. There had been some changes before the election of 1878, but the returns then were 148 Democrats and 130 Republicans. The 15 Greenbackers, Nationalists, and whatever else they called themselves could easily hold the balance of power when a few Democrats were absent, but in the main they sided with the Democrats anyway. The real gain for the Democrats came later, when the state legislatures convened and changed the almost even Senate tie of 1877 to a standing of 42 Democrats, 33 Republicans, and 1 Independent in 1879.[58]

Hayes, for the remainder of his administration, got no more support from Congress than was necessary for appropriations and the routine matters for keeping the government going. As far as accomplishments are concerned, the Forty-sixth Congress might as well be ignored, but the campaign of 1878, nevertheless, is a revealing one. The state conventions disclosed the wide divergencies within the parties and the great number of questions that could be welded into country-wide problems as time passed. Nearly every issue of the next twenty years was aired in the various platforms.

During the last half of Hayes's term, even without supporting legislation, he found it possible to achieve a part of his civil service program. In the New York customhouse, naval office, and surveyor's office competitive examinations, based on the merit system, got under way early in 1879. Thomas L. James, one of the Stalwarts who had been postmaster in the city of New York since 1873, received encouragement for the working out of civil service reform in the greatest post office of the country. In October, 1880, the New York Civil Service Reform Association, under the leadership of George W. Curtis and Everett P. Wheeler, began campaigning for adequate Congressional sanction. George H. Pendleton, Democrat from Ohio, had already introduced a reform bill in the Senate, but the New York association considered the proposed measure inadequate and began preparation of an improved bill.[59]

POLITICAL STRENGTH OF PARTIES IN CONGRESS,
1877–1891
(At Time of Organization of Each Congress)

		HOUSE OF REPRESENTATIVES			SENATE		
Congress	Years	Demo-crats	Repub-licans	Others	Demo-crats	Repub-licans	Others
45	1877–79	156[a]	136		36	39	1
46	1879–81	148	130	15	42	33	1
47	1881–83	129	152	12	37	37	2
48	1883–85	201	119	5	35	40	1
49	1885–87	180	138	2[b]	34	42	
50	1887–89	169[c]	152[c]	4	37	39	
51	1889–91	154	173	1[d]	37	47	

[a] The filling of a vacancy from Louisiana made this 157 in the third session.

[b] Five vacancies.

[c] One representative changed his party and in the second session there were 170 Democrats and 151 Republicans.

[d] Two vacancies.

Source: McPherson, *Handbook of Politics*, 1878, pp. 1–3, 141–43; *ibid.*, 1880, pp. 95–96, 98–99; *ibid.*, 1884, pp. 1–3, 129–31; *ibid.*, 1888, pp. 1–3, 89–91; *ibid.*, 1890, pp. 1–3, 245–48.

SPEAKERS OF THE HOUSE AND PRESIDENTS PRO TEM
OF THE SENATE, 1877–1891

Congress	SPEAKER OF HOUSE			PRESIDENT PRO TEM OF SENATE		
	Name	State	Party	Name	State	Party
45	Samuel J. Randall	Pa.	Dem.	Thomas W. Ferry	Mich.	Rep.
46	Samuel J. Randall	Pa.	Dem.	Allen G. Thurman	Ohio	Dem.
47	J. Warren Keifer	Ohio	Rep.	David Davis	Ill.	Ind.
48	John G. Carlisle	Ky.	Dem.	George F. Edmunds	Vt.	Rep.
49	John G. Carlisle	Ky.	Dem.	John Sherman	Ohio	Rep.
50	John G. Carlisle	Ky.	Dem.	John J. Ingalls	Kans.	Rep.
51	Thomas B. Reed	Maine	Rep.	John J. Ingalls	Kans.	Rep.

Chapter IV

GARFIELD AND CONFUSION

IN THE early balloting at the Republican national convention in 1880, Grant and Blaine led, by far, all other candidates for the Presidency. Though Conkling, Cameron, and Logan, the Old Guard triumvirate, the Stalwarts, strongly supported Grant for the nomination, the growing party schism only partially explained their stand. There had been a festering animosity between Conkling and Blaine since 1866, when in a Congressional debate, Blaine had struck back at the jeering and taunting Conkling, comparing the latter with a "singed cat," "a whining puppy," and a "dunghill," and referring to Conkling's "majestic, supereminent, overpowering, turkeygobbler strut."[1] At least partly in retaliation for this humiliating counterattack, Conkling had blocked Blaine's nomination for the Presidency in 1876, and now he was out to duplicate the feat. On the other hand, Grant's inability to gather added strength during the long balloting was because of the Blaine faction's hostility to the Old Guard and because of the repugnance of many delegates to a third term as President for Grant or any other man. George Washington had set the precedent of a limit of two terms, and Jefferson had warned against breaking the tradition. Between Jackson in 1832 and Lincoln in 1864, no President had been elected for a second term, though Martin Van Buren had run in 1840, and Grant was the first since Jackson to serve two full terms. But Grant, itching with inactivity and prodded by an ambitious family, anxiously sought the nomination.

The Republican convention met in Chicago's Expedition Building on June 2. After the delegates were seated and the galleries filled, Cameron, chairman of the National Committee, called the convention to order and nominated Senator

George Frisbie Hoar of Massachusetts as the temporary chairman, a choice quickly affirmed by acclamation. Then the fireworks began with an effort to unpack the Committee on Credentials, which was a Grant stronghold. Conkling first tried to stop the movement by debate and then Logan brought in five hundred pro-Grant Civil War veterans to set the pace in the galleries for a Grant demonstration, thus saving the day for Conkling.[2]

The most significant event on the second day was a vote taken by states on the adoption of the unit rule. This was a device used by the Democrats, allowing the majority of a state's delegation to cast the vote for all. There was an element in the New York Republican delegation that Conkling could not control, and the unit rule would bring the recalcitrants to heel.[3] If the convention adopted this rule, not only could Conkling hold the entire New York delegation in line, but Logan and Cameron could do the same for Illinois and Pennsylvania. With such support as could be won over from other states, this hard core of delegates might secure the nomination of Grant. James A. Garfield of Ohio, who was heading the movement to secure the nomination for fellow Ohioan John Sherman, was also the leader of the anti-third-term movement in the convention. He presented the resolution against the unit rule, which carried by a vote of 406 to 318.[4] This was Conkling's first major defeat in the convention, and it foreshadowed the ultimate end for Grant's chances.

On the third day, Conkling suffered another setback when he tried to oust three West Virginia delegates for refusing to promise to support the nominee of the convention, whoever it might be. Again, Garfield led the opposition until Conkling partially saved his own face by withdrawing his motion.[5] During the roll call of the states, on June 5, an Illinois delegate, free now from the threat of the unit rule, presented the name of Elihu Washburne of that state. Maine put up its perennial favorite son, Blaine, and Minnesota offered its own William Windom. Then Conkling rose to his last act of effectiveness in pointing out the superior merits of Grant, the man who had saved the Union and on whom its future security depended. Garfield, who already had become a prominent man in the convention, next asked for the nomination of Sherman. Vermont completed the list with the name of favorite son Senator George F. Edmunds.[6] The next day was Sunday and Hoar would not hear to open convention activities on that day, which instead was spent in jockeying for votes for the various candidates. Few of the delegates attended church, but Garfield was one of this small minority, and he was probably wiser politically than he knew in his pious remark that he placed more faith in the prayers of Christians than in the political conniving of the convention.[7]

Balloting on the candidates occupied most of the next two days. Grant started out with 304 votes, needing 379 for the nomination, and held them consistently to the end, but never gained more than two or three. Blaine held his position in a like manner, starting with 284 and ending with five less, while Sherman stuck close to the low nineties through all the 28 ballots cast on Monday. Early the next morning there was an effort mainly by the Edmunds following to stampede the convention for Sherman, but it soon collapsed. Then, on the thirty-fourth ballot, the Wisconsin delegates shifted from Washburne to the dark horse Garfield, and two votes later he got the nomination.[8]

Garfield's success, so soon after he had blocked Conkling's unit rule, added gall to the resentment of the New York boss, who had the reputation of being "the implacable enemy of anyone who had successfully crossed his path."[9] Garfield took his place alongside Blaine on Conkling's blacklist. But there was still some balm in Gilead. As a consolation prize, the convention, on the first ballot, gave the vice-presidential nomination to Chester A. Arthur,[10] Conkling's special pet. This action was also a dig at Hayes who, as the Stalwarts thought, had treated Arthur shabbily. Arthur was an honest man of otherwise unproved merits, but he was also a machine politician of long standing and a perennial beneficiary and practitioner of the spoils system. Nobody seemed to consider that the haphazard choice might soon become President-by-accident. Had Conkling kept his temper in the following year, he might yet have had a President meeting with his approval as he continued his domineering role in the Senate.

The Republican platform gave praise to Hayes (as a campaign necessity) and to the Union veterans of the Civil War (as a matter of vote getting) but, first of all, applause to the Republican party for suppressing the rebellion, freeing the slaves, maintaining the integrity of the dollar, establishing prosperity (the depth of the depression was almost visibly past), reducing the public debt, and paying pensions to the old soldiers. But their "we affirm . . . that the reviving industries should be further promoted . . ." was perhaps more of an admission of Republican inadequacy in 1873 and following than the delegates realized. For this, however, they atoned by affirming "that the pensions promised should be extinguished by the full payment of every dollar thereof." Then, as a final settlement of the Civil War, they placed the federal courts above those of the states in the determination of what powers the Constitution delegated to the nation and which ones were reserved to the states. The recommendation for federal aid to education was not greatly helped by their upholding as a standard "not by the genius of any one State, but by the average genius of all." As the Fourteenth Amendment was not for many years to be so interpreted as to make the federal bill of rights place the same prohibitions on the state legislatures as on Congress, the plank calling for a Constitutional amendment to forbid any state "to make any law respecting an establishment of religion" or to appropriate "public funds to the support of sectarian schools" was truly progressive.

The thinly disguised protective-tariff plank declared that duties for revenue "should so discriminate as to favor American labor." This brought applause from the convention, as did the ensuing condemnation of polygamy, the "twin barbarity" of slavery. The demand for a "just, humane and reasonable" restriction of Chinese immigration, if not applauded, at least secured acclamation. Though it was the duty of Congress "to develop and improve our water-courses and harbors," there should be no more land grants "to any railway or other corporation," and "further subsidies to private persons or corporations must cease." In other words, Republicans must abandon their practices of many years now that there was no foreseeable opportunity of continuing them.

The rest of the platform, except for a final amendment regarding the civil service, might as well have been shortened from three paragraphs to four words: "The Democrats be damned!" They were unpatriotic, lustful of office and patronage, had debauched the electorate and used "methods vicious in principle and tyrannical in practice" in attaching partisan riders to appropriation bills, had "crushed the rights of individuals," had "endeavored to obliterate the sacred memories of the war," and had "advocated the principles and sought the favor of rebellion against the Nation." Above all things, the Solid South should be softened up. To the undoing of all these Democratic atrocities, perpetrated during Republican administrations and Congresses, the Republicans pledged their full support. Thus did they denounce the same Hayes whom in an earlier paragraph they had endorsed. Then, shifting ground again, they adopted "the declaration of President Hayes that the reform of the civil service should be thorough, radical, and complete." Congress should provide "that fitness, ascertained by proper, practical tests, shall admit to the public service." But they struck out the further clause that tenure "shall be made permanent during good behavior."[11]

While the Republicans were still balloting for a presidential nominee, the National Greenback party also convened in Chicago on June 9. Richard F. Trevellick, a leader in the Ship Carpenters' and Caulkers' Union, the National Labor Union, and other economic and political labor groups since the 1860s, became the presiding officer. On the first ballot James B. Weaver of Iowa became the candidate for President, with B. J. Chambers of Texas in second place on the ticket. If ability and energy in campaigning meant anything, Weaver should have won the election in the following November.

The Greenback platform declared that the national banking system should be abolished and all money should emanate from the government and be legal tender; that the government should pay off the national debt by substituting greenbacks for bank notes and by the unlimited coinage of silver as well as gold. The labor plank called for enforcement of the federal eight-hour law, failing to demand like state legislation for workers in general; for the abolition of convict-labor contracts; for a bureau of labor statistics; for the ending of employment of children less than fourteen years old; and for the payment of wages in cash. Because the unfair competition of Chinese labor caused slavelike conditions among American labor, they asked for the abrogation of the Burlingame Treaty of 1868. Demands for the recovery by the government of railroad land grants for nonfulfillment of contract, and for federal regulation of rates for transportation and communication, accompanied a denunciation of monopolies of all existing kinds. The Greenbackers also accused the Republicans of favoring the bondholders of the Civil War debt in preference to the veterans. Then, among a list of general recommendations for decency in government, came the demands for a graduated income tax and for the enfranchisement of "every citizen of due age, sound mind, and not a felon," which could be interpreted to cover woman suffrage.[12]

The Democratic convention assembled in Cincinnati on June 22. George Hoadley of Ohio became the temporary chairman. Serenity was established during the first day's proceedings. New York had two sets of delegates, one chosen by the "regular" Democrats, the other by Tammany. Tammany had been cool toward Tilden in 1876 and now John Kelly, the Tammany boss, openly declared that the organization would not support Tilden in another campaign. The convention settled this problem by refusing to seat the Tammany slate of seventy delegates. Assurance of peace followed the reading of an elaborate letter from Tilden, after he got thirty-eight votes on the first ballot, indicating that he preferred not to make the race again.[13]

On the second day, thorough harmony prevailed while states and individual delegates presented nearly a score of candidates for the Presidency. There were two each from New York, Ohio, and Pennsylvania; Tilden and Horatio Seymour, Henry B. Payne and Allen G. Thurman, Samuel J. Randall and Winfield Scott Hancock. The second highest name on the first ballot was that of Thomas F. Bayard of Delaware. Candidates from California, Illinois, and Indiana were Stephen J. Field, William R. Morrison, and Thomas A. Hendricks. When the roll call of the states reached Pennsylvania, Daniel Dougherty, who had made an eloquent speech for James Buchanan in the convention of 1856, now proposed the name of Hancock "who on the field of battle was styled the 'superb,' yet won the still nobler renown," while military governor of Louisiana and Texas, "by proclaiming that the military rule shall ever be subservient to the civil power." The first ballot, on June 23, showed Hancock well in the lead, with 171 votes. The second ballot, on the next day, gave him 320 and the third 705, Indiana's vote still being for Hendricks. William H. English of Indiana then unanimously received the place as tail of the Democratic kite.[14]

The platform, adopted with like expeditiousness, was primarily a document of revenge for "the great fraud of 1876–77, by which, upon a false count of the electoral votes of two States, the candidate defeated at the polls was declared to be President . . . this issue precedes and dwarfs every other." This was at least partially a misstatement, for preceding it were six other planks, including, among the usual platitudes about the dangers of governmental centralization, despotism, and sumptuary laws, the need to maintain the separation of church and state, benevolent words about the public schools, a declaration for honest money, and a demand for "a tariff for revenue only." Also, there should be a "subordination of the military to the civil power, and a general and thorough reform of the civil service." The Republicans were guilty of "making places in the civil service a reward for political crime." After some pleasant comments about Tilden, there was a remark against "discrimination in favor of transportation lines, corporations or monopolies"; a demand for the amendment of the Burlingame Treaty, cutting off immigration for permanent residence; a somewhat ambiguous statement about "public land for actual settlers"; and a vague expression of friendship for the laboring man, who must be protected "alike against the cormorant and the commune." Finally, the public must remember that it was the Democratic Congress that had reduced the cost of government $40,000,000 a year and had maintained "prosperity at home and the National honor abroad."[15] In other words, it was a rather colorless platform.

During June, the Prohibition party and the American party also held their conventions, the Prohibitionists nominating Neal Dow of Maine and A. M. Thompson of Ohio, the Americans John W. Phelps of Vermont and Samuel C. Pomeroy of Kansas. The Prohibitionists had a feeble organization that captured only a little over 10,000 votes. The American party, opposing secret societies, particularly Freemasonry, and all other organizations that the delegates denominated anti-Christian, was a mere relic of the past and was hardly heard of after the convention.[16]

The ensuing campaign was rather tame and uneventful. The personalities of Garfield and Hancock appealed to the voters, and about equally. Garfield was touted as the "canal-boat boy" who had made good. He was a graduate of Williams College and had taught the classics at Hiram College and became its president. He had been a volunteer colonel in the War of the Rebellion, then a brigadier general, and became a major general for gallantry at Chickamauga. Leaving the army in 1863, he entered Congress, where he served the Western Reserve area of Ohio for several terms. He was a supporter of specie payments; was a member of the Electoral Commission, where he consistently voted for Hayes; had been the Republican candidate for Speaker of the House in 1879; and at the time of the election of 1880 was already a senator elect. He had even been a preacher. He had been a consistent party man, though sometimes aligned with factions. The "superb" Hancock was a professional soldier who had distinguished himself in the Mexican War and again in the Civil War. It was his corps that had stopped Pickett's charge at Gettysburg and turned the Confederates back. He was known as the commander who had never made a mistake in battle. His record as military governor in Louisiana and Texas in 1867 overcame in Southern minds any prejudice they might have had against him as a distinguished leader of their battle foes. He was inexperienced and somewhat naïve in politics.[17]

Hancock's war record made the Republican "bloody shirt" issue fall with a plop. On the other hand, the Democrats brought out the old charge of Garfield's complicity in the Crédit Mobilier affair of 1867 and a later paving contract scandal in Washington, D.C., but the voters did not seem to be greatly excited about such ancient activities. More damaging was a supposed letter from Garfield to one H. L. Morey of the Employers' Union in Lynn, Massachusetts, dated January 23, 1880. This letter, released on the eve of the election, made Garfield seem to be the tool of employers of cheap Chinese labor and opposed to the abrogation of the Burlingame Treaty until the labor market was saturated. This letter was not exposed as a forgery until after the election, and it probably cost Garfield Nevada's three electoral votes and five of the six votes of California. He carried Oregon, the only other state of the Pacific group, by less than 700 votes. It is doubtful whether the grudging stump speeches made by Grant and Conkling did him any more good than the Morey letter did him harm. Neither was of much effect. Hancock rendered one Democratic plank useless. Confronted with the charge of free-tradism because of the platform's words "tariff for revenue only," he opined that, after all, the tariff was merely "a local issue."[18]

The election was too close for Republican comfort. Out of some 8,218,000 votes, Garfield got a little over 4,454,000 or 48.32 per cent, while Hancock received 4,445,000, which was 48.22 per cent. Weaver accumulated only 308,000 and some odd ballots, or 3.35 per cent of the total, and Neal Dow gleaned the insignificant remnant. The electoral vote was more solace to the Republicans, with 214 as compared with the Democrats' 155. But if Tammany had not slighted Hancock, the 35 votes from New York might have gone to him and given him the election. This was almost purely a sectional election, each party carrying nineteen states. Hancock got all sixteen of the former slave states, New Jersey's nine votes in the North, and California and Nevada in the Far West. All the rest, plus one lone vote from California, went to Garfield.[19] In the ultimate results, both North and South had voted the way they had shot.

In the House of Representatives, the Republicans acquired a safe majority of 152 to 129, and even the ten Greenbackers and the two Readjusters from Virginia could not change the score. The state legislatures later had twenty-five senators to choose and, the bulk of them being in Republican states, the Democrats lost five and the Republicans gained four, thus tying the parties at 37 to 37. David Davis of Illinois was the one holdover Independent, and William Mahone, Readjuster from Virginia, replaced the fifth lost Democrat.[20]

Even before the inauguration, Garfield was bedeviled with scandals and with dissensions over patronage. The ratification meetings over his election were about all the political harmony he was ever to experience. Before the election, the Republican National Committee had pressed Garfield into a conference with Conkling and other Stalwarts to bargain for their support in New York. Garfield was convinced that he had won the Stalwarts over without any concessions. The Stalwarts were confident they had been promised the chance to name the Secretary of the Treasury. Conkling needed this vantage point in order to control further appointments in the port of New York. Garfield was definitely committed to the Stalwart New Yorker, Thomas L. James, as Postmaster General. With both the Post Office and Treasury departments under his control, Conkling could, by judicious patronage, have the control of New York Republican politics firmly in his grasp. But Garfield had warning from numerous sources as to the far range of Conkling's ambition before a further conference with the New York boss. Here Conkling used all the artillery in his well-stocked arsenal to force the extra cabinet appointment. Garfield, thereupon, took quick action contrary to Conkling's demands.[21]

Even James, though of Conkling's camp, held advanced views on the civil service and patronage that were not to the senator's liking. But Garfield's appointment of William Windom to the Treasury Department was more than Conkling could bear. Then, the crowning insult was the choice of Blaine

for Secretary of State.[22] Further injury added to the insult
was the proposed appointment of William H. Robertson for
Collector of the Port of New York. Robertson, high in the
ranks of the New York Half-Breeds, was a champion of the
reformed civil service that Conkling abhorred. Furthermore,
Robertson had headed the group of nineteen New York delegates who had supported Blaine in the national convention.
In opposition to these appointments, Conkling entered his
last political battle. Along with him was Platt, who had been
elected to the Senate only after winning over some Half-
Breed votes in the legislature. The United States Senate met
in executive session on March 4, 1881, to consider the appointments, but, because neither Republicans nor Democrats
had a majority, the Senate wasted two months in a futile
effort to organize, after which the foes entered a truce to
consider the business at hand. Then, on May 14, when it had
become obvious that the nominations would all be confirmed,
Conkling resigned from the Senate in a huff and Platt joined
him. Both expected the legislature to vindicate them by
prompt re-election. But now the Stalwart power was completely broken and, after many ballots, the legislature chose
Warner Miller, the leader of the Half-Breeds, and El-
bridge G. Lapham to replace the senators. Conkling's days
as a power in politics ended abruptly, and "Me Too" Platt,
as he was now called, remained in retirement for several
years.[23]

If the problems of patronage befuddled Garfield before his
inauguration, they literally dogged him to his death thereafter. Whatever else the new President may have been, he
was certainly no dedicated civil service reformer. In his
four months of activity he made 390 appointments and dismissed 89 officials, or a fifth more than Hayes had removed
in his first year. Garfield had pursued the methods of the
machine politician during the presidential campaign, and
now he had to pay his political debts. But he owed no debt
to Thomas W. Brady, the second assistant postmaster general, who was a holdover from Grant and Hayes. For years
there had been rumors of scandalous activities in the Post
Office Department, and Garfield had been President less than

a week when, on March 9, he gave James permission to investigate the affair. On April 19 came the cabinet-advised
request for Brady's resignation. On the following day, James
and MacVeagh presented Garfield with evidence of fraud by
high officials so serious that they feared the activities would
result in a Democratic Congress in the election of 1882, unless the administration took drastic action. A day later,
April 21, James gave to the Associated Press a list of ninety-
three star routes in the Southwest on which financial irregu-
larities were found—and Brady was in charge of the star-route
contracts and business.[24]

Meanwhile, Brady retaliated for the investigation by publishing a letter Garfield had written to Jay A. Hubbell, the
Republican Congressional chairman who during the preceding campaign had assessed each officeholder 2 per cent of his
annual salary as a "voluntary contribution" to the campaign
fund. Addressing him as "My dear Hubbell," Garfield asked
about Brady's own contribution, hoping that Brady was doing
all he could for the cause. Here, without doubt, Garfield
was bringing pressure to bear on appointive officials, especially in the Post Office Department, but the letter could also
be interpreted as an effort to extort additional funds from
Brady himself or from the star-route contractors who were
dipping illegally into the federal treasury.[25]

The star-route fraud was a conspiracy between federal
officials and the contractors for privately operated mail routes,
to mulct the public by excessive charges. The companies delivered mail particularly in the remote West, poorly supplied
with railroads. They received contracts calling for delivery
with "certainty, celerity, and security." Because of the asterisks pointing up these words there arose the name "star
routes." In order to keep pace with the mushroom growth of
new Western postal centers, the federal statutes and the
postal regulations permitted extensive alterations in contracts,
to meet new conditions, and the carriers got into the habit of
utilizing these loopholes for their own pecuniary advantage.
The favorite method was to take advantage of the law allowing increased payment for augmented or expedited service.
Having obtained contracts in due legal form, by submitting

the lowest bids, the carriers would petition the Post Office Department to be allowed to give more or quickened service at a much higher rate. In this way, government payments multiplied by as much as ten times the original bid, with no ascertainable improvement of service. Brady was the official who arranged these accommodations for the contractors, without even the semblance of an investigation into the merits of the changes.[26]

This situation was really one of long standing, going back to Grant's first term and continuing under Hayes. As early as January 2, 1872, the *Washington Post* had published a denunciation of postal frauds, and the *New York Sun* followed with editorials on the subject. There had been Congressional investigations of the matter in 1872 and later, most of them of a halfhearted nature until 1880, when the Post Office Department boldly demanded an additional appropriation of $2,000,000 to make up a deficit. At this time the *New York Sun* pointed out suggestions of a conspiracy, and the *New York Times* demanded an investigation. The *Times,* after checking the kind of service rendered by the star routes, asked why such an inadequate accomplishment should cost so much. Because both Republicans and Democrats were involved in the frauds, this did not become a political issue in the campaign of 1880.[27]

As early as 1878 the name of Senator Stephen W. Dorsey of Arkansas appeared prominently in the list of culprits; yet he became Garfield's campaign manager two years later. Then, in 1881, James and MacVeagh pointed to him as the leading conspiratorial contractor. Dorsey's brother-in-law was also involved along with others, including the Salisbury firm, which was even larger than the Dorsey ring. By far the majority of the star routes were under the control of such combinations. Brady had conspired with these contractors and had shared the loot with them. On 134 routes, which by contract should have cost about $143,000, the spoils increased to nearly $623,000. In one Dakota district, where postal receipts amounted to $240 a year, the charge to the United States rose to over $6100. Brady, in addition to his government position, owned the *National Republican,* published in Washington, D.C., which he utilized to fight the investigation instigated by the Attorney General and the Postmaster General. By the same means he had fought their appointment to the cabinet. By this time, Garfield had reason to wish he had paid more attention to Blaine's warnings about Dorsey during the presidential campaign.[28]

While Garfield hung between life and death for more than eleven weeks after July 2, everything was in confusion. Thereafter, the new Attorney General, Benjamin H. Brewster of Pennsylvania, had to do something about the star-route conspirators. But the new Postmaster General was Timothy O. Howe of Wisconsin, whose son-in-law, Enoch Totten, joined Robert G. Ingersoll in the imposing array of defense counsels. The case for the government was ready by the spring of 1882. Besides Brady and Dorsey, the defendants were John W. Dorsey, John R. Miner, John M. Peck, Harvey M. Vaile, M. C. Rerdell, and William H. Turner, who were indicted on March 4. The charge of conspiracy was based on nineteen routes where the contract price had risen from $41,135 to $448,670.90, while the revenue was a mere $11,622.36. From the beginning of the trial the prosecution met repeated obstacles. Two of its own investigators betrayed the government's plan of action to the defendants. Rerdell backed down on an earlier confession. Brady's newspaper conducted a vicious attack on the prosecution, the jury, and the judge, this also serving to intimidate the witnesses.[29]

The trial in the District of Columbia court became about as bad a scandal as the star-route frauds themselves. The prosecution seemed almost in collusion with the defendants, making conspiracy (a difficult thing to prove) the only charge. Once the trial got under way, the defense attorneys raised a constant barrage of objections and searched for loopholes throughout the hot Washington summer. The indictment of the foreman of the jury for accepting a bribe and the discharge of several government officials for officious tinkering added to the confusion. So, on September 10, 1882, a confused petit jury found Miner and Rerdell (small participants) guilty, Peck and Turner not guilty, and brought in no verdict at all on the major offenders. A retrial from

December 7, 1882, to June 14, 1883, cleared all the defendants, including Miner and Rerdell. Thus had the mountain labored.[30]

Though the murder of Garfield came during the early stages of this comic-opera brawl, the act cannot properly be called a direct consequence of the patronage system. Charles J. Guiteau was clearly not only a crank, but definitely insane as well, though the jury, swayed by the general indignation at the deed, did not give this fact serious consideration. Shortly after nine o'clock on Saturday morning, July 2, 1881, Guiteau was lying in wait for the President in the Baltimore and Potomac Railroad depot, where Garfield was intending to catch a train to New York and from there to Williamstown, Massachusetts.[31] As Garfield and Blaine reached the middle of the waiting room, Guiteau drew a large revolver from his pocket and fired two shots, the second of which entered the left side of the small of Garfield's back. The assassin then meekly submitted to arrest, saying "All right, I did it and will go to jail for it. I am a Stalwart and Arthur will be President." This political motive was mentioned also in some letters he had carried with him to the depot, to be sent to the newspapers and prominent people in justification of what he called the "removal" of the President as "a traitor to the men who made him" and as a peril to "the life of the Republic." Guiteau considered himself a tyrannicide doing a noble and praiseworthy deed. Of Garfield he said that "his death was a political necessity. . . ."; of himself, "I am a lawyer, a theologian and a politician."[32]

On the basis of premeditation alone this was murder in the first degree, for these letters had been written before the act. But Guiteau's activities, statements, and writings for the preceding score of years revealed delusions of grandeur, a persistent feeling of being the victim of persecution, and a conviction that he was in alliance with the Almighty to wreak vengeance in a holy crusade, all of which are the common characteristics of religious fanatics and other paranoid-schizophrenics. Aided by a skilled psychiatrist, Guiteau might have concocted the autobiography printed in the *New York Herald* as evidence to be used in a plea of insanity. But there was no help given him as he sat in jail. Furthermore, there is no reason to believe that his earlier career, chock full of aberrations, was planned for a defense in an ultimate murder trial. There was a considerable amount of proved insanity in the Guiteau family, which, taken in connection with the assassin's own activities, may be pertinent testimony.[33] In spite of Guiteau's boast, he was so little a Stalwart that he had taken the stump for Garfield in 1880. After the inauguration, he dogged Blaine's footsteps and figuratively hammered at the door of the White House, until he received orders to stay away. This continued until a few days before the assassination.[34] Disappointment no doubt was the culminating factor in the overthrow of an already diseased mind.

Guiteau's bullet punctured no vital organ, and Garfield might have had a better chance of survival with no medical attention at all than with the kind he got. Asepsis was but poorly practiced in the United States at that time. The platoon of physicians during that hot summer kept probing and irrigating the wound with a catheter, following paths not made by the bullet, and let the patient die (September 19, 1881) of secondary hemorrhage, blood poisoning, a retroperitoneal pus pocket, and localized peritonitis.[35] As for the end of Guiteau, the jury rejected his lawyers' arguments about insanity, and the hanging occurred on June 30, 1882.[36]

The public, concurring with the jury's decision that Guiteau was legally sane, decided that he had assassinated Garfield solely because of his failure to secure an appointment. Consequently, there was a strong incentive for civil service reform under Arthur, though the groundwork laid by Hayes might have resulted in the change just as soon, and without so drastic an urge.

Chapter V

ARTHUR AND HIS KNIGHTS

"CHET ARTHUR President, good God!" This expression was heard and repeated by many citizens when they realized that the man nominated and elected Vice-President, almost as an oversight, had suddenly become the chief executive. Arthur was known only as a Stalwart machine politician, probably financially honest, but tied to Conkling's apron strings and to the old but not revered spoils system. Contrary to the forebodings, however, it happened that Arthur made a better record as President than his past activities and associations portended. There is no reason to believe that Hancock would have done better, and there are grave doubts about Garfield.

A matter that received some attention during Garfield's incapacity and following his death, but no legislation for five years, was that of the presidential succession. Since 1792, the law had provided that when the offices of both President and Vice-President were vacant, the president pro tem of the Senate and the Speaker of the House stood next in succession. There were several things left up in the air. Who was to decide when the President was incapable of performing his duties? When and how should the Vice-President take over? Should he be acting President or should he succeed to the office for the remainder of the term? Who should decide whether or when the disabled President was capable of resuming authority? These questions have never been answered by Congress. During the first three weeks of Arthur's administration, neither house was organized, and there was nobody to assume the office had another crank taken a successful shot at Arthur. Had Guiteau made a clean job of both Garfield and Arthur at the same time, the complication would have caused real trouble. As it was, with Conkling and Platt gone and their successors not yet seated, the Democrats had control of the Senate for the first few days of the extra session and made Bayard of Delaware the president pro tem. With the arrival of Miller and Lapham to succeed Conkling and Platt, and with the tardy swearing in of Nelson W. Aldrich of Rhode Island, the Republicans had a majority of one, but they made David Davis president pro tem as a possible means of averting delaying tactics by the Democrats.[1]

Now that business could proceed as usual, civil service reform had to receive some attention because of the public clamor for it. Though greater problems were crying more vociferously for a solution, a little tinkering with the civil service would cause less anguish and outcry against interference with the American way of life. At the time, it was only to be expected that the Republicans would look with more favor on a little reform than would the Democrats. After all the desirable jobs were filled with deserving Republicans, the law could be applied only to future appointments. Should the Democrats then win in 1884, they would find it embarrassingly difficult to oust legally entrenched place holders to make way for their own appointees.

Nevertheless, the leadership in the movement was taken in the Senate by a Democrat, George H. ("Gentleman George") Pendleton of Ohio. In January of 1881 he introduced a bill drafted by Dorman B. Eaton and other members of the Civil Service Reform Association, but with no success. He tried again in December, but even the death of Garfield could not put the bill through at this time. Meanwhile, the National Civil Service Reform League had grown out of the old New York organization, and it put its full force behind the Pendleton bill.[2] At once it made the most of a new political scandal. "My dear Hubbell" of the Garfield assessment letter of 1880, now chairman of the Republican Congressional committee for the campaign of 1882, on May 15 of that year sent a form letter to every employee of the government, including even soldiers, page boys in Congress, laborers on public works, janitors, and scrub women, telling them that the committee, including Senators Aldrich, William B. Allison of Iowa, and Eugene Hale of Maine, expected a campaign contribution from each. A later circular stipulated 2 per cent of the individual's annual income.[3]

Hale's excuse for this extortion was that the Democrats had done the same thing before the Civil War and that the circular was the same one that the "civil service reform president, Hayes," had approved in 1878 and 1880. But Curtis, Wheeler, and William Potts of the reform league promptly informed the same employees that if they complied with the demands they would be liable to prosecution under an Act of 1876 prohibiting such assessments or the payment of them. As representatives and senators were not employees, Attorney General Brewster absolved the members of the Congressional committee from guilt. But General Newton M. Curtis, an employee of the Treasury Department and chairman of the New York State Republican Committee, incurred a fine of $1000, which the party paid after the United States Supreme Court, on December 18, 1882, upheld his conviction under the 1876 law. The reform movement received further strength when Arthur, the old spoilsman, executed an about-face and let the employees know that their jobs would not be put in jeopardy by refusal to contribute. In December, 1882, he also endorsed the Pendleton bill as a protection for employees and a release of the Chief Executive from the endless chore of interviewing applicants.[4]

Arthur's conversion was not as abrupt as it appeared. His appointment of the spoilsman Howe as Postmaster General had been a surrender to the system, and that department had more patronage to hand out than any other. From time to time the President advanced his stand, and—especially after the Democratic sweep of the House of Representatives in the election of 1882—suggested, among other things, that the patronage might slip out of Republican control after 1884. Also, the reformers stepped up their propaganda in 1881, using the press, the clergy, petitions, and pamphlets to influence Congress and the people. The opposition also warmed up their arguments. Thurlow Weed of New York insisted that the bill would end political devotion, gallantry, and love of country. Again, this being a period when the baiting of England was considered a good way to gain votes, other politi-

cians decried the copying of British precedent for the
changes. But Arthur, bowing to political exigencies, came out
thoroughly for the measure in his message to Congress in
December, 1882.[5]

After all the publicity, the opposition could not long post-
pone Congressional action. On December 27, 1882, debate
ended in the Senate, which passed the bill and sent it on to
the House, where again there was approval after eight days.
Arthur signed it on January 16, 1883. The remarkable thing
about the voting was not so much the wide division within
the parties, but the fact that only an even half of the senators
and ten more than half of the representatives cared enough
about the measure to want their votes recorded in its favor.[6]

The Act provided for a Civil Service Commission of three
members, not more than two of the same political party, appointed by the President. Each was to receive $3500 a year
and necessary traveling expenses. At the President's request,
they were to provide for open competitive examinations; appointments to the classified service from among those scoring
the highest examination grades; and the apportionment of
offices in Washington, D.C., among the states, territories, and
the District of Columbia according to population. The Commission also was directed to establish rules prohibiting political contributions of any kind from employees, or any other
sort of political coercion, under penalty of a $5000 fine or
three years' imprisonment, or both. Within sixty days after
the passage of the law, the Secretary of the Treasury and
the Postmaster General were to put in the classified list
certain clerks in the District of Columbia and all subordinate
officials in customhouses and post offices employing fifty or
more persons each. There could be further extensions of the
classified list in any department of the government at later
times. All existing appointees were covered in and exempt
from examinations to retain their positions, but after six
months there could be no promotions or new appointments in
the classified list, without examination. There were special
indulgences for veterans, and not included in the classified list
were persons not employed by an executive branch of the
government and ordinary day laborers wherever utilized. No

person could receive appointment whenever two or more members of his family were already in the public service, thus guarding against nepotism. There was no stipulation about the tenure of the commissioners, but the law specifically provided that the President "may remove any commissioner" and fill any vacancy.[7]

This hazardous sort of tenure could easily make the commission a political tool. Furthermore, the lack of a provision to select for appointment the candidate making the highest grade on an examination could be utilized to keep appointments fairly well restricted to candidates supporting the party in power. Again, the groups specified in the Act for immediate classification numbered only about 14,000 out of the 100,000 civil servants.[8] Then also, there was no real assurance of tenure for members of the party out of power. According to a circular letter sent out by Postmaster General William F. Vilas of Wisconsin, in 1885, almost any classified person risked dismissal not only for offensive partisanship in behalf of the party out of power, but for publishing objectionable statements, for making stump speeches or being a member of a political committee, for taking any obvious part in a political campaign, or for using his subordinates in a like endeavor.[9] This laid the way open to the henchman of a member of Congress to prefer flimsy charges, secure the dismissal of an officeholder after a packed hearing, and receive appointment to the position as one of the group who had passed the examination only close to the top.

The chairman of the commission that Arthur appointed was none other than Dorman B. Eaton, the other two members being John Milton Gregory (a former president of the University of Illinois) and Leroy D. Thoman of Ohio. With the example of the good work already performed in the post office and customhouse of New York and what had been accomplished by Schurz in the Department of the Interior, the commission set to work in earnest. In addition to the passing of the examination, the chosen one had to submit to a probation of six months. Then, an examining board passed on the neophyte's efficiency and good conduct, and if he failed this test there was a new appointment.[10]

Succeeding years revealed that the weaknesses of the Pendleton Act were persistent and violations were frequent. In 1885, one Aquilla Jones, appointed by Cleveland as postmaster for Indianapolis, engaged in an orgy of firing Republicans, always giving other reasons than party affiliation. Toward the end of the same administration, there was publicity about other activities of a similar kind, resulting in an investigation and a report to the Senate. Cleveland, however, was not a party to such chicanery. Instead, he issued warnings against it. He went further and added over five thousand employees in the Railway Mail Service to the classified list. He wanted the ruling to go into effect promptly, but the Civil Service Commission had to work on the task until after the inauguration of President Benjamin Harrison, who, with his cohorts, made merry with the firing of Democrats before the commission's orders could be applied in May of 1889.[11]

Meanwhile, the states began copying the precedent by establishing civil service commissions. The New York reform bill passed on May 4, 1883, and the job of classification was completed in the following year. The cities of New York, Brooklyn, and Buffalo also exhibited an interest, and in May, 1884, the legislature made the reform obligatory in the larger cities of the state. In the same year, Massachusetts adopted a more comprehensive measure than that of New York.[12] A beginning had been made, national and state; conditions improved only gradually but the reformers were justified in their feeling of gratification.

Other problems faced by the Forty-seventh Congress were polygamy, the tariff, the modernization of the navy, Chinese immigration, and, of course, political fence-mending in anticipation of the election of 1882. There had been an Antipolygamy Act as early as 1862, applying to the territories in general but specifically annulling certain acts of the Utah legislature which tended to support polygamy. This law, sponsored by Vermont's Justin S. Morrill, was rigorous in its prohibitions and penalties, but it was unenforceable because of dependence on local juries dominated by Mormons.[13] An amendment of June 23, 1874, named for Vermont Representative Luke P. Poland, presumably strengthened the earlier law, but four years later George Reynolds, Brigham Young's private secretary, emerged as the only man ever convicted under the act. This came about only because of Reynolds' "voluntary confession for the purpose of contesting the constitutionality of the law."[14]

A petition to Congress from the non-Mormons of Utah, the unanimity of antipolygamy sentiment in the several party platforms of 1880, Hayes's specific demands for a more rigorous law in his message to Congress on December 6, 1880, Garfield's strictures in his inaugural address, and Arthur's like denunciation in December, 1881, all were indications that the time was ripe for new legislation. The non-Mormon petitioners highly resented what they considered the Mormon tendency to vote as a unit on all controversial matters. According to estimates of 1880, 120,000 of the 144,000 people in Utah were Mormons,[15] who could utterly swamp the "gentiles" in any election.

A contest in 1880 over the election to Congress of a delegate from Utah hastened the enactment of new legislation. The non-Mormon candidate, though getting only 1357 votes, claimed the election over the Mormon who polled 18,568, because the latter was a polygamist and his supposed majority was presumably composed largely of female votes. The contest lingered on until January 25, 1882, when the House Committee on Elections refused to seat either candidate.[16] On December 12, 1881, a third Vermonter out to reform Utah, George F. Edmunds, presented his antipolygamy bill in the Senate. This bill continued the penalties of the Act of 1862 that included a fine of $500 or imprisonment up to five years, or both, for bigamy. Children conceived by plural wives after the law went into effect were to be illegitimate. Polygamists and persons who believed in polygamy would not have the right to serve on juries hearing polygamy cases, and polygamists could not vote or hold office. A commission of five persons would supervise elections, apply the test oath on belief in polygamy, and qualify candidates for office. This provision for thought control raised serious objections even among men who did not approve of polygamy. Edmunds had been influential in the passage of the Fourteenth Amendment to the Constitution, which declared that all persons "born or naturalized in the United States, and subject to the jurisdiction thereof" were citizens and were, along with all other persons, entitled to "the equal protection of the laws." This dictate applied to state legislatures, but Senators George G. Vest of Missouri, John T. Morgan of Alabama, and Wilkinson Call of Florida wanted to know why the same obligation did not rest on the federal government as well. A commission depriving an adult citizen of the right to vote, because of his beliefs, was classifying the victim as a criminal, and without due process of law. But while constitutional lawyers and historians may debate these points, political history must record that the bill promptly cleared both houses of Congress and became law on March 22, 1882.[17]

On June 23, President Arthur appointed the Utah commission, headed by Alexander Ramsey of Minnesota. The commission arrived at Salt Lake City on August 18, went zestfully to work and in two years disfranchised about twelve thousand individuals and replaced all polygamous officials with men who would take the oath that they were not of the same practices. The Mormons themselves, confident that the commissioners were violating constitutional rights, considered it a duty to continue in polygamy. Hundreds, especially the leaders who were opulent enough to afford more than one wife, fled to Canada, Mexico, and other foreign places, from which officials governed the church by remote control. Some prominent leaders, like A. O. Smoot, had secret hiding places. Smoot had a room under the floor of his house, reached by means of a trap door. It became a matter of pride to be a plural wife; and so many honorable men went to prison that even this became a distinction among Mormons. In spite of the fact that the enforcement of the law worked hardships, the indomitable Saints remained more determined than ever.[18]

In one case of prosecution, the court set a precedent of denying bail, pending appeal, which decision the United States Supreme Court upheld on January 19, 1885. All the marriages took place in the church, in secrecy, and there were no public records of them. Consequently, it was difficult to prove polygamy but not so hard to convict for unlawful co-habitation. Between 1882 and 1887, there were 289 convictions for the latter and only 14 for the former. Among those hunted were John Taylor, president of the church, and George Q. Cannon, one of the Twelve Apostles. Cannon was arrested while heading for Mexico, escaped his captors and was caught again, jumped bail, remained in seclusion for two years, gave himself up in 1888 on promise of clemency, and was fined $450 and imprisoned for 175 days. Taylor remained so well concealed by trusted friends that he escaped detection until his death in 1887.[19]

On January 11, 1884, Shelby M. Cullom of Illinois made a speech in the Senate, granting that the Utah commission had done some good but that the situation was still far from satisfactory. He would remove all political power from the people of Utah and place the territory under a partial dictatorship until the situation was thoroughly cleaned up. Cleveland, in his December 8, 1885, message to Congress, also stressed the need for an amendment to the Edmunds Act.[20] But there was no further legislation until the Edmunds-Tucker Act of March 3, 1887, which became law without Cleveland's signature. It provided for the dissolution of the corporation of the Mormon church, tightened up on the rules of evidence in polygamy trials, abolished woman suffrage in Utah Territory, and expanded the voters' registration oath to include a statement denying any intention of aiding, counseling, or advising others to defy the antipolygamy laws.[21] The latter provision was almost as silly as some of the antisubversive oaths of the 1950s.

After the passage of the Edmunds-Tucker Act, the Mormon resistance began to crumble. Though individual church leaders continued to uphold the divine authority for polygamy and to proclaim that the "gentiles" were using this issue simply as a cover for their general hostility to Mormons, the hierarchy was beginning to waver. Wilford Woodruff, who became president of the church in the year of the new law's adoption, could read the trend of the times better than his predecessor, John Taylor. The economic and mental strain on polygamous husbands must have been all but unendurable, and many of them may have longed for a theocratic rule relieving them of the burden. But two events in 1890 certainly hastened the capitulation of the church. On May 19, the United States Supreme Court upheld the confiscation of the property of the church, thus affirming the constitutionality of the Edmunds-Tucker Act. The second influence was the effort at passage of the Cullom-Struble bill in Congress. This bill would have provided for the disfranchisement of every person who belonged or contributed to, or encouraged in any way, any organization that taught or sanctioned polygamy. Prominent Mormons assured the sponsors that, if they would delay action, the church itself would renounce polygamy.[22]

True to this promise, on September 24, 1890, President Woodruff proclaimed for the church that during the preceding year no plural marriages had occurred in the Temple; that on rumor of one such marriage in the Endowment House in Salt Lake City that house, by his order, was "taken down without delay"; that the church was no longer teaching or permitting further polygamous marriages; and that he intended to abide by the federal law on the subject and use his influence to see that the membership of the church did likewise. "And I now publicly declare that my advice to the Latter-Day Saints is to refrain from contracting any marriages forbidden by the law of the land." The Mormon general conference confirmed this manifesto on October 6, 1890, and again a year later.[23] Not everybody was satisfied by this declaration, and as late as the 1950s some polygamy was discovered in a remote corner of Arizona. Even so, from the date of the mandate the problem rapidly waned, thus paving the way for the long-delayed entry of Utah as a state of the Union in 1896.

Whatever credit or blame the Forty-seventh Congress may have deserved for the Pendleton and Edmunds acts, no one can judiciously say anything in favor of its tariff-tinkering. The miscarried Act of 1883 was nothing for a lame-duck Congress to be proud of, and the Democratic effort of the Forty-eighth Congress in 1884 was a complete fiasco. Largely political though this issue undoubtedly was, the tariff from

1877 to 1890 can best be handled separately in the following chapter.

The upset of the Republicans in the election of 1882 was partially conditioned by the Reapportionment Act of February 25, 1882, which enlarged the membership of the House of Representatives from 293 to 325, and the Democrats gained slightly.[24] But reapportionment alone could not explain the large Democratic gain. To some observers, the landslide seemed to have grown out of the abuse of the patronage, and these reformers took Arthur to task for using "the power of his office for the advantage of a faction." The Pennsylvania Independent Republicans' platform of the year had declared that their purpose was "to take up the work which fell when Garfield fell." Overlooking Garfield's own factionalism, these Pennsylvanians were beginning to view him as a martyred reformer.[25] Some state Democratic platforms also denounced the Republicans for the spoils system, for elevating to high office men who were known to be dishonest, and for a "systematic levy of black-mail upon the clerks and minor office-holders," for the evils of the "Dorseyites," and for making "a grand auction" of elections.[26]

John Sherman laid the blame for Ohio reverses on "the failure of Congress to pass the bill relieving the people from the burden of internal taxes no longer required" and on "the temporary stringency in money matters." Delaware's Senator Bayard and others pointed to the unreformed tariff, and Representative Randall of Pennsylvania indicted excessive expenditures by the general and local governments.[27] Furthermore, there had been an economic setback during the year, caused by a severe drouth that had reduced farmers in large areas to less than normal subsistence. In industry, stock watering had reduced dividends on stocks and bonds. There had been over ten thousand bankruptcies during the year. Rising costs of living led workers to strike for higher wages which the employers claimed they were unable to pay. In the iron and steel industry alone strikes shut down 116 firms with 35,000 employees.[28] Obviously, in 1882 the Republicans, who two years earlier had taken credit for improved economic conditions, were now paying the penalty for hard times.

On the other hand, the Prohibition party polled nearly 92,-000 votes and made its influence felt on the politics of Ohio. The Republicans in that state, overestimating the temperance appeal, called for effective control of the liquor traffic, thus giving John Sherman cause to attribute local party losses to "the demand of a portion of our people for free whiskey and no Sunday." In California, Nevada, and Oregon there was some disaffection from the Republicans because the Chinese Exclusion Act of 1882 was not total in its effect. This may have explained the solidly Democratic delegations to the House of Representatives from California and Nevada.[29] Most certainly the voters, whether wisely or not, were considering economic problems as they marched to the polls. The lure of the Greenbackers no longer tempted;[30] the Socialist groups lacked strength, cohesion, and a native American support; and the Antimonopoly party was a mere froth on the political stream. It was to the Democrats that the voters turned for a change.

The Democrats gained 72 seats in the House, while the Republicans dropped 33. In addition to the four Independents, one Greenbacker represented the party that was definitely on the way to oblivion. The shift in the Senate was slight, the Forty-eighth Congress starting out with 40 Republicans, 35 Democrats, and William Mahone, the Virginia Readjuster elected in 1881.[31]

Perhaps the most significant development in the second half of Arthur's administration was the movement to create an up-to-date steel navy. During the Civil War the United States had taken the lead in the building of ironclads and monitors and in 1865 had one of the greatest navies in the world. Less than a score of years later, when imperialism was encompassing the globe and the greater powers were racing to outdo each other on the sea, the American navy was a sorry collection of obsolete and nearly useless vessels. In 1881, of the 140 craft of all kinds on hand, 25 were tugs and the rest were unseaworthy. At this time Admiral David D. Porter said, "There is not a navy that does not have the advantage of us in ships and guns." But at this same time, interest in the navy began to revive. The first Naval Advisory Board convened on July 11, 1881, under the leadership of Rear Admiral John Rogers, and remained in session until November 7 following. This board had instructions from Garfield to advise the Secretary of the Navy on the number, class, size, and displacement of any new vessels needed; the materials and form of their construction; the ordnance, armament, and equipment of each; and other details, including costs.[32]

The board recommended prompt construction of two first-class steel cruisers of 15 knots speed and 5873 tons displacement, six like cruisers of 14 knots and 4560 tons, ten second-class steel cruisers of at least 13 knots and 3043 tons, twenty small and slow wooden vessels, and a number of other items in the mosquito fleet, at a total cost for all of $29,607,000. On December 6, 1881, President Arthur stressed these recommendations and added his own hearty endorsement. Congress, however, was loath to shift from iron to the initially more expensive steel. Marine experts testified that steel was not only more effective but was cheaper in the long run, and the House Naval Affairs Committee, headed by Benjamin Harris of Massachusetts, agreed that something should be done. Blaine's meddling in South America had brought Chile close to naval attack on the United States, and the unfinished monitor *Monadnock* was in no condition to defend San Francisco. In case of a Chilean attack, a tribute levied on this city was a thing to anticipate with some degree of shock. Faced by this possibility, Congress passed the Naval Appropriations Act of August 5, 1882, which neatly side-stepped the Rogers report. It appropriated $1,750,000 for repairs and construction, and, if enough was left over after repairs, the remainder could go for two new steel cruisers. It also created a new Naval Advisory Board that retained only one member of the earlier group.[33]

This small effort marked the beginning of a new navy. Also, it stimulated technological advances in the production of better and tougher steels. Through contracts, starting with the Bethlehem company, the navy laid down rigid standards for armor plate that the industry had to accept in order to get business. And so the armament race entered a new phase, with the United States as a participant—a race not only between nations but between armor that no gun could pierce and guns that could pierce any armor. Arthur appointed a board to study the facilities of the various navy yards, which soon demonstrated that their antiquated mills could not produce adequate armor plate, and the task reverted to private industry. Furthermore, naval men quarreled over procedure and designs before the progressive element in the Navy Department won the fight. So, by the end of 1882 the new Advisory Board had adequate plans to spend both the money available and that in prospect, as Arthur softened up Congress for additional appropriations.[34] In line with these developments, but only after prolonged debate, Congress passed the Naval Appropriations Act of March 3, 1883, authorizing the new vessels recommended by the Advisory Board, providing for the location of a government gun foundry, and appropriating $1,100,000 to carry out the work. Although Congress allocated too much of the money for the completion of already outmoded monitors, it also provided another $1,300,000 for the construction of up-to-date steel cruisers.[35]

From this time on, work continued with such speed that on December 4, 1883, the President told Congress that the steel cruisers *Chicago, Boston,* and *Atlanta,* as well as the steel dispatch boat *Dolphin,* were already under construction. He observed that "we have no wish for foreign conquest" but the new naval strength should be sufficient to protect harbors, commercial interests, and national honor. He also assured the legislators that "it is no part of our policy to create and maintain a Navy able to cope with that of the great powers of the world." Arthur could hardly have foreseen that in another fifteen years, his modest project would mushroom out of control and that foreign conquest and equality with the greater navies would be the order of the day. But momentum gathered only slowly. For a time Congress lagged behind the President's requests, causing him to appeal for more ships on March 26, 1884, and again in his last annual message to Congress in the following December.[36] By the end of his administration, the three cruisers and the dispatch boat were not only not yet in commission, but were also criticized for their lack of power. Secretary of the Navy Chandler justified their slowness of speed (in comparison with the fastest passenger ships) as a sacrifice for their necessary heavy armament. The monitors were also still under construction, and $4,250,000 were called for to get them in readiness.[37]

After Cleveland's inauguration, the modernization of the navy was speeded up. The same period saw a rising criticism of previous efforts. The lack of public confidence in the shipbuilders was an issue aired in the presidential campaign of 1884. William C. Whitney of New York, Cleveland's Secretary of the Navy, was interested in the fact that John Roach, the contractor for the four vessels near completion, was a heavy contributor to the Republican campaign fund. The performance of the dispatch boat *Dolphin* called for the sharpest criticism. In nearly every way it failed to meet the specifications. Whitney organized a new Advisory Board headed by Admiral George Belknap, after whose report the Attorney General finally determined that nothing short of an act of Congress could make possible the acceptance of the vessels.[38]

With the work of modernization well under way, Cleveland and Whitney experienced few of the difficulties that plagued their predecessors. In 1885, Congress began including appropriations for new vessels in the regular naval appropriation bills, thus assuring prompt hearings on requests. In that year, too, Whitney secured models from English firms for the *Charleston* and some other vessels, and in the next year the *Maine* was constructed. There was great delay in the building of the *Maine*. As Rear Admiral Robley D. Evans pointed out, it took more than a month to decide about the removal of a small section of pipe from the foundation area of a plate-bending machine. Incidents such as this increased the desire of Congress to have ships built in private yards, with all the attendant graft and multiplied expense. The navy's own cumbersomely bureaucratic practices, comparable to those of the army, thus worked in the interest of heavier expenditure of public funds. After the *Maine,* fourteen additional ships were authorized before 1889, including the *Olympia* and the *New York.* But it was not until 1890 that, after heated debate, Congress authorized the first large battleships, capable of commanding the high seas. It was at this time also that Captain Alfred T. Mahan began to dominate naval construction.[39]

Mahan had a long military background. He was born at West Point, where his father was professor of engineering and the author of books on that subject. The son graduated from the Naval Academy at Annapolis in 1859, and from 1886 to 1889 and 1892 to 1893, was head of the Naval War College at Providence. In 1890, he published the first volume of his lectures under the title of *The Influence of Sea Power upon History, 1660–1783.* This and later books on sea power had a vast influence on military thought the world over.

Details concerning the development of armor plate, ordnance, and machinery; controversies over designs, methods, and means of construction; Congressional bickering, criticism, and delay; dubious contracts, involving chicanery and kickbacks; and official muddling can be searched out in the various naval histories. It must suffice here to observe that, during Arthur's administration (1881–85), appropriations for the navy amounted to $77,878,000; from 1886 to 1889, $80,-957,000 more was accounted for; and that by the time of the War with Spain in 1898, the total cost since 1880 had reached $496,715,000.[40]

Chapter VI

TARIFF PROTECTION AND POLITICS

EVEN Arthur's most ardent panegyrists, when assessing his administration, could work up little enthusiasm over the Tariff of 1883. This offspring of political and industrial misalliances, nondescript in anatomy and disowned by its parents, well deserved to be called the "Mongrel Tariff." Before the enactment of this law, the Morrill Tariff Act of 1864 had set the pattern of tariff rates. Presumably the purpose of the wartime measure had been to procure additional revenue, but Morrill and Thaddeus Stevens had so guided the measure through Congress as to provide sharply increased protection to every interest that vigorously presented its claims. Because of high wartime internal revenue duties on home manufactures, the rates on competing imported goods became about 20 per cent higher than could be otherwise justified, the hypothetical average for all schedules being 47 per cent. When the internal revenue duties on domestic manufactures were repealed in the early postwar years, this repeal acted as an equal amount of additional protection. But in the same years, especially 1867 to 1870, a series of "popgun" bills still further augmented the tariff on a few items, such as woolens, copper, steel rails, marble, flax, and nickel, while certain noncompetitive raw materials went on the free list, thus keeping the average of all rates the same as in 1864 while further intensifying protection for the manufacturers using the articles put on the free list. The horizontal reduction of 1872 and its cancellation in 1875 would have been only a temporary aberration in the tariff curve had not the raw materials cuts been retained after 1875, thus again benefiting manufacturers. So, for nineteen years, protection in most of the lines of advanced production went up by steps, while the buying public heard only that rates were on an even keel.[1]

Meanwhile, the Democrats, with traditionally the more liberal view of the leading parties on the tariff issue, had been totally ineffective. Since the war, the Presidency, and except for 1879–81, one or both houses of Congress, had been in Republican hands. In 1868 the Democrats had hedged on the tariff, in 1872 they sold out to the Liberal Republicans who would make no stand at all, and in 1876 the Democrats had stressed reform in general with no particular emphasis on the tariff. Though they had denounced the existing tariff as "a masterpiece of injustice, inequality, and false pretense," and went on to demand that all tariff "taxation shall be only for revenue,"[2] they had not made much use of the declarations in the campaign of 1876. Then, in 1880, Hancock's declaration that the tariff was a local issue counterbalanced the platform's outspoken stand for a tariff for revenue only. Democrats in Congress had made no more than feeble and unavailing efforts to achieve this end. In the first session of the Forty-fourth Congress, William R. Morrison of Illinois offered a reform tariff bill that was under consideration for two days and was heard of no more. Again, in 1877, Roger W. Mills of Texas offered to the House a resolution to instruct the Committee on Ways and Means to revise the tariff so as to make it for revenue only. Though the resolution got 60 Democratic and 7 Republican votes, the opposition of 64 Republicans and 12 Democrats killed it. Such a bill had no chance anyway, with a Republican Senate and President, but Mills apparently hoped to put the Democrats on record as favoring such a revision. Fernando Wood of New York then offered a drastic reduction, but high-tariff Democrats joined with the Republicans to strike out the enacting clause by a vote of 134 to 121.[3]

Representative Samuel J. Randall of Pennsylvania headed the protectionist faction that had developed, by 1883, in the Democratic ranks. Pennsylvania had been a manufacturing state from the early days of the Republic, and, from Thomas FitzSimins in the Tariff of 1789 to Joseph R. Grundy in the Tariff of 1930, its sons, of whatever party, were protectionists whenever they had an industrial constituency. The Morrill Act of 1861, abandoning the low rates of 1846 and 1857 and returning to the pattern set by Henry Clay in 1842 and ear-

lier, could not have passed without the consent of President
James Buchanan, a Democrat from Pennsylvania. Though on
other issues Randall's counsel was valued by the Democrats,
on the tariff he was a consistent insurgent. He represented a
Philadelphia district where the campaign contributors favored
high protection, and his views corresponded with those of
the donors.[4] This stand seriously affected Randall's position
in national affairs. In a letter of Thomas F. Bayard's concerning the presidential nomination of 1876, he expressed high
respect for Randall's courage and ability, but pointed out his
weakness as a candidate because of his tariff views. Randall
had great influence as Speaker of the House from 1876 to
1881, and it was he and his following of Democrats from the
northeastern industrial states of Pennsylvania, New Jersey,
New York, Connecticut, and Ohio, and from the sugar state of
Louisiana, who during those years had blocked tariff reform
measures in a Democratically controlled House of Representatives.[5]

Not only the protectionists, but also other business pushed
tariff reform into the background. For a few years after 1875
the problems of resumption of specie payments, greenback
agitation, and the silver question attracted the most attention, and between 1877 and 1880 the outcome of three tariff
bills was to put quinine on the free list. No argument over protection and free trade brought on the Act of 1883; rather, it
resulted from the embarrassment of an excess of revenue over
expenditures. In the 1880s there was nearly always between
$100,000,000 and $150,000,000 lying idle in the Treasury, at
a time when soft-money men were pointing cogently to the
need of more currency as a cure for economic ills. Between
the reports of 1881 and 1882, this surplus rose from $100,-
069,000 to $145,544,000. So the surplus financiers of Congress
set about solving the dilemma and mending political fences
at home by devising ingenious methods of spending. One
never-failing vote getter was to enlarge the pension rolls and
magnify the donations. On January 25, 1879, President Hayes
signed the Pension Arrears Act, which added 23,372 new
claims in the next month and pushed up the total new increment to 184,709 by the end of June. In the next six years

this generosity cost the people $179,404,873, and still there was a treasury surplus. The Republican platform of 1880 promised higher pensions for Union soldiers, so they got them, if not in a lump sum of arrears since discharge, averaging about $1000 each for successful claimants,[6] then by means of private bills. There were numerous party workers whose military records were nothing to brag about but who were valiant in getting out the vote; so, by the logrolling method, these veterans of the polls became beneficiaries of a long series of one-man pension bills, thus getting monthly stipends far above the general level.

The venerable pork barrel also made inroads on the surplus. Congressional districts where the incumbents' chances of re-election appeared slim got federal buildings or a dredging of rivers or enlargement of harbors that the residents had not even thought of requesting. Creeks so tiny that waggish critics suggested paving as the more economical conversion for transportation, were instead made navigable. Ever since the war, river-and-harbor bills had been growing in proportions until by 1881 Congress had appropriated over $11,000,000 for such purposes. Then, on August 2, 1882, by a bipartisan vote, Congress passed over President Arthur's veto a bill appropriating $18,743,875 to be spent in almost five hundred localities for public works. *Harper's Weekly* justified the President's veto by stating that "nobody denies that the bill was a vast aggregation of jobs, a net of swindles and steals. . . . It is a huge log-rolling bill, in which one job balances another, and one jobber is as deep in the mud as another in the mire." *The Nation* observed that "when it comes to draining the Treasury, a large majority of the chosen men of one party will harmoniously cooperate with a majority of the other like a band of brothers. They fight for the first seats at the table and embrace in the gutter." The act made appropriations for one port where the annual revenue collected amounted to only $23.25, and to another where there was no commerce at all. One rill that was to be made navigable was so small that all the water could flow through a twelve-inch pipe. This same Congress appropriated nearly $100,000,000 for soldiers of the War of 1812 and their dependent relatives, and in another law passed on the pensions of veterans of the Civil War, after their death, to their widows and children. When a widow remarried, the children of the veteran should get the pension until the age of sixteen years.[7]

Between 1879 and 1883 the government also retired $577,-000,000 of the public debt, much of this before the bonds were due; but largely because of expanding tariff revenue the annual Treasury receipts from 1879 to 1882 grew $130,000,-000, and there was still an embarrassing surplus.[8] The absurdity of further contraction of the public debt and the concomitant deflation of the national currency just as business was showing signs of revival, the impoliticness of maintaining a huge surplus with like deflationary effect, and the stench aroused by the spending policies of the surplus financiers made patent the fact that the next measure would have to be tariff reduction. Accordingly, William W. Eaton, Connecticut Democrat, early in 1880 pushed through the Senate a bill that would have set up a tariff commission to study the problem; but the act died in the House. Two years later, after President Arthur recommended the establishment of such a commission in his first address to Congress, that body responded. "The work of the Commission," reported one journal, "is not to decide whether or not there shall be a protective tariff, but to make a protective tariff."[9]

Thus Arthur appointed nine commissioners, most of them being professed advocates of high tariffs and none a free trader. John L. Hayes, a long-time lobbyist for the National Association of Wool Manufacturers, was the chairman. Austin M. Garland of Illinois represented the wool growers, Duncan F. Kenner of Louisiana took care of the sugar interests, and Henry W. Oliver of Pennsylvania gave zealous attention to iron and steel. Thus there was assurance that any recommendations for changes in the rates would come from the friends of protection. These men had but little over six months to investigate, listen to industrialists, and make their report by the December 4, 1882, deadline. They traveled as far west as Minneapolis and as far south as Atlanta, not neglecting Philadelphia; listened to 604 witnesses; and took 2625 pages of testimony, most of which was just what might have been expected from persons with axes to grind. The way the witnesses besieged, dogged the footsteps of, and entertained the commissioners, says Ida M. Tarbell, "did more to demonstrate . . . the peculiar evils inherent in any protective system than reams of the ablest theoretical teaching could have done." Yet, the commissioners declared in their report that "a substantial reduction of tariff duties is demanded, not by a mere indiscriminate popular clamor but by the best conservative opinion of the country." They thought that manufacturers could stand a 20 per cent reduction, and that the rates in their proposed bill would average about 25 per cent, ranging from virtually nothing to 40 and 50 per cent.[10] If protectionists could grant this much, the question was as to how much more reduction could take place without harm.

The report of the tariff commission being made on time, both houses of Congress promptly commenced debate on the proposed bill. The arguments during this second session of the Forty-seventh Congress fill approximately a third of the 3777 pages of the *Congressional Globe,* and a summary might become boresome. The Senate, using a parliamentary fiction, tacked the customs measure onto an internal revenue bill held over from the first session, calling the tariff an amendment. So the senators did not need to wait for the House to write the tariff bill and send it on. The Senate bill passed by better than a two-to-one vote, with the aid of ten Democrats, and was a respectable downward revision, setting some rates lower than those suggested by the tariff commission. It was a different story in the House. Ruses to delay action became so numerous and ingenious that the parliamentarian Thomas Brackett Reed, rehearsing for the time when, as Speaker of the House, he would acquire the nickname of "Czar," maneuvered the acceptance of some new gag rules to expedite matters. Even so, the end of the session drew near and still the House had no bill of its own to offer, so it simply rejected the Senate measure and sent it into a conference of the two houses.[11]

John Sherman chaired the conference committee. Because the House severely castigated the Senate for taking the initiative on a revenue measure, the Democratic appointees for the

Senate refused to serve, and two Republicans took their place. After the Senate had juggled the rates in the bill drafted in accord with the tariff commission's report, until they were unrecognizable, the lobby for the protected interests exerted its noblest effort in the conference committee. Hayes, as an expert on the commission, was honest in agreeing that rates could with safety be lowered. Then, as the representative of the woolens men, he, again honestly, told Congress what the industry really wanted, and the legislators seemed to be far more interested in the lobbyist than in the advisor. Thus, they kept everything on an honorable plane. The steel and sugar interests had like able support, but Sherman neglected to look out for the wool growers of Ohio. Essentially drafting a new bill, the committee in a number of instances set higher rates than proposed by the tariff commission or by either house of Congress. For example, Congress had supported the commission's recommendation for fifty cents a ton on iron ore. Then the conference committee raised it to seventy-five cents. When Democrats protested that the committee was exceeding its authority, the reply was that the Senate had made but one amendment to the old internal revenue bill of the House, and this amendment embraced the whole tariff. The House had rejected the entire amendment, and this left the committee free to fix rates without consideration for the House debates on an entirely different bill.[12]

The Senate's approval of the conference report, by a vote of 32 to 31, came only after the winning over of a Democrat and Independent David Davis. William D. Kelley of Pennsylvania, who had fought to the last ditch for the iron and steel schedule, who came to be known as "Pig Iron" Kelley, and whose name shares that of "Mongrel" in the popular designation of the Act of 1883, reported the bill back to the House. Here, on March 3, after more debate it passed by a vote of 152 to 116. Twelve Republicans, including William McKinley of Ohio, who thought the rates should have been set higher, voted with the opposition, while Randall, true to form, headed a group of nineteen protectionist Democrats for passage. Sherman bemoaned the triumph of logrolling over principle and later expressed the wish that, as chairman of the conference committee, he had managed to kill the bill. Thomas B. Reed is reported to have said that "the only place you can pass a perfectly balanced tariff bill is in your mind: Congress certainly will never pass one."[13]

This act, which Arthur signed on March 3,[14] was a masterpiece in that it lowered the average of rates from 47 per cent to 43 per cent by increasing the duties in the individual schedules. Congress achieved this feat of legerdemain by shifting items from a lower schedule to a higher one without lowering the rates in either group; by reducing the tax on noncompetitive goods, where the tax was purely for revenue, and increasing it on articles where elastic demand could make the duties still more protective; by lessening the levy on raw materials, such as wool, and putting others on the free list, while retaining the fullest protection for manufactures using the raw materials; and by putting the products of young industries under low protection, after they had demonstrated that they could prosper without this infant pap, and averaging the new, low schedules with the higher ones, thus reducing the average for all. As the infant industries grew stronger, they could demand a larger share from the public trough. The steel schedule was an outstanding example of augmented protection by reclassification, while textiles illustrated the cutting down of duties on noncompetitive grades while other goods got more bountiful protection. There was some of the latter type of juggling in the steel schedule as well. Congress lowered the duty on rails from $28 a ton to $17, which duty, because of inelastic demand, was still prohibitive, giving the maximum of protection without producing revenue. Oddly enough, the suave lobbyist Hayes made a slip that brought a real protection cut for worsteds, but the McKinley tariff of 1890 corrected this error. Even this early, the tariff makers were befuddling the farmers by placing duties on produce that the tariff could not affect, while still using the home-market argument of the Clay era. In 1883, the farmers' duties were little changed except for a lowering of the rate on wool, but the farmers still adhered to their faith in the tariff.[15]

Randall's triumphs in 1883 and earlier were merely a warm-up for victories to follow, though his personal political fortune was already on the wane. As noted in the previous chapter, in the Forty-eighth Congress the Democrats had seventy-seven more votes than the Republicans and Greenbackers combined. But the Republicans had picked up enough Senate seats to give them a margin of four over the opposition. Quite clearly, the Democrats were in no position to enact party legislation, but they should have been able to get a tariff measure through the House as a promise of what to expect if the electorate in 1884 continued its trend of 1882 and chose a Democratic President and Congress. The first victory in the House, indeed, went to the low-tariff Democrats. Randall, after the two-year Republican interlude under Joseph Warren Keifer of Ohio, expected to return for a fourth time as Speaker. But his opposition in the caucus, headed by John G. Carlisle of Kentucky and Morrison and joined by the new tariff reformer William L. Wilson of West Virginia, put a sprag in Randall's wheel, and Carlisle emerged as Speaker, which position he held through three successive Congresses. The fact that Carlisle had been one of Randall's bitterest opponents in the preceding tariff free-for-all made the Pennsylvanian's ignominy fully as great as that of the ineffective and unpopular Republican runner-up, Keifer.[16]

But Randall's power was not ended, "half-Democrat" though he was sometimes called. On March 11, 1884, Morrison, chairman of the Ways and Means Committee, presented a bill to show the people what to expect from a Democratic tariff. His bill put salt, coal, and lumber on the free list, maintained the high rates on the luxury items of liquors and silks, and administered a horizontal reduction of 20 per cent on everything else, with a maximum of 40, 50, and 60 per cent on cotton goods, metals, and woolens respectively. Yet, no rate was to be lower than in the Morrill Act of 1861. This was far from free trade, and some critics called the bill an unscientific approach, but none could explain when or how any tariff had followed scientific principles. Horizontal reductions had worked well enough from 1833 to 1842, and the similar feature of the tariff from 1873 to 1875 had surely harmed no industry. Morrison's motion to have the bill referred to the Committee of the Whole carried by 140 to 138

at a time when Randall was ill in Philadelphia and could not
keep his following fully in line against the attack of the tariff
reformers. Debate continued from April 15 to May 6, by
which time it was understood that William McKinley would
move to strike out the enacting clause. The humiliation of
the regular Democrats was complete when, instead, another
Ohioan, the Randallite Democrat George L. Converse offered
the motion, and the House killed the bill by a vote of 159 to
155. Here, at the climax of his strength, Randall headed the
forty-one Democrats ("Randall and his forty thieves") who
mutilated the Democrats' chance to make an issue of the
tariff in the coming presidential campaign. Party harmony
received this blow at a most unfortunate time.[17]

Yet the consequences were not as serious as they may have
seemed. Almost wholly on the basis of other issues, as will be
seen in a later chapter, in 1884 the Democrats carried the
Presidency for the first time since 1856, received a comfortable majority in the House of Representatives, yet remained
helpless as long as the Senate continued in Republican hands.
The Democrats had no chance to show what they could do
with a tariff until 1893 to 1895. Then the Wilson-Gorman
Act of 1894 proved almost a complete betrayal of their promises. The next opportunity was in 1913 when the Underwood
Act finally satisfied the demands of a Democratic platform,
but proved futile a few months later when European war
and its aftereffects played havoc with imports from abroad.
Then came twelve more Republican years and, by the time
the Democrats were fully in power again (in 1933), the tariff
was a subordinate issue. They muffed the only two chances
they had in the days of great tariff debates.

They might have stood a better chance at least to show
their intentions in 1886 if Cleveland had shown some leadership. But the New York school of politics, which was his only
alma mater, had not trained him widely on national issues.
After inauguration he had to learn from the ground up, and
he did not start with the tariff. He had little to say on the
subject in his annual messages to Congress in 1885 and 1886
because, as he admitted to Carl Schurz, he knew little about
it. The Democratic platform of 1884 had used weasel words

on the subject, and furnished no real guidance to party leaders. Naturally, it denounced the Act of 1883 and declared that taxation should "not exceed the needs of the government." But so effective was Randall in his divisive force in the party that the most the convention could conjure up was a promise "to revise the tariff in a spirit of fairness to all interests" and not "to injure any domestic industries, but rather to promote their healthy growth." Randall working alone could not have devised a statement more to his liking. The Republicans had pledged themselves to correct tariff abuses without lessening protection.[18]

Under these discouraging circumstances, the veteran Morrison presented a new tariff bill to the House on April 14, 1886. Much care had gone into the drafting of this bill, and David A. Wells, the free-trade economist who had been special commissioner of the revenue under President Johnson, had assisted. Cleveland, who by now was waking up on the subject and was no longer under the tutelage of Randall in tariff matters, along with Carlisle offered advice. The bill thus drafted, in spite of the free-trade sponsorship, was quite moderate in nature and did not violate the platform of either major party to any great extent. It abandoned the horizontal principle of 1884 and simply offered a moderate downward revision. By this time Morrison and Randall were barely on speaking terms, and party relations were badly strained. On May 29, Representative Abram S. Hewitt, who was not only a steel manufacturer but soon was to become the Democratic mayor of New York, made a speech in Randall's own Philadelphia criticizing his Congressional colleague, though in a somewhat disguised fashion, for his stand on the tariff. But Randall prevailed again. On June 17, Morrison asked for the Committee of the Whole to begin discussion of his bill, but his motion lost by a vote of 140 to 157. This time the Randallite vote fell from 41 to 35, but it was still sufficient, and tariff reform went over to the second session of the Forty-ninth Congress. In December of 1886 Morrison brought the measure again before the House where another time he suffered defeat, by a vote of 148 to 154. Only twenty-eight of the Morrison group remained intransigent, and this was the last battle between Randall and Morrison. Morrison was a lame duck who had already failed of re-election. The able and forceful Randall was broken in health and had only forty months yet to live.[19]

Yet, one more time the indomitable warrior was to take his stand, on the Mills bill of 1888. Before this occasion Cleveland had acquired ample information about the treasury surplus and the tariff, and in his message to Congress on December 6, 1887, he made the tariff the principal issue on which he would fight for re-election in the following year. In fact, he devoted the whole speech to that subject. But he was a little too late to accomplish anything in his first administration. The election of 1886 reduced the Democratic lead in the House from about 40 to 17, and gave the Republicans a majority of two in the Senate. Disregarding warnings that he might be cutting his political throat by creating a new issue after a generally popular administration, Cleveland pointed to the cumbersomeness of the Act of 1883, with its incomprehensible schedules and four thousand or more individual duties. He did not demand tariff for revenue only, or free trade, but only that the taxes be reduced to what an economically administered government needed. To earlier criticisms that he did not follow any definite tariff doctrine, he replied in his message with the not particularly brilliant, but popular, remark: "It is a *condition* which confronts us, not a theory." Equivocal as the message may have been—and liberal economists could detect serious flaws—it was the most advanced stand any President or presidential candidate had taken in thirty years.[20]

In the Fiftieth Congress, the mantle of Morrison fell on the new chairman of the Ways and Means Committee, Roger Q. Mills, who had been following the free-trade line for more than a decade. His was the task of putting Cleveland's message before the people in the form of a new tariff bill. Not only did he give the Republican members short shrift in the committee proceedings, but for the first time in the memory of most of the legislators he excluded the lobbyists. This high-handed treatment of "the third house of Congress" so shocked the feeders at the trough that, likening it to the ways of burglars, they referred to the Mills proposal as a "dark lantern bill." The measure reported from the committee on April 2, 1888, followed the line of Cleveland's argument more than the free-trade principles of Mills. It offered genuine reduction to replace the illusions of 1883, the clarified schedules averaging not above 40 per cent. It placed nearly all raw materials on the free list and substituted ad valorem for many specific duties. Since specific duties gave higher protection the lower prices fell, this provision was not relished by the industrialists. The Democrats, scarcely deigning to reply to Republican criticisms, suppressing all amendments, and enforcing strict party discipline, passed the bill on July 21 by a vote of 162 to 114. Randall, firm in the faith to the last, was one of the four Democrats who voted against it, and this lost its sting when six Republicans voted for it. Cleveland had cut off Randall's patronage, thus ending his prestige in the House and breaking up his leadership in Pennsylvania politics. But he had already done his work. If the National Association of Manufacturers knows the meaning of gratitude, it should erect an obelisk in Randall's memory taller than the Washington Monument. The Senate, working over the Mills bill in a forecast of the later McKinley bill, returned it to the House on January 22, 1889, and there it died.[21]

The Mills bill had served its purpose. Before the election of 1888, the Republicans in the Senate, like the Democrats in the House, had shown the electorate what to expect of them in the way of tariff amendments. If, in the election of 1888, the people spoke their favor in one way or the other, their voice, like one shouting down an empty rain barrel, reverberated back in confusion. Cleveland received the most votes, but Benjamin Harrison carried the Electoral College. The Republicans also moved into control of both houses of Congress. Both parties could claim a victory on the tariff issue, but the Republicans alone could do anything about it.[22]

The House of Representatives in the Fifty-first Congress chose Thomas B. Reed as Speaker, while the consolation prize, the chairmanship of the Committee on Ways and Means, went to William McKinley. McKinley, the son and grandson of iron masters, the ablest student in "Pig Iron"

1. Soldiers Firing on Strikers at Baltimore, July 20, 1877

2. The Burning of the Roundhouse at Pittsburgh, 1877

3. Allan Pinkerton

4. Franklin B. Gowen

5. The Wandering "McKenna" (McParlan) Arrives at Pat Dormer's Saloon

MAJOR PARTY CANDIDATES IN 1876

6. William A. Wheeler

7. Rutherford B. Hayes

8. Thomas A. Hendricks

9. Samuel J. Tilden

10. A Radical's (or Carpetbagger's) Conception of the Fate of the Republican
Party in the South, 1877

MAJOR PARTY CANDIDATES IN 1880

11. William H. English

12. Winfield S. Hancock

13. Chester A. Arthur

14. James A. Garfield

REPUBLICAN AND LEADING MINOR PARTY CANDIDATES IN 1884

15. James G. Blaine

16. John P. St. John

17. John A. Logan

MAJOR PARTY CANDIDATES IN 1888

18. Benjamin Harrison

19. Levi P. Morton

20. Grover Cleveland

21. Allen G. Thurman

Kelley's school of politics, also had represented an iron-producing district in Ohio since 1877. As a member of the Committee on Ways and Means from 1880 on, he had fought every Democratic tariff measure since Fernando Wood's bill. He was not a leader in politics, but tried to follow the wishes of his constituency, and kept his "ear to the ground." The industrialists' wire was grounded close to his listening post, and the voice he heard from the campaign contributors, saying "higher protection," he took to be the voice of the people. He would present no dark-lantern bill to Congress. Instead, he called the prominent lobbyists into the committee room to take part in the deliberations. In the great tariff debate of 1888, he had flourished a $10.00 suit of men's clothing before the edified House to prove that the tariff worked no hardship on laboring men, whereupon Mills demonstrated that, minus the tariff costs, that suit could have sold for the bargain-basement price of $4.98.[23] MicKinley would demonstrate that the way to prosperity for all was paved by protection.

The Republican platform of 1888 had proposed to solve the surplus problem by lowered duties on tobacco and alcoholic beverages and, if more were needed, it said, "we favor the entire repeal of internal taxes rather than the surrender of any part of our protective system. . . ." Prohibitive duties on competing imports would also help lessen the revenue.[24] President Harrison, in his address to Congress on December 3, 1889, asked for an improvement in the Act of 1883 in matters of uniformity, administration, and inequalities, "but the protective principle should be maintained and fairly applied to the products of our farms as well as of our shops."[25] Then Reed facilitated the passage of the McKinley bill by getting some changes of the House rules, using steam-roller tactics to achieve his victory. It might prove difficult to keep a small majority of Republicans in line and always alert, so among the new rules was one giving the Speaker authority to count all members physically present (even if in the cloakrooms) whether they answered the roll call or not, for the purpose of forming a quorum. Another rule was that the presiding officer had the right to refuse to entertain a clearly dilatory motion.[26]

McKinley's committee contained Nelson Dingley of Maine and Sereno E. Payne of New York, while Nelson W. Aldrich of Rhode Island did valiant work for the bill in the Senate. The names of all three were later attached to other Republican tariff measures. Working in close unison under the new rules, the leaders rushed the bill through the House in two weeks, the final vote of 164 to 142, almost on straight party lines, coming on May 21, 1890. The Senate passed the bill, after 496 amendments, by a margin of 40 to 29, and sent it back to the House on September 10. In the conference committee the House acceded to 272 of the Senate amendments and compromised on 173, the Senate yielding on the rest. Harrison attached his signature on October 1, 1890. In view of the Senate's alterations, perhaps this should be called the McKinley-Aldrich Act.[27]

The people were soon to find what their confused voices in the election of 1888 had called out of the political forest, and they did not like the monster that sprang upon them. In preceding decades they had heard talk of tariff for revenue only or for revenue with incidental protection, but here was an act declaredly for protection mainly, revenue being the incidental feature. The reduced duties on tobacco and alcohol, amounting to about $10,000,000 annually, was but a small part of the way the architects built the McKinley Act so as to lessen revenue. Another method was to remove the duty of two cents a pound on crude sugar and pay a subsidy to American growers as a substitute. This would lose the Treasury from $50,000,000 to $60,000,000 in duties and from $6,000,000 to $8,000,000 in bounties each year and be popular with consumers. For that matter, if an industry must be protected, this method is the cheapest one in the long run. The price of the product goes on a competitive basis and the people pay a subsidy only to the domestic producers. Under a tariff they pay the increased cost on the imports as well. If further revenue is needed it is no more expensive to pay it in the form of other taxes. Next, there was a left-handed variety of reciprocity, thrown in as a sop to Secretary Blaine of the State

Department. To patch up some of the sores caused by Blaine's diplomacy in Latin America, the law put hides, coffee, tea, sugar, and molasses on the free list, but the President could restore the old rates against countries that discriminated against imports from the United States, as Harrison did against Venezuela, Colombia, and Haiti two years later. The virtue of this section of the law was that it tended toward freer markets to the south, and gave American consumers the advantage of lower prices. But it was not the sort of thorough reciprocity that reformers desired.

Prohibitive duties for the benefit of the greater industries were disguised in various ways. One was to extend greatly the number of specific rates and to go further than Clay would have deemed possible in the application of the minimum-valuation principle. There were some woolens on which the specific duties equaled 100 per cent if translated to ad valorem equivalents, but which also got an additional 40 or 50 per cent ad valorem. Another ruse was to juggle minimum valuations so that the higher taxes applied to cheaper goods than they did in the old schedules. Any rates that the act lowered were uniformly on noncompetitive items. As to the agricultural schedule, the duties on wheat, corn, flax, and hemp went up. But farmers produced a surplus of wheat and corn, which therefore sold according to the world price and could not be protected by a tariff alone, while the growers of flax and hemp were so few as to be inconsiderable. Technically, the McKinley tariff average was 49.5 per cent, or not much more than that of 1864, but real protection for the industries that had powerful lobbies was about twice that of the wartime measure, and considerably above that of 1883.[28]

With the McKinley Act, the time was past, if it ever existed, when protection could be gauged by schedule and general averages. No duty will give the same degree of protection year after year. Only a device that will show how much more an industry profits with and without the tariff can reveal the percentage of tariff protection.[29] Some goods, like whiskey and automobiles, will sell in very slightly diminished volume, regardless of the price charged. For them, almost any rate of tariff can be fully protective. But when prices go too high on bacon and bread, people can do with less of them, and a tariff ceases to be protective when it would push the cost above what the public will buy in adequate quantities. In such a case, 1000 per cent of tariff might not increase the price more than a 50 per cent levy would. But the higher rate cuts off imports and produces no revenue.

From the point of view of the surplus financiers, the law was an unqualified success. The surplus dwindled to nothing by 1893 and in the following year there was a deficit of $61,000,000. The deficits continued, down and up, year by year until that of 1899 was $89,000,000.[30] Farmers of the West seemed to believe that the five cents a bushel extra on wheat and corn was at least well intentioned, and for many years in the future were convinced protectionists. A like amount on rice would have been of real help to some sections of the South. But there were no Republican votes to be gained there, so there was no tax. A convincing evidence that the industrial schedules furnished more protection than the averages indicated is seen in the race of the *Etruria,* a Cunard liner, into the port of New York just a matter of minutes before the new law became effective. By doing so it saved a million dollars in duties. Day laborers had more painful evidence. The cost of living rose so sharply because of the "McKinley Bill" that in November they went to the polls to oust Bill McKinley. By that election the Republican majority in the House vanished before a Democratic landslide of nearly three to one. McKinley himself was voted into retirement. Thomas B. Reed reported in the *New York Sun* that the stories told by drummers to storekeepers, of the imminent rise in prices, hurried the advance in retail charges, thus angering the women customers, who next informed their menfolks how to vote. A tin peddler in the pay of the Democrats is supposed to have elevated the price of his wares in McKinley's home town of Canton, Ohio, to such a ridiculous peak that his sales were nil, and McKinley went down with them.[31]

Chapter VII

THE GROWTH OF MONOPOLIES

THE American tariff policy was one of several factors stimulating the rise and growth of monopolies in industry. Some of the early trusts, the American Tin-Plate Company, for example, grew directly out of such protection from foreign competition. Others, like the American Tobacco Company and the beef trust, might well have grown up even under free trade but, here also, their profits depended largely on the tariff. The Standard Oil Company, though the strongest of the nineteenth-century trusts, had no competition from abroad and could have none, because virtually all of the crude petroleum before 1900 came from American wells. Its power grew from its absorption of the petroleum fields, special favors from the railroads, a firm grip on nearly all of the important pipelines, and the ingenuity and sometimes the ruthlessness of its officials. Congress bestowed immense grants of land on certain railroads, mainly in the Far West, and seldom bothered to investigate the activities of these corporations. An exception occurred when Representative Oakes Ames of Massachusetts bribed certain Congressmen to suppress an investigation of the Crédit Mobilier in 1867, which led instead to further investigation of the building of the Union Pacific Railroad, and a censure against Ames, in 1873.[1]

Additional governmental activity (and inactivity), benevolent in effect on the rise of monopolies, included lax state corporation legislation, various sympathetic court interpretations of restraint of trade as defined in the common law, and the application of parts of the Fifth and Fourteenth Amendments to the United States Constitution so as to include corporations as "persons" from whom the federal and state governments could not take property "without due process of law." Business also invoked the economic doctrine of *laissez faire*, misinterpreting it to mean that governments should never regulate, but do everything in their power to foster business enterprise. In a later generation, when antitrust laws and the Interstate Commerce Act were galling a few tender spots on the economic body, business changed the name of its theory to "rugged individualism." Then, in the bankrupt 1930s, when waggish individuals interpreted the new term to mean "ragged individualism," the expression "free enterprise" supplanted all earlier designations. But *laissez faire*, rugged individualism, and free enterprise were all myths from the time when one corporation or combination rose to sufficient power to dominate its field. When the New Deal attempted to save capitalism by putting it under restraint against its own excesses, the cry arose that the government was strangling free enterprise. But a very recent economic treatise shows that private monopoly has been a greater hindrance to the economic freedom of the unaffiliated company than has any legal restraint; that the government has fostered private monopoly, with a resulting decline in competition; that such legal regulation as has arisen does not protect the consumer; and that monopoly has grown in power economically, legally, and politically, while regulatory bodies have become the servants of the monopolies.[2]

Though this tendency has become intensified since 1900, the same was essentially true at any time since the Civil War. Contractors for army supplies and services came out of the war with huge fortunes and a desire to watch them grow still larger. Accustomed to seeing their capital multiply by integers, they were impatient with fractional or percentage gains, and saw in the organization of huge corporations a chance to control a large amount of public investments with a relatively small outlay of their own. By manipulating the stock and performing sleight-of-hand tricks with accounts, they could skim off the cream of the profits for themselves. Monopoly control was the ideal means of accomplishing this end. That once achieved, there would be no competition, whereupon the favored few could limit output, raise prices, cut down on the number of salesmen, pry concessions from transportation agencies, and dominate the market so as to give the enterprisers—certainly not the consumers—the benefit of the savings. In the rough-and-tumble between businessmen for mastery, the one who was shrewdest and most ruthless had the best chance of coming out on top, so giving credence to Herbert Spencer's doctrine of the survival of the fittest in the social and economic struggle for existence. Thus it was that Jay Gould's reputation as an ogre so fearful that parents used his name to scare their children into obedience (the children thinking their parents were talking about a ghoul) came from the aspersions of his own associates. It was for these more strenuous of the masters of capital that Matthew Josephson popularized the designation "robber barons."[3]

This term had a considerable vogue for several years before the writers of official business histories began to assail it. Organizations sprang into existence after 1940 with no other apparent purpose than that of glorifying every industrialist, financier, merchant, public utilities magnate, and transportation or communications leader against whom their contemporaries made charges of unethical or dishonest activities. Sometimes the apologists tell of the impeccable family life, community leadership, and church interests of the accused, as if those matters had anything to do with the indictments. Someday, it is to be anticipated, a countermuckraker will demonstrate to his own satisfaction that Edward S. Stokes did not kill James Fisk in a brawl over Josephine Mansfield. Ned and Jim, as former business associates, were discussing a renewal of their relations while Ned was cleaning a gun. The gun went off accidentally, and Josie's name did not enter their discussion. Ned, while serving four years at Sing Sing, still keeping his carriage and span of driving horses, was overwhelmed with grief over his awkwardness. Other revisions have gone almost this far; why not this one? In fact it was in 1951, if newspaper reports of a speech before a history conference at Stanford University are accurate, that Allan Nevins said there never had been any robber barons in the United States, and spoke of the "feminine idealism" of historians who used such an expression.[4] In other words, you are a sissy if you stop to consider the existence of a seamier side of business.

The new business-history argument runs somewhat as follows: If a man steals his neighbor's calf, and from it builds up a large herd from which he supplies the whole community with dairy products (at an adequate price), whereas the former owner of the calf would probably have butchered it for veal, the later great service of the dairyman excuses his earlier transgression. Then, anyway, who saw him steal the calf? In a like vein, one can excuse the robber barons of the Middle Ages. Perhaps, when they stole half the freight of a passing merchant, they also protected him from other robbers and probably saved his life thereby. Consequently, there were no robber barons in the Middle Ages either. In an entirely elevated frame of mind, contemplating the zestful atmosphere about the lofty castles of those same medieval knights, Lynn Thorndike once said, one "can to some extent sympathize with the robber baron's descents from his stronghold in order to procure a round of beef or saddle of mutton from such sheep and cattle, or a cask of wine and mess of fish from such traveling merchants, as strayed within his ken. . . ."[5] But Thorndike soon receded from this whimsey, and elsewhere dealt with the robbers as they deserved. Fads in the writing of history have come and gone, and there is no particular reason to believe that this one about the complete benevolence of *all* nineteenth-century masters of capital will survive for long.

The most vigorous of the buccaneers before 1877 concerned themselves in the combination of railroads and the manipulation of their stocks. Of the four horsemen of the Erie War and their political protagonist William Marcy Tweed, only Gould was active after the seating of Hayes as President. The departure of Fisk at the age of thirty-seven in 1872 has already had sufficient elaboration. Cornelius Vanderbilt died just two months before Hayes was inaugurated. Daniel Drew, bankrupt by 1876, existed only until 1879. Tweed was moldering away in the Ludlow Street Jail in New York City, where he died in 1878. Drew had commemorated his name by the founding of a Methodist theological seminary, Vanderbilt with a university; Gould left the matter of philanthropy to his daughter, after his death in 1892; if Fisk and Tweed were ever guilty of any benefactions, the matter has not come to light. Nevins, before he began to eschew the term "robber barons," described these railroad wreckers and their activities in a chapter he named "The Moral Collapse in Government and Business," where he called them "great railway freebooters" and "robbers," and followed with an account of the desperadoes Cole and James Younger and Jesse James.[6]

By 1877, the first period of railroad consolidation was drawing to a close, with the completion of most of the trunk lines running from the Atlantic coast to Chicago and the Mississippi River and on to the Pacific coast. Then the crass habit of bribing legislators, governors, and judges to legalize or wink at the illegality of sharp practices did not diminish in intensity, but became less obvious, being overshadowed by newer tactics for eliminating rivalry between competing lines. As parallel railroads from New York, Philadelphia, and Baltimore reached Chicago, and others contested for the carrying trade between Chicago and Omaha, Pittsburgh and St. Louis, St. Louis and Kansas City, and elsewhere, there were occasional rate wars in the 1870s, greatly relished by shippers who could take advantage of them though they were all but disastrous to the carriers themselves. For a time in 1870 and afterward the charge for a carload of cattle from Chicago to New York was one dollar; occasionally a railroad would carry a shipment free, and there were cases where the company actually paid a bonus in addition for the favor of getting the business. In such instances, as in less spectacular contests, when the competition reached the point of absurdity the result was a rate agreement or a pool which set charges amply high enough to erase all red ink incurred by the rate war. By 1873 the Pennsylvania, New York Central, and Erie railroads formed the "Evener Combination," pooling the cattle traffic between Chicago and New York and charging $115 a carload except to the favored shippers, known as the "Eveners," who paid only $100. This arrangement, which lasted until 1878, was not the earliest of the pools, but it was an example also of rebating and discrimination between rival shipping points. The rate from St. Louis to New York during the same years was so high as to give the bulk of the business to the Chicago favorites.[7]

The inducement to further rate agreements and pools came from continued rate wars in 1877 and the time following. Thomas A. Scott of the Pennsylvania declared that no line made any profit on "through competitive freight" in the first half of that year. As a consequence, before the year was gone the New York Central, Erie, Pennsylvania, and Baltimore and Ohio officials made a rate agreement for freight from New York to Chicago and St. Louis, putting the proceeds from that business in a common pool to be divided between the lines on a 33, 33, 25 and 9 per cent basis respectively. Also, they cut wages 10 per cent to help cover past losses in operation, which act contributed to the beginning of the big strikes of 1877.[8] But by 1881, the New York Central, not in violation of this pool, was cutting rates to ten cents a hundredweight from Chicago to New York.[9] Farther to the west, in 1882 the old Chicago-to-Omaha pool of 1870, between the Chicago and Northwestern, Rock Island, and Burlington lines, began transformation into a series of traffic agreements that could not prevent another rate war in 1884. In 1887, when the Interstate Commerce Act outlawed pooling, these railroads transformed their arrangement into the Western Traffic Association,[10] which was no less effective than the earlier pools. The Southwestern Railway Rates Association of 1876 pooled the traffic between Chicago and St. Louis, and in the early 1880s had a strong centralized control.[11] The Southern Railway and Steamship Association, created by Albert Fink of the Louisville and Nashville system, also worked effectively until compelled to change its form but not its purpose in 1887. By this same date there were also some pools with interlocking directorates to presage the greater consolidation that was to follow.[12]

In the same years there was, by lease, sale, and other means, a great deal of railroad consolidation of a sort that outmoded rate agreements and pooling. Between 1883 and 1893 the Boston and Maine and the New Haven lines took over the bulk of the railroads of New England, while in Ohio from 1875 to 1890 there were ninety-four mergers, and by the latter date "a dozen large companies and their affiliates" controlled over "half the railroad mileage of the South. . . ."[13] Based on a high degree of social control, most of these consolidations would have been beneficial to shippers and the buying public alike, but the methods of achieving monopoly as exemplified by Gould and Collis P. Huntington and associates have not been successfully justified. Gould controlled the Union Pacific until 1882, as well as the Kansas Pacific (from 1878), the Texas and Pacific, the Wabash, and the Missouri Pacific, which between them in 1884 had over fifteen thousand miles of track. Also, by means of the Pacific Mail Steamship Company and the Panama Railroad, he dominated the Panama route to the West. Failing to block the extension of the Burlington to Denver, he retired from that area and concentrated on the Southwest, where he had monopoly control before he started to unload on less perspicacious victims. He got connections with the Central Pacific in 1881 and then helped Huntington check the advance of the Santa Fe. Gould, using his properties purely for speculative purposes, let them deteriorate "until they became a synonym for bad management and poor equipment." The Missouri Pacific and the Texas Pacific failed in 1884, but he had taken his profit and retired from active management before the crash.[14]

Huntington, associated with Leland Stanford, Mark Hopkins, and Charles Crocker, used the Central Pacific to get a monopoly of transportation in California and then extended eastward.[15] During the decade after 1875 they spent $500,-000 a year in graft. In the same period the transcontinental lines and other railroads disposed of millions of dollars "in Washington, state capitals, county seats, and city halls to get land grants, loans and subsidies, and then spent millions more to maintain their grants inviolate."[16] The Southern Pacific had such political control, handled by Huntington, that in 1890 he boasted a candidate for constable had to come to his office for permission to run. In 1885 he secured from the state legislature the election of Stanford as United States senator.

Until 1895, the Southern Pacific held the veto right on nominations for governor of California.[17] The situation in the South, with other railroads responsible, was comparable. But there were exceptions among railroad presidents. Charles Francis Adams of the Union Pacific resigned when he learned in 1890 that Gould was again taking over the reins. Adams had tried to win better public relations, but competition kept him from sweeping reforms, and he could not abolish rebates, passes to prominent men, and other discriminations. Nor could he overcome the troubles caused by overcapitalization. James J. Hill began in 1875 to expand the railroad that became the Great Northern, and without federal aid. He reached a high point in his career by 1890, and, though he also strove for monopoly, he was in other respects frequently cited as the admirable railroad magnate.[18] But some of his later activities cast a little doubt on this characterization.

While the railroads were thus forming pools and mergers, the shippers and the public had other reasons for complaint. Charging all the traffic would bear resulted in ton-mile rates in the West and South frequently as much as three times those for the same goods between Chicago and New York, while from 1877 to 1889 the Burlington charged four times as much west of the Missouri River as east of it.[19] Even in the regions of ample railroads, shippers at noncompetitive points had to pay higher rates for a short haul than customers paid for a longer haul where there was competition. The old account of Pittsburgh merchants sending goods to Cincinnati and from there back through Pittsburgh to Philadelphia to circumvent the monopoly rate between the two Pennsylvania cities has a much later counterpart involving the same Pennsylvania system. For some years around 1900 a wholesale butcher in Brazil, Indiana, shipped cattle from St. Louis over the Vandalia line of the Pennsylvania system, right past his slaughterhouse, to Greencastle, eighteen miles to the east, where there was competition from St. Louis by way of the Big Four. Then he would spend the night driving the cattle back to Brazil, often with icicles hanging from his mustache, declaring that if he could always make as much money in so short a time from his regular business, he would soon be a rich man.[20]

Rebates to favored interests, as those paid to the Standard Oil Company, not only stimulated industrial monopoly but also were made up in higher charges to the less-favored shippers. Railroads engaging in industry, as in the anthracite region of Pennsylvania, by hauling their own products free of charge could drive competitors out of the field. Free annual passes to such persons as could enact, administer, and adjudicate laws or to others with influence over public opinion, such as editors and preachers, meant higher fares for the general traveling public. Many a Western locality voted county or city bonds to donate to railroads to get them to come their way. Before 1892 forty-three Nebraska counties of small population gave nearly $5,000,000 to companies for the building of railroads, "some of which never built a mile of track." One such Missouri county that did not get its railroad spent until 1938 in paying off its bonds.[21]

Such activities led to a widespread demand for regulation of the common carriers. Early in 1877 the United States Supreme Court, in Peik v. the Chicago and Northwestern Railroad, upheld one of the Granger laws that allowed Wisconsin to fix rates on shipments to points in other states, unless or until Congress decided otherwise.[22] This ruling applied to any state that chose to take action, but the need for a more systematic approach through federal legislation was apparent. Between 1874 and 1885, the House of Representatives considered upward of thirty such bills, but such of them as passed died in the Senate. Among these was one presented by John H. Reagan of Texas in 1878, which would have left it to the courts to stop rebating and pooling and enforce equal rates.[23] President Arthur on December 4, 1883, called upon Congress to act, declaring that it "should protect the people at large in their interstate traffic against acts of injustice which the State governments are powerless to prevent."[24] The railroads themselves did not mind restoration of order, as long as the restrictions were not oppressive. In 1885, the Senate rejected another Reagan bill and the House did likewise with a bill by Senator Shelby M. Cullom for an interstate commerce com-

mission. Then in the following year came the Supreme
Court's decision in the Wabash, St. Louis, and Pacific Railway
Company v. Illinois, putting an end to interstate rate-fixing
by states.[25]

Likewise in 1886, the Cullom Committee of the Senate
gave its report, condemning all the practices just recounted
and adding the distribution of dividends on watered stocks
and the improper issuance of interest-paying bonds. Now that
not even the states could say anything about interstate rates,
Congress had to stop its horseplay and pass some sort of legislation. The fact that the Interstate Commerce Act of February
4, 1887, got through the Senate by a vote of 43 to 15 and the
House with a margin of 219 to 41 in itself should have revealed that it was a stopgap measure without teeth. The law
forbade pooling, rate agreements, excessive rates, and rebates, and placed restrictions on the charging of more for a
short than for a long haul. All rates should be open for public
inspection, but they could be charged on notice of ten days,
and there was no requirement that any little shipper should
receive such notice. Thus, favored customers of the roads
could have forewarning when to ship under a lowered rate,
and the others could have a like advantage if they just happened to ship before the schedule went up again. There were
prescribed penalties up to $5000 for each offense, and every
day of violation was a separate misdemeanor. An amendment
of 1889 also authorized imprisonment for guilty officials. The
Interstate Commerce Commission administered the law, its
members being appointed for six years each by the President
of the United States. This commission was mainly a fact-
finding body with authority to inspect the carriers' books for
information. It could decide on the reasonableness of a rate,
on complaint from a shipper who felt he was injured, and
could issue cease-and-desist orders. And that was just about
all. The commission had no authority to enforce its decisions,
and complaints could be carried to the courts only by the dissatisfied customers. Such cases might linger in the courts for
years before settlement, during which time the offending railroad could continue the old practices.[26]

The commission received over seven hundred such complaints during its first three years of operation but, out of the sixteen cases that went all the way through the courts up to 1905, the Supreme Court decided fifteen in favor of the railroads. For a brief time the commission had some success in breaking up some pools in the West and in modifying certain long-and-short-haul abuses, but when, in 1890, it turned its attention to the cherished rebate system, the railroads fought back and the supposed power of the commission began to wither. It may be said that the weakness of the act itself, together with the courts' habit of overriding the commission's findings and orders, by 1897 turned the commission into, as Associate Justice John M. Harlan saw it, "a useless body for all practical purposes." In 1890, the Supreme Court, in the Minnesota Rate case, also decided that a state had only very limited powers of rate-fixing even within its own borders, the final word being that of the courts. Thus was the Peik decision almost totally reversed, and the railroads were left to do pretty nearly what they planned, just as before any Granger legislation or Interstate Commerce Act.[27]

Acting with the most expensive legal advice obtainable, the railroad companies soon began firing through the loopholes in the law. Renewed rate wars in 1887 and 1888 led to the formation of several traffic associations, particularly in the West. Also at this time the New York bankers, and especially John Pierpont Morgan, began to take over the financial management of the railroads. As early as 1879, Morgan had made an arrangement with William H. Vanderbilt for handling sales of New York Central stock, and in exchange became a director of the system so that he could have a voice in management and thus protect his investment. In a somewhat similar manner, in 1880, Morgan got directors on the board of the Northern Pacific, and in 1885 he had the power to induce the New York Central and Pennsylvania to buy competing lines in order to end competition. Before 1888, he had helped in the reorganization of several weak companies, including the Reading, the Baltimore and Ohio, and the Chesapeake and Ohio, always working in the interest of smoother financial operations and understandings with rivals—in other words, for monopoly. In 1889, he began working out communities of interest, over which in a few years he was obtaining a form of administrative control that came to be called "Morganization." In 1889, he held a conference of the presidents of twenty-eight systems that controlled over four-tenths of the mileage of the country. Here he paved the way for future rate agreements. He was convinced that if there was to be orderly business among the carriers he would have to enforce it himself. In other words, he would tend to the regulation that the government had declined. He took good care of solvency and profits and did not concern himself with public relations. Finance capitalism in control of the railroads was getting into full swing before 1890.[28]

The admonitory slap on the wrist given by Congress to the railroads was quite comparable with its treatment of the trusts three years later. Industry was slower in its movement toward consolidation than was transportation, but by 1890 several branches were effectively monopolized and serious concentration on furtherance of progress toward a complete system of monopolies was achieving notable gains. Though the word "trusts" was in common use to describe monopolistic concerns for many years after 1900, such combinations on a large scale, in the legal and technical sense, existed only in the 1880s and shortly afterward. A writer of that period described them as composed of a group of trustees representing the majority of the capital in a given interest who induced former competitors to turn over to them the stock in their own corporations and receive trust certificates in return. The trustees then, by owning outright the greater part of the certificates, elected the directors of each corporation and managed the whole business in the interest of greater profits for all. They had the power "to cause one concern to be closed, limit the production of another, consolidate the different establishments, or centralize production at one point." The different companies looked to the trust, and not to their own factories, for profits.[29] Another writer of the same year, almost anticipating the later extralegal gentlemen's agreements, described what he called "monopoly in its most concentrated form. Suppose the presidents of all the incorporated companies in a given branch of industry . . . assembled, and one of their number in whom they all have perfect trust—hence the name—was selected to perform the function of *absolute* manager, with power to determine, autocratically, how much each company is to produce, and consequently its share in the proceeds, and you have the 'trust.' "[30]

There had been only a slight trend toward monopoly in industry before the Civil War. Numerous mergers and consolidations had occurred, but there had been only a few attempts at price-fixing, and these were not effective. In 1860, the cordage manufacturers formed a pool, and others followed. In 1868, the Michigan Salt Association based itself on a pooling agreement to purchase the total output of the big producers in the Saginaw Valley. The Standard Oil Company was essentially a pool for a decade following 1872. Throughout the 1880s, the cotton-bagging pool controlled about two-thirds of the national product. The Western Exporters' Association, or whiskey pool, organized in 1882 or probably earlier, limited output of the distilleries to 40 per cent of capacity at one time and to 28 per cent another time, and also levied assessments on all members for exporting the surplus at a loss so as to keep up the price in the domestic market. Such combinations as these had inherent weaknesses. Usually an outgrowth of price wars, they generally broke up when prices were good. Also, the common law against restraint of trade, as applied by the courts, was a deterrent force, especially as no person knew beforehand what, in any case, would be the judicial distinction between reasonable and unreasonable restraint.[31]

The Standard Oil Company set the pattern for a new kind of organization which, operating in secrecy and with no charter, seemed to be less liable to prosecution than the pools. Before 1877, John D. Rockefeller and his brother William, Henry M. Flagler, Samuel Andrews, Stephen V. Harkness, Henry H. Rogers, Oliver H. Payne, and later John D. Archbold, had secured a monopoly of the petroleum business, about 90 per cent perfect. They had not been squeamish about the methods they employed. They got rebates from the railroads, not only on their own oil shipments but on those of their competitors as well, who soon thereafter either had to sell out, merge, or go out of business. By 1876, through any means that seemed suitable, they had acquired control of all the important pipelines. By 1879, some independents had built a pipeline from the oil fields to Baltimore, only to find the Rockefeller interests in possession of it two years later. Meanwhile, using the most advanced of business methods, Standard Oil hired the best researchers available to work in advanced laboratories, began making its own barrels and acids, developed by-products, and got possession of facilities for ocean shipment. In order to keep down production, it closed down many wells and let others flow on the ground.[32] Allan Nevins who, in his life of Rockefeller, takes a rather benign view of this whole situation, a few years earlier referred to the "octopus grip" of Standard Oil and spoke of its "harsh and at times unethical" practices. "In the path which Rockefeller had left were strewn ruined men and abandoned plants; before him lay an unquestioned control over tremendous sources of wealth."[33]

While a railroad rate war was going on in 1876 and 1877, Rockefeller not only cut prices to drive the last competing pipelines into his snare, but elsewhere made monopoly profits on coal oil at prices from fifteen to twenty-five cents a gallon. Then, in 1877, he drew the New York Central, Erie, Pennsylvania, and Baltimore and Ohio railroads into a pool that gave Standard Oil not only rebates on its own shipments, but drawbacks on the freight transported by rivals, just as in the old South Improvement Company days of 1872, whereupon some of the few remaining refiners began falling into Rockefeller's hands. Meanwhile, his methods included nearly everything short of arson, and he was accused of that. He organized the whole country into districts and subdistricts, with a hierarchy of officials, and each local official was to get a monopoly of sales. There were big rewards for success and dismissal for failure. The tactics included spying on rivals and bribery of employees and dealers. Standard companies under bogus names befuddled competitors, who could not discover the source of the contest. Rockefeller's justification for all this was that "the coal-oil business belongs to us." By 1878, with a monopoly of transportation and with all but about

5 per cent of the refinery capacity of the entire business, Rockefeller could extort monopoly prices on finished products and beat down rates paid for crude petroleum. It seemed that every time he made some philanthropic gift, the price of coal oil went up or that of crude petroleum fell. Yet, in one of the numerous investigations into monopoly practices, in 1880, he swore that he had no control over numerous transportation agencies and refineries that were integral parts of his oil empire.[34]

This was during a trial in Pennsylvania, under an indictment for conspiracy. In this case, after many delays, there was a compromise with the complainant, the Producers' Union, which dropped the charge on payment of $40,000. Thereafter, the independent producers began to drop out of the hopeless contest. Wearied by experiences such as this, in 1882 Rockefeller found a temporary solution in the organization of the Standard Oil trust. Following a plan used for expansion a few years earlier, he issued stock certificates to the amount of $70,000,000 and exchanged them for the stock of the different companies, the Standard Oil group holding the majority. Then the nine trustees, all Rockefeller men, were in a position to evade state laws curbing corporations. On these certificates he paid dividends of 10 per cent. Thereafter, for a few years, the trustees had things just about as they desired them. By 1883, other new attempts at a rival pipeline having been squelched, the trust started building longer and more capacious tubes than any preceding ones, thus bringing the shipment of crude oil by rail virtually to an end.[35]

In the courts and in politics the trustees also had their successes. In 1885, the Buffalo Lubricating Oil Company brought conspiracy charges against five Standard Oil officials, including Archbold and Rogers, for methods of sabotage including the bribing of the Buffalo manager to overheat oil to the point of danger to life and property. Archbold and Rogers secured acquittal while, in 1888, two of the group received fines of $250 each and a year's jail sentence which was suspended. In a civil suit the Buffalo company also secured damages of a paltry $85,000, the judge seemingly being in the pay of the trust. Most of the Standard Oil officials were Republicans, but in Democratic states they were Democrats. Thus, Oliver H. Payne, treasurer of Standard Oil, lubricated the Ohio legislature to the point of electing his aged father, Henry B., to the United States Senate in 1885. G. F. Hoar was quite discomfited when the Senate smothered an investigation of the election. But the railroads had William B. Allison of Iowa and Stanford of California in the "Millionaires' Club"; why should not industry also be represented?[36]

Meanwhile, especially as new trusts with great power sprang into existence, the public became concerned and soon there was a new series of investigations. Before the New York Senate in 1888, Rockefeller again swore that he had never been involved with the South Improvement Company, that he had never received rebates, and that he had always been open and aboveboard in his righteous dealings with competitors. After all, perhaps being cynical about women, the officials had not even told their wives about the trust relationships and they had carried on their correspondence under assumed names. How could anybody prove guilt! But the federal House of Representatives held its own investigation in the same year, and here both Rockefeller and Flagler had to admit some of the charges they had so long denied. Yet nothing came of the inquiry except a huge report. The trustees had "made no agreements, signed no contracts, kept no books," the trust "had no legal existence." The subsidiaries had done the dirty work. How could there be a conspiracy?[37]

Further basis for public concern lay in the multiplication of trusts in the 1880s. The distillers and cattle feeders trust and the sugar trust took form in 1887 and the American Tobacco Company with $25,000,000 capital and trust-like proportions in 1890. Carnegie Brothers and Company got started with $5,000,000 capital in 1879 and began extending its control until by 1891 it had absorbed several other concerns and changed its name to the Carnegie Steel Company, with $25,000,000 in stock. The Illinois Steel Company, a combination of plants around the southern edge of Lake Michigan, started out in 1889 with $25,000,000 and doubled this amount two years later, by that time probably being the largest producer in the world. The Tennessee Coal, Iron, and Railroad Company of 1881 and the Colorado Fuel and Iron Company of the same approximate date, which by 1892 had $13,000,000 capital, were others of the regional trusts that in the next decade were to effect further combinations until the United States Steel Corporation emerged in 1901. Henry Demarest Lloyd needed eight pages to record "a partial list of trade combinations, or trusts, achieved or attempted, and the commodities covered by them" to 1894. Included in the list was the United Shoe Machinery Company of 1890, which was in time to take a dole, through the leasing of the machines, from the price of every pair of shoes manufactured in the country.[38]

From the Marxist point of view, the rise of monopolies was both inevitable and desirable. Even the abuses of the trusts, if not condoned, could be accepted with complacency, for they would hasten the time when the people would see the necessity of taking over the businesses to operate for use instead of for profit. But other persons, less zealous in economic doctrine, but outraged at corruption and the mulcting of the public, took up their pens and demanded reform. Lloyd summed up and elaborated his "Story of a Great Monopoly," and numerous other articles of the 1880s, in his magnum opus of 1894, so vital that half a century later it was still a source of controversy. Henry George, as early as 1879, expounded the single tax on the unearned increment of land values as a panacea, and single-tax clubs continued into the 1950s. William Godwin Moody assailed the monopoly in land in a trenchant book in 1883, but his was a voice crying in the wilderness and he was soon forgotten. In 1888, Edward Bellamy, in an imaginative novel, proposed a brand of Utopian Socialism as a cure, and followed it up with a series of tracts along the same line. His main weakness was the assumption that capitalists would give up their advantage without a struggle.[39] Bellamy clubs and enthusiasts also continue to flourish, especially in Los Angeles, the mecca of the devotees of probably every prophet who ever existed.

Third parties had been agitating the monopoly question

since 1878, and the Antimonopoly party of 1884 made a special issue of it. A 1500-page report from the House of Representatives in 1888, the bulk of it devoted to the Standard Oil Company, was an indication of the probability of legislation to follow. Then, in 1888, the major parties had to take a stand, the Democrats assailing the tariff as the cause and the Republicans deploring the situation that had grown worse during the administration of their opponents, regardless of the earlier Republican origins. The general idea was that bigness alone was an evil. In 1889 and the following years, several states and territories adopted antitrust laws, and ultimately all states did so except New Jersey, Delaware, and West Virginia. Consequently, monopolies threatened by the states in which they were chartered, moved into the wide-open states where, under the "full faith and credit" clause of the federal Constitution, they were free to do business in every other state. Clearly, in view of the temper of the times, Congress had to bestir itself. So, on July 2, 1890, it passed the law generally called the Sherman Anti-Trust Act, though John Sherman had precious little to do with its drafting and passage. It was a brief statute, and its essence lay in the first sentence following the enacting clause: "Every contract, combination in the form of trust or otherwise, or conspiracy, in restraint of trade or commerce among the several States, or with foreign nations, is hereby declared to be illegal." Every person making such a contract or taking part in "any such combination or conspiracy, shall be deemed guilty of a misdemeanor . . ." and be subject to a fine of as much as $5000 or imprisonment up to one year, or both.[40]

This, to the nonlegal mind, should seem clear enough. The contract, the combination, and the conspiracy—each was illegal, and the person who violated one or all of the prohibitions was guilty and was subject to the penalties. But, in the manner in which the courts interpreted and applied the act, it meant exactly nothing, which development no doubt the lawyers in Congress anticipated. Even the provision that persons damaged by such restraint of trade might recover through civil suit three times his loss in addition to court costs and attorneys' fees, was of little effect. The Republican

Senator Orville H. Platt, one of the opponents of the measure, said in effect that the law was rushed through Congress simply to tide the Republican party over the next election. If this is true, then the act was still worse a failure, in view of the Democratic landslide the following November. Senator Cullom, not as cynical as Platt, said that strict enforcement of the measure would bring all the business of the country to a halt. But as perceptive a remark as any was that of Mr. Dooley to Mr. Hennessy: "What looks like a stone-wall to a layman is a triumphal arch to a corporation lawyer."[41] Most eloquent of all was the vote on the measure—only one opposing voice in the Senate and none in the House. Platt had cause for his jeers.

The administration of the Sherman Act belongs in another volume. Only a few conclusions can come here. Before any application of the Sherman Act, Louisiana attacked the cottonseed oil trust and Nebraska instituted proceedings against the whiskey trust, both in 1887. In the following year, New York assailed the sugar trust, and in 1890 Ohio set about to dissolve the Standard Oil trust. By court decisions, all apparently broke up into their component parts. This dissolution, however, was a mere sham. The whiskey trust converted itself into one solid corporation, the sugar trust did the same, and the Standard Oil combination became for the time being a community of interest before transforming into holding-company management. The Sugar Refineries Company at once began to expand, brought Claus Spreckles into its fold, and enlarged its capital stock to $50,000,000. During depression years following the Panic of 1893, there was a slackening of monopoly growth, yet in 1897 there were sixty-three trusts. Talk about repeal of the futile Sherman Act dropped off in a few years, when business found that it had one point of strength—it could be used to break up labor unions. Then, under the aegis of the Sherman Act, in the last three years of the century the number of trusts multiplied threefold, reaching 183 in 1900; and the greatest of all the monopolies were to come in the new century.[42]

Monopolies moving into New Jersey, Delaware, and West Virginia found protective laws suited to the formation of holding companies. These devices were corporations owning the majority of the voting stock of each subsidiary, which could be only a small fraction of the operating capital. They differed from trusts in that there was no wholesale exchange of stocks, each subsidiary had some autonomy over inside affairs, but the holding company had the final voice in matters of policy. Holding companies gained some headway during the 1880s especially over public utilities, the idea probably being furnished by Francis L. Stetson for the Metropolitan Traction Company of New York. Under special legislation, The Pennsylvania Company in 1870, the American Bell Telephone Company in 1880, and the Southern Pacific Company in 1884 received such charters. Then New Jersey adopted a general act legalizing such combination, requiring only that the corporation have desk space, display a sign somewhere in the state, and make an annual report of no importance. As stated in the report of the Industrial Commission, the effect of the antitrust laws was to drive corporations "from the old forms which often contained the seeds of disintegration" into more powerful combinations. The monopolies of the future were "promoted by laws intended to prevent them."[43]

As an anticlimax, one might view with compassion John D. Archbold as, before 1890, he saw the Pennsylvania oil fields dwindling and being replaced in other states by new fields that Standard could not completely monopolize. He had once declared that he would drink all the petroleum discovered outside of Pennsylvania.[44]

Chapter VIII

THE ELECTION OF 1884

MONOPOLIES and the tariff played only a small part in the political campaign of 1884. This was a contest over personalities rather than issues. Republicans and Democrats mouthed inane phrases about the tariff, while the Greenbackers declared it to be "a convenient issue" used primarily to divert the people's attention from more important urgencies, such as the monetary question. Democrats and Republicans alike spoke disapprovingly of land monopoly, especially by alien and absentee control, and suggested the confiscation of railroad land grants where the companies had violated the conditions on which the gifts were made. The Greenbackers spread a little wider to cover "railroad, money and other corporate monopolies," while the Antimonopoly party became somewhat more specific in its denunciation. All platforms asserted that the classified civil service was a good thing, and there was more or less agreement that it should be extended. The cadaver of polygamy was handy for all to thump, and nearly all pledged themselves to a strict limitation on Mongolian immigration, an exception being the American Prohibition party (the old American party), which instead would extend "civil equality" to "Indians and Chinamen." Democrats and Republicans agreed on the maintenance of a sound dollar, but the Republicans went so far as to advocate an international conference to establish a proper ratio of value between silver and gold, a matter of which the Greenbackers took a dim view. Each party, naturally, had a monopoly of virtue and honesty, which among the Prohibitionists and Americans extended to Christian guidance, under which they would enact sumptuary legislation. The Greenbackers would not join the two prohibition groups in offering woman suffrage, but they would submit that to the states, along with prohibition, in the form of constitutional amendments.[1]

As far as the platforms went, if the laboring man asked bread he could expect to receive a stone, unless he turned to the Socialist Labor party, and then he might starve before he got it. Between 1876 and 1879 the Workingmen's party, which later became the Socialist Labor party, had achieved some success and elected a few candidates in Cincinnati, Chicago, and St. Louis, but then for a few years the trade-union element was in the saddle and the political actionists had marked time. After the anarchists split off in 1883, for a time there were only 1500 Socialist Labor party members, whereas two years later the anarchists claimed eighty groups, 7000 members, and eleven newspapers. In the Socialist Labor convention at Baltimore, December 26–28, 1883, there were only sixteen delegates, fourteen of them from the New York and Baltimore areas. Nevertheless, they adopted a resounding platform calling for social control of "land, the means of production, public transportation, and exchange," and included a list of immediate demands going well beyond those of the Greenbackers. They condemned the anarchists, but decided not to take political action except for propaganda purposes. By calling for the abolition of the Presidency, they excluded themselves from nominating leaders of the ticket and gave the workingmen nobody to lean on for immediate strength. A further split in the ranks before 1886 left the party still more ineffective until Daniel DeLeon, a brilliant young political scientist of Columbia University, took over in 1890, and remained the party's lawgiver until his death in 1914. However much influence socialism may have had in the labor ranks during the Centennial years, its action at the polls was limited to a few candidates in still fewer localities.[2]

With so little to choose from in the platforms of the major parties, the public would have had almost nothing to entertain them during a long campaign had not personalities, scandals, and slanderous charges and countercharges assailed them from all sides. Andrew Dickson White, president of Cornell University, called it perhaps "the vilest political campaign ever waged." Despite both candidates' disapproval (except on an occasion or two) of the methods employed by their supporters, "the vile flood of slander raged on."[3] As most of this rancor developed between Republicans and Democrats following the nomination of candidates, a consideration of the party conclaves must intervene.

Chicago was the principal convention city of the year. The Antimonopoly party met there on May 14 and nominated Benjamin F. Butler of Massachusetts on the first ballot. Having been in and out of various parties, and with charges of arbitrary acts and corruption as military governor of New Orleans (1862) still hanging over him, he was not a strong choice. But the Greenbackers, assembled in Indianapolis two weeks later, endorsed Butler by a 3 to 1 vote over all opponents. There was also an Equal Rights party with Belva A. B. Lockwood of Washington, D.C., the first of her sex to practice law before the United States Supreme Court, as its distaff candidate.[4] The Prohibitionists flocked to Pittsburgh on July 23 and on the following day nominated John P. St. John, former Republican governor of Kansas. Up to this date, the Prohibitionist platform did not extend beyond liquor and woman suffrage. One thing that can be said for the 1880s is that they were remote from the time when the major parties could think of trying to keep their little rivals off the ballot. The Prohibitionist St. John was the only one of the minor candidates who really had any effect on the outcome of the election, but the Greenbackers talked biggest, explaining why "we point with pride to our history" as a "great, harmonious party," by taking credit for every progressive legislative achievement in the preceding eight years.[5]

The Republican and Democratic frolics in Chicago were five weeks apart. Observers of the Republican powwow of June 3–6 apparently saw it according to their own predilections. Nicholas Murray Butler in retrospect called it "quiet indeed" when contrasted with the assemblages of 1880 and 1888, but Andrew D. White described an overwhelming mob that "endeavored to sweep the convention in the direction of its own whims and fancies . . . [and which] took possession of the convention and became almost frantic. . . ."[6] Blaine, deprived of the presidential nomination for two consecutive times because of suspicions against him based on the Mulligan letters and other shady dealings, now felt that the past would be forgotten or forgiven, and he was clearly the favorite of the convention. But Arthur also had ambitions and stood second in popularity. Senators Edmunds and Sherman were sufficiently in the running that if either were chosen he could hardly be rated as a dark horse. John A. Logan of Illinois had twice the strength of Joseph R. Hawley of Connecticut, whose name also was in formal nomination. The complimentary votes for William T. Sherman and Robert T. Lincoln may have been intended to keep them under observation in case a deadlock prevented any other choice, as in the case of Garfield in 1880.

Though, from the start, Blaine had the edge on all other candidates, he held seventy-seven less votes than a majority on the first ballot, and there were strong elements in the convention determined to stop him if possible. The sores of factionalism dating from 1877 had never entirely healed. Blaine's opponents were only in part from the old Stalwarts, and the more respectable ones now called themselves Independents. The first test came in the selection of a temporary chairman. Powell Clayton of Arkansas was the choice of the National Committee, but Henry Cabot Lodge of Massachusetts put forward the name of John R. Lynch, a Mississippi Negro, in opposition. Speeches by the Independents George W. Curtis, Lodge, and Theodore Roosevelt stopped the Blaine forces and secured the election of Lynch. Though this preliminary skirmish may have prevented Blaine's nomination on the first ballot, it also showed that the Ohio vote for Sherman was divided. The seating of a respectable Southern Negro in place of a rather discredited carpetbagger might have been good politics eight years earlier, but it had little effect in 1884. In the campaign that followed Sherman loyally supported Blaine, speaking daily on his behalf from August 30 until the election.[7]

Arthur, who started out with 278 votes, remained a strong contestant through all four ballots. But of the original number, 196 delegates were from the South, where Arthur had used the patronage to build up a strong anti-Bourbon force

in his support. Some of Arthur's former associates shunned
him because he had not made a clean sweep of Half-Breed
officeholders, and others because he had favored tariff revision.[8] The Independents were for Edmunds of Vermont,
who got 93 votes on the first ballot. After Blaine's nomination, some of the Independents bolted the ticket.[9] They afterward were called Mugwumps. The definition of a Mugwump
as a bird who roosts on a fence, with his mug on one side
and his wump on the other, is probably spurious, though it
has some applicability.

The first blunder of the Blaine forces was the selection of
Stephen B. Elkins of West Virginia as manager. The financial
and transportation activities of Elkins brought attention too
readily to the Little Rock and Fort Smith scandal of a decade
before, in which Blaine's role was somewhat short of illustrious. It was quite natural for voters not under the sway of
Blaine's magnetism to think of birds of a feather. The campaign was hardly under way when newspapers began anew
printing the Mulligan letters. Cullom of Illinois, who presented
John A. Logan for the Presidency, later thought Logan would
have been a stronger candidate than Blaine, because there
would have been none of the scandal that attached to Blaine.
During the first three ballots on Friday, June 6, Blaine gained
slightly, Arthur's vote was relatively unchanged, while
Edmunds, Logan, and Sherman each lost some votes. Then
Logan telegraphed Cullom to turn his vote over to Blaine.
Next, Foraker withdrew Sherman's name, thus giving Blaine
541 votes on the fourth ballot, or 130 over bare majority.
At the evening session Logan got nearly the entire vote of
the delegates for the Vice-Presidency. Blaine was the
party's choice, expressed without official pressure or the use
of patronage, and if he proved to be an unworthy candidate,
the blame lay with the rank and file of the Republican party.
Logan, though a Stalwart, a boss, and a follower of machine
methods, had always shown more regard for public opinion
than many of his associates, but his name on the ticket did
nothing to attract the support of the Mugwumps.[10]

The Democratic convention, July 8–11, quickly got into a
deadlock over the chairmanship of the Resolutions Commit-

tee. The contest was between the low-tariff men, backing
William R. Morrison of Illinois, and the Randall following, supporting George L. Converse of Ohio who, just nine weeks
before, had introduced the motion killing Morrison's tariff bill.
Ultimately, the choice went to Morrison but this did not end
the struggle.[11] The tariff plank that emerged was a sorry
sort of compromise, and the high-tariff Democrats were determined that the presidential candidate, if not one of their
own following, should be neutral on the subject. Randall and
Converse had done their work well in May, and now the
Democrats were afraid to nominate a genuine tariff reformer.
Loyal friends put Randall and Carlisle on the list, but Randall got only 78 votes out of 820 on the first ballot and
Carlisle a mere 27. Of middle-of-the-road possibilities there
were Hendricks and Joseph E. McDonald of Indiana, and
Thurman, Payne, and Hoadly of Ohio. Tilden, the old hero of
'76, telegraphed the convention that he would refuse even a
unanimous nomination, yet he received 1 and 2 votes on the
first two ballots. There was also Bayard of Delaware, who
ran second in the voting, but his Free Trade League connections were against him, and some people remembered that
in 1861 he had favored letting the South leave the Union
peaceably.[12]

This left Cleveland as the favorite. His record as a reform mayor of Buffalo and governor of New York, since 1881,
had received wide approval, especially his efforts at civil
service reform.[13] As sheriff of Erie County and mayor of
Buffalo, he had attracted attention by his devotion to duty,
and by his reform and efficient reorganization of the city
government. On his record as mayor, in 1882 he received the
Democratic nomination for governor of New York and won,
over Secretary of the Treasury Charles J. Folger, by the
prodigious and unprecedented plurality of almost 193,000.
This made him a natural candidate for the nomination for
the Presidency in 1884. His record as a reform governor had
enhanced his availability, even though he had incurred the
enmity of boss John Kelly and his Tammany Hall. Tammany
rationalized its hostility on the assumption that Cleveland
had antagonized the Antimonopolists, the laborers, the Cath-

olics, and the Irish, but the disciples of the saint of Gotham could not dominate the New York delegation, and the unit rule prevailed. The rank and file of the party were becoming indisposed toward an organization that had opposed Tilden in 1876, and in 1880 had stabbed Hancock in the back.[14]

Before the Democratic convention opened, the Mugwumps who had walked out on Blaine and Logan called upon the Democrats to make nominations that they could support. Edwin L. Godkin, the acidulous editor of *The Nation* and the *New York Evening Post*, through whose columns he influenced American thinking until the end of the century, estimated that there were over eighty thousand Independents in the state of New York alone. The prominent man of letters George W. Curtis declared that Cleveland, if nominated, would carry most of this vote and, with it, the state. Carl Schurz warned Bayard not to carry his rivalry too far and thus play into the hands of Tammany. Other Independents such as White, Lodge, Roosevelt, Edmunds, and Hamilton Fish refused to join in the Republican secession movement. Roosevelt seemingly tried to escape supporting Blaine by hurrying out to Dakota Territory for the summer, where he played cowboy and built up a somewhat dubious reputation as a "roughrider," but he was back in the East by October to stump for Lodge for Congress, in Massachusetts, and to lend a grudging hand to Blaine. Thus did he maintain his regularity.[15]

Among the New York Democrats was the wily politician David B. Hill, who was running for governor. He worked hard for Cleveland, hoping to ride on his coattails into office, and waited four more years to throw his leader into the tiger's cage. By July 8, it was clear that, with Tilden's support, Cleveland was sure of the New York delegation, and some of the Southern ones as well. It was to be a fight between Ben Butler and Kelly on the one hand and Cleveland's friends on the other. Daniel Manning, by assuring Randall the patronage in Pennsylvania, secured his agreement to retire in Cleveland's favor on the second ballot. On the other hand, Bourke Cochran, "the Mulligan Guard Demosthenes," stood side by side with Kelly, honing his razor for the still sharper attacks he was to make on Cleveland in 1888. The first ballot was taken late at night on July 10. The next morning Senator Daniel W. Voorhees of Indiana withdrew McDonald's name and tried to start a stampede for Hendricks. But Randall's retirement before the voting began threw 37 Pennsylvania votes to Cleveland, and other states fell in line. Cleveland was now close to the necessary two-thirds, when Hendricks turned the Indiana vote to him. Most of the Bayard and Thurman strength also went over and Cleveland became the nominee by a wide margin. After a recess, the convention nominated Hendricks for Vice-President, with no dissent. He, being popular in the West, lenient on monetary reform, and a machine politician, helped reconcile elements that feared an Eastern, hard-money, reform candidate for President. His strength in Indiana was to play an important part in carrying the state.[16]

A word more about Butler is in order. A Massachusetts delegate, he favored the candidacy of Hendricks. As a member of the platform committee, when he could not get his ideas adopted he submitted his own minority report. He defended it in a long speech in which he condemned the obvious attempts to evade the tariff issue, and threatened the party with the loss of support of his following unless the delegates accepted his protectionist and prolabor ideas. Failing in all of these efforts, he left the convention and belatedly accepted the nominations of the Greenbackers and Antimonopolists. Thereafter he slipped into obscurity, but shortly before his death he spoke the final word of wisdom on the Democratic tariff plank: "Some mongrel resolution was adopted which meant anything or nothing as one chose to construe it."[17] His vote in November was eighteen thousand less than that for St. John.

At the beginning of the campaign the Mugwumps set the pace. They wanted reform and they did not want Blaine, so they did not make the most of what should have been important issues. The old parties did not take up the challenge of the social questions that had arisen since the war. Neither of them had any clearly defined policy on the problems of

the farmer and the industrial laborer. Between 1883 and 1886
business seriously stagnated. In 1884, about 350,000 fewer
persons had work in industrial occupations than two years
before. Both parties felt that the labor vote would play an
unusually important part in the election. In their platforms
they gave considerable space to the situation, but their recommendations were vague, and there was no noticeable
cleavage between them. As to the civil service, the wording
alone was different. White and Foraker induced Blaine to
come out strongly on the subject in his acceptance speech,
but Independents remembered that his record was against
him. On the other hand, Cleveland was so sound on this issue
that he had vetoed a mangled tenure-of-office bill in 1884
with the approbation of its original author. As to the tariff,
the Mugwumps declared it no issue and asserted that the
Republican concentration on the topic was for the purpose of
diverting attention from Blaine's disgraceful public record.[18]

About one thing Cleveland could rest easy—the Republicans could not reproach him for his lack of a military record.
That could wait until he was in the White House and began
to veto pension bills. The point was that Blaine was as innocent of service in the army as himself. When men were being
conscripted, Blaine could sit in his draftproof cellar in Congress, which that body had provided for its indispensable
members. The three Cleveland brothers had drawn straws to
see which one should remain at home and provide for their
mother, and Grover drew the short one. So he hired a substitute. Congress had hailed this kind of service as honorable
and desirable, but a score of years later it did not rank with
Congressional immunity as an excuse. Outside the minor
parties, Logan alone had been in the war, and he could not
prate on this subject without harming his superior on the
ticket. Blaine, who had "waved the bloody shirt" in 1876,
was a different man in his acceptance letter of July 15, 1884,
where he cried down the issue and used soft words to win
Southern votes to his support. Yet, while campaigning in
Indiana he warned his hearers against the Democrats, with
their connections in "the old South with its bitterness, its un-
reconciled temper, its narrowness of vision, its hostility to all

Northern interests, its constant longing to revive an impossible past."[19]

The dyed-in-the-wool Republican George S. Boutwell of Massachusetts (who later became an anti-imperialism Bryan Democrat) wrote a small book with a long title in support of Blaine. In a chapter on the issues in the campaign, he devoted two pages to the bad record of the Democrats, three to banking and the currency, three to the tariff, a single paragraph to civil service reform, and four pages, the longest of all, to the Democratic suppression of the Negro vote and the issue of the "solid South." The relief of Southern Republicans from Democratic suppression he declared to be "the paramount question to which every other is subordinate or incident." Senator Lucius Q. C. Lamar of Mississippi retorted to this sort of argument with a perfervid defense of white supremacy, to which the *New York Tribune* replied after the election, calling Lamar a traitor who had regained all of his antebellum rights and privileges while "Jefferson Davis, even, has not been hanged on a sour apple tree. . . ."[20]

The lagging nature of the start of the campaign left the postern gate wide open for the Mugwumps' attack. Before Blaine's nomination, they had republished all the details of his early financial escapades, and then they uncovered, in the possession of James Mulligan, some more letters he had written to Warren G. Fisher, which coincided with the Mulligan letters of 1869 and following, exposed in 1876. In the middle of September, these appeared without comment in a Boston newspaper. Day after day, Godkin printed in the *New York Evening Post*, in parallel columns, Blaine's contradictory statements, and the Independents circulated them in hundreds of thousands of pamphlets. As a further indication that Blaine was overly friendly to privilege-seeking corporations and would not enforce laws to control them, they pointed to his brief term in the Senate, when he had proposed an amendment to a bill to oblige the Union Pacific to pay off its debts to the government, which if adopted would have prevented Congress from passing any other laws to regulate this railroad for a period of twenty years.[21]

But times are hard indeed for a politician when he cannot

find some moral lapse in the life of an opponent who is an old bachelor. From the dens of vice in Buffalo, that Cleveland had tried to suppress, came the vengeful story that he was the father of an illegitimate child. Blaine rushed this story to the Republican National Committee, and it appeared in print in a Buffalo newspaper on July 21, vouched for by two Buffalo preachers. Cleveland admitted the original charge and told his aides to "tell the truth."

But the truth was not enough for the Republican National Committee. So "now from every drinking-den and brothel there was sent forth a swarm of vile and slanderous stories, . . ." suggesting a lifetime of debauchery, the abduction of the woman in the case, and the kidnaping of her child. This brought forth a reply from another Buffalo clergyman, well acquainted with the facts, who denied all but the original charge. "There was no seduction, no adultery, no breach of promise, no obligation of marriage, . . . no abduction, . . . " and "after the preliminary offense, . . . his conduct was singularly honorable. . . ." This exposition of the truth should have satisfied all but the most meticulous moralists, and Godkin, who was fairly strait-laced himself, suggested that it would be better to have for President a man "who, like Cromwell, Franklin, Hamilton, and Webster, had been unchaste," than a man who had used his public office for dishonest gain and then destroyed evidence of his guilt. A Chicago Independent expressed somewhat the same idea with more wit: "We are told that Mr. Blaine has been delinquent in office but blameless in private life, while Mr. Cleveland has been a model of official integrity, but culpable in his personal relations. We should therefore elect Mr. Cleveland to the public office which he is so well qualified to fill, and remand Mr. Blaine to the private station which he is admirably fitted to adorn."[22]

A descent from the libelous to the ridiculous was the remark attributed to Robert Ingersoll, who in 1876 had dubbed Blaine the Plumed Knight, that Cleveland could slip his collar off over his head without unbuttoning it. There were few votes to be gained by such persiflage. Yet the Democrats thought up some of their own, in a couplet playing on

Logan's supposed carelessness of grammar as well as a coolness that had sprung up between him and Blaine, which had Logan saying

> We never speak as we pass by,
> Me to Jim Blaine nor him to I.[23]

Opposition to Cleveland came from within various quarters of the Democratic party as well as from without. Henry Watterson of the *Louisville Courier-Journal*, for example, called him an impossible candidate because he was inexperienced and opposed to Tammany, and also because (as Tammany said) he was hostile to organized labor and to the Catholic hierarchy. Charles A. Dana, the influential owner and editor of the *New York Sun*, opposed Cleveland from the beginning and kept up the attack even after Tammany itself capitulated. Butler called Kelly the strongest man in the state of New York and declared that this boss "represented the opposition to Mr. Cleveland," while Kelly himself had called Cleveland "no Democrat" and a potential traitor to the party. Even the Republican head of the Pension Bureau, while drawing a federal salary, devoted all of his time to mobilizing the old-soldier vote for Blaine. Randall failed to patch up the trouble with Butler, who was subsidized by the Republican Stephen B. Elkins of West Virginia. Butler centered his efforts in the state of New York, whose population contained half a million Irish. The voters among this group were generally Democratic but doubtful about Cleveland and might be won away from him in large numbers. It was Hendricks, for whom Kelly had a high regard, who finally won Tammany over to Cleveland. On September 12, its general committee voted 810 to 87 to support the national ticket. But Kelly's support was hardly more than a thin pretense, and Tammanyites in large part divided their strength between Butler and Blaine.[24]

The uncertainty about the labor vote made especially invidious the Tammany and Greenback interpretation of Cleveland's stand. Cleveland remained in Albany during most of the campaign, making only two speeches, one at Newark and the other at Bridgeport, both late in October. In these

addresses he stressed the need for further civil service reform and reduced taxation, and dwelt on his friendliness
toward labor. Depressed business conditions showed no tendency to ease up, and in May, 1884, there had been something
of a financial panic on Wall Street. Business failures grew
from 4350 in 1880 to 10,299 in 1883, and to 11,620 in 1884.
Such conditions did nothing to alleviate unemployment, and
except for the continuous sniping at Cleveland's labor attitude, it would have been expected that labor would be turning
from the Republicans to him. But labor had little solidarity
or awareness of its real interests. Otherwise it would have
rejected both of the major parties. In the hope of quelling
the suspicions about him, in July Cleveland wrote to Mayor
Carter H. Harrison of Chicago, protesting his good will to
labor and promising that "there will be pamphlets printed
in a few days on this and other subjects concerning which I
have been grossly misrepresented."[25] It is altogether uncertain just how labor finally divided in its support, but the
supposition is that, like the general vote, that of labor was
fairly evenly split.

In so close a contest, it seemed that the outcome would
depend on what happened in New York, New Jersey, Connecticut, and Indiana. Considering the strength of Hendricks
in Indiana, this may explain why Cleveland thought it better
to speak in only New Jersey and Connecticut. The election
fell on November 4, and by the following morning it was
clear that Cleveland had carried all of the South besides
three of the doubtful states of the North. But the 36 electoral
votes of New York would be decisive, and the count there
was long delayed. By the third day it seemed reasonably
certain that Cleveland had carried his own state also. Even
the *Sun*, supporting Butler to the last ditch, conceded Cleveland's election. But the *New York Tribune* would not back
down, nor would the Republican National Committee. For
two weeks the nation agitatedly awaited the answer. Many
cities feared mob violence. In New York, the nervous throngs
got the idea that Jay Gould, who was in control of the Western Union Telegraph Company, was adding to his career of
nefarious activities by delaying the returns, supposedly to

profit by gambling on the results. The mob descended on his office and threatened to hang him, whereupon he telegraphed Cleveland, congratulating him fulsomely on his election. On November 18, the official count showed that Cleveland had won New York and, thereby, the election, by a margin of just 1149 votes.[26] Cleveland received 219 electoral votes and Blaine 182.

Pundits, from historians to politicians, have pondered the returns, trying to show how some trivial incident or another shifted enough votes from Blaine to Cleveland to decide the election. The account would be incomplete without a resurvey of the evidence. For one thing, Blaine's chickens of 1866 came home for a final roost. Conkling had never forgiven him for his slurring remarks during their Congressional debate over the bounty brokers. After the experiences of 1876 and 1880, Blaine should not have expected any change of heart. But he felt desperately in need of votes in New York, and thought Conkling could bring them to him. Conkling was busily engaged in practicing law, and had let Platt take over the job of Republican leader in New York and earn the title of the "Easy Boss," but still had a following that he could influence. "Can Conkling be induced to speak for us?" Blaine asked a friend, soon after the convention. "It would be an immense thing for us. How can he be induced to do it?" A delegation of Blaine workers made Conkling a flattering offer to make even one speech for Blaine, to which his sardonic reply was: "Gentlemen, you have been misinformed. I have given up criminal law." News of this conference could not have helped Blaine. Thereafter, Conkling was commonly supposed to be secretly helping Cleveland. On October 24, a letter signed by 146 Oneida County Stalwarts appeared in the *Utica Daily Press*, setting forth their reasons for not voting for Blaine, but Conkling's biographer could find no evidence that the retired boss instigated the letter.[27]

Perhaps more influential in the final outcome than the Stalwart opposition was that of the Prohibitionists. After the Democratic platform declaration against "sumptuary laws which vex the citizens and interfere with personal liberty,"

there was no overpowering reason why the drys should lend
Cleveland even incidental support, especially as the Republicans had remained mute on the question. But St. John got
his feelings hurt. He refused to withdraw his candidacy at
the behest of the Republicans, whereupon their newspapers
began a systematic attack on him, which so irritated him
that he canceled all other speaking engagements and went
to New York to fight Blaine where he could do him the most
damage. He was strikingly successful. Whereas in 1880 the
nationwide Prohibition vote was barely over 10,000, in 1884
it rose to 150,000. Butler's 17,000 votes in the state of New
York were less damaging to Cleveland than St. John's 25,000
were to Blaine. In New Jersey the vote for St. John was twice
that for Butler. Also, many German-Americans turned to the
Democratic ticket on the prohibition issue. The influence of
Schurz attracted many others. A large meeting of Germans in
New York on September 29 was enthusiastic for Cleveland.[28]

During October it seemed unlikely that the Irish and
Greenback defections from Cleveland would be offset by the
hostility of the Mugwumps and Prohibitionists for Blaine.
Then, among Blaine's runs, hits, and errors, there were two
of the latter category that harmed him sorely when he
marched into the New York arena. Both blunders occurred
on October 29, less than a week before election day, one in
the Fifth Avenue Hotel and the other at the famous Del-
monico's restaurant. On the first occasion Blaine received a
group of clergymen and listened to a speech by one of them,
Samuel D. Burchard, who, probably to offset St. John's attacks, perorated the fatal sentence: "We are Republicans,
and we do not propose to leave our party and identify ourselves with the party of Rum, Romanism, and Rebellion!"
There sat Blaine, exhausted and in poor health, perhaps
also benumbed by the boresomeness of the occasion, and he
did not catch the remark. Neither did the newspapermen
present. But Arthur P. Gorman, scouting the occasion for the
Democrats, and a shorthand reporter along with him both
heard the remark, and within a few hours the words were
spread over the front pages of the newspapers. Blaine's
mother was a Catholic and his sister was the mother superior

in an Indiana convent. The Irish vote was at stake, yet he failed to correct Burchard when he crucified the Catholic Church between John Barleycorn and Jefferson Davis. This may have been the determining factor in the election, though one cannot be sure. But Chauncey Depew wrote (improbably) that he knew "personally of about five thousand votes which were changed in our State, . . ." and this was far more than Cleveland's majority.[29] Burchard's family tells that he also could not live down the witticism.

Shortly afterward the stricken Blaine sat down with Jay Gould, Henry H. Rogers, Cyrus W. Field, Russell Sage, Herman Ossian Armour, and other captains of industry and finance at what by the next day was to be called the "Millionaires' Dinner." The *New York World* carried on the front page a cartoon by William McDougall denominated "The Royal Feast of Belshazzar Blaine and the Money Kings." Actually, millionaires were not the only attenders, prominent people of all respectable kinds being present. But, in a time of recession, Blaine had appeared at a banquet organized by wealth and privilege and had made a speech to the taste of that audience. By this one act he possibly lost the votes of thousands of workingmen. For days the Democratic and Independent newspapers carried stories of the fabulous sums garnered for the campaign fund at this dinner.[30]

As an anticlimax, one can mention that election day was a rainy one in New York, and it could be that enough virtuous, moral Blaine men in the upstate farming regions got stuck in the mud on the way to the polls to lose him the election. The post-mortem was a particularly lugubrious one. There were claims and counterclaims about Democratic falsification of the returns and of counting Butler's ballots for Cleveland. Sour grapes were cheap in 1884. It is futile to try to match one set of incidents against another in an analysis of the vote in New York, but many have made the attempt.[31] More to the point is the fact that, taking the nation as a whole, the people had spoken for Cleveland and gave him a plurality of 63,000 over Blaine in the popular vote and a majority in the Electoral College. The Forty-ninth Congress was to meet with 180 Democrats, 138 Republicans, and 2 others in the House of

Representatives, with 5 temporary vacancies to alter the results slightly as their places filled. This represented a Republican gain of about twenty over the preceding Congress. The Democrats also lost one Senator and the Republicans gained two, that body having 34 Democrats and 42 Republicans.[32]

Chapter IX

CLEVELAND AND RESPECTABILITY

SO EFFECTIVE had been the campaign of slander against Cleveland that, as in the cases of Jefferson and Jackson, he entered office under grave suspicion from a considerable minority of the people. The handsome, suave, courtly, and dignified Arthur, so it was said, gave way to the gross, repulsive, uncouth libertine Cleveland. Consequently, there was widespread amazement when Cleveland wrote a short but scholarly, moderate, unassuming, and, in spots, eloquent inaugural address,[1] and then announced a cabinet of distinction. The State Department for Bayard was the customary prize awarded to the convention runner-up, but he was more than ordinarily able. Secretary of the Navy Whitney soon aroused suspicions regarding his relations with the Standard Oil trust, thus foreshadowing his much later shenanigans in the Metropolitan Traction Company, but his official activities were above reproach. Lamar, the scholarly type of Southern gentleman, could not use the Department of the Interior as a vehicle for white supremacy. Early in 1888 Postmaster General Vilas succeeded him in the Department of the Interior and Don M. Dickinson of Michigan became Postmaster General. Since 1862 there had been a Department of Agriculture of subcabinet rank, and when in February, 1889, Congress raised this to the executive level, Cleveland immediately elevated the commissioner, Norman J. Colman of Missouri, to the position of Secretary of Agriculture.[2]

The new President remained a curiosity for a considerable time, and must occasionally have been annoyed by the hordes of inquisitive sight-seers, some friendly and others not, who dogged his footsteps. The culmination came on June 2, 1886, when the forty-nine-year-old bachelor married Frances Folsom, a quarter of a century his junior. Buchanan, the only other bachelor President, had never become so brave.[3] Perhaps even more vexing than this surveillance was the attrition from Democratic office seekers and placers, having little faith in his insistence on an orderly civil service, and the sniping of Republican critics who assumed that all his pretensions were a mockery. Leaning backward in probity, Cleveland was unbecomingly curt with Tilden, who asked permission to nominate the Collector for the Port of New York. On another occasion, when a Democratic senator urged him to take better care of the interests of the party, the reply was: "I suppose you mean that I should appoint two horse-thieves a day instead of one."[4]

Although, with a divided Congress, the President could not expect to initiate any controversial legislation, the *Statutes at Large* reveal the usual plenitude of laws passed by the Forty-ninth Congress. Nonpartisan or bipartisan measures included not only the customary appropriations acts, with ever increasing allotments to the navy, but also the Interstate Commerce Act, the Dawes Severalty Act for the gradual absorption of the Indians as citizens of the United States, the repeal of the Tenure-of-Office Act of 1867, which had resulted in the impeachment of President Johnson, a strengthening of the laws against polygamy, and the withdrawal of the Bland-Allison trade dollar from circulation. By now, it was also timely to adopt a new Presidential Succession bill. Hendricks' death on November 25 left no person to succeed to the Presidency should Cleveland also die before Congress met and organized in December. Senator Hoar had presented a bill in 1882 to correct this situation, but it had died in its sleep. Other proposals were no more successful, and now Hoar introduced a new bill fashioned along the lines of his original one. Omitting the president pro tem and the Speaker, the succession was to devolve upon the constitutionally qualified members of the cabinet in the order in which the offices had been established by Congress. Senator Edmunds objected bitterly to the possibility of a President thus choosing his successor, and John Sherman, as president pro tem of the Senate and next in line to the highest office under the existing law, could see no merit in the proposed change. Opposition in the

House came from McKinley and T. B. Reed, who asked their fellow Republicans if they preferred Bayard to Sherman. But hostility was confined to only a few, and the bill passed both houses by large bipartisan majorities and became law on January 19.[5]

There were still serious deficiencies, besides the objection pointed out by Edmunds. A cabinet officer had to be confirmed by the Senate before he could qualify, which could produce a deadlock even in a special executive session right after the inaugural ceremonies, and it was possible for a vacancy to occur in that short interval. It was not until after the Twentieth Amendment to the Constitution in 1933 and the Presidential Succession Act of 1947 that this matter was finally put on a safe and democratic basis. Somewhat of a companion to the Presidential Succession law, but passed in the second session, was the Electoral-Count Act of February 3, 1887, making impossible the recurrence of such a scandalous situation as had happened in the Hayes-Tilden disputed count. Repenting rather tardily of that brawl, Congress now decided that each state should settle its own squabbles of that nature and, if the tribunal in any state could not come to a solution, Congress should act only by an agreement of both houses acting separately. In case of a lack of accord, the word of the governor of the state would be final.[6]

As another wreath on the grave of Reconstruction, Hoar, desirous of winning for the Republicans some of the sympathy that had been going to Cleveland in his differences with the Senate, proposed the repeal of the Tenure-of-Office Act, much to the disgust of John Sherman and others. All but four of the Republican senators voted against repeal, but it passed by a margin of 30 to 22. In the House, the vote was 171 to 67 in favor, and Cleveland added his approval on March 3, 1887,[7] remarking that the old law had already fallen into "innocuous desuetude."

Some of the legislation, abortive bills, and vetoes of the second session of the Forty-ninth Congress may be classified as unfortunate, ill-advised, or hard to explain. One of these was the Dawes Severalty Act of February 8, 1887. Senator

Henry L. Dawes of Massachusetts had for years been interested in the Indian problem, and well knew the multitude of evils that had developed in the white man's relations with the aborigines. He wanted to do something for them. The Indian wars that had been going on since 1862, sometimes with violence and again in desultory fashion, had attracted much unfavorable attention. In 1881, Helen Hunt Jackson had aroused moral indignation in the minds of thousands of Americans with her book *A Century of Dishonor,* a circumstantial and documented account of brutality inflicted on many Indian nations. Three years later her novel *Ramona* touched many more hearts in its depiction of persecutions in California. Cleveland, for one, was deeply stirred by these writings. Even Edward Z. C. Judson (Ned Buntline, died 1886) may have roused sympathies he had not anticipated (revulsion against his exaggerated portrayal of bad Indians) in his blood-and-thunder tales of the West. Public feeling was running high, so it was not difficult for Dawes to secure the passage of his bill.

The law gave the President the authority to end tribal government on reservations when he thought conditions so warranted, whereupon each head of a family should receive 160 acres of land, with women, children, and unmarried men getting smaller amounts. An amendment of 1891 changed this to 80 acres for each Indian, regardless of family or marital status. Although the Indians became United States citizens at once, the government was to hold the land in trust for a period of twenty-five years so as to guard the recipients against hasty disposal. The government was to sell whatever was left of the reservation after the division, and deposit the proceeds in an educational fund. The consequences of the act were anything but those anticipated. On reservations in the arid regions, the allotments were not enough from which to dig a comfortable living. As much land went to speculators, at low prices, as to the Indians, and when the latter got complete title to their tracts they were as likely as not to be cheated out of them. Furthermore, the government had no business to encourage the breakup of a form of life that suited the Indians' disposition, and to subject them to the kind of competition that already kept poor white people in permanent servility to forces they could not alter. After any number of amendments to the law, many years later the government saw the light and went back to the policy of making the most of the red man's cultural background instead of trying to make an imitation white man of him.[8]

On the same date as the Dawes Act, a law passed to recover some 300,000 or 400,000 acres of land granted to a little Southern railroad that had not lived up to the terms of the gift. Oddly enough, at about the same time, a bill to recover most of the more than forty million acres of land grants to the Northern Pacific along right of way where there had been no construction or where the laying of track had taken place after the time for such building had expired, died in a House committee after a similar bill had passed the Senate.[9] It was, apparently, not politic to antagonize so powerful a corporation. At the end of the session Cleveland pocket-vetoed a bill for arbitration of labor-management disputes on interstate common carriers. Another bill, passing the House by a huge majority and the Senate without division, would have prohibited the federal government from letting contracts for supplies or for public works to companies that employed convict or other prison labor, persons who were not bona fide residents of the United States, or aliens who had not filed their intention to become citizens.[10] Cleveland's pocketing of this bill lent some credence to the persistent rumors of his lack of warm sympathy for the workingman. Bills and resolutions tabled, killed, or interred by committees included one to repeal the Preemption, Timber Culture, and Desert Land laws, another "to aid in the establishment and temporary support of common schools," and a resolution to submit a woman-suffrage amendment to the states.[11]

By 1886, Cleveland was drawing attention to himself by vetoes of private pension bills, passed by Congress because the claims were so preposterous that the Pension Office could do nought but laugh at them. It was inevitable that some notice of this would appear in the Congressional campaign of

1886. It is no uncommon thing for the party in power to lose some strength in the off-year elections, but in this canvass there were complications working both for and against the Democrats. Business conditions were beginning to improve, but, or perhaps because of this, labor was seeking to recoup its losses of the preceding years, and the great upheaval was at its climax when the campaign began. The Haymarket bomb of May 4 had spread fears of anarchy through multitudes of slightly informed voters, and it was altogether uncertain whether the Democrats could gain as much strength from economic betterment as they would lose because of the strikes and the violence, both of employers and laborers, that accompanied the disturbances. By the process of filling vacancies, Democratic membership in the House of Representatives built up to 183 before the end of the Forty-ninth Congress, but in the election the party lost thirteen of this number. What were the reasons for this setback? An examination of conditions in a few of the districts at stake may help to answer this question.

The most illustrious among the casualties was William R. Morrison, whose Illinois district included Madison and St. Clair counties, directly across the river from St. Louis, and containing the industrial cities of Alton, Belleville, and East St. Louis. An ardent tariff reformer could easily get into difficulties in such surroundings. In October of 1886, one John Jarrett invaded this district with the single purpose of unseating Morrison in favor of the Republican candidate Jehu Baker. Jarrett spent money from the Republican war chest in great profusion. In the Morrison bill of 1886, the tariff rates on pig iron, steel rails, and window glass were in the list of reductions. Foundries, rolling mills, nail mills, glass houses, and allied industries, all presumably sensitive to tariff changes, abounded in the area, and their operators longed to guard their profits. It was still possible to indoctrinate laborers of nonanalytical habits with the hoary wages theory of the tariff. Jarrett, who was secretary of the American Tin-Plate Association, attributed his funds to the "Workingmen's Tariff Club." He hired men at three dollars a day and "legitimate expenses" to talk to the workers in the mills and factories and to organize them against Morrison. Threats of boycott against the merchants if they did not fall in line probably had some effect, and the *Chicago Daily News* declared that the "saloonkeepers were also dragooned into opposing him." Even the Knights of Labor lent their assistance to Baker, while Morrison assiduously avoided the tariff issue. With such valiant backing, Jehu drove furiously into the seat Morrison had occupied for sixteen years, fourteen of them continuously.[12] Morrison was given the consolation prize of a seat on the Interstate Commerce Commission, and eventually became its chairman.

Another Illinois Democrat, William M. Springer, slipped through by a margin of only 388 votes out of a total of over 35,000, and he bluntly told the Associated Press that his reduced majority was due to "the efforts of the tariff monopolists outside the district."[13] The Democrats of Indiana lost three seats, apparently in the same way.[14] William D. Hill of Ohio, opposed by the Ohio Wool Growers Association because of his vote for the Morrison bill, also lost by a small minority. The *Cincinnati Enquirer* had suggested that Ohio Democrats who had been unorthodox in such fashion had better fear other interests as well as the wool growers. In general, it was in the newly industrialized Old Northwest that the tariff issue worked hardest against the low-tariff men.[15] In the nation at large it was noted that only thirteen of the thirty-five Democrats who voted against the Morrison bill achieved re-election.[16] On the other hand, in Massachusetts the Republican William W. Rice lost to a free trader, leading the *Boston Herald* to speculate on the impending downfall of protection. In New York, where the tariff issue was pretty thoroughly confused, the Republicans gained three seats and lost two.[17]

Blaine brought up the issue in Maine, and placed particular stress on the benefits of a protective tariff, blaming the Democrats for entailing "upon the country a vast loss" because of their actions, though the Democrats had had no influence on tariff legislation since 1857. Reverend Professor William Graham Sumner, whose voice probably did not reach many of the common people, became quite sardonic in his analysis of Blaine's arguments. But the free trade clubs in the two old protectionist strongholds of New York State and Boston unquestionably made themselves heard where the arguments would be most effective. They assisted the Young Men's Democratic Club in electing Samuel S. ("Sunset") Cox of New York to the Congressional seat to which he had been appointed in April (on the resignation of Joseph Pulitzer). This enabled the humorist of the House, as Cox was known, to round out twenty-seven years in that body, eight from Ohio and nineteen from New York.[18]

As a result of the election, the House of Representatives in the Fiftieth Congress convened with 169 Democrats and 152 Republicans. This was a more comfortable majority than the Republicans retained in the Senate, where their loss of three seats left them with an advantage of only 39 to 37.[19] A sampling of opinion and of election returns in the districts of greatest party turnover seems to indicate that no other factor was as great as the tariff. The fact that the Democrats retained the House and made gains in the Senate would seem to indicate that the people were expecting reform, but their voice was not quite strong enough.

As far as legislation is concerned, the outcome of the election made little or no difference. The Democratic gains in the Senate were not enough to secure passage of the Mills bill (see Chapter VI) and the Republicans had fired their heaviest shells in the preceding two years. But Cleveland had his hands full and his wastebasket overflowing with complaints over his vetoes of pension and pork-barrel bills and concerning his hesitation waltz on the distribution of patronage. Senator Hoar later recalled that few Democratic senators liked the President personally,[20] and this seems to be an accurate estimate. After a long effort to hold the fort against the spoilsmen in his party, Cleveland gradually gave way before the pressure, especially that of Vilas and of First Assistant Postmaster General Adlai E. Stevenson of Illinois, thus making it possible for Hale of Maine to lay before the Senate a list of 55,608 appointive offices in which the President had authorized 42,555 changes.[21] Cleveland's relaxation of vigilance came too late to appease the Democrats in

Congress, but in ample time to incur the excoriation of the Mugwumps and civil service reformers. Vilas and "Adlai and his ax" got all the credit and Cleveland all the blame.

Sometimes Cleveland vetoed pork-barrel bills, but not always the most flagrant of them. The River-and-Harbor bill adopted on August 5, 1886, was one he could have slain. Calling for an appropriation of $15,000,000, it initiated over a hundred new projects mainly useful for electioneering purposes in the various districts, while allowing money for the completion of only five out of sixty-three improvements already begun, for which the government engineers were urging support. This simply meant that the next Congress would be asked to set aside more money to continue work on the deferred old jobs, thus creating a cycle of increased spending. In opposition to this bill, Representative Robert M. La-Follette of Wisconsin said: "I believe that the tendency of such legislation is to debauch the country and dull the moral instincts of the American Congress."[22] Yet, in the following year, the President pocketed a measure equally obnoxious but for only approximately $10,000,000. Albert Bushnell Hart (a distinguished Harvard historian) estimated that the bill was made up mainly of expenditures that would benefit only the owners of waterfronts, contractors, and the workers employed.[23] Twelve vetoes between June 19, 1886, and August 27, 1888, only two of them overridden by Congress, were of bills of the kind that Joseph C. Cannon of Illinois loved to introduce in the House so as to keep himself in favor in his Danville district. These were for public buildings such as post offices, federal courthouses, and old-soldiers' homes. Even though only some of the most obviously unneeded of these proposed structures met this fate, these vetoes were not designed to curry favor with the hungry popularity seekers in Congress or with the party leaders.[24]

Yet these vetoes were but mosquito bites to the members of Congress as compared with the hornets' nest torn down in front of Cleveland when he became active in vetoing pension bills. Old-soldiers' votes were as highly coveted in the 1880s as the farmers' votes threescore and ten years later, and were almost as numerous in proportion to the total. Veterans of the polls who found it embarrassingly difficult to reveal a war record, but who were diligent at rounding up floaters on election day, surely should have some reward. Cleveland read and studied each bill before giving or withholding his signature, and soon found private-pension bills of which he became suspicious. The public became fully aware of the President's cautiousness when on May 8, 1886, he vetoed the Andrew J. Hill pension bill, saying incidentally that on one day Congress had sent him 240 such measures, of which 198 were claims already rejected by the Pension Office.[25]

Cleveland, in his first annual message to Congress in December, 1885, made clear that he favored adequate pensions to deserving veterans, but extensions of the system "should not be vitiated by the introduction of any fraudulent practices. Therefore, it is fully as important that the rolls should be cleansed of all those who by fraud have secured a place thereon, as that meritorious claims should be speedily examined and adjusted."[26] His study had shown that for years the Pension Office had been used to keep the veterans' votes solidly Republican. Commissioner William W. Dudley, who had performed this service in the Blaine campaign, resigned before inauguration day, thus relieving Cleveland of any possible feeling of compunction against kicking him out bodily. Dudley had made a tour of the doubtful states, granting pensions only on condition that the recipients should vote Republican. His successor was General John C. Black, who immediately overhauled the office, not only sweeping out the existing political favoritism but also giving close examination to all pension claims.[27]

Cleveland was interested in economy as well as in orderly procedure. The Arrears Act of 1879 had nearly doubled the number of pensioners, who in 1885 numbered over 345,000 and received $65,000,000. This sum was one of the larger costs of government, and Cleveland wanted further extensions at least to be made to deserving persons. As it was, private bills had been passed on claims that no Commissioner of Pensions could sanction, allowing considerably larger sums than those provided by the general acts of Congress. Some of these grants went to soldiers who had been dishonorably discharged and to slackers who had evaded conscription by shooting off a finger or a big toe.[28] Cleveland restrained this trend for a time, but he could not forestall the pressures of later years.

After General Black tightened controls in the Pension Office, private bills multiplied until on one day five hundred of them passed the Senate. Cleveland vetoed only the most scandalous of the claims, which amounted to one-seventh of all passed in four years. One man had broken an ankle while on his way to enlist, thus presumably entitling himself to a monthly indemnity for the rest of his life. Another had fractured his skull in a fall from a ladder in 1881. A man with eye trouble laid it to an attack of diarrhea during the war. Another had broken his leg while at home picking dandelions. Many were deserters. Cleveland could not personally examine the merits of all bills, so he let through the bulk of them where he was not assured of fraud. The fact that he had hired a substitute now came up against him in full force. He was a rebel at heart and had an ingrained hostility toward the brave boys in blue. Yet, Congress passed only one such bill over his veto. Perhaps the members realized that Cleveland was actually protecting the honest claimant against the corrupt one.[29]

One measure, attached to an appropriation bill, the President had to let pass on June 7, 1888, rather than kill the entire law. This broadened the Arrears Act of 1879 so that widows' claims should become retroactive no matter when filed.[30] Also, on January 29, 1887, he had approved a pension of eight dollars a month to honorably discharged veterans of the Mexican War who had incurred disabilities in consequence of service, provided they had not later joined the rebel forces (and to their unremarried widows) if the claim did not make a total pension paid to the individual more than eight dollars.[31] This was merely in line with the basic principles of Civil War–pension legislation and contained nothing invidious.

Simultaneously, there came a determined effort to reduce the troublesome surplus in the treasury (discussed in Chapter VI). This was the Dependent Parents' and Soldiers' Pension bill brought to a vote in the House on January 17, 1887. It clarified the status of dependent parents of men who died in the war and made their claims nonretroactive. But the main purpose was to allow any honorably discharged persons who had served the United States in any war for as much as three years and who were physically incapacitated not as a "result of their own vicious habits or gross carelessness," twelve dollars a month from the time of filing claim in the Pension Office. This bill passed the House at once and the Senate ten days later; Cleveland vetoed it on February 11; and the House failed to override the veto on February 24. The long veto message dwelt mainly on the revolutionary nature of the bill and the unnecessary expense involved. Speaking of the vagueness in reference to disability, one sentence of the message is both illuminating and amusing: "For such disabilities there are now paid one hundred and thirty-one different rates of pension, ranging from $1 to $100 per month."[32]

The Republican Senator Henry W. Blair of New Hampshire, who actively supported the bill, estimated that it would cost anywhere from $35,000,000 to $50,000,000 a year, but the numerous critics claimed that it would cost more than any person could calculate. Putting the veteran who became incapacitated after the war on a par with the battle casualty would encourage men to feign disablement so as to get the pension. The veto brought the full wrath of the Grand Army of the Republic down upon Cleveland's head, although many of the large newspapers favored the action taken. Petitions, editorials, and outcries of all kinds had no effect, and Congress made little effort to revive the bill as long as Cleveland remained in office.[33]

After the political campaign of 1888, in which the opposing forces fought out this issue, the victorious Republicans in the Fifty-first Congress (known as the "Billion-Dollar Congress") promptly repassed the Dependent Pension bill, and President Harrison signed it on June 27, 1890. The treasury surplus in 1890 was still above $85,000,000, but in 1894 there was a deficit of $61,000,000; the pension act, supplemented by a general business depression, had eliminated the surplus.

The numbers on the rolls rose immediately from 350,000 to around 550,000 and to 1,000,000 ten years later, while the cost grew from $65,000,000 to $150,000,000 a year, or nearly a third of the annual budget of even a billion-dollar Congress. The new Commissioner of Pensions, James Tanner (known as the "Corporal" and as "God help the surplus" Tanner), also did his bit in the game of surplus financiering. He was so determined to grant pensions, even illegally, that his own party members were soon glad to accept his resignation.[34] Thus, the lull in treasury raiding under Cleveland was but a brief one.

Cleveland manufactured additional Republican campaign thunder by his "rebel-flag order" of May 26, 1887. It all came about in a humdrum routine way. In April, after the adjournment of Congress, Adjutant General Richard C. Drum suggested to Secretary of War William C. Endicott of Massachusetts that the battle standards of the various states, stored in Washington, be returned to the states from which the regiments had been recruited. These included many Confederate flags captured in battle. From time to time the department had made a practice of returning Union flags at the request of states or individuals. Cleveland approved the order, but upon its publication the indignation was so great that he withdrew it three weeks later, saying that he had exceeded his power and that Congress alone had the authority to dispose of the flags.[35] This, however, did not end the commotion. General Sherman assailed Drum as a noncombatant in the war who, therefore, had no sympathy with the men in uniform, an accusation that at least one of the President's biographers tore to pieces. Drum was a Republican, a member of the G.A.R., and had decorations for his service in the Mexican War.[36] General Lucius Fairchild, national commander of the G.A.R., worked up more froth than most, even of his organization: he asked the Almighty to palsy the hand, head, and tongue involved in the order, thus earning for himself the title of "Fairchild of the three palsies."[37]

Mayor David R. Francis of St. Louis had invited President Cleveland to attend the national encampment of the G.A.R. in that city, whereupon many posts threatened to boycott the assemblage, while others talked of insulting or injuring the President. Because he did not want to see the office of the Presidency belittled, Cleveland refused the invitation. This had the effect of putting the Grand Army on the defensive. Governor Joseph Foraker of Ohio, referring to the rescinding of the order, said that Cleveland had sneaked out like a whipped dog. On the other hand, many Southerners looked upon the proposed flag return as a courtly gesture, and even in the North Cleveland found some support. *Harper's Weekly* and *The Nation* showed approval, the latter saying that if Fairchild wanted Cleveland killed he should do it himself, and not invoke the supernatural powers that had already allowed enough slaughter in the War of the Rebellion! As one biographer stated it, "President Cleveland's ceaseless activity for civil service reform, and for the purification of the pension rolls, had made for him and his administration a body of enemies who eagerly seized upon the incident of the flags as a rallying cry."[38] The ironic sequel of the whole affair was that, by a resolution of February 28, 1905, a Republican Congress returned the flags.[39]

This change of heart of nearly a score of years later could not be foreseen by the parties ready to engage in another presidential campaign. The pension question, along with Cleveland's supposed attitude toward the veterans, became one of the leading issues. There were still far more old soldiers off the pension rolls than on, and a Republican vote seemed to be the surest way to get a snout in the federal trough. This may have been the decisive factor in the campaign. A further rationalization of this vagary in voting could be found in the rebel-flag order and in the fact that Cleveland had once gone fishing on Decoration Day, sacred to the memory of the dead Union warriors. His veto message on the Dependent Pension bill rounded out the required reading of the old soldier. Cleveland's poorly veiled animosity toward the newspapers served to line many of them up against him, and they did their part to add to the suspicions of the disgruntled veterans.[40]

A newly formed Union Labor party, merging the remnants of the Greenbackers with elements from the Knights of Labor, the Grange, the Agricultural Wheel, the Farmers' Alliances, and other agricultural and labor groups, was beforehand in the campaign. Meeting at Cincinnati on May 15, 1888, it named Alson J. Streeter of Illinois for the Presidency and submitted a platform demanding public ownership of the means of transportation and communication, revision of the monetary system, sweeping labor reforms, pensions for all old soldiers, a graduated income tax, the prohibition of importation of laborers under contract, Chinese exclusion, woman suffrage, and the direct election of senators. "The paramount issues," said the Laborites, "are the abolition of usury, monopoly, and trusts, and we denounce the Democratic and Republican parties for creating and perpetuating these monstrous evils." A splinter group, the United Labor party, met in Cincinnati on May 15 and, with Robert H. Cowdrey as their standard bearer, worked for Henry George's single-tax plan. The American party, pitifully weak, made its last Know-Nothing stand; it nominated James Langdon Curtis of New York and James R. Greer of Tennessee; Greer refused to run, and Curtis might as well have joined him.[41]

The Socialist (still officially "Socialistic") Labor party, while favoring the abolition of the Presidency, centered its campaign on a few local offices.[42] The Prohibitionists gathered in Indianapolis on May 30 and, climbing up toward their all-time peak of strength, which would come in 1892, broadened their platform to include a tariff plank that at one point sounded like free trade and at another protectionist! Among the molecular groups were the Industrial Reform party (stillborn), the Equal Rights party again backing Belva Lockwood, and the Independent Labor party, which decided to support the Republicans. The Greenbackers declared their principles for the last time and decently interred their party, some years too late.[43]

The Democrats assembled in St. Louis on June 5. Regardless of the disgruntlement of many of them, it was clear that they could make no favorable stand in the campaign unless they renominated Cleveland. They would also have to make something better than a pretense of endorsing his policies. The only thing wide open was the vacant Vice-Presidency which, to keep peace in the family, should (and in a way did) go to a contrasting candidate, more of the Hendricks stripe. The resolutions committee was divided as to the amount of support to give the Mills tariff bill, but finally came out strongly in its favor. Cleveland's tariff message of the preceding December 6 had been far from an advocacy of free trade, and the plank in the Democratic platform of 1888 was equally wide of the mark. The words "a fair and careful revision of our tax laws, with due allowance for the difference between the wages of American and foreign labor, must promote and encourage every branch of such industries and enterprises by giving them assurance of an extended market and steady and continuous operations" should have caused no tremor of fear among manufacturers. The following sentence: "In the interests of American labor, which should in no event be neglected, the revision of our tax laws contemplated by the Democratic party should promote the advantage of such labor by cheapening the cost of necessaries of life in the home of every workingman, and at the same time securing to him steady and remunerative employment," with no reflection on its rhetorical purity, was to offset the usual wages theory of the Republicans.

Praising themselves for carrying out civil-service-reform promises and for effective exclusion of Chinese laborers (under an act passed in Arthur's administration), the delegates then endorsed the granting of statehood to the territories of Washington, Dakota, Montana, and New Mexico. The matter of self-praise and condemnation of opponents having been settled to their satisfaction, they nominated Cleveland by acclamation and chose as his running mate Allen C. Thurman, of Ohio.[44]

The Republicans, congregating in Chicago on June 19, adopted a platform eloquent in condemnation of their opponents: "We denounce the hostile spirit shown by President Cleveland in his numerous vetoes of measures for pension relief, and the action of the Democratic House of Representatives in refusing even a consideration of general legislation." No longer ambiguous on the tariff, as in 1884, the delegates were "uncompromisingly in favor of the American system of protection. . . ." They would "favor the entire repeal of internal taxes rather than the surrender of any part of our protective system. . . ." On the territorial question the Republicans followed the lead of the Democrats, but with a reservation against the suspectedly Democratic New Mexico, which did not become one of the "omnibus states" of 1889–90. A telling blow at their opponents was the declaration that the Democrats owed their current enjoyment of power "to the suppression of the ballot by a criminal nullification of the Constitution and the laws of the United States." A reading of the Mugwumps out of the party; a bid for the vote of the Irish, by endorsing autonomy for their ancestral homeland; an antitrust plank; a pledge to recover unearned railroad land grants; a denunciation of Cleveland for his "efforts to demonetize silver"; one-cent postage; civil service reform; and an appeal for bigger pensions helped round out the platform.[45]

The choosing of candidates was not a problem as easily settled as the adoption of a platform. A number of prominent Republicans were reluctant to give up the hope that they could persuade Blaine to bear the main burden a second time, but as early as January he had written to the chairman of the national committee that, for personal reasons, his name was not to be presented to the convention. Not contented with this declaration, staunch supporters continued the pressure until on May 17 Blaine wrote from Paris to Whitelaw Reid, editor of the *New York Tribune*, that "if I should now, by speech or by silence, by commission or omission, permit my name, in any event, to come before the convention, I should incur the reproach of being uncandid with those who have been candid with me. . . ." Consequently, if the nomination came his way he "could not accept it at all."[46] A large number of favorite sons and other prominent Republicans then promptly entered the race. Among these were Benjamin Harrison of Indiana, Senator William B. Allison of Iowa, Russell A. Alger of Michigan, and Governor Jeremiah M. Rusk of Wisconsin. The Illinois delegation put up Walter Q. Gresham of Indiana; Chauncey M. Depew was the choice of his New York group, though they were unpledged; and there was some support for Senator Joseph R. Hawley of Connecticut, William Walter Phelps of New Jersey, and Senator John J. Ingalls of Kansas.

The labor of selecting a candidate must have been a fatiguing one, for eight ballots and an extra one for the running mate consumed three days. John Sherman was in the lead until the final ballot, but never with as much as a third of the votes; Gresham, half as strong, made early gains and then dwindled; while Alger showed growing promise until after the fifth ballot. Ingalls, Depew, Rusk, and Phelps dropped early by the wayside, while another half a dozen hardly left the starting line. Even the oratory of Robert Ingersoll could not help Gresham. During the recess over Sunday there was time for the customary political horse trading. By the last ballot on Saturday (the fifth) it appeared that Sherman had reached the limit of his strength and that Harrison, who had been gaining considerably, had no better chance. The results of the bargaining were revealed when after the seventh ballot Allison's votes switched to Harrison, other states began jumping on the band wagon, and Harrison won the nomination. Levi P. Morton of New York, sixty-four years old and destined to live another thirty-two, drew second place.[47]

In the ensuing campaign, Cleveland set the pace in his letter of acceptance on September 10, by dwelling long and earnestly on the tariff and the treasury surplus. The Republicans accepted the challenge, and the opposing forces resorted to everything short of brass knuckles in fighting out the issues. Blaine returned from Europe in August and, besides campaigning in Maine for its September elections, toured the West and spoke to large crowds. Both parties spent most of their effort in the doubtful states of Connecticut, New York, New Jersey, and Indiana. Neither presidential candidate took an active part in the canvass, but Harrison made a few short talks to delegates visiting him in his home, thus setting the example for McKinley eight years later.[48]

The Republicans collected a huge campaign fund. John Wanamaker, Philadelphia merchant and famed Sunday-school superintendent, and Senator Matthew S. Quay of

Pennsylvania, a political boss of devious tricks, used ingenious methods to "fry all the fat out of" interests expecting a continuation of high tariffs. Then Quay, assisted by the malodorous William W. Dudley and James Tanner, used the boodle to buy voters away from the Democrats in Indiana. Dudley was treasurer of the Republican National Committee, which directed party workers in that state to "divide the floaters into blocks of five and put a trusted man with the necessary funds in charge of these five, and make him responsible that none get away, and that all vote our ticket." In one precinct over a hundred of the drifters were loaded on wagons and presented at the polls at sunrise, before the Democrats could get at them first, and in time to haul them on to another precinct. In eight years the cost of such votes had risen from two dollars to about fifteen dollars.[49] The slogan "vote early and often" was paying its way in 1888. A highly laudatory biographer of Wanamaker admitted that his hero contributed $10,000 to the campaign and induced at least ten other businessmen to lay down as much. He and his group alone raised upward of $400,000, and Wanamaker became Postmaster General as a reward.[50]

"Corporal" Tanner concentrated his attention on the old-soldier vote in Indiana. He "went about 'representing Cleveland as an inhuman monster and Benjamin Harrison as an angel of mercy carrying a purse hanging mouth downward.' Tanner said afterward that he had 'plastered Indiana with promises' that more money would be paid out for pensions if Harrison won the election."[51] To finance the counterattack on this kind of campaigning, the Democrats had no wealthy patrons, so they fell back on the old but hardly respectable method of assessing the officeholders. Political clubs played an important role for both parties, the Republicans claiming 6500 of them, organized into a nationwide league and having a million members. The Democrats had a somewhat smaller number.[52]

A piece of blatant trickery, perpetrated too late for the Democrats to expose fully before election day, probably helped the Republicans. One George Osgoodby of Pomona, California, was the supposed author of a letter to Lionel

Sackville-West, the British Minister to the United States. He signed his name as Charles F. Murchison, claimed to be a naturalized American of English birth, and asked Sackville-West which way he ought to vote in the coming election. The minister replied that he believed the administration was trying to be conciliatory toward England, thus seeming to imply that a vote for Cleveland would be in the interest of Great Britain. This correspondence appeared in the newspapers on October 24, and the Republicans made immediate use of the letters in the last days of the campaign. "Twisting the lion's tail" had been a favored American political sport for years, and great capital could be made of the assumption that Cleveland was truckling to Robert Gascoyne-Cecil, Marquis of Salisbury. Cleveland would have done better to ignore the incident, but instead, on October 30, he dismissed the minister and sent him home, which so annoyed the British that they would not appoint his successor until after the inauguration of Harrison.[53]

The influence of this incident is uncertain, but another matter is more sure. If Cleveland had carried New York, he would have won the election, but he lost his own state by 13,002 votes. For this fact he could blame the Democratic machine, including Tammany. David B. Hill was thirsting for re-election as governor, and at political rallies his followers carried banners with the inscription "Harrison and Hill." Democratic speakers urged the voters to register their approval of Hill at the polls, and remained innocent of having the name of Cleveland on their tongues. Hill gained his point and won. As many voters as supported him could also have put Cleveland ahead.[54]

Cleveland won all sixteen of the former slave states, and the doubtful Connecticut and New Jersey as well. Harrison carried all the other states, including Indiana where the floaters and veterans helped him win a majority of 2340. Out of a total vote for the two parties of about 11,000,000, Cleveland had a plurality of slightly over 100,000. But his huge majorities in most of the South could not offset small pluralities for Harrison in the North. The electoral vote was 233 to 168 in favor of the Republicans. The House in the Fifty-first

Congress was to have 173 Republicans and 154 Democrats, the Senate 47 and 37 in the same order.[55]

Harrison's beginning cabinet was made up almost entirely of party workers. Blaine became Secretary of State; Wanamaker, Postmaster General; Governor Rusk of Wisconsin, Secretary of Agriculture; and William H. H. Miller of Indiana, Attorney General.[56] There was little more in Cleveland's administration worthy of note that belongs in this place. On inauguration day he rode with Harrison to the ceremonies. Four years later Harrison rode with him. This much, at least, is unique in the history of the Presidency.

Chapter X

FINANCIAL AND AGRARIAN PROBLEMS

PROBLEMS of public finance and agrarian unrest come in the indistinct borderland between political and economic developments. Like the tariff, the monetary question persisted throughout the Centennial years, just as it had long before and would long after. In the dozen years between the adoption of the Bland-Allison Act of 1878 and the Sherman Silver Purchase Act of 1890, there were five Presidents, each a gold-standard man in an era of generally declining farm purchasing power and of a resultant swelling agrarian demand for a reflation of the currency.[1] The per capita circulation of money, which stood at slightly over thirty dollars in 1865, fell to about half that by 1876, then increased gradually to twenty-two by 1890.[2] Even this increase was a financial mirage, for the expansion of business was exceeding the monetary supply, and the development of instruments of credit was not taking up the slack in purchasing power. The index of general prices fell nearly 50 per cent between 1866 and 1879; then, with some wavering, below the halfway mark by 1890.[3]

Manufacturing and transportation had their ups and downs during these years, but technical advances cheapened their costs of operation and generally kept them afloat, regardless of price trends. For the farmer the situation was different. He had about the same financial outlay each year, whether or not crops matured and regardless of what they brought on the market. He was a member of no monopoly to restrict output. Few, if any, tariff rates supplemented his income, though they increased the cost of many of his necessary purchases. The factory or mine could keep expenses at a minimum by closing down when the market was slack; the railroad could run fewer and shorter trains when traffic demand fell off; but if chinch bugs, Hessian flies, blights, drouth, frost, excessive heat, or flood laid waste the farmer's crops, he had to redouble his own efforts and retain his hired hand in hope of salvaging enough to pay expenses. Crop insurance was not even a dream of the future. If inflation and deflation struck each part and each individual in the economy uniformly and simultaneously they would not cause much trouble except to statisticians. The farmer's difficulty was that, in the long downward curve, the prices he received between 1877 and 1890 were constantly well below all other commodities.[4]

It must not be forgotten that the quotations of prices of farm products on the exchanges were, especially in the West North Central states, almost always far above what the tillers of the soil received. The same was largely true of the South. Charges made by middlemen for handling the crops and by railroads for transporting them came out of the pockets of the producers. On top of this, the shortage of banking facilities and credit brought interest rates so high as to make agriculture hazardous. This situation, bad in the 1870s, worsened in the next decade. When the Nebraska farmer moaned that it took one bushel of corn to pay the freight on another, or when his neighbor in Dakota Territory made the same complaint about wheat,[5] he sometimes understated the case. When each heated his home with the cereals, he was simply making a wise adjustment to a topsy-turvy economy. In the 1880s, freight rates in the South, and west of Chicago, were often two, three, and four times as high as in the West. In 1879, when the ton-mile charge on the Lake Shore and Michigan Southern line was 64.00 cents, on the Burlington between Omaha and Denver it was 3.74 cents, and on the Galveston, Houston, and Henderson Railroad 4.07 cents.[6] In the following year, a small line in Arkansas and Louisiana had a rate of 44.00 cents.[7] This situation improved considerably during the following decade, but not to the point of equity before the end of the century. The Granger laws of the 1870s, scrupulously fair to the carriers and the shippers alike, undoubtedly contributed somewhat to this change, though other, possibly more important factors entered into the picture. For one thing, especially before the Interstate Commerce Act of 1887, there was the ever present fear of more drastic legislation.[8]

Again, the embattled farmers of the 1870s, in the various laws they had forced through the state legislatures, had by no means fought the middlemen to a standstill. Complaints about the discriminations and overcharges of elevator companies, dictation by the packers on the price of live animals, and the way in which the terminal exchanges rigged the markets continued through the 1880s and beyond. Kansas corngrowers may have been unreasonable in complaining at the offer of ten cents a bushel for their crops when the product was selling at from four to seven times as much in Chicago and a dollar in New York,[9] but their discontent can be understood.

Another sore spot was the perennial shortage of operational capital, except at exorbitant interest rates. The crop-lien credit system lay at the bottom of this trouble in the South. In the West, a succession of years of ample rainfall in the early 1880s led to an excess of optimism about the future. Railroads, drumming up business, did their part in fostering this delusion. The Burlington and the Union Pacific lines, between them, spent close to a million dollars advertising Nebraska. "Follow the prairie dogs and Mormons," a Burlington pamphlet effused, "and you will find good land." From 1879 to 1886, rainfall out to the Rocky Mountains was adequate, though in 1881 there was serious drouth in the wheat states along the upper Mississippi River. The railroad advertisements encouraged people to believe that the Timber Culture Act of 1873 and irrigation had worked a miracle. Heavy settlement and cultivation would revolutionize the weather of the Great Plains for good. There was a real need for farm expansion, for tilled acres were beginning to lag behind the growth of population in the cities. But hard-pressed laborers often could not buy all they would have liked of agricultural produce, and foreign markets, particularly for cereals and meats, were sluggish.[10] The much-vaunted free, or anyway cheap, land of the new country, while furnishing no safety valve for Eastern laborers, did lure farmers into unfamiliar surroundings where relatively few would be able to make good.[11]

While the mania lasted, they flocked into Minnesota and into the tier of states from Kansas to the Canadian border, and the banks in the larger cities from St. Paul to Denver eagerly lent them money at usury. Down to 1900 and later, Western interest rates were commonly 12 and 15 per cent, while, in the East, banks were glad to accept 3 or 4. Ubiquitous agents of loan companies in the East encouraged the old and the new among Western farmers to take out mortgages to make a start, or for purposes of expansion, and the propaganda-infatuated farmer snapped at the bait, assured that his earnings would soon make of the extra cost a mere bagatelle. By 1890, in the five states just mentioned, there were more mortgages than there were families.[12]

In some areas speculation ran wild. Improvements alone could explain the doubling of land values between 1881 and 1887 in some Nebraska counties that were not affected by the craze. But a farm near Abilene, Kansas, worth $6.25 an acre in 1867 and selling twenty years later at $270.00 an acre, needs another explanation. The same land a few years afterward would have done well to go at $60.00. Boom towns were the order of the day, from Omaha and Lincoln to Kansas City, Atchison, and Topeka. But the prize of them all was Wichita, where in January–May, 1887, land sharks sold forty-two square miles of farm land for town lots at a total cost of $35,000,000. Promoters in such towns talked the citizens into voting bonds for buildings they would never need and to subsidize the construction of unnecessary and heavily overcapitalized railroads. Somebody got rich, but it was not the townsmen or farmers.[13] A traveler through Wichita, as late as 1911, could see rotting houses, never inhabited, and others abandoned before completion, miles from the city on "town lots" sold in 1887.[14]

By 1886, the prairie and plains farmer began to realize that a cycle of wet years did not signify a permanent change in the climate. A disastrous winter of blizzards and ice storms in 1886–87 brought the serpent of insecurity into the cattlemen's Eden on the high plains. The lower prairies began

drying out. In the next ten years there were only two crops
worth harvesting. Chinch bugs, accompanying the drouth,
and hot winds, shriveling the wheat when it was yet immature, completed the work dryness had begun. Before the end
of 1887, hordes of farmers, mainly west of the ninety-seventh
parallel, realizing that their land was worth far less than the
mortgages, let the loan companies foreclose. In the plains
from Kansas northward, large areas became almost depopulated before 1892. Eastward-moving wagons loaded with migrants bore such laconic signs as "In God we trusted, in Kansas
we busted." Numerous ghost towns took the place of once-
promising metropolises, one in Kansas displaying a $30,000
theater and a $20,000 schoolhouse.[15]

In the bluestem pasture lands of the Flint Hills in the
eastern part of the same state, the New England Loan and
Trust Company appears in the county books, ten or twelve
times to the page for long periods in the 1880s, for foreclosures of mortgages.[16] After surviving land-grabbers, grass-
hoppers, hailstorms, prairie fires, rattlesnakes, and ants, the
freeholders succumbed to the loan company or to the county
sheriff after one manifestation too many of unfriendly natural
forces. Many of them stayed on, trying as tenants on their
former possessions to struggle through to a new ownership.
Though owners of small farms escaped with relatively fewer
foreclosures than their speculative neighbors, nemesis was
catching up with all, including the usurer.[17] In a strip of
counties running northward through the middle of Kansas,
Nebraska, and Dakota Territory, the farmers were rather
firmly entrenched, yet threatened with mortgage foreclosures.
Most of them were ready to fight nature, man, and the devil
to keep their farms. Drouth had not yet completely whipped
them. They became the hard core of the Western Populist
movement; they were the ones who listened reverently to
Mary Elizabeth Lease's admonition to "raise less corn and
more hell." In the easternmost parts of the same states, the
drouth was less pestilential than in the counties to the west.
Lawrence, Kansas, often has luxuriant crops, when around
Manhattan, eighty miles to the west, the corn at knee height
dies and does not make even good hog fodder. Heavy settle-

ment also made the land in the eastern counties less speculative. So political conservatism persisted there, when the western counties were so depopulated that there was little activity of any kind, and when the central counties were in revolt.[18]

Short and intermediate loans, needed to grow and move the crops, had long been hard to get, and the interest rates on them were far above even the high charges on long-term mortgages. As early as 1868, E. L. Godkin had condescendingly reminded the Westerners that their banks held a fair ratio of the nation's greenbacks in excess of their reserves, but the bankers had to be cautious about making loans at any rate of interest because most of the demand for greenbacks was to settle accounts in the East. These United States notes were the only legal tender in circulation, and every time a customer drew out a dollar of them, this lowering of the reserve held four other dollars out of circulation, thus producing the high interest rates. The businessman, as well as the farmer, had to pay. What Godkin said almost explicitly was that the agriculturists must mend their ways and stop owing so much to firms in other sections, totally disregarding the fact that these debts were made inescapable because of the Eastern financial suzerainty.[19]

This was not a very palatable doctrine to men who knew that the conditions the editor had so obligingly expounded applied mainly to the past. Deflation was actively under way. The money that the government had issued during the war was for the North alone. The collapse of the Confederacy had left its currency completely valueless, instead of just nearly so. A dozen years after the war, counting the restored Southerners and the natural increase in population, there were only half as many United States notes per capita as there had been in 1864, and these greenbacks remained the only bank reserves. By the time that the Treasury resumed gold payments in 1879, farmers who had not yet settled debts for expansion during the war and who were denied renewals of their mortgages were not loath to let the creditors foreclose and bear their share of the loss. Such men were demanding inflation at least to the point of avoiding a renewal of their difficulties, and Godkin, with vitriol on his pen, said they were merely seeking personal gain, and that the government should ignore their outcry.[20]

Other deflationary factors had also been at work. The act of Congress approved on February 12, 1873, outlawing any further coinage of the standard silver dollar,[21] came at a time when few persons were aware of what was happening to the silver markets of the world. For nearly forty years, monetary legislation had undervalued silver, the consequence being that the silver dollar was worth more than the gold one, and so went out of circulation. In 1873, the two metals reached parity, and the price of silver continued to fall so rapidly that in 1876 the bullion in the dollar was worth only 89.22 cents on the market.[22]

The reason for this sharp decline was mainly that contemporaneously with American demonetization, several European countries were doing the same thing, while the Western mines were beginning to produce silver in unprecedented quantities. Only once before 1870 had the domestic production been as much as 10,000,000 ounces; then it skyrocketed from 12,000,000 ounces in 1870 to nearly 28,000,000 in 1873 and, with some fluctuations, to 63,500,000 ounces in 1892. This point was not reached again for another twenty years. In 1893 and following, at the height of the scare over a silver-flooded nation, production was actually on the downgrade.[23]

The silver-mining interests were the first to raise the hue and cry and to call demonetization "the crime of '73" when the price fell below parity, and they soon had the hagridden debtors joining in the chorus. Low prices at the mine and on the farm would not have happened had it not been for this "crime." To "right-thinking" people the use of such an epithet was nauseous, and for eighty years they frowned at it. But thoughts do change. In 1954, a British economist, Roy Harrod, with his nation's financial interest in mind, said that "highbrows incline to bimetallism, while the naive and simple-minded favour monometallism," and concluded that the Act of 1873 really was "objectively a crime."[24] The trade dollar, heavier than the standard dollar so as to induce silver-standard Oriental countries to accept them in settlement of trade balances, was authorized by the Act of 1873, but this provision was soon repealed and the trade dollars left the country.[25]

Further deflation had taken place under the Resumption Act of 1875, which provided not only for the payment of gold for greenbacks on demand, beginning on January 1, 1879, but also that the existing volume of $382,000,000 in United States notes be reduced to an even $300,000,000.[26] In an effort to make this palatable to Greenbackers, five dollars in national-bank notes were to replace each four dollars in greenbacks canceled. But this meant that ultimately there would be a reduction instead of an increase in currency, and the reason was simple to debtors who studied the subject. National-bank notes were most plentiful in boom times when a little deflation would have a salutary effect, and were scarce during business depressions when a little inflation might prove helpful. This was because the bank notes were secured by government bonds which national banks could buy cheaply from speculators in a rising market, and thus expand their note issues, whereas in hard times people with any money to invest preferred safe government bonds to blue-sky stocks, thus encouraging national banks to sell the bonds back at a nice profit, and reduce their note issues accordingly. But this happened just when more money was needed to inject life into business.[27] From 1875 to about 1900 this "inverse elasticity" followed almost a mathematical formula. Consequently, the issuing of $102,500,000 in national-bank notes for $82,000,000 in greenbacks was not attractive to the soft-money men. Thus, it was not only politic, but perhaps unintentionally wise, of Congress to halt the retirement of greenbacks by an Act of May 31, 1878, leaving ever afterward $346,681,016 in greenbacks, less such bills so completely destroyed as to be irreplaceable.[28]

When the date for resumption of specie payments arrived, Secretary of the Treasury John Sherman had $133,000,000 in gold on hand, most of it procured by the sale of bonds, but over a third from surplus revenue, tariff duties being payable in gold, thus adding to the protection of American manufacturers. As the year 1879 approached, confidence in the Treasury's ability to redeem them built up the value of greenbacks to a par with gold, the consequence being that, in January, people favored the paper money and exchanged more gold for greenbacks than the reverse.[29] A five-dollar gold piece was too much the size of a nickel and to horny-handed toilers the weight made little difference. Paper notes were not so apt to disappear through a hole in the pocket, nor mistakenly be dropped into the collection plate on Sunday.

No special fund as yet existed for redemption, so Congress took partial care of this shortcoming in the Act of July 12, 1882, which fixed the gold reserve at a minimum of $100,-000,000, though it reached nearly twice that figure by mid-1890. Not until the Panic of 1893 was this fund raided, during which interval people were glad to cling to their gilded greenbacks.[30] This situation lent cogent argument to the Greenbackers' cause, whose adherents were especially bitter in their opposition to the national banks. They wanted government money and not private notes; they opposed corporate profit from both notes and bonds; and they feared the political influence of the bankers. Even in the Treasury Department there was a faction showing a preference for greenbacks. Western and Southern debtors, hostile to a money power centered in the East, led the opposition to federal policies. The contention, after 1878, was that the bankers were constantly plotting against the general welfare.[31] The substance of the greenback argument was a plea for a managed currency, automatically adjustable to the price level of the average of all products.

The pure theorists of the 1870s and 1880s would make United States notes the sole money of the country, except perhaps for small change, these notes being convertible into federal bonds paying 3.65 per cent interest. This cent a day on each $100 they called the "natural" rate. Then, each tendency toward a fall in prices would cause the hard-pressed to convert bonds into cash, thus providing the necessary stimulus to a revival. Conversely, in boom periods, more than enough small investors would repurchase government securities to offset stock gamblers selling bonds for speculation in the markets, thus again tending to restore the horizontal price line. The validity of the second guess is less apparent than the first.[32] Something more was needed, and the hostility of Greenbackers toward the stock and produce exchanges suggests the answer. So much for the theorists. The Greenback *party* was always ready for opportunistic compromise, and the doctrine should not be confused with the stand of its political advocates, whose campaign activities appear in earlier chapters. Only Weaver, of the party's three presidential candidates, could inspire public confidence both as to honesty and capability.

The Greenback party barely made a good start when the free-silver movement started pushing it into the background. Many voters had the feeling that paper could never really be money; there was something dishonest about the idea. Gold was another matter entirely; its acceptance had the sanctification of the ages. But there was not enough of it. So why not go back to the bimetallic standard of their fathers and restore the free and unlimited coinage of silver at approximately the ratio of 16 to 1? Single-standard advocates replied that the ratio would work just as long as the market values of the two metals remained stationary at exactly 16 to 1, but they never had and they never would. In a day when the actual ratio was 20 to 1 and getting larger every year, the world's silver would inundate the American mints at a huge profit to the possessors of the bullion and would bring disastrous inflation.

The gold men invoked Gresham's immutable law to prove that the cheaper money would drive the dearer out of circulation and leave the United States on a purely silver basis. The silver men retorted with the equally immutable quantity theory of money. Their metal was declining in price no more rapidly than other commodities, thus proving that gold was rising instead of silver falling, and that a silver standard would restore stability to markets in general, their price curve becoming the ideal horizontal line almost exactly parallel with that of silver. In the middle and late nineties, when the silver in a dollar got down to forty-nine cents in value, it was still following the general price curve. If nothing else came out of

DEMOCRATIC POLITICIANS

22. William R. Morrison

23. Samuel J. Randall

24. John G. Carlisle

25. David B. Hill

REPUBLICAN POLITICIANS

26. Roscoe Conkling

27. Shelby M. Cullom

28. Alonzo B. Cornell

29. John Sherman

MERCHANTS
OF NOTE

30. Frank W. Woolworth

31. Marshall Field

32. John Wanamaker

33. W. H. Vanderbilt

34. Thomas A. Edison

35. Leland Stanford

36. Cyrus W. Field

37. Chauncey M. Depew

38. William B. Allison

LABOR LEADERS

39. Terence V. Powderly

40. Uriah S. Stephens

41. Peter J. McGuire

42. Samuel Gompers

STRIKE LEADERS

43. Joseph R. Buchanan

44. Peter M. Arthur

45. Frank P. Sargent

46. Martin Irons

RAILROAD PRESIDENTS

47. Jay Gould

48. Charles E. Perkins

the controversy, at least it gave the gold-standard economists a chance, ultimately, to re-examine one of their sacred laws. If they could not repeal the quantity theory of money, anyway they could amend it.[33]

Though free-silver agitation was later to be associated with Populists and Democrats, it was no less prominent a Republican than "Pig Iron" Kelley, who on July 18, 1876, introduced a bill of that nature into the House of Representatives. A week later, Richard P. Bland of Missouri offered a measure of a similar character. Bland, a Democrat, chaired the House Committee on mines and mining, and when young had worked in the Nevada silver mines. He was soon to be known as "Silver Dick," for he kept up the fight until his death in 1899. Neither bill got through the House during that session or the next, while Kelley and Bland, disregarding party lines, worked hand in hand. The Forty-fifth Congress was barely under way in extra session when Bland presented Kelley's bill with slight alterations, which passed 163 to 34, under suspended rules and without debate on November 5, 1877. This was strictly a measure for free and unlimited coinage at the old 16 to 1 ratio of 1834 to 1873. The vote was decidedly bipartisan. Among the Republicans, not only Kelley but Jay A. (My Dear) Hubbell, the later Speaker of the House Keifer, and another Ohioan, named William McKinley, voted alongside of Bland, Simon Bolivar Buckner and Carlisle of Kentucky, and the two Coxes, Jacob D. of Ohio and "Sunset" of New York. Notable among the opposing Democrats was Hewitt of New York. The bill encountered rough sledding in the Senate where, under the leadership of Allison of Iowa, it underwent so many changes that it ought to bear his name alone instead of Bland-Allison. The House, for lack of anything better, accepted the amendments. Hayes returned his veto on February 28, 1878, after which, on the same day, Congress repassed it by far more than the necessary two-thirds majority.[34]

The free-silverites accepted the law as a little better than nothing, but did not for an instant give up their determination to replace it with an outright repeal of "the crime of '73." The key words of the Bland-Allison Act directed the Secretary of the Treasury "to purchase . . . silver bullion, at the market price thereof, not less than two million dollars worth per month, nor more than four million dollars worth per month, and cause the same to be coined monthly, as fast as so purchased . . ." into dollars. Profits from such coinage were to go into the Treasury. Holders of the dollars could exchange them for silver certificates of ten dollars and upward in value. There was also a provision for the calling of an international monetary conference to work out a common ratio between silver and gold.[35]

During the lifetime of the measure, each President allowed the acquisition of only the bare minimum authorized. Meanwhile, purchase totaled approximately $308,279,000, which produced over $378,000,000 in coin. Between 1879 and 1889, to take the first and last years of the full operation of the law, the bullion value of the dollar, with some variations up and down, fell from 96.8 cents to 72.3, based on the average for each year.[36] Bland and his followers saw a little saving grace in this fact when combined with the hidden sliding scale of purchases sanctioned by the law. The cheaper the price of silver became, the more ounces a fixed sum would buy. This would have some effect in stabilizing the silver market and, at the same time, would increase inflation. Thus, at prevailing prices, the minimum purchase would result in $2,257,336 of new coin each month in 1880, and half a million more, or $2,776,251 in the lower market of 1889. The greatest protest was against minimum buyings, for the maximum would either double these figures or else so bolster the silver market as to prevent or lessen the decline in price.

While monetary conditions thus remained fairly static during the 1880s, the farmers began to take steps toward helping themselves out of their difficulties. There are numerous claims as to the "first" farmers' alliances, mostly of no merit. The mere fact that some local club in early Granger days bore the name of "alliance" does not signify that it was the germ of the great movement. Certainly none was of much importance before 1880, when *Western Rural* editor Milton George, at Chicago, led in the movement that established the National Farmers' Alliance (popularly dubbed the Northwestern Alliance). Almost simultaneously, Texans chartered their Grand State Alliance, which, after various reorganizations and renamings, became the National Farmers' Alliance and Industrial Union (or more simply, the Southern Alliance).[37]

Unlike the earlier Grange, both of these movements started from the grass roots and drew membership and certain educational and cultural features from previous farmers' clubs and from the Grange. Many of the farmers disliked the secrecy of the Grange, felt it was not aggressive enough, and wanted more political action than it would sanction. From the beginning, the National Farmers' Alliance combined the educational and recreational features of the Grange with economic and political activities. The original group became Cook County Alliance No. 1, declaring in its motto that its object was "to secure the triumph of right." So vigorous was the initial organizational work that five months later the officers claimed between 200 and 300 local alliances.[38] A year after this the national secretary reported about 1000 locals with a combined membership of 24,500 families. Kansas, Nebraska, Iowa, Wisconsin, and even New York had state organizations before the second annual meeting, at which there were also delegations from Indiana, Illinois, Michigan, and Minnesota.[39] Within the next ten months, Michigan and Minnesota also had state alliances, the movement was growing strong in Missouri, and a Negro alliance had developed, operating in Arkansas. George was opposed to the color line in his organization, but in the South he had no other choice.[40]

Soon, the National Farmers' Alliance boasted of 2000 locals and 100,000 members. Just before 1880, the Northwestern farmers' yields were fair but prices were execrable. In 1880 and 1881, prices improved somewhat but there was severe drouth in Nebraska, Kansas, Iowa, and Minnesota, the states of earliest alliance growth. There was slackened interest in 1883 and 1884, as conditions again eased up, followed by low prices for wheat and a striking growth of membership in the wheat belt. By 1887, the Northwestern Alliance was talking about free silver and competition by the federal government with the railroads. At the convention in Minneapolis that year it also flirted with the Knights of Labor, but consummated no union. In 1890, Kansas claimed 130,000 members, while Nebraska, the Dakotas, and Minnesota trailed closely behind.[41] For a time, it looked like a genuine display of class consciousness. But there were setbacks as well. The Southern Alliance penetrated Kansas and the Dakotas, breaking up solidarity. In 1887, Milton George, who was not an easy man to get along with, lost his dominant influence. He was especially caustic about the claims of the Southern group, and resisted efforts at union.

There were other Northern farmers' organizations operating independently. The main one in the western portion was the Farmers' Mutual Benefit Association, apparently founded in Johnson County, Illinois, late in 1883, by five farmers who were disgusted with the local grain elevator's manager and decided to do their own grain marketing. Although it centered largely in southern Illinois, before the end of 1889 it included seventy-five county assemblies and 2000 subordinate lodges in nine states, extending from Kansas to North Carolina. In 1890, it had 4224 lodges with 200,000 members, and soon it was to boast half a million. The state of Illinois issued the F.M.B.A. a charter in 1887, authorizing it to assume interstate activity.[42] Because of its cooperative efforts, discontented elements in the towns of Egypt, and across the river in St. Louis, vied in their efforts to make something out of the initials by which the organization was generally known. A St. Louis newspaper came out with the not particularly brilliant Farmers' Mutual Blindfold Association, and an aspiring wit showed that he had halfway realized his ambition when he called it "Fill My Bottle Again."

Greatest of all, in size, strength, and influence, was the Southern Alliance. It grew out of certain vigilante clubs in Texas, whose members were interested in catching horse thieves but who indulged in cooperative buying and also coped with land monopolists and the cattle barons who were indifferent to the rights of the small operator. As the idea spread, the pioneers set up a Grand State Alliance in 1878, only to split up presently over the greenback issue. In 1880, it secured a charter as a secret society with benevolent features. Five years later it laid claim to 50,000 members in 1200 lodges. Its most significant work was opposition to the country merchants and the crop-lien system, aimed at getting higher prices for crops. By 1886 it was demanding, among other things, high taxes on railroads and speculative land-holdings, the abolition of alien land monopolies, an increase in paper money, and laws to end dealing in futures. It was at this time that Charles W. Macune joined, and in 1887 he was in control. His first achievement was to effect a merger with the Louisiana Farmers' Union. Under a federal charter, the combination assumed the name of Farmers' Alliance and Cooperative Union. In the following year came the absorption of the Agricultural Wheel, which had grown out of a tiny debating society of 1882, but in five years had spread from Arkansas into eight states, and proclaimed a membership of half a million. Its main contributions to the farmers' movement were proposals for the limitation of crop acreages; opposition to corporations, national banks, and protective tariffs; and a demand for a graduated income tax. By 1890, the new combination claimed three million members and was co-operating with Benjamin R. Tillman's Farmers' Clubs in South Carolina. The Alliance took credit for electing Tillman to the governorship in 1890. Considering the gentleman's later career, this was nothing to brag about.[43]

For a year, the consolidation of 1888 went under the name of Farmers' and Laborers' Union, and then it was changed to the National Farmers' Alliance and Industrial Union. In 1889, the Southern Alliance also came to an understanding with the Knights of Labor on certain national policies, but the mutual distrust of farmers and industrial laborers prevented them from doing anything more effective. At this time the Southern Alliance also made inroads in Kansas and the Dakotas, as mentioned earlier, to the intense dissatisfaction of Milton George. The race line in the South was stronger than any class solidarity, so the Negroes, who could not work in the same organization with white men, formed their own colored alliances which, at Houston in 1886, combined into the Colored Farmers' National Alliance and Cooperative Union. In 1890, this group claimed 1,250,000 members. Many figures such as this raise doubts. If they are accurate, whole families must have joined, for in some localities there were not as many farm operators as alliance members, and only rarely did they have strength enough to control politics.

At St. Louis in 1889, an effort to unite the various farmer and labor groups proved unsuccessful, even though there could be no striking economic or political achievements without it. The Knights of Labor expressed feelings of solidarity but would go no further. The American Federation of Labor remained entirely aloof. The Colored Alliance had not a ghost of a show. The Northwestern Alliance shrank from being absorbed by the huge Southern affair, and objected to the secrecy and to the separation of the races of Macune's group. The lard and butter producers of the North wanted a legal ban on substitutes, which proposal was singularly unappealing to the cottonseed-oil interests. Macune, on the other hand, could not get the North even politely interested in the subtreasury scheme, his own answer to the crop-lien credit system of the South.[44]

Macune's plan evolved from his study of experiences in his own state of Texas. There, the Grangers and farmers' clubs of the 1870s had tried cooperative marketing in an effort to break the grip of the country merchants, and all through the early 1880s the Texas Alliance built on the earlier efforts, but never could succeed. Then, in 1887, Macune took over the effort and set up the Farmers' Alliance Exchange of Texas, which also was on the downgrade by 1889, when he gave up control and became editor of the *National Economist*, the official organ of the Southern Alliance. The Exchange failed in 1890, but the evidence showed that Macune's management had been honest. The whole trouble was that the farmers never could raise enough capital to make sure of filling their contracts with cotton buyers, who therefore were unwilling to deal with the cooperative marketing agencies. Macune had tried to solve this difficulty. The Exchange treasury would not only sell stock in the enterprise to the farmers, but would also issue interest-bearing notes secured by such cotton as was in the Exchange warehouse. These notes, paid to farmers for cotton, could then be used as money in buying supplies from the Exchange until the time the next crop was ready to market. This would allow the farmers to hold their cotton for sale when the price was better than it usually was during the picking season.

Before the bankruptcy of the Exchange spoiled this plan, Macune was evolving the idea on a national scale to submit to the St. Louis convention of the Southern Alliance in December, 1889. This was the subtreasury plan. The federal government, Macune reasoned, could succeed with a system that was too much for a weak farmers' cooperative. Instead of depositing all its surplus funds in national banks, the government should set up subtreasuries, where the farmers could deposit nonperishable crops in exchange for federal treasury notes to the amount of 80 per cent of the crop's current value, the loans to mature within a year and cost 1 per cent in interest. Any county that produced as much as $500,000 worth of cereals, cotton, tobacco, wool, or sugar, or a combination of these commodities, should have one of the subtreasuries. The farmer, when he deposited his warehouse receipts and got the treasury notes in exchange, could use them for money, reserving the right to sell the deposited crop for whatever it would bring beyond the money he had already received from the government. The purchaser, when claiming the goods from the warehouse, would then pay to the subtreasury its original advance, plus the interest and the charges for storage and insurance. The treasury notes, being good for only one year, could be redeemed from current funds at or before the expiration of that time, and retired from circulation, thus preventing an endless chain of annual inflation.

There have been efforts to attribute this scheme to persons other than Macune, but no other such plan appeared until after the Texas experiment on which Macune built his idea, so it is his. Though the St. Louis conference did not endorse the idea, it did get into the Populist platform of 1892. The Northwestern Alliance, being interested in the sale of meat animals, butter, and other perishable goods as well as the cereals, felt that too much of the benefit of the plan would go to the South, and it was for this reason that its members would not accept the idea.[45]

Though the alliance failed to come to any agreement at St. Louis, they went ahead offering political platforms embodying most of the later Populist planks, including a flexible greenback currency geared to business needs, free silver, the abolition of national-bank notes, government ownership of the railroads and other means of transportation and communication, the recovery of land grants from the railroads, an end to alien land monopolies, a graduated income tax, and labor reforms.[46]

Although the two great Alliances continued to follow separate paths until swallowed up by the People's party, their force was enough to impel Congress to adopt a new silver purchase act. The admission of six new Western states to the Union in 1889 and 1890 converted the Senate into a free-silver body, and the House, seeking Western support of the McKinley tariff, was willing to make concessions. The Silver Purchase Act of 1890 so modified the law of 1878 that in effect, if not in fact, it constituted a repeal and replacement. As approved on July 14, it required the Secretary of the Treasury to purchase "silver bullion to the aggregate amount of four million five hundred thousand ounces" each month, paying for it in treasury notes in denominations ranging from $1 to $1000. The bullion was to go into the treasury vaults and only enough should be minted to redeem such treasury notes as their holders demanded silver for instead of gold.[47] But the mine owners who received the notes nearly always asked for gold, and neither Harrison nor Cleveland would refuse their demand, so, during the three years that purchases continued, very little silver was coined, and this did not add to the supply of money. It simply replaced notes that immediately afterward went to the crematory.[48] This was a strictly partisan measure—the votes for it were all Republican and those against were all Democratic. For some mysterious reason, as John Sherman had almost nothing to do with its passage, it took the name of Sherman Silver Purchase Act. Not until it went into the conference committee of the two houses did he play any part in its construction. Even here,

Sherman was merely one of the majority who reported it back to the Senate for passage. He said afterward: "I voted for it, but the day it became law I was ready to repeal it, if repeal could be had without substituting in its place absolute free coinage."[49] The old watchdog of the Treasury, therefore, is mainly remembered for two laws, this and the Anti-Trust Act of the same year, neither of which should have borne his name.

No free-silver men really liked the law, and the only reason why any voted for it was because, temporarily at least, it provided for the purchase of more silver than the Treasury was currently buying under the old act. Even this soon proved to be a mistake, from the silverites' point of view. Unlike the Bland-Allison measure, this law provided for the purchase of exactly the same amount of silver each month. The substitution of "ounces" for "dollars worth" was the joker. Only the cost went into circulation as an addition to the monetary supply, and this amount would depend entirely on the state of the silver market. At the average price in 1890, this would mean $4,738,500, which may be compared with the $4,944,-376 under the Bland-Allison law if the President had insisted on the maximum purchase rather than the minimum. What the silver interests should have insisted on was a measure of one sentence, repealing the words "not less than two million dollars worth per month, nor more than," in the Act of 1878. Because of the increased mass of silver purchased, the price went up 11.7 cents an ounce in 1890. But this was an artificial level, based on a lack of realization of the true nature of the new law. By 1892 it had fallen 17.7 cents, and in 1893, another 9.4 cents. At that time, even the minimum under the Bland-Allison Act would have bought almost as much as the Sherman Act, and the new money going into use would also have been up in a like ratio. The repeal of the purchase provision of the law in 1893 may have affected the decline of an additional 14.2 cents in 1894, putting the price at an even 64.0 cents an ounce. In that year, supposing that the price would have been the same if either act had been in effect, even the minimum purchase under the Bland-Allison principle would have added $4,073,319 to the circulating medium each month, as compared with $2,880,000 under the Sherman law.[50]

Free-silver agitation now entered into a new phase. The farmer was destined to get into far more desperate straits than he had experienced in all of his previous life, before he started on the path to recovery. When that time came, it could be laid to anything other than the achievement of policies for which he had fought so hard and so long. Yet, inflation played an important part in the improvement that started at the close of the century, an inflation based on a vastly increased world supply of monetary gold and on a manifold rise in the supply of national-bank notes, in addition to the growth of bank credit.

Chapter XI

THE FARMERS

WESTERN and Southern farmers, bedeviled by low prices and hard terms of credit, and the Eastern ones, trying desperately to adjust themselves to Western competition, continued to increase their output, though not more rapidly than world needs warranted. But world needs and world means to purchase are not even vaguely similar, which fact is enough to explain any surpluses at any time since the Civil War, except excesses of luxury items, and American farmers did not produce those. Except for cotton and tobacco, particularly after 1865, the foreign demand for agricultural goods has been infinitesimal compared with home consumption. Even so, the advantageous disposal of this minuscule surplus often meant the difference between comfort and want in the farm home. No tariff wall protected domestic prices of agricultural commodities, so they brought only what world-market conditions dictated. As Governor Frank O. Lowden of Illinois told the Midwest farmers in 1920, a 10 per cent surplus can beat prices down several times as much. It would be better to dump the excess into the ocean rather than to unload it in the foreign market, considering the consequent reprisals.[1]

Reasons for European reprisals were not always apparent. In 1879, Italy charged that American pork was unwholesome, and started banning imports of it. Portugal, Spain, France, Germany, and Austria-Hungary soon followed the example. The heaviest buyers had been France and Germany, so their policy hurt the most. Yet American packers had been shipping better meat abroad than they put on the home market.[2] Exports of "crude foodstuffs," that is, wheat, rye, and their flour, suffered even more after 1880, falling off $179,741,000 by 1888. Although there was a slight gain in cotton exports at the same time, the decline in tobacco as well as the cereals and animal products dropped the total exports of agricultural commodities in the second half of the decade well below the total average for the first half.[3] Another part of the picture shows the year 1880 to be the high point in the percentage of farm products shipped abroad to the total of all exports. This situation could well be anticipated as industry continued its ascendancy over agriculture in the nation's economy.[4]

There was further evidence that the farmer was taking the back seat in everything but politics. Three-fifths of the people lived on farms in 1860, but only slightly over a third in 1900. In those forty years the farm population grew from 19,000,-000 to 28,000,000, while the nonfarm element grew from 12,000,000 to 48,000,000, or eight times the rate of strictly rural growth. A fair share of this change came during the Centennial years, during which the farm percentage of the total population declined approximately a fifth. The languishing condition of the foreign market had slight effect on demand, since for every new person to take hold of the plow handle there were twenty new mouths to feed in the city, town, and village, and two more at home. Even on a minimum of subsistence, the six million immigrants of 1877 to 1890, inclusive, would far more than offset the loss of foreign demand—whether the alien settled in town or country—for it must be remembered that the farmer is one of his own consumers.[5]

Here was potentially a greatly increased outlet for agricultural products. But although the consumers of the nation had increased a third in number and those in town by five-eighths, their demands on farmers had not kept pace. The amount of cropland, which had remained almost stationary throughout the 1870s, expanded a third in the 1880s, pastureland increased by a fifth,[6] but the number of agricultural workers had grown only one-twelfth. From 1877 to 1890 the corn crop expanded only slightly (one-sixteenth), wheat a bit more (one-eighth), and potatoes the most (one-quarter). Because of this slow over-all increase, the per capita consumption of these most important staples could have done nothing but decline, for imports of foodstuffs grew hardly at all, and there was no compensating improvement in the output of other food crops. Potatoes were the only product approaching sustained consumption. A two-thirds increase in hay[7] may have had some significance to others than horses and cows, for it added to the meat supply. The hog population rose by half in the 1880s, thus indicating a slight rise in per capita consumption, but the 70 per cent growth in the number of beef cattle[8] is less convincing. So many of the added increment were scrawny, undersized Western brutes that the amount they contributed to the beef supply is uncertain. The cotton crop nearly doubled, held at fairly stable prices,[9] and apparently reflected the constancy of foreign demand. There is nothing in these data to indicate overproduction as a basis for farm depression. More likely the trouble reflected the decline in the purchasing power of the urban centers.

After credit, prices, and markets, other factors, such as migration, government land policies, improved machinery, and scientific advances influenced farm life. After 1880, migration from the Atlantic coast and South Central states was little more than the migration into them. The center of the outward movement was the five states of the East North Central (Old Northwest) group, including Iowa and Missouri. Their net loss was 1,087,000, out of the 1,363,000 for the whole nation. Illinois, for the second decade, was the greatest loser, closely followed by Iowa. The great gainers were the states west of the Louisiana to Minnesota tier. There, Kansas had led in the 1870s, but Nebraska took the lead with 240,-000 in the 1880s. The migration of 126,000 into the Dakotas, plus the natural increase there, helped them to statehood in 1889. The same was true of Washington and her 153,000 addition. Colorado's 100,000, Montana's 40,000, Idaho's 27,000, and Wyoming's 22,000[10] indicated that there, in the higher Great Plains and the open places of the Mountain states, a new agricultural frontier, destined to be the last, had opened. This held true even though the livestock and mining businesses, in some areas, still attracted the bulk of the newcomers.

Even though these figures are impressive, they did not reflect a mass exodus of children of the Eastern brickyards to the free lands of the West, as the once-lively proponents of the labor–safety-valve theory had maintained. Nearly all of the moving population came from Midwestern farms, and more of them settled in Western towns and mining camps than on the land, whether free, expensive, or rented. They represented only a minor fraction of the surplus farming population of the era that escaped to the urban centers. If there ever was a safety valve it was the industrial city, and it operated in such a way as to relieve rural discontent.[11] The spectacular race for homesteads in Oklahoma, on the opening of a part of that territory for settlement by white men in 1889, and the succeeding runs into new strips, until one of the most dramatic of them all in 1893, simply meant that homesteads in a region where there was reasonable assurance of enough rainfall to grow crops were getting scarce, not that free land was gone. There were far more homestead entries after 1893 than before that date, but most of them were in the drier West where there could be little successful agriculture without irrigation or dry-farming methods.

Organized inducements to migration and immigration, so frequently the resort of state governments, railroads, steamship lines, and immigration agents in earlier decades, continued with some abatement down through 1890. By 1880 the Dakota boom was on, and Hamlin Garland was soon to be one of those who listened to the call, though he remained only long enough to take a good look at the country before trekking off for New York. His family was one of many on the rich prairies of Iowa who listened to the talk about the still-more-fertile black land of the lower plains, where bonanza farms were beginning to flourish, and who were apparently little concerned about scantier rainfall and hard winters. The inordinately deep freezes, they heard, kept moisture in the soil late in the spring, assuring crops regardless of the shortness of the frost-free season, so they ignored the lecturers at the farmers' institutes who urged diversification of crops as the real road to prosperity. They were wheat men, and they would follow their specialty to a supposed region of free homesteads,[12] not realizing that any land near enough to a shipping point to make anything but subsistence farming a success would have to be bought from a railroad company or, in the government-reserved sections, at a minimum of $2.50 an acre. Homesteads in such favored spots were limited to eighty acres, tracts too small for a successful wheat economy in that climate.

Kansas had colonies that sprang up for a variety of purposes. Near Hutchinson was a large settlement of German Mennonites, who previously had sojourned in Russia and chose their new location after the legislature had exempted conscientious objectors from militia service. Their descendants remained as a German-language group. Shortly before 1880, misguided philanthropists helped several thousand impoverished Southern Negroes to settle in Graham County, where some of them founded the town of Nicodemus. In the same longitude as Dodge City, it was a location where only by the most desperate effort could one make a go of farming, but they continued the struggle, though their town was never more than a few score in population. In the southeastern part of the state, near Humboldt, a colony of vegetarians took their stand. Rainfall was adequate here, but the settlers were not, so they soon left the land to other vegetarians such as jackrabbits and prairie gophers, with enough coyotes to make life interesting for them. Spectral inhabitants could not subsist on such a diet, so not even a ghost town remained, but the name survives, attached to Vegetarian Creek. Finally, one Ned Turnley set for himself the hopeless task of rehabilitating worthless sons of the British nobility. This effort soon collapsed when the sires gave up confidence and withdrew their support.[13]

There was even proof that, with sufficient financial support furnished by benevolent companies, rare groups of Eastern laborers could build homes on farms not too far west. Thus some Western bishops organized the Irish Catholic Colonization Association; and an incorporated group in Illinois, with a book capital of $100,000, established Irish colonies in Minnesota and Nebraska before the effort collapsed in 1891. Bishop John Ireland of New York also had settled eight hundred Irish families in various parts of Minnesota, and there were other clusters of them as far south as Virginia, Georgia, and Arkansas. One of the records, showing that it cost $1174 to put up a modest house and plow thirty acres on a homestead,[14] reveals the reason why industrial laborers, who required every cent they could collect from their employers just to subsist, could not hope to make such a new start in life unassisted. Unfortunately, there were too few philanthropists, and their resources were too small, to furnish any measurable relief for conditions in the Eastern factories. Governments aided not at all, unless propaganda can be listed as assistance.

Immigrants continued to pour into the industrial centers, competing with erstwhile farm boys for any available jobs, but a fair share of the aliens were also arriving in the farming states of the North Central group and westward. Hordes of Canadians came into Minnesota, Iowa, the Dakotas, Nebraska, and Kansas before the hard times of the 1890s slowed the movement almost to a complete halt. By 1900 there were more than a million of them in the United States.[15] A new wave of Germans rolled over the country after about 1880 and added to the already large number of their compatriots in Wisconsin and elsewhere. By 1900, nearly a third of the population of Texas was German or of that descent. The arrivals before 1860 had done much to build up America's farming country, but the late-comers included a much larger number of day laborers and artisans.[16]

Scandinavians were among the first settlers along the Atlantic coast, and they trickled into the country for the next two centuries. Then, after 1865, they became an important portion of the population of the Central states bordering the Mississippi River, and by 1900 there were over a million of them in America and twice that number of their children. In the 1880s, some of the Swedes were moving into Dakota Territory, but they later gave way to Norwegians there and centered their attention on Minnesota. Danes were less numerous but widely scattered, except for concentrations in Iowa and Minnesota. Ireland was the only European country that lost a larger portion of its people to America in the nineteenth century than did Norway. Half of the Scandinavian population in the United States in 1890 was Norwegian. Over a quarter of the Swedes remained farmers, which exceeds the percentage of Americans or Germans, but the rate among Norwegians was still higher. There were also Swiss, Dutch, Welsh, French, and various other elements of the immigrants who went to farming, Bohemians being prominent in central-eastern Iowa and in northern Illinois.[17] It was also in the 1880s that immigration from southern and central Europe began to show prominence. Most of the newcomers from these countries remained in the cities, though many Italians became truck gardeners around the larger urban centers, north and south.

Migrants, immigrants, and established farmers alike, especially in the North Central states which already had become the larder and granary of the nation, profited from the inventive genius, mainly of prairie farmers, in the evolution of labor-saving agricultural machines that multiplied the productivity of the persons using them. It was the farmer who operated such equipment that managed to hold his own under the otherwise adverse conditions of the last third of the century. After the work of William Morrison, John Lane, and John Deere of Illinois in the building of steel-faced moldboards, it was not until 1877 that James Oliver of Indiana got a patent on the first successful chilled-iron plow, which brought complete turning of the soil to perfection. But, in the regions of serious wind erosion, a partial turning that leaves the stubble of the preceding crop protruding as a windbreak proved more effective. The later disk plow was the more useful there. Gang plows turning multiple furrows, that the operator could ride, added proportionally to the work accomplished by a driver. Attempts at steam-tractor propulsion in 1859 had only indifferent results, but by 1890 huge, earth-packing tractors were pulling as many as twenty-four disks in the wheat fields of the Pacific coast. These proved too cumbersome for wide adoption, so the horse held his supremacy in the field until after the coming of gasoline tractors in the next century. The lister, a double plow throwing soil in both directions and planting corn in the furrow, came about 1880 and proved most effective in regions of scanty rainfall. Deep rooting came as cultivation threw the ridges down into the furrows while the corn was growing. Improved harrows, seed broadcasters, and drills kept pace with the development of plows.

Mowing machines, tedders, rakes, and hay loaders accompanied the soil-working implements. Between 1875 and 1890, a company at Sterling, Illinois, developed a combined rake, carrier, and loader that would put a ton of hay on a wagon in five minutes. By 1880, steam-operated balers were beginning to displace the old horse-drawn rotary sweeps, but the idea was not widely adopted before the gasoline age. The self-binder for wheat and other small grains reached virtual perfection with the twine knotter, developed by Jacob Behel of Illinois and John F. Appleby and sold to the Deering company in 1878. The McCormick company and others soon copied the device, which speeded up the process of threshing, because there were no wires around the bundles to be clipped. As wheat-growing extended into western Kansas, the header came into use, leaving most of the straw on the ground and reducing the bulk to be threshed. It was not of much value in a climate of greater moisture. By 1880, huge combines were coming into use in California, being pushed by a monstrous steam tractor and cutting a swath as wide as 52 feet. The main utility of steam was in the transportation and running of threshing machines. Separators handling as much as a thousand bushels of grain a day were known by 1890. No great advance was achieved in the harvesting of corn, but in 1875 and the following years Manly Miles of the University of Illinois popularized the silo, thus aiding in the economy of cattle feeding.

As an example of the savings effected by mechanization, one hour's labor in the best-managed wheat fields of 1896 was worth eighteen hours in 1830. A fair amount of this development took place between 1877 and 1890.[18] Not many of the inventions before 1890 did anything to lighten women's work, unless they went into the fields, but an exception can be made for the centrifugal cream separator, introduced into America in 1879, and also for the centrifugal home cream tester, invented by Stephen M. Babcock of the University of Wisconsin in 1890. The latter was valuable as a check on thieving dairy companies.

Although scientific advance was slower in seizing the imagination of farmers than was improved machinery, it also had its devotees and, through the efforts of state experiment stations and the extension work of the agricultural colleges, the ideas gradually spread. The Department of Agriculture at Washington set the pace. The Commissioner of Agriculture under Hayes was William G. LeDuc, followed for four years by George B. Loring, then by Norman Colman, who was succeeded as Secretary by Jeremiah Rusk. It was Loring who brought Harvey W. Wiley into the department in 1883 and soon made him chief chemist. In 1884, he also made Elmer Salmon chief of the newly created Bureau of Animal Industry, with the immediate task of stamping out pleuropneumonia, which was threatening the existence of the cattle business. Within eight years this mission was a complete success, at a cost of a mere $1,500,000. A further safeguard for cattle came when Theobald Smith, by 1890, got a good start at the conquest of cattle-tick fever.[19]

Colman, recognized as the ablest of the six commissioners since the creation of the Department of Agriculture under Isaac Newton in 1862, had much to do with the adoption of the Hatch Act of March 2, 1887, under which he established the Office of Experiment Stations. It was Rusk who announced the extermination of pleuropneumonia and who got the chemists out of the basement of the Agriculture Building in Washington. They had been something of a nuisance in that location, their fumes often almost suffocating visitors and staff. On one occasion, one of their explosions had blown a commissioner out of his chair.[20]

The Division of Entomology started about 1885 to use poison sprays, at first arsenic, to destroy insects, and it also made basic studies for the later control of Hessian flies and certain cotton worms. It was not until 1892 that the boll weevil invaded Texas from Mexico, creating an entirely new problem. The divisions of Pomology and of Vegetable Pathology came in 1886–87. There was also some wasted effort in the department. Between 1884 and 1891 there came another of the experiments that had been tried since the earliest colonial days, to produce silk. As always before, silk resulted, but at too high a cost to compete with the foreign product. Other experiments in 1881 and following, to make sugar from cornstalks, ended with the same verdict: "scientifically possible but commercially impractical."[21]

Meanwhile, state boards of agriculture, succeeded by departments, carried the work forward on a more local scale; the experiment stations in every state and territory rolled thousands of pamphlets off their presses for the benefit of such farmers as would ask for them; and the agricultural colleges turned out increasing numbers of book farmers who also had deep funds of practical knowledge. The colleges also tried to educate the students' elders in the farmers' institutes. Sometimes it was individuals who set the pace. Such was the case of Seaman A. Knapp, who in 1885 left the presidency of Iowa State College to participate in a land-promotion scheme in Louisiana, only to remain and become the great agricultural leader of the South.[22] But many of the lessons remained unlearned by most of the farmers, who dreamed at the plow handles in fields that had never experienced a rotation of crops, who wondered at diminishing yields as they dumped the barnyard manure in the chuckholes of the road, and who "calculated" that, having run through two good farms and reaching bottom on another, there was nothing these college slickers could teach them. In the science of agriculture, as in so many other things, the period following Reconstruction was one of planting, deep rooting, growth, and budding. The flowering and the fruits were left for a later gathering.

The bonanza farmers of the Red River valley in Dakota Territory exemplified the highest use of improved implements and little regard for science. In 1875, the land grant for the receivers of the bankrupt Northern Pacific Railroad induced other officials to promote sales of more of the generous grants that the railroad had received by planting wheat on eighteen square miles in the neighborhood of the later city of Fargo. The manager, Oliver Dalrymple, was to get half of the entire outfit if he succeeded. In 1877, he averaged twenty-five bushels on each of 4500 acres, whereupon capitalists started buying depreciated Northern Pacific bonds to exchange for bonanzas of their own, and little farmers crowded in from neighboring states, hoping to share in the prosperity. Before long, Dalrymple was managing about 100,000 acres and several other holdings ranged between 20,000 and 40,000, the average of all being around 7000 acres, while little farms of two or three square miles each were not worth counting. It cost $9.50 an acre to produce a crop of 20 to 25 bushels bringing $0.90 each. The Grandin bonanza employed from 250 to 400 men in the harvest season and as few as 10 during the winter. Dalrymple used 125 broadcast seeders and 200 harrows to start the crop and 155 binders and 26 steam separators for the harvest and threshing. Only the greatest operators got rebates from the railroads on their shipments, which helped squeeze out small competitors. Migratory workers, called tramps by the newspapers, worked thirteen hours a day for from $9 to $13 a week in addition to bed and board during the harvest; year-round employees received $18 a month.

Good times for the speculators did not last long. Between 1885 and 1890, the ground dried out, crops dwindled, prices fell, and taxes rose. Then the bonanzas broke up and gave way to tenant farms, though Dalrymple held on until 1896.[23] While the movement was at its height, nothing but praise issued from the chambers of commerce and the newspapers. Only the rare intrepid individual, such as William Godwin Moody, would speak out against all land monopolies.[24] But, as a recent authority on land problems has said, the bonanza farms were "an amazing commentary upon our so-called democratic land system."[25]

The wheat belt, as in preceding generations, clung to the frontier, with the unplowed cattle range to the west. In the North Central states, where in 1879 more than seven-tenths of the nation's crop was grown, the same sort of machinery was used as that on the bonanza farms, and the procedure was the same except that wheat was more often a part of mixed farming and the individual grower had only one binder and other implements in proportion. Groups of farmers moved from one's fields to another's to do the threshing, along with the owner of the equipment who worked on a custom basis. Half of these twelve states, four east, one west, and the other straddling the Mississippi River, accounted for a little over half of the crop of the United States. In order of importance, they were Illinois, Indiana, Ohio, Michigan, Minnesota, and Iowa. Ten years later, the seven west of the Mississippi (Missouri to Minnesota and Kansas to North Dakota) achieved permanent ascendancy, but as yet three of the leaders were in the Old Northwest. Minnesota was first, California temporarily taking second place. The rest in order were Illinois, Indiana, Ohio, and Kansas. Minnesota remained on top for another decade, after which, in another score of years, it sank out of sight below the leaders, though retaining pre-eminence in milling, from wheat raised to the west. First North Dakota and then Kansas became the champion.[26]

The corn belt, as usual, remained just east of and overlapping the wheat belt, but again largely confined to the Midwest. In 1859, the South, which in the two preceding censuses had grown from half to three-fifths of the corn in the United States, still had five states among the ten leaders. By 1879, these had been reduced to two. The rise of a one-crop economy in the cotton belt helps explain the shift, but the more adaptable climate of the expanding North Central fields must also be considered. Now, approximately four-fifths of the corn grew in Illinois, Iowa, Missouri, Indiana, Ohio, Kansas, Kentucky, Nebraska, Tennessee, and Pennsylvania, in that order. Ten years later, the same states were again the leaders, with a slightly larger percentage of the national crop, except that Texas had replaced Pennsylvania and the order was different. At that time, Iowa was ahead, followed by Illinois, Kansas, Nebraska, Missouri, Ohio, Indiana, Kentucky, Texas, and Tennessee. Wheat and corn growing continued in the East in almost undiminished quantity, but as its population multiplied the crops did not expand noticeably, and increasing dependence had to be placed on the West.[27]

The supremacy of the North Central states in the growing of cereals is no indication that the section was lagging in other respects. At the end of the century, with an even quarter of the land area of America, 54 per cent of the improved acres, and 56 per cent of all farm property, by value, this Midwest produced commodities in the following percentages: corn 71, wheat 64, oats 77, hay, barley, and potatoes 58 each, and rye 52. Of animals it had 64 per cent of the hogs, 52 per cent of the horses, and 23 per cent of the mules, this latter figure being hardly pro rata by area only because of the constant shipping of broken mules to the South. Even in sheep the Midwest had 22 per cent on its 25 per cent of the land, and Ohio almost equaled Wyoming or Montana. The supremacy extended also to cattle, the section containing 47 per cent of all in number and 53 per cent by value, the ratio being about the same both for beef and dairy animals. Iowa and Kansas, with a combined area but little over half that of Texas, had as many beef cattle at a value 74 per cent greater. Counting both beef and dairy cattle, these two states were ahead of Texas by 28 per cent in number and 113 per cent in value. Texas cattle were still scrawny.[28]

The Midwest's strong leadership in hogs resulted from its predominance in corn growing. It was more profitable for the farmer to feed his corn and sell the swine. Cattle feeders also learned to keep one hog to fatten on the corn that each four cattle wasted. The resulting pork was almost clear profit. Also, it had long been noted that a bushel of corn would put ten or twelve pounds of weight on a pig,[29] so it became a rule that if hogs were selling at five dollars a hundred pounds the grower could afford to feed them fifty-cent corn, or ten-dollar hogs on dollar corn. If the ratio widened, say to 12 to 1, farmers were loath to sell any corn, preferring to feed it all and expand their droves. But when the ratio shrank, as in the case of eight-dollar hogs with corn at a dollar, the tendency was to sell the grain and let commercial feeders take the risk. What usually happened then was that immature swine along with the fat would be sold until a scarcity of pork brought its price up, and the extra corn on the market brought its price down to parity again. Then the cycle, usually taking from four to six years at that time, began all over again. So, whatever price the consumer could or would pay for pork had much to do with the price of corn and the amount of it planted.[30] In later years, hogs that fattened in six or eight months instead of eighteen greatly abbreviated the cycle. It was such things as the combining of corn growing and live-stock feeding, and the larger acreage that one man could handle with improved implements, that kept many farmers solvent in spite of other adversities.

Because of these Western developments, farmers in the North Atlantic states had to make numerous and repeated adjustments, abandoning one crop after another and experimenting with new ones. Nowhere was this more evident than in New England where, though much of it was fit only for pasture, sheep growing had become hazardous and the fattening of cattle totally impractical.[31] Before 1900, there was some increase in barley, hay, and dairy cattle, but in proportion to population growth this was a negative development, and it was not enough to offset the decline in volume of other crops. The labor cost in growing an acre of corn was from seven to nine dollars in the West, but approximately seventeen dollars in New England.[32] The amount of improved land in the North Atlantic states in the last forty years of the century diminished only slightly, because while New England lost over four million acres, or about a third, the Middle Atlantic states gained just a little less. Most of New England's improved land was in the parts of Maine and Vermont where something like frontier conditions prevailed. Less than half of Connecticut's farm acreage was improved.[33]

An observer in 1900, noticing conditions that had existed for a quarter of a century, said that "the most unobservant of travelers through the agricultural districts of the Nutmeg State cannot fail to note the bush-grown highways, the down-fallen walls, the decayed fences, dilapidated buildings and neglected fields which mark the decadence of the true agricultural spirit." He heard complaints that "farming does not pay," and that "most of the hired labor . . . is of foreign birth, transient, ignorant and unreliable. . . ." This left the impression that "notwithstanding the many splendid, well kept farms in the state, Connecticut farming has fallen far below its high standard of a half century ago."[34] At about the same time, Secretary of Agriculture James Wilson, referring to the abandoned farms of New England, remarked that "a Personal inspection of some of these farms shows that they are not abandoned on account of sterility of soil, but are in many cases capable of affording a good living to industrious farmers, and under more favorable auspices than are farms in some of our newer States, on account of nearness to market, educational institutions, and other desirable environments."[35] One such farm of sixty acres, with twelve "suitable for culti-vation," was offered for sale about 1890 or shortly afterward. It had a five-room house "in need of some repair," a "small barn, in good repair," adequate water, and thirty-two fruit trees. It was six miles from a railroad depot and post office and was priced at $400, "cash at sale, $100; interest on balance, four per cent."[36]

For many of these farms, abandonment was the wisest policy; they never had amounted to much, and the families were better off elsewhere. In one case near New Haven, on the breakup of the home, one son went to California, another bought a much larger farm in the West, and two more got rich from coal mining. There is no later report on the one who went hunting for gold. Often, even in those days, commuters from the cities bought these farms to build up as show places.[37] A minority on the submarginal tracts held on by taking in city boarders for the summer. Many owners moved to the nearby cities, in search of day labor or even to engage in business or professional life. The reported success of one lured many more,[38] helping to glut the industrial labor market.

The New England farmer saw no virtue in scrabbling for an existence on stony acres just for the good of his soul, and there was always a chance that he would do no worse for himself in town. It was not necessarily the more intelligent men who remained behind and succeeded, but generally it was the ones with the better lands who, therefore, could take longer to experiment with new methods. As a result of their efforts, changes for the better were taking place before 1890. The contributions of the agricultural colleges proved to be another influence. In this direction, Connecticut got a late start when, in 1881, Charles and Augustus Storrs gave to the state 170 acres, buildings, and $6000 for equipment as a beginning toward a college. Two years later the state chartered the school as Storrs Agricultural College, which more than half a century later became the University of Connecticut. Because the stinginess of nature compelled them, the Yankees had to listen more attentively to the educators than did their Western competitors. When a farmer paid heed and began to diversify his crops, his consequent growth in prosperity became an incentive to his neighbors. Thus, the idea spread. The more broken topography and the smaller fields of New England made the region less adaptable than the prairies to the use of heavy machinery. Yet, the farmers in increasing numbers began hanging up their scythes and abandoning their antiquated plows, and adopted improved implements to the limits of their utility and of the means of the purchasers.[39]

In a larger account, more attention might be given to the Middle Atlantic states. It must suffice here to say that, as in geography, their problems lay between those of New England and the Midwest, and that they partook somewhat of both. New York's dairies and orchards gave her a greater degree of diversity than some of her neighbors, but Pennsylvania maintained a respectable position in the growing of wheat and corn. Before 1890, a considerable shift had taken place in the dairy industry from New York to Wisconsin and Illinois; tobacco went through some changes both as to technology and geography; while horticulture, truck gardening, and plant breeding spread widely.[40] Each of these developments is worthy of a special study. The problems of the cotton belt have been considered as far as they can be taken here, in an earlier chapter. The diversified agriculture, including truck gardening and horticulture, of the Pacific coast belongs to the story of Western adjustments to new ways of life, and will add something to the romance of the history of the West. This summary disposal of important matters is unpalatable but necessary, in order to give space to problems maybe no more significant but certainly more intricate or perplexing.

The final item in the latter category pertains to the status of the hired laborer and the tenant. In 1880, about 43 per cent of all persons receiving income directly from agriculture were wage laborers, and approximately 16 per cent of the total were female. The great bulk of Negro and female laborers were in the South, and most of the alien employees were in the rest of the country. In 1899, a South Carolinian testified before the Industrial Commission that he paid day laborers 30 cents, three-fourths of it to be traded out at his store at 50 per cent profit. Workers by the month received $5.20 for 26 days of toil, on the same basis. He deemed that he was one of the more liberal employers of his vicinity. A Georgian said he paid from $2 to $6 a month, and food. This was cheaper than slave labor ever was.[41]

In 1880, the average monthly wage for South Carolina was $10.43, or $7.95 with board. Thus, it seems, food for one person cost about $2.50 a month, and this reveals what the wage really meant. A man could feed three others besides himself; but on what? Item for item, for goods and services of equal quality, living in the South has always been more expensive than in the North. Furthermore, living consists of other things besides eating. Only by the work of each member of the family, from toddlers to totterers, and by consuming the minimum for subsistence, of the coarsest sort of goods, could the families exist at all. By way of comparison, one might notice the wages of South Carolina and those of Montana or Nevada, but this is hardly fair because of the higher cost of nearly everything in the neighborhood of the Western mines. Nevertheless, food allowances there were sometimes as high as $15 a month, not only on account of higher prices of groceries, but also because the laborers demanded something better than the fat back and corn pone of the South. A better comparison is that between the South and the North by major census divisions. Comprehensive figures available for this purpose show only the brighter lights, for they deal with average rates for outdoor labor of grown men alone, when hired without board and by the year.[42]

MONTHLY WAGES OF MEN EMPLOYED IN AGRICULTURE

Year	South Atlantic	South Central	North Atlantic	North Central	United States
1877	$11.49	$14.88	$20.42	$20.73	$16.79
1890	13.94	16.10	24.72	22.25	19.45

A brief survey of the possible living standards of farmers is now in order. In 1890, the lowest point for agriculture had not yet arrived, and, by 1899, there was enough recovery so that the conditions were about equal at both ends of the decade. A study of the states at the time of the twelfth census reveals several interesting facts. The gross income of the average farm in the United States, including goods consumed by the producer, was $656, and in the Midwest, the most important agricultural section, it was $815. The total number of farm-income receivers in the whole country was 10,700,000, those in the Midwest 3,625,000. The average that each worker got, before subtraction of operating expenses, was $352 for the nation at large and $496 in the Midwest. In this section, 37.8 per cent of the gainfully employed were wage laborers receiving, on the average, $117 a year. Comparative figures for the Far West were $353, for the North Atlantic states $174, and for the South Central section $32. The average for the United States was $81. At this time, by skimping and cutting all possible corners, a family of average size could live in considerable discomfort on $500 a year. At unskilled labor, it usually took more than one wage earner in the family to achieve this goal. At $1000 a year, a family that was not too ambitious could live in a certain degree of ease.

In the Midwest about half the hired laborers were members of families operating the farms, thus helping them to break even. Only 8.9 per cent of the gross farm receipts went to these employees, who were three-eighths of all farm income earners. Another 17.6 per cent were tenants, some more prosperous than many owners and others indescribably poor, who usually paid one-third of their produce to the landlord for rent. Less than 1 per cent were hired managers. After

making another small subtraction for farms operated both by
owners and tenants, it is found that 43.2 per cent of the
income receivers were owner-operators. A depressing amount
of involved but disinterested arithmetic enters here to show
that, out of each 1000 owners, tenants, managers, and wage
laborers, 724 were receiving below $500 a year and 276
were making both ends meet. Of the latter number, 84
were getting along comfortably or were prospering on $1000
and upward. But this is not conclusive. How much interest
were owners and tenants paying out of their supposed in-
comes? Oddly enough, the census takers of 1900 did not take
this into consideration. Such figures exist for 1890 and 1910,
but an average between them, because of the depressed mid-
nineties, would have no validity. It may be that by 1900 so
many farmers had been "frozen out" and had not yet recovered that the number of mortgages and their total value
were considerably below those of a decade earlier or later.
It seems rather definite, though, that the real benefits of
farming were going largely to the moneylenders, wherever
located.[43] Yet, as the years passed, the tendency was for
values of land, improvements, and livestock to advance. But
this blessing would be reaped only in the future and did not
clothe the backs of the present generation.

Chapter XII

THE BIRTH PANGS OF LABOR

L IKE the farmers, the industrial laborers had continuing difficulty adjusting themselves to the increasing dominance of capitalism over society. In earlier decades the labor movement had included a strongly idealistic factor. There was a feeling that to be "born equal" was incompatible with one man working under the domination of another and under the complete control of the employer.

In the old guild system, the apprentice and journeyman labored, and often lived, with the master, and each had a chance to set up a shop for himself when he acquired adequate proficiency. This system broke down when labor-saving devices, invented by the men themselves, became the property of merchant capitalists who then paid wages for the operation of the machinery. Had the guilds been pliable enough in their organization and rules to hold on to the machines for their own use, instead of fighting against their adoption, they might have developed a form of cooperative management and control far different from the factory system that grew up in its place. But before the guilds could break down tradition to the point of joining in and dominating the new movement, the merchant capitalists had evolved the factory out of an earlier domestic system and, with cheaper processes, undersold and drove the guild members into the ranks of wage earners. As always before, nature and labor of hand and mind continued to supply the raw materials. Labor devised the inventions, reproduced them, and alone made them profitable to the owners. But the inventors, unable to finance the putting of the machines on the market or to organize for their cooperative ownership and control, sold out, and then, likely as not, found the fruits of their genius putting them out of work. On the other hand, the employers, through the power of ownership, perpetuated their control and informed their employees that wages were purely the munificence of capital and that, naturally, the smallest sum on which a man could live was the highest the industry could pay.

The laborer was slow in accepting this point of view, but yielded rather than starve. Just the same, his leaders held tenaciously to the thought that they might restore some of the old comparative freedom of action. For the first three-quarters of the nineteenth century, unions were made up largely of the old artisan class that adhered to this tradition and in periods of full employment relied on bargaining over wages and working conditions, falling back on cooperatives and cure-alls only in times of depression. They sought equal power with employers in the bargaining, to protect their unions, job tenure, health, and bodily safety, as well as to fix wages according to needs and to the contribution of labor to the whole economy. Shorter workdays, limitations on female and child labor, the closed shop, restriction of immigration, and the abolition of the sweatshop were means to this end. They strove for free education, a homestead act, and easier credit, sometimes embracing Greenbackism. For some, the final aim was a cooperative commonwealth, in which they, through trusted officials of their own selection, would in effect be self-employed. But American laborers were seldom class-conscious enough to seek this end, and even if they had been, they were a distinct minority within a society that generally cared little for caste. Only after seventy years of failure, not often well understood except by some of the leaders, did they begin to become opportunistic.[1]

The expansion of the factory system, the irruption into the cities of the surplus farm population, deeply rooted in rural individualism, and also the arrival of poor immigrants from Europe helped swell the labor market. The bulk of the new increment was devoid of artisan skills and too innocent of any knowledge of a labor philosophy even to ignore it, much less to become indoctrinated. The newcomers, in the main, took up the rougher tasks, where they were largely out of touch with the skilled artisans, who in turn looked to the protection of their own crafts. The unions sought to keep the rabble out of the aristocracy of labor, and rarely did a leader see the desirability and ultimate necessity of a common front against the employers. The solidarity of labor, as described by one school of historians,[2] simply did not exist. Yet an awareness of common problems, and prompt action, was imperative. As a single example, the slums that housed the poorer laborers were as horrible and unhealthful after 1877 as Nevins has so well pictured them before that date,[3] and their menace extended far beyond their own environs. In 1878, at the time of the yellow-fever visitation in Memphis, the Gayoso Bayou was an open sewer, carrying the filth of the slums right past the homes of the rich. It was foolish to ignore the need for unity, but multitudes succeeded in keeping their heads in the sand.

The plight of the mass of common laborers rested in large part on their need to compete with the wages of underpaid women, children, and immigrants under sweatshop conditions, and with contract labor both of the prisons and poorhouses and from abroad. There were in the 1880s men who had authority in their families. When such men permitted, encouraged, or ordered their wives and children to take employment, so as to make life a little easier, the head of the family soon found himself taking wage cuts brought about in part by competition with the puny stipends his erstwhile dependents received. Thereafter, all had to work, no longer for comforts but as a necessity. In 1886, children went to work in New Jersey at an average age of nine years. Their employment ranged from ten to fourteen hours a day for a wage of not over two dollars a week. Such children were subject to corporal punishment by their employers, and the small change they brought home on payday helped support their fathers, who were thrown out of work by their competition.[4] Furthermore, the work was often harmful to the child's health, and it deprived him of an opportunity for education.

The census of 1870 showed 739,164 of the gainfully employed to be between the ages of ten and fifteen, most of them being on the farms but 114,628 in factories. The total grew to 1,118,536 in 1880 and to 1,750,178 in 1900. The data for 1890 are not comparable because of the use of a different form of classification. There was no accounting of the numbers below the age of ten, and the whole system of enumeration has been called "notoriously inadequate." When a Maryland law of 1906 required permits for employment of children under sixteen, Senator Albert J. Beveridge of Indiana noted that the number of such permits obtained was twice the number reported as working in that state at the time of the last preceding census. The factory owners as well as the parents were simply withholding information. For what the figures may be worth, in the factories the percentage of children under the age of sixteen to all employees in the United States was 5.6 in 1870, 6.7 in 1880, and 3.2 in 1900. By the latter year, wariness of reporting was becoming notable. There had been a few rather feeble state laws for the limitation of child labor before 1860, and in 1866 and 1867 Massachusetts became quite stern about factory employment of children under ten, and against more than sixty hours a week for those under fifteen, who were also supposed to have three months each year for schooling. Illinois and Wisconsin adopted some indefinite legislation in 1877, and Michigan in 1885, but it was a later generation that took the matter firmly in hand.[5]

While the labor of children seemed to decline in proportion to all employees, that of girls and women was on the increase, actually and in proportion to population growth. In 1870, the percentage of all females over nine years of age gainfully employed was 13.0; in 1880, 1890, and 1900, 14.7, 17.4, and 19.0 respectively. In 1880, a fifth, and in 1900, a quarter of all girls and women in the various occupations were working in trade, transportation, manufactures, and mechanical pursuits. As in the case of children, excessive hours and unhealthful surroundings were damaging to the individual, and underpayment was a threat to the wages of all competitors. Like the children, women often accepted submarginal pay to supplement the family income. Also, the ephemeral nature of so many of their occupations made them hard to organize. As late as 1908, a survey in Pittsburgh showed that of more than 22,000 women employees, three-fifths received between three and six dollars a week, while only one-fifth got eight dollars or more.[6]

As mentioned earlier, the main difficulty with immigrants was their willingness to work very cheaply. This was a serious matter from 1877 to 1890, when labor was in upheaval and the arrivals numbered over 6,162,000. This was half again as many as in the preceding fourteen years and nearly double the 3,727,000 of the great period dominated by Irish and German immigration from 1846 to 1859 that had resulted in rampant antialienism. In the like period between 1891 and 1904, there was an increase of only 5.4 per cent over 1877–90. The 789,000 of 1882 remained the record for any one year until 1903.[7]

The most deplorable feature of immigration from the Civil War onward was the practice of importing gangs of labor under contract, to beat down industrial wages and serve as strikebreakers. Federal legislation in 1885 and 1887 did not entirely correct this evil.[8] Also, steamship companies "systematically violated the law" governing their activities, by scouring Europe for steerage passengers, the backbone of profits in the passenger business. This helps to explain the 17.6 per cent of all immigrants in the 1880s that came from Austria-Hungary, Italy, Russia, and Poland. In the next decade they became half of the total. These people came to take over much of the heavier and more disagreeable work. They were tolerated by society because they were cheap, and for the same reason they were dreaded by labor organizations. Why buy expensive machinery when wearing out immigrants or letting them lose their lives at dangerous tasks cost the employer nothing? There are no dependable estimates before 1908 on how many of the aliens returned to their former homes. The Bureau of Immigration then guessed that in the preceding decade 68 per cent of all had remained in America.[9]

Legislative bodies did little to ameliorate the conditions created by this inflow of cheap labor. The federal Act of June 3, 1882, barred the insane, persons with criminal records, and potential paupers,[10] but did nothing about the greater problem. By 1884, four states had bureaus of labor statistics, Massachusetts pointing the way in 1869 with the appointment of Carroll D. Wright as commissioner. Wright was an ideal man for the task and, by the careful accumulation and analysis of information, he prepared himself for making judgments and recommendations for legislative action. The federal government followed the example by an Act of June 27, 1884, and then Wright became commissioner of the national bureau. So effective was his work in the study of prison contract labor, together with other unfavorable publicity, that within a few years that blotch on the face of America began to fade. After his able analysis of the Southwestern Railroad strikes of 1885–86, Congress, by an Act of June 13, 1888, raised the bureau to the rank of a subcabinet department,[11] perhaps for the later benefit of the armies of labor even if of no immediate help.

A numerically rather insignificant element in the immigration of the period was that of the Chinese. Employers welcomed them because of their docility and willingness to toil almost incessantly for less than enough to keep an Occidental alive. For these same reasons, many labor leaders favored exclusion of Asiatics. One of the restrictionists was that still rather young veteran of the labor movement, Andrew C. Cameron, who, in 1869, had said, "Bring them along, Chinamen, Japanese, Malays, and monkeys, make voters of them all; acknowledge them as men and workers; mix them all up together, water down the old Caucasian race." A Know-Nothing of 1856, an American Protective Associationist of 1892, or a Ku-Kluxer of 1924 or 1965 could hardly have been more bitter. The pioneer socialist Adolph Douai deplored Cameron's attitude of racism, but agreed on banning the Chinese because of their apparently lower standard of living and the feeling that it might take a century to Americanize them.[12] Change from Douai's point of view was slow. More than forty years later, in 1910, Morris Hillquit secured the adoption by the Socialist party of a resolution opposing "the immigration of strike-breakers and contract laborers, and the mass importation of workers from foreign countries, brought about by the employing classes for the purpose of

weakening the organization of American labor, and of lowering the standard of life of American workers." Thus far he
said nothing that Samuel Gompers of the American Federation of Labor might not have endorsed. But the rest of the
resolution was a thoroughly straightforward appeal for the
United States to remain "as a free asylum for all men and
women persecuted by the governments of their countries on
account of their politics, religion or race."[13]

From the first census listing in 1820, through 1853, only
88 Chinese came to America through regular channels. With
the opening up of Oriental trade in 1854 and down to the
Burlingame Treaty of 1868, inclusive, there were 77,042.
Yet, the tendency of these Celestials, as they were often
called in those days, to return to China with a piddling stake
that in their home country passed as a handsome compe-
tency, was so great that, though another 12,874 entered in
1869 and an unknown part of the 15,740 of 1870 before the
census takers got around in that year, only 63,042 of Chinese
birth were enumerated in the United States in 1870. Another
116,823 arrived in 1869–76, after which there was a decided
slowing down until the eve of 1882, in which year there
were 39,579 entries crossing the line in time to evade the
Exclusion Act. This was nearly twice as many as in any
previous year, but it was only one in twenty of the total
immigration of 1882. Thereafter, there was a sharp decline
until only 10 came over in 1887, followed by a sudden rise
to 1716 in 1890. From 1877 to 1890, the total was 96,703,
and in seventy-one years the aggregate amounted to 290,656.
Yet, the entire number of Chinese birth counted in 1880
was only 104,468 and in 1890 there were 106,701. The total
number of Chinese, counting those of American birth, in the
two census years swelled the numbers only about a thousand
each time. In 1900, the figures for foreign-born and all
Chinese were 81,534 and 89,863.[14]

No doubt, the two-thirds of all such immigrants who returned home took a great deal of American money with
them, but they left behind a far greater amount of wealth
that they had created for their employers. For their exploiters, the Chinese, going or coming, were a wonderful invest-

ment. It was the native day laborer who suffered, and nowhere worse than in the Pacific states. Hostility to the Chinese started in California and extended to the East after the completion of the first transcontinental railroad made it possible, in 1870, to rush them into North Adams, Massachusetts, to act as strikebreakers. For some time, Eastern interest in the question remained academic, except on occasional repetitions of the North Adams escapade. But in 1877–78, rowdyism burst into violence in California. Denis Kearney, a teamster who boasted of having acquired wealth in business ventures, had little sympathy for his fellow man, especially if a laborer, but he had a healthy ambition for political advancement. Finding the major parties unenthusiastic about his talents, he deserted the "pick-handle brigade" of businessmen who had been breaking up assemblies of anti-Chinese demonstrators, and became the leader of mobs in San Francisco, demanding that "the Chinese Must Go." He completed his rightabout by organizing a branch of the Working Men's party of the United States, in California. His dictatorial practices and evidences of his willingness to desert the cause for a price soon ended his leadership, but the party itself started a movement that later brought about notable reforms in the constitution and laws of the state, while continuing to fight the importers and employers of coolie labor.[15]

In 1877, the Working Men's party of the United States, a coalition of various socialist organizations, assumed the name of Socialistic Labor party. Popularly known as Socialist Labor, it continued under its original secretary Philip Van Patten. Kearney was not such a socialist as to advance in the new party's ranks, and in 1884 he left politics for the remaining twenty-three years of his life.[16]

There were understandable reasons why California socialists, if not hostile to the Chinese as a race, were bitter against their exploiters. A few great companies controlling their labor had, without question, beaten down wages for all competing laborers. In the shoemaking business, as an example, there were four Chinese employees for each white one, and the wages for all fell between 1870 and 1878 from twenty dollars a week to nine dollars.[17] With this situation in mind, the members of Congress from California secured the appointment of a joint committee to study the situation and make recommendations. The dying Senator Oliver P. Morton of Indiana was chairman, but the California senators had most to do in drafting the report of 1877 urging that the President negotiate a modification of the Burlingame Treaty, "confining it to strictly commercial purposes; and that Congress legislate to restrain the great influx of Asiatics to this country." The committee felt that the Chinese government would willingly agree.[18]

In response to this plea, Congress considered various resolutions, and President Hayes had to veto one bill for proposed violation of the existing treaty, but he asked George F. Seward, Minister to China, to negotiate a new treaty. On Seward's failure, James B. Angell replaced him and, in 1880, got China to agree that the United States might regulate, limit, or suspend the immigration of coolies. Chinese nationals in the United States should have protection as before. It was strictly a unilateral agreement, in which China conceded everything but an outright boycott of its people.[19] Shortly after the ratification of the new bargain, Congress passed a bill that President Arthur felt obliged to veto because it provided for a suspension of immigration of laborers for twenty years, which was the same as the outright prohibition that the Chinese government had refused to accept. But he signed the next bill on May 6, 1882, though it differed from its predecessor only in limiting the exclusion to ten years.[20] It seemed that a slap in the Chinese face was less insulting than a sound cuffing. After a renewal of the ten-years' ban in 1892, Congress made it permanent a decade later, in total disregard of the treaty. Many people thought the Act of 1882 was too lax, so Congress passed an amendment, approved on July 5, 1884, seemingly closing the loopholes.[21]

The early legislation did not avert further outbursts of violence. In 1885, a mob of coal miners at Rock Springs, Wyoming, killed twenty-eight Chinese, wounded fifteen more, and played havoc with their property. In November of the same year another riotous group drove seven hundred out of Tacoma, and in 1886 a few determined and law-abiding citizens prevented a similar outrage at Seattle. There were numerous expulsions of Chinese, destructions of their homes, and thefts of their goods in California towns, for which the Chinese government could procure no reparation or apology from the federal government because it would not hold itself liable for acts committed by individuals.[22]

Perhaps because of such mob violence, in 1886 the government at Peking offered to assume the obligation of prohibiting the emigration of coolies to the United States. Instead of accepting this generous and probably sincere proposal, in 1887 Cleveland authorized negotiations for a more airtight treaty. While this matter was in progress at Peking, Representative William L. Scott of Pennsylvania, who was to be the President's campaign manager in the coming election, brought forward a bill to put the provisions of the proposed treaty into the statutes. Though such premature action was a flagrant insult to the Chinese diplomats, the bill secured easy passage and approval on October 1, 1888. The act provided that Chinese who had resided legally in the United States and had gone back to visit their old homes, or should do so in the future, could not return, and that the old certificates of identity were no longer valid for re-entrance into the country. Presumably, such certificates had become an article of commerce, letting entirely new immigrants over the wall and, as the officials are supposed to have summed up the situation, "all Chinamen look alike to me." This meant that more than twenty thousand Chinese were barred from return. In fact, some six hundred of them who were on the way over when the law went into effect had to turn back on arrival in Western ports. Many of them had families and property to leave behind. The Scott Act did not put an end to fraud and evasion of earlier legislation; all it did was to keep the more desirable Chinese element, who had gone on visits, from resuming their lives in the country of their adoption.[23]

Some of the Chinese laborers discovered a certain entertainment value in the evasion of the exclusion laws. They could land in Canada or Mexico and step over the border on a dark night. As an immigration inspector at San Diego said in 1889: "The children on the streets of this city laugh at me when I inform them that the punishment of a Chinaman, under the 'Scott exclusion act,' is to put him across the line into Mexico, as they know full well the Mongolian will be in our Chinatown early next morning for breakfast."[24]

The British inventor Hiram S. Maxim summed up another phase of the situation, both for South Africa and the United States, in a series of ironical remarks. A few excerpts will give the flavor. "They [the Chinese] worked too many hours in a day, too many days in the week, and too many weeks in a year. . . . The natural condition of a white man appears to be a state of rest." He observed later that "mobs were organized, and many of the little heathen farms were destroyed. But there seemed to be no end to the iniquity of these degraded heathens, for no sooner did they find their plants destroyed, than they went fishing on Sundays, and managed to catch as many fish in one day as the local fishermen could catch in a week." The Californians wanted "John Chinaman" to depart without money, but the Orientals "had the effrontery to say that they would be pleased to allow their money to remain in the country if they were also allowed to remain and invest it in business, but they absolutely refused to be separated from their money. They said if they were forced to return to their own country, they proposed to take their earnings with them, much as they loved California. . . . It is only too evident that the heathen Chinee is a hopeless case. No one can make money out of him except the man who gives him a job."[25]

The final sentence from Maxim applies equally well to the many other immigrants, as well as to the women and children, who were victims of the sweatshop. The employer made the money, while the toilers either went about their tasks half-starved or else procured further sustenance from almost equally impoverished relatives or, in the form of charity, from society, which in this way showed its benevolence to the sweatshop managers. A great deal has been said about the charity of the rich to the poor; this was a case of charity of the poor to the rich. Much the same thing applies to the entire wage and profit system of the period.

Sweating occurred in foul shops in the tenement houses of the larger cities, but a favorite method was to recruit the victims by use of advertisements in newspapers and magazines, urging women to "earn money in your spare time." This was often an outright swindle, requiring the correspondent to advance a few dollars to cover the cost of materials. On receipt of a dime's worth of cardboards of a uniform size, covered with outlined designs to be painted into acceptable greetings, the woman found the task beyond her skill and had lost her investment. Should she have the requisite talent, she might collect two or three dollars a week for some fifty or sixty hours of eye-straining endeavor. There was a great number of such household tasks, especially in needlework and the making of artificial flowers, requiring the nimble fingers of children and women, the great advantage of the sweatshop employer being that he did not have to bear the overhead cost of furnishing the room, light, heat, ventilation, or even machinery that he would need if employment were in his own establishment. No pay for imperfect work, and fines deducted for materials allegedly spoiled, were certain assurance of no risk involved. Cigar making flourished both in the home and the centralized shop. The requirement of sealing cigar wrappers with spittle could not have been pleasant even to the workers.

Conditions in tenement workshops have been so eloquently described by a Russian immigrant, who managed to emerge from the squalor,[26] that any attempt at a paraphrase would be a travesty. The boss, in his insanitary shop, was essentially a parasite. Receiving a percentage of the piece-wage allotted to each employee, it was to his interest to reject and refuse pay for work that would pass inspection when turned in to his own employer, thus keeping the entire sum to himself. Anything he got beyond his just remuneration as a supervisor was extortion from the worker. During a period of heavy Jewish immigration into New York, between 1876 and 1882, the task system, unique to that locality, sprang up in the clothing industry. It required a high degree of teamwork paid

for by the day, during which time each person must keep
even pace with all the rest on the assigned task. The tendency
was to assign so much work for each day that the laborers
could not complete it at top speed in less than twelve or
fourteen hours. There was no need of supervision, final inspection being the sole criterion. Many persons stuck to this
kind of sweating just to be free of a boss constantly "looking
down their collars."

The courts of the day were not above finding excuses for
such exploitation. In 1885, the New York Court of Appeals
declared unconstitutional a law forbidding cigar making in
tenement houses. The "hallowed associations and beneficent
influence" of the homes would protect the children's health
and morals. Then, too, the court must uphold the worker's
"liberty" to toil wherever the boss ordered him and under
conditions thus imposed. As a sample of the wages paid as
late as 1907, New Yorkers who made artificial roses in their
homes, flowers that sold at seven cents each, received six
cents for the manufacture of 144 of them, and that was the
main cost to the industry.[27]

Sometimes, the situation was, in sheer tyranny, worse than
this. The period opened with tragedy in the anthracite mining industry around Pottsville, Pennsylvania, where in 1877
and 1879 twenty men were hanged for murders. Some of
them were undoubtedly innocent, while others got off scot-
free for acting as state's witnesses.[28] The newspapers and
the public called them Molly Maguires.

There had been trouble in the same region in the early
1860s, the accused then being known as Buckshots. After
fighting against the brutality of mine bosses, some of them
joined in resistance to the military draft in 1863. The newspapers referred to them as Irish, that nationality being under
particular odium at the time, as the most recent large wave
of immigrants. Among the arrested "Irishmen" were persons
with such names as Bressler and Stutzman.[29] There was no
more serious rioting until the summer of 1875 but, for some
years before this, there had been tension between the operators and the employees over intolerable conditions in the
mines. Whether or not the Molly Maguires took the leader-

ship of the miners after the breakup of their union in a long and unsuccessful strike, or whether such an organization had any real existence, is altogether uncertain. It was almost impossible for unions to survive in the open, much less accomplish anything, and there were several secret groups active, quite naturally including "illiterate, drunken, quarrelsome" individuals. Among the Irish miners were many members of the Ancient Order of Hibernians, some of whom undoubtedly "did use their positions in the society to bring about the murder of three bosses. . . ." But this was less an indication of a labor conspiracy than of just plain, low-down orneriness, for they were also concerned in the killing of three other men "who had nothing to do with labor problems."[30]

It is altogether unnecessary to picture the convicted men as inoffensive Marxians, quietly going about the business of a law-abiding class struggle, as one author has quite skillfully and accurately done, except for the omission of some damaging facts.[31] More convincing is the friendly statement of another historian of the movement: "The groups were crude and rough, often to the point of lawlessness, but their general purpose, in so far as it was related to labor problems, was legitimate." Individual Irishmen, members of the Ancient Order of Hibernians, also engaged in "shady political projects."[32] Possibly some good Presbyterian Republicans did the same. Some of the convicted men, who by their own confession were murderers, had nothing to do with the labor movement. The rest were convicted almost solely on the testimony of James McParlan, a hired Pinkerton thug, with some corroboration from "highly disreputable accomplices who secured immunity for their own crimes by testifying."[33]

One should now pay a little attention to the sequence of events, not necessarily following a *post hoc, ergo propter hoc* manner of approach. In 1873, the young Franklin B. Gowen, president of the Reading Railroad and of its anthracite monopoly, though professing his abiding friendliness for and sympathy with the coal diggers, asked Allan Pinkerton, notorious for fostering labor trouble so as to have a lucrative part in its settlement, to send in an agent to investigate the labor leaders. The man Pinkerton chose was McParlan, who proceeded to prove himself a perjurer by joining the Hibernian order, swearing that "should I hear a member illy spoken of, I will espouse his cause, and convey the information to him as soon as possible for me to do so," knowing full well that his intention was to get as many of them in trouble as possible. Also, he had ingratiated himself with the criminal element by claiming to be a murderer, an illegal collector of military pensions, and a passer of counterfeit money—"shoving the queer," it was called. He worked diligently at his task for three years until, in 1876, he had to drop it, on discovery by his associates that James McKenna was really James McParlan, Pinkerton man. But he had done his work well, and he could not be an effective agency man unless he could foment trouble. By 1875, hell was popping in the coal fields. After a series of farcical trials, the innocent along with the guilty became crowbait on the gallows.[34]

Late in 1889, Gowen, then only fifty-three, revisited Pottsville and then blew his brains out in a Washington, D.C., hotel room. But there is little to support the theory that he was suffering any remorse ten years after the hangings. It was not his nature.[35] As to McParlan, he was never the little tin angel as pictured by Arthur Conan Doyle in "The Valley of Fear," constantly pursued by a ruthless nemesis. In fact, he cropped up thirty years later (1907) in his old role of assistant to the prosecution in the Haywood-Pettibone-Moyer trial for the murder of ex-Governor Frank Steunenberg of Idaho. Here, McParlan coached Harry Orchard in the art of perjury to the point where he was confessing to the murder of persons who had died in accidents, pointing to the men on trial as his instigators. His lies were so obvious that he thereby unwittingly helped Clarence S. Darrow, with the support of Eugene V. Debs and Samuel Gompers and the organizations they led, to secure an acquittal of the men at the bar.[36] As to the Pennsylvania miners, their oppression continued into the next century. As the biographer of Gowen has said in his preface: "The facts show that there was far more terror waged against the Mollies than those illiterate Irishmen ever aroused." In concluding the episode, he stresses much the same thing by saying that "other mining corporations, seeing Gowen's success, adapted his methods until the term Coal and Iron police became a synonym for terror, a far more actual terror than any inspired by the Molly Maguires."[37] The members of that supposed organization suffered the fate of the contemporary proverb: "Give a dog a bad name and then take him out and hang him."

Faced with conditions such as these, common labor tried to organize. Some strong unions had emerged from the Civil War period and others had grown up afterward. But the failing strikes of 1877 left the whole movement in a demoralized condition, while the mass of the unskilled had no leadership and often no faith in combination. An effort to break down this lassitude came in 1878, when Frederick A. Sorge and J. P. McDonnell objected to the political-action program of the Socialist Labor party and joined forces with Ira Steward, George E. McNeill, and George Gunton of the eight-hour leagues to launch the International Labor Union for the particular benefit of those who needed organization most. Both groups held to socialism as the ultimate goal. Sorge wanted to achieve this by union activity, while Steward subscribed to the visionary philosophy that the eight-hour day would increase the laborer's wants and wages to the point where management's profits would vanish and the cooperative state would emerge without conflict. But Sorge's theories, carried from the old Socialist International, prevailed in the organization. The group started out with members in eighteen states, but had little appeal outside the textile industry, particularly in Paterson, Fall River, and Hoboken. The last-named local claimed about eight thousand members before the end of 1878, but the union dwindled and passed out of existence in 1887.[38]

Of earlier origin, less doctrinaire, and for some years quite successful was the Noble and Holy Order of the Knights of Labor—rather an aristocratic title for an organization dedicated to the uplift of the proletariat. In 1869, it grew out of the futility of the Garment Cutters' Association of Philadelphia in its struggles with the employers. The principal founder was Uriah S. Stephens, who had been educated for the Baptist ministry and carried the missionary spirit into the order.

It was a secret society, even the name being unknown to anyone but members until 1878, and aside from its name it remained secret throughout its period of activity. Meanwhile it was generally known as the "five stars" for the row of five asterisks heading its public notices. Until the great strikes of 1877, it was only of local importance and confined largely to the clothing industry. The consequent disaster to the trade unions gave it a chance to expand.

In 1878 it took on national scope with Stephens still the Grand Master Workman, but in 1879 he gave control to Terence V. Powderly, with whom he was soon at odds over changes in the ritual. Stephens died in 1882, still scarcely on speaking terms with Powderly, though hardly realizing how futile the new Grand Master was to become. In 1878, several of the leaders ran for political office on the Greenback ticket and Powderly was elected mayor of Scranton, which office he held for six years. Several craft unions sent delegates to the first general assembly in 1878, and so many such unions submerged themselves in the new organization as to lead the officials to the unjustifiable conclusion that the day of the separate exclusive bodies was over. At this same assembly, the Knights adopted the preamble and much of the constitution of the little-known earlier Industrial Brotherhood. The constitution presumably created a highly centralized body of workingmen operating as one big union, but in reality the leaders had to follow the demand of the local and district assemblies.[39]

If not always holy, the Knights had a noble, though in some parts impractical, set of principles. They adopted the motto: "An injury to one is the concern of all." Yet they did not always live up to this precept, notably in 1887 when the order deserted Albert R. Parsons and let him hang for a crime of which he was not guilty. They admitted Negroes and, with some reluctance, women, to whom they gave "due but not excessive consideration." The organization brought a solidarity into the labor movement that the American Federation of Labor did not continue when it reached ascendancy in 1886 and the following years. Under an able leadership, the Knights might have become the foundation of a labor movement for all workers, perhaps even developing into a labor party of real vigor. Actually, it was a dreamy religious organization. The sympathetic Norman J. Ware described the Knights as "serious-minded, high-falutin, sentimental, a little ridiculous, but engaged in a crusade of some sort which in some way seemed to them important." Their great contribution grew out of their knowledge that the industrial revolution was breaking down the old trades, that the reign of an aristocracy of labor was ending, and that skilled and unskilled workers must combine as a unit for the good of the whole— that they could swim together or drown separately. Disgusted, after 1878, with the political approach as much as with trade unionism, they leaned most heavily on reformism, which they called "education." In 1878 they had a "brave platform" but did not know what to do about anything. "They were in sympathy with everything and involved in nothing."[40]

Stephens had good reason to regret his choice of Powderly as his successor, though the founder did not live long enough to realize how well grounded was his doubt. Powderly was vague, uncertain, and vacillating. As a friend of the movement has said: "He was a windbag whose place was on the street corner rousing the rabble to concert pitch and providing emotional compensation for dull lives." Yet, though he frequently begged for acceptance of his resignation, the faithful Knights held on to him until 1893, years after the order had ceased to be important. It was only in these later years that he became dictatorial, and then only when he wanted to oust an enemy. When he got a grand idea he would not follow it out or cling to it long, as in 1884 when he proposed to "abolish the wage system." He did not believe in strikes, did not want labor disputes, and was a failure as an arbitrator. By confession, he took part in the Southwestern Railroad strike of 1886 only when the trainmen forced his hand, and the same was true of all the rest of the strikes. He called off the Chicago stockyards strike of the same year just as the men were on the point of winning, yet they followed his instructions. He let the Knights' locals go on their own in the Reading coal and railroad strike of 1887–88, lest the public might not approve. He did his best to prevent the strike against the New York Central Railroad, which failed in 1890, probably from weakhearted support. When he could not deter the Knights from a strike, his one thought was to end it, even on disadvantageous terms.[41] He finally wound up as a bureaucrat in the administration of McKinley and kept an important position in the Bureau of Immigration until three years before his death in 1924.

On one thing Powderly did act positively. He believed in cooperation, but the only enterprise supported by the central organization was a coal mine near Cannelburg, Indiana, purchased in 1884. Bad management seems to have been more potent than foul practices on the part of the local railroad and competing mines in the failure of the venture two years later.[42]

The growth of the Knights of Labor was slow and wavering for a few years. Individuals and whole unions joined, received inspiration, found nothing more of value, and dropped out. The initiation fee was only a dollar, membership fees were negligible, and there was no compulsion to contribute for benefits. The membership late in 1879 was over 9000, whereas by Gompers' estimate the total in the trade unions at about the same time was only 50,000. After tripling in 1880 and losing a third in 1881, membership grew steadily to above 111,000 in 1885. Then, the success of strikes in that year brought the total to nearly 730,000 by the middle of 1886, 703,000 of them being paid up in their dues and in good standing. The losing strikes of 1886 cost a quarter of the members in the following year, and by 1890 only 100,000 were left. Thereafter, though the Knights did not close shop for good until 1917, they never again made the number of their membership public. In the days of their glory, in 1884 and 1885, they established assemblies in England, Belgium, Australia, New Zealand, and Ireland.[43]

Chapter XIII

INDUSTRIAL STRIFE, 1877–90

THE great railroad strikes of 1877 were an indication, scarcely realized at the time, that the depression following the Panic of 1873 had reached bottom and that, on the slow upclimb of the business cycle, labor was asking for its share of the benefits. Railroaders had taken their wage reductions while the downward swing was on, lest they have no jobs at all. But when the Pennsylvania, Erie, New York Central, and Baltimore & Ohio systems declared a second 10 per cent cut on June 1, 1877, this was asking too much, and the men walked out. Now, first-class freight conductors would get but $2.12, second-class $1.91, and brakemen $1.45 a day, and far less of them than formerly would be working at all, for the lines also doubled the length of the trains so that they would have to pay fewer full crews. The companies were trying to insure dividends on watered stock, the laborers were anxious to continue eating, and a horde of hoboes, of whom there was an uncommon abundance after four years of desperately hard times, were anxious to act as camp followers behind any strike and commit whatever depredations against property suited their fancy, well knowing that they had nothing to lose. A legislative committee in Pennsylvania described the strikes as "the protest of the laborer against the system by which his wages were arbitrarily fixed and lowered by his employer without consultation with him, and without his consent."[1]

Thus, there began a movement that would bring reprisals on the railroaders in the form of secret police (Pinkertons), the use of the state militia and of federal troops, a revival of conspiracy laws and trials aimed by the states particularly against boycotts, and injunctions. It was only to be expected that the operators would do all in their power to win, but one might be naïve enough to assume that intervention by the governments would be solely for the purpose of maintaining law and order. Instead, the legislators, administrations, and courts acted in general as though every management pleases and only labor is vile. It is small wonder, then, that the strikers used force against duress.

Their greatest disadvantage was that they had no well-established unions to lead them. The Brotherhood of Railroad Engineers dated from 1863, and since 1874 had been under the leadership of Peter M. Arthur, who was as much a pacifist as the preceding Grand Chief Engineer against whom Arthur, protesting such tactics, had secured election. The Order of Railway Conductors, founded in 1868, had a rule forbidding strikes, never rescinded at least until after 1890. The Brotherhood of Locomotive Firemen, organized in 1873, consisted of men hoping as individuals someday to step into the shoes of their fellow cab mates, so they followed in the footsteps of Chief Arthur. The Brotherhood of Railroad Brakemen came along in 1883, aping the conductors as the firemen did the engineers. So they also opposed strikes and did not even have a grievance committee for collective bargaining until 1888. Section hands and shopmen had no leadership at all. Arthur had used up all of his initial zeal in late 1876 and early 1877 when he won three small walkouts and lost the same number, primarily against the Boston & Albany and the Reading lines. Reduced pay was the motive in the one case and Gowen's efforts to break the union in the other. Having destroyed an earlier union and then the Molly Maguires, Gowen was now whetting his ax for the locomotive engineers, telling them to withdraw from the brotherhood or be discharged. They submitted, but first struck. Pinkerton men and scabs quickly ended the revolt, and thereafter Chief Arthur emulated the currently famous Chief Sitting Bull, if remaining aloof for eleven years from such plebeian activity as strikes could so qualify him. The sycophantic firemen followed his lead.[2] This left the way open for spontaneous combinations and for the Knights of Labor, in time, to take over in emergencies.

The organization that took up the challenge against the

railroads was a secret Trainmen's Union headed by Robert
H. Ammon, a young brakeman. His first effort at a strike, to
begin on June 27, broke down because of rumors spread by a
discontented element that it had been called off. During the
next month, as the union began to reassert its control, several
outbreaks occurred in the form of strikes and riots. The first
came at Martinsburg, West Virginia, on July 16, in which the
members of the Brotherhood of Locomotive Engineers on that
division, without sanction of their officers, helped to the extent
of retarding train service. The state militia in that area would
not fight their neighbors and relatives to uphold the cause of
the Baltimore & Ohio Railroad. So the governor of the state
induced President Hayes to send in 256 of the regular army.
Under the Constitution, the army in such a circumstance
could be used only to protect "against domestic Violence," but
when the soldiers arrived two days later, it was to uphold
the railroad and end the strike. Immediately, the men carried the movement to Baltimore and Cumberland, Maryland.
The governor, learning from the Martinsburg experience not
to depend on the local militia, on July 20 ordered a regiment
and two companies to proceed from Baltimore to Cumberland. The two companies had a hard time getting away. The
angered populace of Baltimore besieged them in the armory,
from which they could not escape without a battle, the mob
using brickbats and revolvers, while the militia fired their
rifles, killing nine and wounding thirty or more. Then the riot-
ers set fire to the depot and threatened to kill anybody who
tried to save the building. The police then took over and
let the fire engines do their work. The next day, federal soldiers arrived and ended the strike throughout the state.[3]

It was getting to be an established policy for Hayes to em-
ploy the army not merely to prevent violence, but to support
the railroad companies. On the request of governors and federal marshals in control of lines in receivership, he also sent
forces into Pennsylvania, Indiana, Illinois, and Missouri.[4]

Just as the trouble on the Baltimore & Ohio was coming to
a head in Maryland, rioting attained its most dramatic force
in Pittsburgh. Citizens of all classes there had been incensed
at the Pennsylvania Railroad Company because of its long-

and-short-haul discrimination against the city. This brought them into almost a unity of sympathy with the strikers. On July 19, when the rule about double-header freight trains went into effect, the railroaders took command of the switches, refusing to let any trains enter or depart. Mill hands, boys, thugs, and tramps joined in the fun. The Pittsburgh militia quite naturally fraternized with the trainmen, so the governor sent in six hundred troops from Philadelphia. Then the real trouble began. The armed force fired into a crowd trying to obstruct its progress, killing twenty men, women, and children on the spot and wounding twenty-nine more. The enraged mob, multiplying in numbers, then drove the militia into the roundhouse, tried to cannonade it, and set it on fire. When the treed refugees poured out they had to retreat from the city, peppered with shots from all sides. On the following day the triumphant victors indulged in arson, general destruction, and looting until they made away with about $5,000,000 of railroad property and exhausted themselves into quiescence in the process. There was little organization in the movement in Pittsburgh. But across the river in Allegheny city (later incorporated into Pittsburgh), Ammon, his Trainmen's Union having recovered from the debacle in June, maintained order and operated the passenger and mail trains, as they were not affected by the strike, for four days uninterrupted.[5]

The Pennsylvania system had further interference in many places, particularly at Altoona, Harrisburg, Reading, Scranton, and Philadelphia. At Scranton, more coal diggers participated than railroaders. A posse of "secret police," a term ordinarily used to designate Pinkertons, killed three of the miners. In Reading, federal troops did what the militia refused. On the Erie line, there were disturbances particularly at Buffalo and Hornellsville (or Hornell). The attorney general of New York reported one "rioter" killed on the spot and several fatally injured in a fracas near Buffalo, but the governor told the legislature that the militia had handled all the outbreaks "without bloodshed."

To the west, Toledo, Chicago, Louisville, St. Louis, and San Francisco were involved. At Chicago, police and the

mounted militia killed nineteen persons and injured more than
a hundred while dispersing crowds. Police, militia, and the
regular army soon quelled the workers and their hangers-on
everywhere. In this year for the first time, federal troops,
legally supplied, suppressed strikes, and in an apparently unconstitutional manner. More ominous in perspective was the
re-enactment of state malicious-conspiracy laws and the first
extensive use by the courts of blanket injunctions and imprisonment for their violation, to render labor activities futile.[6]

Just when courts first made criminal equity in labor cases
a usurper of the common and statute law, issuing injunctions
and imposing penalties fixed according to the whim of the
magistrates, thus combining in one man the functions of legislature, judge, and jury, is not altogether certain, but it was
long before the Debs case, carried to and settled in the United
States Supreme Court in 1895 (*In re* Debs, 158 U.S. 564).
There is mention of a vaguely similar judgment in the United
States as early as 1809.[7] In 1877 and following, the practice
was for a federal judge to publish notices to laborers and the
public in general without mentioning specific names (the
blanket injunction), ordering them not to interfere in the
operation of railroads in receivership, under penalty for contempt. Instructions went to the United States marshals to hire
enough deputies to protect the properties.[8]

As an outcome of the strike of the Brotherhood of Locomotive Engineers against the Boston and Maine Railroad in
February, 1877, a federal court in Maine convicted six of the
men of conspiring to obstruct the mails, and at least one person received sentence in Pennsylvania for a similar offense. In
two cases at Chicago and Indianapolis, in July and August
of the same year, federal Circuit Judge Thomas Drummond
gave twenty-three men who had violated his injunction
against interfering with the operation of railroads in receivership short jail sentences for contempt of court, though he
had no way of showing how they could disobey an order not
addressed to them. On the same July 31 that Drummond inflicted his first penalties, a colleague of his, District Judge
Samuel Hubbel Treat of the court in Springfield, Illinois,

handed down the first of several similar decisions of his own, none of them reported in *Federal Cases*. This one involved twenty-six shopmen, firemen, and engineers who in Urbana, Illinois, had obstructed traffic on what was later called the Peoria and Eastern Railroad. Each of the men drew ninety days' imprisonment for contempt. In the course of the next ten days Treat handled six more cases, resulting in the locking up of eleven more men on the same charge and for a like time. Not one of the sixty in this series of trials had been found guilty by a jury of any crime or misdemeanor. The contempt decisions brought punishment without due process of law.[9] Drummond's decisions became the precedent for later court action in a number of instances following 1880, and especially during and after the great railroad strikes of 1884–86.

Jay Gould was the principal target of irate laborers in the 1880s. He was in something like a frenzy of buying, breaking, selling, recovering, and throwing railroads into receiverships so as to have federal protection and assistance in efforts to banish the unions. By 1886, he had a network of 4115 miles of right of way, largely in Missouri, Texas, and Kansas, and he had the employees seething in resentment of his treatment of them.[10] The first protest came from the telegraphers, who wanted eight-hour shifts, a six-day week, and 15 per cent more pay. By 1882, the Knights of Labor had begun to relent in their opposition to strikes and in 1883 they encouraged the telegraphers to silence their keys, but then failed to support them. The widespread loathing of Gould caused the public and many newspapers to uphold the movement, but elicited no war chest. After failure, the men had to sign the ironclad oath (yellow-dog contract), and many were blacklisted.[11]

Next came the railroaders, especially on the Union Pacific and Gould's Southwestern System. The credit for victories in 1884 and 1885 belongs mainly to Joseph R. Buchanan, who had joined the Knights in 1882, rather than to the Noble Order as a whole, and not at all to Powderly. Buchanan's place would be secure even if he had not written a book about his work as an agitator. The first struggle came early in 1884 on the Denver & Rio Grande. Buchanan won this round, thus lending encouragement to the shopmen on the Union Pacific at Denver. On May 4, these men struck against reductions in pay, and Buchanan came to their assistance. A day later, every shop from the Missouri River to Ogden, including the side lines, was tied up for thirty-six hours, whereupon the company surrendered unconditionally. The success of this five days (in all) was due solely to good leadership and the zeal of the men, not to any financial assistance from the general executive board of the Knights of Labor, which never had a strike fund of over $7000. In both of these early tests of strength, Gould and his chief lieutenant H. M. Hoxie seem to have been playing a cat-and-mouse game, as though deliberately inviting trouble. Scarcely more than three months later, twenty Knights in the Denver shops, the center of the initial strike, got their "walking papers" and fifteen machinists at Ellis, Kansas, looked into 10-per-cent-lighter pay envelopes. The ensuing strike lasted only during August 13–18, whereupon the company gave in again, restoring the men's jobs and former pay and promising to negotiate future disputes. Once more, Buchanan, and not the national Order of Knights, had achieved the victory.[12]

Before the end of the year, trouble was brewing again on the Gould system. In October, the Missouri, Kansas & Texas (Katy) line ordered a 10 per cent cut in wages, and on February 26, 1885, the shopmen on the Wabash suffered a like reduction. On the twenty-seventh, the Moberly, Missouri, shopmen walked out and very soon the workers on the Katy and the Missouri Pacific joined the Wabash protest. Even the trainmen, many of whom were Knights, participated and brought the number of strikers up to 4500, but the brotherhoods refused to take any part. The Union Pacific members of the Order sent Buchanan to Kansas City with the offer of $30,000 to help in the movement. Such united action brought temporary victory in less than a month. But hardly were the Moberly shopmen back to their tools again when the company expelled several of them for no other ascertainable reason than that they were among the great number who had joined the Knights of Labor after the strike.

Gould was now ready to nip the flowering Order in the

bud, discharging all leaders whenever his underlings found them. On June 16, he locked out all employees except a few scabs at Moberly, in flagrant violation of the recent agreement. This made a strike on the Wabash inevitable if the Knights were to retain their old and new membership and continue to grow. On August 18, the movement began. After the general executive board, now forced to act in order to preserve its existence, failed to receive an audience with the receivers of the Wabash, it asked all Knights to stop handling any of that railroad's equipment on the Union Pacific and every branch of Gould's Southwestern System. What had begun as a lockout developed into a strike and concluded as a boycott. The tying up of twenty thousand miles of track was more than the financier could face at the time; so, declaring the enduring nature of his love for the laboring man, he gave in again. Powderly now showed his dubious skill as a negotiator. Meeting representatives of the Wabash and the Missouri Pacific on September 3, he accepted an agreement that the railroads would cease discriminations against the Knights and that all old employees would be reinstated before the employment of any new men. But Powderly also agreed that there would be no future strikes before conference with the employers. This was a peculiar leadership. All the managers had to do in order to tie the hands of the Order was to refuse a conference, as they had done before. Buchanan thought that Powderly was overawed at dealing with such prominent men. Furthermore, Powderly left the men who were striking again on the Denver & Rio Grande in the lurch. They lost their intermittent contest and Buchanan faced the threat "of being lynched by the better element in Denver."[13]

The Gould strikes of 1885 centered in Missouri, that of 1886 in Texas. Labor unrest was not altogether unknown in the latter state. In 1885, it ranked ninth among the states in the number of striking workers. In 1883, there had even been a strike of cowboys against five great land corporations for more wages, respectable food, and the rights of small landholders. Two years later the International Granite Cutters Union boycotted the Capitol Syndicate for using convict labor at sixty-five cents a day to quarry stone for the state capitol. The syndicate then imported eighty Scotsmen under contract to do the work, in blatant violation of the new Anti-Alien-Contract-Labor Act of February 2, 1885, that the Knights of Labor had almost singlehandedly pushed through Congress. Under prosecution backed by the granite cutters, the court fined the contractor $1000 on each of the eighty counts. Both the Knights and the new American Federation of Labor were incensed at Cleveland's commutation of the penalty. The Knights had established themselves in the state in 1882, and the membership naturally grew during the great inrush all over the country in 1884-85. Railroaders there had enough to complain about. Though the average wage of skilled and common labor on the lines in St. Louis was $2.00 a day, and the stated week's work was sixty hours, in Dallas it was $2.34 and the hours were the same.[14] The slight difference was hardly enough to compensate for the location.

These wages were only averages. Section hands and many other unskilled laborers in Texas worked seven days a week, getting $1.15 for a shift of eleven or twelve hours and nothing for overtime. This was a situation that the officers of District Assembly 101 of the Knights, who had supervision over the Order on the Southwestern System, deemed hardly fair. Both they and Gould were watching for a chance to bring on a showdown. In scorn of the promise of 1885 not to discriminate against Knights, petty officials of the companies made themselves pestiferous in many little ways. The Knights for ten months had been watching for an overt act that would give them the chance to force through the demand for a minimum wage of $1.50 a day and recognition of the Order. This opportunity came with the discharge of a shop foreman on the Texas and Pacific at Marshall, Texas. The strike began on that line on March 1, 1886. Five days later, the Knights on the Missouri Pacific and all of its subsidiaries joined in a sympathetic movement. Approximately nine thousand men on five thousand miles of railroad were involved. The railroad brotherhoods, as usual, remained aloof until the strikers used the threat of force to make the enginemen stop work. Martin Irons signed the Missouri Pacific strike order while in Moberly, but only when a stranger held a cocked pistol on him.

Irons, bound by the Knights' oath of secrecy, would not reveal the name of the bumptious individual, even if he knew the identity. There has been speculation as to whether the man might not have been an agent of Hoxie, using the device as an excuse to smash the order.[15]

Irons was an experienced leader, with a deep social conscience. He considered this a war against capitalism that he must fight to the finish. Revealed in his picture as a robust and handsome man by the hirsute standards of the day, he was also a powerful orator and a prolific writer. A newspaper called him "one of the finest mechanics that ever worked in the West." He was honest and earnest but inclined to be overbearing and harsh. Had he won the contest he would doubtless have become the great hero of labor. When he lost, there were no epithets too foul with which to pelt him. So, by 1906, Harry Thurston Peck probably thought he was leaning over backward to be fair when he said that Irons was "sly, ignorant, and half an animal. . . ."[16]

Soon after the trouble began, the governors of Missouri and Kansas asked Gould to negotiate, but he refused and later spurned arbitration until the men would come back to work. Meanwhile, the strikers were using effective methods to keep the trains from moving, such as setting fires at strategic places, loosening rails, and crippling locomotives. This latter consisted of putting out the fire, letting the water out of the boilers, and disconnecting parts that only an expert knew how to reassemble. Congress appointed a committee to investigate the affair and it came to the anticipated conclusion that, though the workers had real grievances, they should not have struck against a railroad in receivership. The general executive board of the Knights had money enough to spend about $50,000 for a headquarters building and to pay Powderly $5000 a year, but nothing with which to help the strikers. So, after two months of sabotage and some bloodshed growing out of attacks by strikebreakers, police, militia, and federal marshals and their deputies, the whole effort failed dismally on May 4. The Knights of Labor received a blow from which they never recovered, and the blacklisted members had to take employment elsewhere, if they could find it. Irons, with all his skill, could never get a job in a machine shop during the remaining fourteen years of his life and rarely could find employment of any kind. Harried and persecuted wherever he wandered, even when using an assumed name, he became so poor that he was once put on the rock pile as a vagrant, fastened to a ball and chain. At other times, as the rancor of the earlier years became dim, he seems to have made a little money from lectures whenever he could find a curious audience.[17]

After the locomotives started rolling again, Pinkerton men secured the arrest of forty-one men in the St. Louis area on various charges, including arson, but could procure no convictions. At Sedalia, Missouri, there were sixty-five indictments for "train wrecking" (probably locomotive crippling). On the Texas & Pacific there were some three hundred arrests for contempt of court, and a few other arrests elsewhere, but not many convictions.[18]

As in 1877, so again in 1884–86 the receivership expedient had its day in court. Judge Walter Q. Gresham had inspired Drummond's action, and he passed it on. As a consequence of the Wabash strikes, some participants had to enter the federal court of David J. Brewer and Samuel J. Treat in Missouri in March, 1885, and received sentences for contempt that were reversed on rehearing by another judge on jurisdictional grounds. Treat also added to his reputation in an unreported decision by sentencing nine strikers from the shops at Springfield, Illinois. Some of the Knights on the Denver & Rio Grande got the same treatment.[19] Then a group of the brothers brought impeachment charges against three judges, including Brewer and one of the Treats, because of their contempt decisions, and got exactly nowhere;[20] Brewer received appointment to the Supreme Court in 1889. The Southwestern strike resulted in the sentencing of ten in one of the nation's courts in Texas, and there were some unreported decisions elsewhere.[21] The sentences were usually for three and six months, again as in the later Debs case.

The failure of the Southwestern strike came just after the beginning of the May Day strikes for the eight-hour day and on the exact date of the Haymarket bomb. But before considering these startling events, another impressive revolt of railroaders deserves consideration. This one, on the Burlington system, was the longest and one of the most doggedly fought of them all. It started on February 27, 1888, and did not end until January 8, 1889. Still more remarkable is the fact that the brotherhoods of locomotive engineers and firemen waged this one. Peter M. Arthur of the engineers took pride in his organization as the strongest and most respected of the trade unions of America, but the basis of such a reputation would naturally be the ability to protect the members and improve their conditions, and they had grievances that no efforts at collective bargaining had ameliorated. There had been no strikes of the brotherhoods except for a few wildcat affairs in 1876 and 1877, which came only after wage reductions and efforts, such as that of Gowen on the Reading line, to break up the union. Arthur had opposed these early attempts, and now in 1888 he tried to talk the engineers out of their determination. In spite of his continued supercilious attitude toward the firemen, Frank P. Sargent, their chief, used the same sort of language to his men. Yet, both leaders insisted they would back the movement if they could not avert it. Eugene V. Debs, secretary of the Brotherhood of Locomotive Firemen, was one official who would not follow in the obsequiousness of Sargent. The conductors and brakemen remained aloof through all the dismal struggle, but the switchmen participated.[22]

The principal demands made on the Burlington company by the enginemen were the abolition of wages paid by the trip classification system and the substitution for it of a wage scale geared according to the standard of three and a half cents a mile on all passenger trains. The practice was to pay by the trip, the result being that the men got nothing for overtime caused by delays over which they had no control and for which they were not responsible. Furthermore, under the classification system it was too easy for the company to hold down costs by delayed promotions. The Burlington's reply was that it would pay the same as competing roads and no more. The president of the system, who received the demands, was Charles E. Perkins, a social Darwinist who opposed all railroad regulation and arbitration. His company alone should decide on wages and working conditions. If the poor and ignorant chose to propagate their kind, they should accept the penalties that accompanied the act. His chief associate was George W. Holdredge, who believed that a striker was disloyal to the company. The laborer was guilty of thinking of his own welfare instead of that of his benefactor, a thing that sound men should abhor. Harry B. Stone, the general manager, had an aloofness and unbending spirit that made him unfit to deal with strikers. There had been a severe rate war going on, in which the Burlington had taken a leading part, and these officers were determined to keep all operating expenses down to a minimum, except perhaps their own salaries, so as to protect the dividends of the holders of watered stock.[23]

The strike, called after adamant refusal of the Burlington company to negotiate, quickly spread through the whole system, including lines it controlled. Arthur resisted efforts to let it spread to independent railroads, but nevertheless some lines struck in sympathy. Efforts at a boycott received no strong support, for fear of the new criminal-conspiracy laws, particularly severe in Illinois, where statutes also gave heavy support to blacklisting. Within a few days the lack of labor solidarity brought its penalty. Hostility between the brotherhoods and the Knights of Labor had encouraged the former to act as scabs against the Knights, thus breaking a strike on the Reading two months earlier. Now, the Knights retaliated by filling the cabs on the Burlington locomotives, and by March 15 Perkins had all the enginemen he needed. Thereafter, the strike was over as far as realities were concerned, but the brotherhoods held out until January 3 of the following year, and the order to go back to work did not come until five days later. The unions might just as well not have issued it at all, for Perkins was not rehiring men who had not remained at their throttles and shovels. Stone had said that "if only one class of men can run this line, they will be scabs." When the capitulation came, Perkins had promised that there would be no blacklisting. Then his actions fulfilled Stone's threat. Perkins had taken back seventy men while the contest was on, as a bait to the rest, but he allowed no more than six to return afterward. Most of them had to hunt jobs elsewhere, but their reputation for efficiency was so great that they were in demand. The brotherhoods themselves took care of a few who were too old for re-employment.[24]

The sympathetic historian of the strike, leaning backward to be unbiased, has condoned the parts played by Perkins and his lieutenants by saying that "it is fairer to judge men's acts and ideas by the standards of their own time than by the standards of some later time when some of the underlying assumptions, which determine whether prevailing opinion considers a course right or wrong, have changed."[25] This is a sage proposition. But, from this, one can draw the corollary that a band of thieves and cutthroats should be judged by the code of ethics of their society. To continue the analogy further, there is also the scholium that in any day society has several standards and that in 1888 far higher principles had warm support than those that Perkins practiced. He was not the only railroad magnate who had expressed warm sympathy for the laborer; Gould had been far more effusive.

In the strike, as could be expected, the Burlington company employed Pinkertons, and there was violence, including the dynamiting of some bridge approaches, but there was no serious damage. Such activity resulted in few convictions, though one man in Illinois drew a sentence of two years. In 1884–85, boycotts had been a frequent resort after failing strikes, but they were used more by the Knights of Labor than by the trade unions, and until the Wabash strikes they had been quite rare on railroads.[26] Powderly declared in 1883 that an injunction prohibited glass blowers in Kent, Ohio, from persuading immigrants to break the contracts under which their employer had imported them.[27] Then, before 1890, there were frequent injunctions against boycotts affecting transportation systems.[28] This happened frequently during the Burlington strike when enginemen and switchmen on connecting lines refused to move Burlington rolling stock. The competing lines at first agreed to the boycott, fearing

sympathetic strikes and continued loss of Burlington transfers
if they refused. But injunctions and threats of others broke
up the effort. In March, 1886, suits began in the federal
courts at Omaha and Chicago. The Omaha judge enjoined
the Union Pacific engineers against laying off when there
were Burlington cars in the train, but the men "continued to
suffer from the colic," and there was nothing the magistrate
could do about it. Nevertheless, a continuing series of injunctions finally ended a boycott on the Santa Fe. But there
was no injunction against the Burlington blacklist, and it was
many years before the brotherhoods could organize on that
system again.[29]

During the depression years after 1883, the few trade unions that had survived the bitter late seventies continued to
exist and many new ones arose. In 1878, there were probably
no more than 50,000 organized in all the crafts, though seven
years earlier the now nearly defunct Knights of St. Crispin
(shoemakers) alone had boasted that number. By 1883, the
combined membership in all the trades was over 200,000
and in 1885 it was 300,000. The leadership in the movement
to federate the trade unions fell to Samuel Gompers, Adolph
Strasser, Peter J. McGuire, and lesser aides. At the same time
that Douai left the Socialist Labor party to attempt industrial
unionism, Strasser and McGuire split off in the other direction, Strasser into straight unionism, where McGuire joined
him after a sojourn with the Knights of Labor. Strasser had
become president of the International Cigar Makers' Union
in 1877, while the strike against the tenement-house system
was on, and Gompers was head of the strongest local, that at
the focal point of the struggle in New York. After the dismal
failure of this effort, the two leaders decided to adopt the
British plan of combination, of which Gompers had become
conscious before emigrating to America in 1863, at the age
of thirteen. This system featured centralized authority, high
dues, a comprehensive benefit system, and "equalization of
funds," so that the stronger locals had to come to the aid of
the weaker. Other trades soon discovered the advantages of
this plan and adopted it with variations to suit their needs.
McGuire organized the carpenters in 1881, and in the same

year, at Terre Haute, Indiana, and Pittsburgh, helped Gompers and Strasser in forming the Federation of Organized Trades and Labor Unions of the United States and Canada, which at Columbus in 1886 was transformed into the American Federation of Labor. Dissensions over political action, and the efforts of the Knights of Labor to bring the skilled trades into their ranks, made this action seem necessary.[30]

The old federation was falling apart before the Columbus convention. The reorganized body was not simply a society for the influencing of legislation, as was the old one. Membership was not open to individuals, but to national unions and such locals that, by the restricted geographical nature of their work, could not achieve a wider scope, each member body to have a vote in the conventions according to its numerical strength. The central office scanned legislation to see that labor got a fair deal, took care of organization in previously nonunionized trades, strove for unification within the national and international unions, had the deciding voice regarding boycotts, and collected funds for use in boycotts and strikes. Dues were $1 from each $200 of the individual's wages. Hostility to the Knights continued; and down to 1889, after which the Noble Order ceased to be of importance, all efforts at coalition went overboard. In 1881, John Jarrett of the Amalgamated Iron and Steel Workers became the first president of the original federation. Samuel L. Leffingwell of the Indianapolis Trades Assembly succeeded him in 1882, and Gompers took over in 1883, to remain in charge until his death in 1924, except for 1894–95 when the socialists temporarily gained ascendancy and put John McBride in control.[31] Gompers was a firm advocate of the eight-hour day as a means of assuring steady work for all. He said in 1887 "that so long as there is one man who seeks employment and cannot obtain it, the hours of labor are too long."

The federation consistently refrained from direct political action, but followed a policy of rewarding friends and punishing enemies in the major parties. It sought improvement for labor within the capitalistic structure, and was willing to have employers pass the increased labor costs on to the consumers, of which the workers themselves were a considerable part. Looking out only for the aristocracy of labor, with a few unavoidable exceptions such as the brewers and coal miners, the A. F. of L. realized that improved wages for its members would come largely from higher costs borne by the mass of unskilled workers that it spurned. The unions rigidly excluded Negroes, regardless of their skill.

By 1886, employers' associations had grown strong and active. The idea was sound in principle, granting that the employer-employee relationship was inevitable and eternal. One committee from the combined management and one from the national union could thus negotiate, settle their differences, and maintain stability within the industry or trade. But this ideal did not arrive during the century. Instead, by lockouts, blacklisting, and "union smashing" in general, the associations set themselves to dominate the labor situation absolutely. The Knights of Labor had ample experience with this stone wall of opposition, and now the A. F. of L. had to confront it.

Before the reorganization, the old federation had fixed May 1, 1886, as the date for a general eight-hour-day strike. In this movement, with the cooperation of some of the Knights, 340,000 men participated. (Of these, 150,000 got reduced hours simply on threat of strikes, while 190,000 walked out, 42,000 of them successfully. But within a month the employers canceled the gains for a third of the nearly 200,000 celebrators of victory, and the number grew. There would have to be a later repetition of this eight-hour movement.[32]) A memorable three days ensued, during which the failure of the Southwestern strike and the explosion of the Haymarket bomb spread gloom through the ranks of the workingmen. A noted labor editor called the latter "a godsend to the enemies of the labor movement."[33]

In conjunction with the arrival in America in December, 1882, of the German-born anarchist John Joseph Most, the Socialist Labor party had begun splitting into factions. One of them formed a branch of the International Working People's Association, or the Black International for short, in Pittsburgh in October of 1883, under the leadership of August V. T. Spies and Albert R. Parsons of Chicago. But Most, then thirty-seven years of age, soon gained control and in the Pittsburgh Manifesto urged force to secure the anarchist utopia.[34] Anarchists in general are starry-eyed idealists, believing in the perfectibility of man by withdrawing the restraints of the state and substituting associations and agreements in place of coercion.[35] In the absence of a fair trial of the system, it is unfair to assert dogmatically that they are wrong. But some of the revolutionists of the 1880s believed in "propaganda by deed," which could mean the use of dynamite.

In Chicago, in 1886, there were two leading anarchist papers, the *Arbeiter Zeitung* edited by Spies and *The Alarm* conducted by Parsons. A letter in *The Alarm* on February 21, 1885, advised the planting of a bomb made of dynamite, cap, and fuse in a piece of one-inch iron pipe "in the immediate neighborhood of a lot of rich loafers," promising a gratifying result.[36] Even though there was no "clear and immediate danger" involved, such a doctrine caused enough panic among enough Chicagoans that they were prepared to hang all anarchists. They had not been excited a year earlier when Thomas A. Scott of the Pennsylvania Railroad recommended a "rifle diet" for all men on strike, or when Theodore Roosevelt in 1886 wanted to lead his Dakota roughriders of earlier acquaintance in a battle to shoot down the strikers in Chicago.[37] But Scott and Roosevelt were not anarchists, and this apparently made all the difference in the world.

Parsons was of Mayflower descent, but not of the first order, for his ancestor had arrived on the second trip to Plymouth. He was a highly esteemed labor leader and had had years of experience in the Socialist Labor party and the Knights of Labor.[38] It was as an advocate of the eight-hour day that he was best known, and on this subject he had addressed the Knights, trade unions, and socialist groups.[39] Spies was German-born and the leading intellectual of the Chicago anarchists. He entered the Socialist Labor party as soon as it was organized, and also belonged to the *Lehr und Wehr Verein,* a workers' militia to oppose the brutal aggressiveness of the Chicago police. He had helped draw up the Pittsburgh Manifesto and was a prominent worker for the eight-hour day.[40] George Engel, also from Germany, came to Chicago in 1873 and at once became engaged in socialistic activities. Finding the *Arbeiter Zeitung* too tame for him, he and Adolph Fischer founded *The Anarchist*, of slight circulation but rivaling in violence Most's own *Die Freiheit* in the East.[41] Fischer, likewise German, had been in Chicago only three years, but he had been a socialist from youth.[42] Michael Schwab, again from Germany, was the most advanced doctrinally of them all. He had been on the editorial staff of the *Arbeiter Zeitung* for four years. Samuel Fielden was a hard-working teamster who had come from England in 1868. He had drifted into the revolutionary movement because of the asperities of his struggle for existence. Oscar Neebe, American-born, had limited intellectual capacities and knew little about doctrinal points. For eleven years he had been a union organizer but was barely connected with the anarchist agitation, except as a friend of some of the others. Louis Lingg, fifth of the Germans in the group, had been in America only a year and was in his early twenties. He was the most uncompromising of all in his views and knew a great deal about making bombs.[43]

It was not the eight-hour strike or any other great one that gave the Chicago anarchists a chance to hold a mass meeting to protest against police brutality. The McCormick Harvester works had been laying off men for union activities, in violation of a promise made in 1885, and the men were demanding a settlement. The company's response was to lock them out on February 16, 1886, and to bring in Pinkertons and the Chicago police to protect the scabs operating the plant. On May 3, Spies was addressing the pickets outside the plant just as the strikebreakers were leaving it. In the fracas between the two forces, the police fired their revolvers, killing one of the strikers on the spot and mortally wounding four or five others. Spies then rushed to the *Arbeiter Zeitung* office and issued a call for a meeting to be held at Haymarket Square at 7 P.M. on the following day, May 4.

A crowd estimated at three thousand assembled there and listened to temperate speeches by Spies and Parsons, denouncing the police for acting as a private army for the em-

ployers and for the savage tactics employed. When Fielden
started the third speech, a rain set in and most of the listeners
departed. Mayor Carter H. Harrison was in attendance and
he also left, stopping at the Desplaines Street police station
and telling Captain John Bonfield not to interfere, for the
assemblage was peaceful and law-abiding. But Bonfield
knew who his real bosses were and marched at the head of
280 policemen to disperse the bedraggled remnant of about
200 earnest listeners. Fielden and Parsons protested against
the interference, and somebody threw a bomb at the front
ranks of the squadron, flattening sixty of them, seven fatally,
and injuring others. The police then shot and clubbed several
spectators.[44]

The murderer could have been a relative or friend of one
of the slain pickets of the previous day. It might have been a
laborer clubbed silly by the police in some earlier raid on
union men. Nobody ever made public the identity. Certainly
it was none of the thirty-one anarchists and sympathizers
who were indicted. The officials were interested only in hanging anarchists, not in finding the killer. Only the eight already named came to trial, where not a shred of evidence
against any of them appeared. As Professor Ware has observed: "It was a case of Society against Anarchy with revenge as the motive."[45]

It was certain that none of the eight had thrown the bomb,
so the charge against them was that of accessories before the
fact in the murder of policeman Mathias J. Degan. In a
farcical trial during a period of frantic excitement when mobs
gathered around the courthouse demanding Mosaic reprisal,
and Judge Joseph E. Gary sided with the prosecution, all
that was needed was to show that the murderer could have
been influenced by the doctrine of violence. As far as the
evidence showed, he might have got such an idea from reading the public utterances of Scott or Roosevelt. All but Neebe
received sentences of death by hanging. He, being only the
messenger boy of the group, got off with fifteen years in the
state penitentiary. Gary refused a new trial and set the date
of the mass hangings for December 3, 1886. But there was a
stay of execution for appeal in the supreme court of the

state, which refused a writ of error. The United States Supreme Court then upheld the legality of the procedure under Gary. Governor Richard J. Oglesby offered clemency to Parsons, who refused it because of the exclusion of his comrades. On November 10, 1887, Oglesby commuted the sentence of Fielden and Schwab to life imprisonment, but on the next day, another Black Friday, Parsons, Spies, Fischer, and Engel danced on air. Just before the event Lingg either committed suicide in his cell by chewing a dynamite cap, as the police said, or else was murdered by them. The whole truth never came out. There were more fragments of explosives in the cell than any conscientious jailer would have left on the person of a condemned man. How did they get there? The most charitable guess is gross carelessness.[46]

On June 26, 1893, Governor John P. Altgeld pardoned Fielden, Schwab, and Neebe with a scathing message denouncing the miscarriage of justice seven years earlier. It was perhaps the least of the defamation piled on the head of the governor for this humanitarian act when Harry Thurston Peck explained the action by saying that Altgeld was "moved partly by the appeals of sentimentalists, and partly by his own instinctive sympathy with lawlessness. . . ."[47]

Not only did the Knights of Labor turn their backs on their brother Parsons, but the Illinois Federation of Labor refused to support George A. Schillings'[48] attack, placing the blame on the Chicago police, and would not demand a new trial. It was not until 1889 that they softened enough to ask the governor for clemency for the imprisoned men. Gompers of the parent body was a little more lenient. Before the executions in 1887 he asked for mercy.[49] On the other hand, the long speeches made at the trial by Parsons, Schwab, Engel, and Fielden—Parsons alone talked for eight hours—defending their revolutionary activities, did nothing to advance the cause of labor. They repeatedly used the words socialist, communist, and anarchist as though they were exact synonyms.[50] A European couple touring America at the time, in the interest of the Socialist Labor party, considered this confusion of terms a hindrance to the working-class movement.[51] The party walked circumspectly for a time after the Haymarket affair, well aware of the common practice of assuming guilt by association, but in 1887 its convention took a stand against the "judicial murder" of the anarchists. It did not lose further members, but rather gained as the Black International broke up and many anarchists, from the most philosophical to the extremists, drifted back into the fold.[52]

The Order of the Knights of Labor was already on the wane, and a great idea too timidly applied was perishing with it. The Haymarket tragedy could do little to speed the descent. The American Federation of Labor grew rapidly as skilled laborers found no other haven of refuge, but it was quiescent for a time, while recovering from the blighting effect of the bomb on the gains made in the eight-hour movement. Revival of activity came when the convention of 1888 planned a new offensive for this objective, to begin on May 1, 1890. The planners intended to open with demands by the strong Carpenters' and Joiners' Brotherhood, follow with the coal miners, and roll along with the rest. The carpenters' effort started on time and McGuire reported complete success in 137 cities and a nine-hour day in many others. But the miners' project failed because of fractional organization, and the project subsided. The high point of achievement, as the era drew to a close, was the success of the Amalgamated Association of Iron and Steel Workers, at the time of its greatest power in 1889, in forcing the Carnegie Steel companies to accept the union's terms simply by threat of a strike.[53] Andrew Carnegie and Henry Clay Frick were not yet prepared for the banishment of unions, which came with the Homestead strike of 1892. In 1890, skilled labor was settling down with a fair degree of unity and clear plans for the future. But the railroad brotherhoods continued to remain aloof, and common workers had no leadership and no welcome from their less unfortunate brothers. Some of the hottest contests were still to come, and the stolid burghers, the hardheaded middle class, were as yet not certain that there was not something criminal in the presumption of workers in thinking that they should have a voice in their own most vital affairs.

Chapter XIV

INVENTION AND INDUSTRY

WHILE the farmers fed the nation and the army of industrial labor took care of the trade, transportation, and industry that supplied the rest of the material wants, another group of workers invented devices and processes that were to add greatly to living comfort and sometimes to anguish. An index of this activity is the increase in new patents: from nearly 86,000 in the 1860s to more than 138,000 in the 1870s and about 218,000 in the 1880s.[1]

In 1877, Thomas A. Edison made his first workable phonograph, which he patented in the following year. Before 1900, he and others, including Alexander Graham Bell and associates, evolved about 250 improvements, including the method of duplicating records.[2] Early in 1880, Edison also patented his incandescent light, which he regarded as his greatest achievement. Following Edison's first exhibition on October 21, 1879, the Pennsylvania Railroad ran special trains for several days to carry curious visitors.[3] In 1892, after a long contest with two inventors who had produced a similar light a year earlier but patented it a year later than Edison, a federal court decided in his favor.[4] In 1878 and 1879 Charles F. Brush received patents for improved arc lights, and Edward Weston did likewise in 1883.[5]

In the ensuing decade, there was a rapid growth in the use of these new means of illumination. The first incandescent lighting system started to function in Appleton, Wisconsin, on August 20, 1882. The Pearl Street station in New York began operation two weeks later, being the first to supply such service on "an extended scale." Within the next two years such lights were widely adopted. The first central arc-lighting system appeared in San Francisco in 1879.[6] Increasing demand for current made improvements in dynamos necessary. In 1883, Edison patented a three-wire system, using two generators for strengthening the current. Nikola Tesla, an Austro-Hungarian living in New York, developed the first split-phase induction motor and in 1888 received six patents for polyphase, multiphase, and rotating currents.[7] The alternating current was in use by 1885, and in 1890 there were over 3300 lights in the state of New York using this form.[8]

With improved dynamos, it was possible to develop electric streetcars. In 1881, Edison had a model electric freight train at his home in New Jersey. In 1885, the first electric car line began operating in Baltimore, and in 1888 Frank J. Sprague completed a successful twelve-mile system in Richmond, Virginia. By 1890 there were over 1200 miles of such lines in the United States, in the control of 144 companies.[9] Among the multitude of other developments, in 1886 Elihu Thomson patented the first electric welding device.[10] By 1890, in New York alone, five medical schools were giving courses in electrotherapeutics and surgery, fifty-one hospitals had reported requests for such treatment, and some sixty physicians had reported its use on sixteen thousand or more patients.[11] Also, the day of electric-belt quackery was at hand. If, by 1888, babies could be ushered into the world by electric light, it may be noted that in the same year the hapless though guilty victims of barbarism found a new exit from the world when New York substituted electrocution for hanging.[12]

In the related field of magnetism, soon after the patenting of the telephone by Bell in 1876, it began to receive favorable publicity, and adoption followed as rapidly as the Bell Telephone Company could manufacture the apparatus. The Western Union company organized a subsidiary to compete with Bell, employing as managers Elisha Gray and Amos E. Dolbear, each of whom claimed prior invention of the telephone. By 1890, over six hundred lawsuits had sprung up over the new means of communication and the improvements that evolved. By 1884, there were wires between New York and Boston. Some cables were put underground in 1881. An important innovation helping make the telephone a commercial success was Charles E. Scribner's multiple switch-

49. Artist's Conception of the Haymarket Bombing

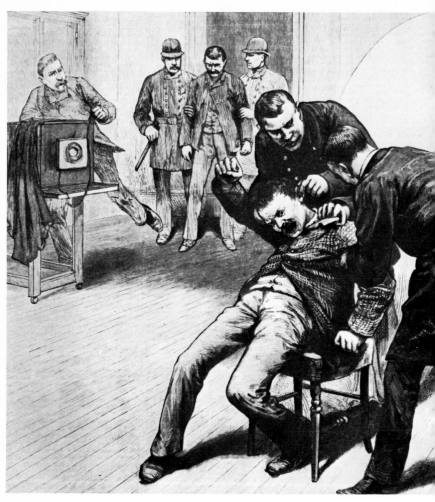

50. The Anarchist Trials: Chicago's New Rogue's Gallery System for Identification of Criminals

ADVOCATES OF VIOLENCE IN LABOR DISPUTES

51. Theodore Roosevelt

52. Thomas A. Scott

53. The Less Fortunate: Execution of the Men Convicted
in the Haymarket Bombing

54. The Chicago Anarchist-Labor Troubles: The Week Following May 3, 1886

THE CONDEMNED CHICAGO ANARCHISTS

55. Samuel Fielden

56. Michael Schwab

57. August Spies

58. Adolph Fischer

THE CONDEMNED CHICAGO ANARCHISTS

59. George Engel

60. Oscar Neebe

61. Louis Lingg

62. Albert R. Parsons

THEIR EXECUTIONERS

63. Judge Joseph E. Gary

64. John Bonfield

board.[13] But it was Theodore N. Vail, entering the Bell company in 1878, who made it prosperous. In less than a year the stock was selling at $800 a share instead of $50. Bell and his original associates, including Thomas Watson, then sold out and no longer had to give stage performances with their invention to supplement their income. Vail absorbed the Western Electric Manufacturing Company for the manufacturing of equipment that later could be charged to the parent organization at enormous prices so as to justify appeals to the state public-utilities commissions for higher service rates. In 1885, he set up the American Telephone and Telegraph Company, thus completing the system. For a long time there were certain drawbacks to rapid expansion, including rates of twenty dollars a month, cursing operator boys, and static from grounded wires.[14]

Advances came also in printing. In 1884, Ottmar Mergenthaler of Baltimore completed the linotype for which he received a patent in the following year. Tolbert Lanston sold his rights in a monotype in 1887, but it was not made practical for another ten years. Presses had developed to the point where in 1880 one in St. Louis could print, fold, and stack 30,000 newspapers in an hour. Within the next few years further improvements enabled printers to make 100,000 impressions in an hour and in as many as twelve colors.[15] But the setting of type and the operation of flat presses by hand kept the editor-compositor and printer's devil occupied in small towns for decades longer.

Perhaps few country editors had much use for the cash register, developed in 1879 and the following years, but many people in offices and in homes could enjoy other inventions of the 1880s. Improvements in the typewriter added to its convenience. In 1884, Lewis E. Waterman produced the fountain pen and William S. Burroughs contributed the adding machine. From 1886 on, the users of such equipment could cool off on summer days with the electric fan, and in time they would find recreation in watching motion pictures, an early step toward which was Hannibal Goodwin's transparent celluloid film for cameras, which appeared in 1885 as an improvement over George Eastman's flexible roll film of

1884. This supplanted the dry plate of 1881 as it had put out of date the wet plate made famous by Mathew Brady and others, which itself had outmoded the tintype, daguerreotype, and pinhole camera. In 1888, Eastman put the first celluloid-film camera on the market.[16] Late in the following year, Edison gave the first demonstration of his kinetoscope or peep-show box, and the motion-picture industry was born, though it needed an incubator for some time to come.

A means of recreation, developing into a craze, came with the introduction of bicycles. In foreign countries, this means of locomotion had been evolving for a century, but the high-wheeled apparatus shown at the Centennial Exposition of 1876 attracted the eye as a distinct improvement over the machines previously imported. In 1878, Albert A. Pope established the first factory for their manufacture in America, at Hartford, Connecticut. For some years the high-wheeled monsters, which required a horse block to mount and had a distressing habit of pitching the rider forward onto his pate, prevailed. Then came the "safety" in 1887, much like the later standard bicycle. The pneumatic tire followed in 1890. The bicycle also contributed precision tools for the later automobile makers.[17] A harbinger of the coming motorcar age was the application of George B. Selden of Rochester, New York, in 1879, for a patent on a gasoline engine for horseless carriages. He did not receive it until 1895, by which time such engines were already in use. What few cars were built in America before 1890 seem to have used steam propulsion, in the tradition of Nicholas Joseph Cugnot and Oliver Evans. Ransom E. Olds of Detroit built one such tricycle in 1887, and S. H. Roper constructed a car in Massachusetts in 1889.[18]

The business of manufacturing such products as these, and of commodities in general, was in a low state of health in 1877, and conditions got worse before there were perceptible signs of recovery in 1879.[19] Business failures declined from 1 in each 64 concerns in 1878 to 1 in 105 the following year, while the liabilities fell from $234,000,000 to $98,000,000.[20] Thereafter, things improved until the depression of 1883–85, which struck the hardest blows at the iron and textile indus-

tries. The building of more than forty thousand miles of railroads in the preceding four years had begun with rails at $70
a ton and, in that premonopoly era in the industry, ended
with the price of $33.[21] The 10,299 business failures in 1883
had been exceeded only in 1878, but the liabilities were
smaller, nearly four-fifths of them being for no more than
$10,000.[22] Five of the largest textile manufacturers declared
that the situation in 1885 was the worst they could remember.[23] Cotton goods revived in the next five years, but the
woolens interests had many bankruptcies as late as 1889.
The labor unrest, a brief stock-exchange panic in December,
1886, and drouth in the grain belts were not enough to prevent a slow but steady improvement in that year, and the
decade closed with much better but not altogether satisfactory conditions. In 1890, the stock market was shaky, and the
failure of the house of Baring in London in the same year cut
off a flow of capital and caused the dumping of many American securities on the United States market.[24]

The index of manufacturing production, with 1899 as the
base year of 100, follows with considerable fidelity the swing
of the business cycle. Starting at 30 in 1877, there is an annual rise varying from two to six points until 1882, only one
in 1883, a decline of three for 1884-85, then a jump of ten
in 1886 with the index at 57, and finally a consistent growth
to 71 in 1890.[25] Capital investment is a more elusive trail to
follow. A labored analysis of such data as are usable seems to
show that the amount of capital mounted 120.78 per cent
from 1879 to 1889 while the increase in value of products was
69.31 per cent. One study, however, gives the latter item as
74.5 per cent.[26] A careful scholar has noted that, from the
outbreak of the Civil War to 1905, in each five years on the
average the growth of value of manufactured goods equaled
the total industrial production in 1860.[27]

In these years, many new products were becoming prominent among exports; high on the list were canned sea foods.
In 1878, canned meats valued at over $5,000,000 went
abroad from Chicago and St. Louis, this being higher than
the figure for fresh beef, while the increase for all such provisions over 1877 was nearly $20,000,000. Cheese, butter,

lard, and cured meats were making gains. Manufactures of iron and steel were already well established, and in 1879 the estimates of exports of locomotives, steam engines, iron bridges and buildings, railroad materials, agricultural and other implements, and hardware came to $15,000,000, not including numerous minor classifications ranging in value from $200,000 to $800,000 each. In 1875, the $92,679,000 for manufactures was 16.57 per cent of all exports, but twenty years later the $183,596,000 was 23 per cent. The recovery of the Asiatic market, lost during the Civil War, added to the growth of foreign trade in cotton goods, but also Americans were invading England with finer grades once the monopoly of that country. Besides the coarser sorts of drygoods, China was demanding glassware, firearms, clocks, chemicals, lamps, petroleum, clothing, prepared tobacco, and flour. American producers were beating a path to the door of the buyer, from London and St. Petersburg to Rio de Janeiro.[28]

Only generalizations, subject to much restriction, can be made about the profits of manufacturing enterprises. In 1890, the Massachusetts Bureau of Labor Statistics made a report on 23,000 establishments that netted under 5 per cent, with no consideration of hidden gains, such as padded payrolls and excessive managerial salaries and administrative costs, that make the data of little value. On the other hand, the annual average dividends of thirty-four mills at Fall River were almost 8 per cent. In 1881, one California woolen mill paid 30 per cent and another 18,[29] but such scattered examples have little value, and no accurate summary of the entire situation seems possible.

As to the shifting geography of manufactures, a glance at the percentages of capital and value of output reveals that the Central states were gaining on the East.[30] The leaders in production in 1890 were, in order, New York, Pennsylvania, Illinois, Massachusetts, Ohio, New Jersey, Missouri, Michigan, Wisconsin, Connecticut, Indiana, and California.[31] Inasmuch as seven-eighths of the output was in a belt from Pennsylvania northward to Massachusetts and westward to Missouri, while the South had a lower percentage rating in 1900 than forty years earlier, a summary of Southern development is in order to show that something was really happening there.

The new industrialization, beginning about 1880, depended little on prewar experience. Much more important was the interest of Northern capitalists such as "Pig Iron" Kelley of Pennsylvania and Edward Atkinson of Boston, a former abolitionist, in exploiting cheap and unorganized workers in a period of returning prosperity and labor unrest. But influential newspaper editors and the country press as well also did their part in encouraging investment. As a consequence of the new development, the number of active spindles in Southern textile mills jumped from 542,000 in 1880 to 1,554,000 in 1890, two-thirds of them in Georgia and the Carolinas, but with considerable numbers in Tennessee, Virginia, and Alabama. But, in the latter year, this was hardly an eighth of the total for the whole country. The fact that, in 1875, Southern mills consumed only 1 bale of cotton to 8.0 in the North, whereas in 1890 the ratio was reduced to 1 to 2.3, is explained by the fact that the newer industry still confined itself largely to the heavier and coarser fabrics. In the decade, the total of all Southern textiles manufactured annually increased from a little over $20,000,000 to nearly $50,000,000.[32]

Richmond, Virginia, had been an iron-manufacturing center from early days, but in 1871 Birmingham began to grow up at a railroad crossing in a cotton field, and soon became an important contender in the iron trade. Chattanooga, already a producer, shared in the prosperity. Alabama rose from seventh among the contenders for pre-eminence in the mining of iron ore in 1880 to second in 1889, being surpassed only by Michigan. In the same years it grew from fifteenth to fourth in the output of iron and its products, as nine Southern states increased their annual production from 615,000 tons to 2,297,-000 tons. Birmingham puddling iron sold at the furnace at $13 a ton and, with water transportation, sold at Philadelphia for $16, which was below the cost of production in Pennsylvania or Ohio. The high phosphorus content of the ore made it unsuitable for Bessemer steel. After the Thomas basic modification of the Siemens-Martin open-hearth furnace in 1878, this ore proved unexcelled for the making of steel, but the adoption of this method was slow in coming and the South did not make much steel before 1890. Coal mining multiplied along with the smelting industry, showing phenomenal development in West Virginia and Alabama, while Maryland, Kentucky, and Tennessee maintained high rank.[33]

Lumber rose to importance in the same decade. Though the South sawed less than 10 per cent of the national total in 1869 and just a little above that in 1879, it reached over 25 per cent in 1889, 40 per cent in 1899, and 53 per cent in 1909 and 1919—after which it slipped back to 45 per cent by 1946, although it stayed ahead of the Pacific states except in 1939.[34] Except for a budding furniture industry in the Appalachian towns, later to extend widely, the section did not advance far in the manufacture of finished wooden products.[35]

Tobacco was the basis of a final industry of much promise. The center of the bright-tobacco culture shifted from Virginia to North Carolina, and with it the marketing and processing. Durham, Winston, and Salem became prominent as a consequence. Richard Joshua Reynolds started a factory in Winston in 1875, and in 1873 Washington Duke moved his little shop to Durham, where his sons began making cigarettes in 1881. The cigarette machine, appearing in 1879 and improved in the following decade, added to the expansion of the industry. Duke produced sixty million in one month in 1887, but as yet New York held the supremacy by a wide margin, and Richmond was more important than Durham before 1890, when after a big cigarette war James Buchanan Duke merged with four other concerns to incorporate the American Tobacco Company with a capital of $25,000,000.[36]

At the base of nearly all manufacturing was iron, and its production required coal, which also was still the source of nearly all the energy for machinery. The development of hydroelectric power came almost wholly after 1890, and, though there were various good turbines in use, they were mainly in the old, established regions such as the mill towns of New England.[37] The output of coal rose more than 85 per cent in the 1880s, exceeding 141,000,000 tons, and this amount nearly doubled in the next decade. Anthracite, de-

clining in smelting and other industrial uses, showed only a
moderate growth. Two-thirds of the bituminous product came
from the Appalachian fields. Some mines had a few pumps
and locomotives run by steam or compressed air, but all the
digging and loading was done by hand, while diminutive
bank mules hauled the cars along the entries.[38] Mining was
a life of danger and drudgery.

By 1880, coke was coming into prominence in the smelting
of iron, and the number of ovens tripled during the ensuing
decade. They were nearly all of the beehive variety, wasting
the volatile elements that themselves could have been valuable to industry. The rest were of still cruder design. Retort
ovens appeared after 1890. The Connellsville region of Pennsylvania still supplied half of the product at this date, but
Alabama was soon to rise to second place among the states.
The abundance of coking coal at the headwaters of the Ohio
River, in conjunction with water transportation most of the
way from the Lake Superior ore fields, was the determining
factor in the centering of so large a part of the iron and steel
plants in the neighborhood of Pittsburgh.[39] Natural gas became a preferred fuel in the regions of its abundance, from
Pennsylvania to Kansas. Extravagant consumption soon exhausted the supplies in northern Indiana and Ohio, and by
1892 hardly a tenth of the factories were using gas. In 1887,
an oil-burning locomotive on the Pennsylvania Railroad between Altoona and Pittsburgh was the pioneer of this development. About a year later a Chicago rolling mill demonstrated
that twenty-one gallons of oil equaled a ton of Indiana coal,
and that in every way it was second only to gas as the most
desirable fuel. The output of petroleum rose from 13,350,000
tierces in 1877 to 44,824,000 in 1890, but most of it was still
for home use. At least one smelting plant used electric power
for the reduction of aluminum and the production of certain
alloys between 1887 and 1890.[40]

By the 1870s, America was producing more iron than it
needed, and the exploitation of new ore regions facilitated the
much faster later growth. Not until after 1878 did the Mar-
quette range come out of the doldrums brought on by the
Panic of 1873, after which it was prosperous for several more

years. In 1875, George C. Stone of Duluth reported an "iron mountain" in Minnesota, but it was left to the searching parties of Leonidas Merritt of the same city to discover the true richness of this Mesabi range late in 1890. Meanwhile, the Menominee range opened in 1877 and was soon turning out 600,000 tons a year. Between 1880 and 1882, Charlemagne Tower of Pennsylvania, depending largely on Stone for practical knowledge, engrossed over twenty thousand acres in the Vermilion range and began shipping in 1884. By the end of the century the Vermilion area had produced about 82,000,000 tons and Mesabi 1,600,000,000. Together with the Gogebic range, opened in Michigan in 1884, these were the more important Lake Superior ore fields. Shipments from all of them exceeded 9,000,000 tons in 1890.[41] Meanwhile, the Iron Mountain and Pilot Knob ranges in Missouri were wearing out, but Colorado and other states were beginning to produce in a small way. Michigan took the lead from Pennsylvania in 1889, only to pass it on to Minnesota a few years later.[42]

In 1880, there were blast furnaces in twenty-four states and Utah Territory and the same number in 1890, with some shift in the arrangement, all the way from the East coast to the West; during this time pig-iron manufacture almost tripled to 9,900,000 tons annually. The count of furnaces declined nearly a fifth, partly through abandonment but also because of replacement by larger units. There was little expansion in New England, while decay was setting in in New York and New Jersey, but capital invested in Alabama multiplied sixfold to $15,700,000. Pennsylvania slipped about 1 per cent in national ratio of pig-iron output but still accounted for almost an even half of all in 1890, followed in that year by Ohio, Alabama, Illinois, New York, Virginia, Tennessee, and Michigan.[43]

Most of the steel was Bessemer, but there was always some of the crucible product for cutlery, springs, suspension-bridge wire, and high-grade tools. Improvements in the open-hearth process resulted in its making inroads on both the other steels, but the cost was still high and the demand limited until about 1897, when railroad and structural engineers saw the need of a grade better than Bessemer. After that, it was not long before the Bessemer process joined the museum class of industries. Between 1880 and 1890, open hearth rose to nearly a fifth of Bessemer and by 1900 it reached half, while crucible steel remained about stationary. Throughout the twenty years, Pennsylvania turned out approximately three-fifths of the steel, Ohio rose from one-eleventh to a sixth, while Illinois declined from a little over a fifth to less than a seventh, later to rise close to the top. These three states consistently made around nine-tenths of the total. Forges and bloomeries became fewer, though the demand of the crucibles kept some in the business. The need of ferromanganese in the Bessemer converters led to a little domestic contribution, particularly in Virginia, Georgia, and Arkansas, but imports from Brazil, the British East Indies, and Cuba supplied most of the trade, and the local supplement diminished after 1890.[44]

The vast expansion of the iron and steel business rested on the demand for rails, locomotives, tenders, undercarriages for cars, bridges, building construction, steel ships, armor plate for the navy, and industrial and agricultural equipment of all kinds. By 1890, the United States was exporting large quantities of machinery, including, for the English market, superior looms. The making of farm implements alone required a capital of about $62,000,000 in 1880 and over $145,000,000 in 1890, while the annual value of the product mounted from $68,500,000 to above $80,000,000.[45]

Among the nonferrous metals, copper, lead, and zinc were the most important. Copper reached great prominence especially after Montana and Arizona Territories began their mining in 1883. In 1879, Michigan smelted five-sixths of all, but ten years later the two Western regions, particularly in Montana, accounted for 56.9 per cent. After that date, the electrolytic process made possible the reduction of low-grade ores, thus contributing to the twelvefold rise in production of the metal in the last twenty years of the century. The Anaconda mines in Montana and the Calumet and Hecla mines in Michigan were the leaders. The Lake Superior region still produced a third of the total in the late 1890s. The national growth in the 1880s was from some 51,600 long tons to almost an even 116,000.[46] After 1878, Colorado quickly wrested supremacy from Missouri in the lead industry, and by 1893 the largest smelteries were in Pueblo, Denver, and Salt Lake City. The total output grew from 81,900 short tons in 1877 to 183,000 in 1889, in which year a trust of monopoly proportions arose, leaving only 5 per cent of the product in independent hands. The main center for zinc was the Illinois–Missouri lead region, projecting also into Kansas. The New Jersey–Pennsylvania area contributed zinc oxide, and in Tennessee and Virginia a third field was expanding in the 1880s. The leadership among the states has shifted often since that time. In the later decades Missouri abandoned her one-time primacy and crept far down on the list. After the day of the washboard and zinc-lined bathtub, the element found extended use in alloys, particularly Connecticut's brass, but much of it along with lead went into paint, while zinc and copper also had many applications in the electrical enterprises.

America never had nickel or tin in sufficient quantities to do more than attract attention to their scarcity. The rare metals invaluable as alloys in steel were not in use before 1890. Chromium, like ferromanganese, later had to be imported, while tungsten, vanadium, and molybdenum became by-products of lead and zinc mining when the demand and the economy of reduction of ores made this necessary. A small amount of pig tin came from the Black Hills in the 1880s, and a few years later deposits were discovered in San Diego County, California, which in 1893 cast 134 of the nation's total of 152 tons. The tin-plate business was just getting a good start in 1890 when the McKinley tariff gave it a mighty impulse, but even before that date a Chicago company had lowered the cost of can-making to a tenth of its earlier level. In 1885, E. H. and A. H. Cowles discovered an improved process for manufacturing aluminum and in the next year C. M. Hall facilitated the development of the industry. The American product soared from 80 pounds in 1883 to 7,500,-000 pounds ten years later, by which time the lowest price on the market was $1.25 a pound. The earlier uses were for dental plates and optical instruments, but by 1890 some cooking utensils could be had.[47]

Of nonmetallic minerals in the basic-industry class were chemicals, fertilizers, stone, brick, cement, and glass. The chemical industry did not branch out far beyond the making of sulphuric acid, alum, lime, phosphorus, and borax. Aniline dyes originated during the period of the Civil War and in 1880 the industry, confined wholly to the state of New York, turned out eighty thousand pounds. Others then got into the business, but it continued to languish. After 1867, South Carolina began exploiting her phosphate rocks for fertilizer, and that state and Maryland struggled along after 1877 in the as yet rather hopeless attempt to convince farmers that it was better to keep up the old farms than to move on to unexhausted ones. Stone for building was abundant in most parts of the country and was seldom shipped far, except for New England marble and granite and the Bedford limestone of Indiana. Brick and tile comprised another industry of many centers serving their own communities. Charleston, West Virginia, in 1875, was the first city to use brick for street paving; three hundred others had begun to do likewise by 1893. Enameled and other fancy bricks appeared in 1876. Also, common bricks often came in from foreign places as ballast to supply the port towns. In the 1880s the capital investment in this industry grew from $28,000,000 to $83,000,-000, and trusts were rising. Hydraulic cement had helped in the building of the Erie Canal and remained in ascendancy long after the Portland variety made its appearance in 1885. In 1890, out of a total of 7,777,000 barrels (376 pounds each) manufactured, only 336,000 were Portland. Glass found its most extensive use in consumer goods, but from 1880 there was rapid progress in the making of plate glass for construction and replacement. In that year there were three plants, located at Crystal City, Missouri, and Albany and Jeffersonville, Indiana, and an idle one in Louisville.[48]

Last among the basic industries to be considered is lumbering. By 1880, the supremacy had passed from New England to the Great Lakes states, where for a time Michigan contributed nearly a quarter of the nation's total output. Wisconsin, Pennsylvania, and Minnesota followed in that order. The once predominant white pine was approaching exhaustion and Southern yellow pine was replacing it while also taking over the turpentine business. Some live oak was still in demand for shipbuilding. The number of sawmills in the country more than doubled in the 1880s, and with improved machinery and procedures their capacity multiplied threefold to 39,320,000 board feet in a year. In 1877, a band saw made in Pennsylvania for use in California was fifty-four feet in circuit and eight inches wide. By that time, gangs of fifty-four saws were known. The lowly cant hook did far more than its design would indicate in speeding up the work and reducing strain on the men.[49] Planing mills kept pace with the saws.

Developments in consumer goods can best be gauged by a consideration of foods, clothing, and shelter. Though a large quantity of meat products came from individual enterprise on the farm, in the local slaughterhouse, or in the back rooms of butcher shops, the concentration that had once made Cincinnati the Porkopolis of the West intensified until in 1880 the Chicago packing houses handled 2,175,000 hogs, Indianapolis being the nearest rival. Swift and Company moved to Chicago in 1875 and other important firms had headquarters there and in Milwaukee. Kansas City, Kansas, was rising in importance, especially for beef, but New York continued to hold high rank. The introduction of mechanical refrigeration was important both in packing and transoceanic shipping. Canned beef developed to the point where, in 1890, England was buying five-sixths of its exports valued at $6,787,000.[50]

Following Oliver Evans' improvements late in the eighteenth century, hardly any change took place in flour milling until 1870; then two millers in Minneapolis met the challenge presented by soft spring wheat, with the hardness, abundant gluten, and flimsy bran that made it difficult to grind and separate into a white flour that would keep. In 1870 and the ensuing years, Edward E. La Croix brought forth the middlings purifier, and in 1874 Charles A. Pillsbury introduced from Hungary the iron-roller process of grinding. Dust collectors, bolters, scourers, sifters, and separators followed, and in 1878 Cadwallader C. Washburn had what has been called the "first complete automatic roller-mill in the world." In 1890, the twenty-four Minneapolis mills had a daily capacity of 44,100 barrels, or nine times that of 1877. Flour was milled throughout most of the country, even the South, where 150 establishments sprang up in 1885 alone.[51] Beer and whiskey furnished additional markets for barley, rye, and corn. Nearly every town of ten thousand or more had a brewery. The whiskey trust has already received attention. Canned beer was unknown in those days, but Maryland and California led the nation in the canning of vegetables, fruits, and fish. The introduction of the autoclave for cooking at high temperatures meant that the products kept better and longer.[52] By 1886, tomatoes went into more cans than any other item.

Experiments to find new sources of sugar went on continuously. The Department of Agriculture tried hard to get a satisfactory product from sorghum, and in 1888 Congress subsidized a few factories to the extent of $80,000. The University of Illinois developed a method of crystallization and in 1893 a factory at Champaign produced about eighty tons, but Kansas was the real seat of this temporary project. Various Eastern states exerted failing efforts with beets, but by 1880 this source proved suitable in California, where one firm made 40 per cent profit on the first five hundred tons in 1883. But cane sugar from Louisiana far overshadowed all other sources except the imported product, which still comprised the major portion. The value of glucose production, $4,500,000 in 1880, rose to $7,757,000 in a decade, the center being in Illinois. Kansas entered the field of salt pumping and mining about 1887, and soon rose to eminence.[53] Between 1870 and 1890, tobacco, the great competitor of sugar as advertisers once assumed (in the belief that it dulled the appetite for sweets), increased in yield from 263,000,000 to 488,000,000 pounds, about half of it from Kentucky. The portion exported grew to three-fifths in the eighties. Virginia manufactured a quarter of the snuff and smoking and chewing tobacco in 1880, after which Missouri made gains. Cigar making was widely scattered in small shops.[54]

Of the various textiles, the greatest expansion was in cotton goods, the other branches of the trade lagging far behind.

Cotton began replacing wool for many purposes, including underwear, and the two fibers often occurred together in cloth of both high and low quality. Before 1890 the words linen and lingerie had become almost obsolete for sheets, pillow cases, and many other items of household and personal use, but the old names clung permanently to the cotton substitutes. Fine laces and embroideries were mainly imports from Switzerland, France, Germany, and the British Isles. The years 1883–86 were critical ones for the cotton trade as well as for others, particularly the Northern firms that continued to compete with the Southern mills in the coarser grades. By 1890, conditions were considerably better than ten or a dozen years earlier. In 1889, the Fall River mills were paying the highest dividends to that time in their history and, in 1890, there were thirty-three of them yielding 10 per cent.[55]

American manufacturers produced about three-quarters of the domestic requirement for woolens, consuming 200,000,000 pounds of raw material in 1870 and 386,000,000 pounds in 1890. The sheep ranges of the Mountain and Pacific states benefited from this demand, but the national supply, expanding from 146,000,000 pounds in 1871 to 337,000,000 in 1884 and standing at 309,000,000 in 1890, left a considerable amount for importation. The principal mechanical innovations in the trade were improvements in combing machinery, thus making Western wool adaptable for worsteds, which were coming into high demand, and the substitution of mules for hand jacks in spinning. The manufacturers preferred Australian wool for the better grades of cloth, but before 1890 they were utilizing a larger part of the domestic clip for such purposes than in earlier decades or after 1893. A lowering of prices for finished goods resulted from an increasing mixture of shoddy in the "virgin wool" cloth, rather than from greater efficiency in production. The industry was particularly sensitive to fluctuations in the business cycle, but a long-range study of prices and output indicates that the management paid entirely too much attention to the tariff as a factor. High rates sometimes led to slipshod practices, overproduction, and lowered prices, while lower rates had a sobering effect, with consequent betterment of conditions.[56]

The silk-goods industry remained comparatively small and wholly dependent on foreign sources of raw material, in spite of all efforts to stimulate American silk culture. Japan encroached steadily on China in supplying these imports, and by 1884 France and Italy began to participate in a lively fashion, in response to the rising market for plain dress goods, which showed the defects in low-grade silk much more readily than the early varicolored patterns. At this time there was also a shift from hand to power looms. Improved throwing machines and the invention of the automatic ribbon loom in 1889 made the employment of many women and girls feasible, the cheaper the better according to the prevailing philosophy. So the center of manufacture shifted from New Jersey to the coal towns and mining towns of Pennsylvania, where the men's wages were so desperately low that the supplementary income of the women was welcome, however slender. The industry grew up under the 60 per cent tariff of 1864 but expanded more rapidly after the 50 per cent tariff of 1883 went into effect. The net income rose from $10,000,000 in 1870 to $34,500,000 in 1880 and $69,200,-000 in 1890. Rayon was not yet a competitor, though experiments were under way in France. Linen no longer was an industry worth considering, though the culture of flax continued to supply seed for oil used mainly in the mixing of paint. Hemp also was giving way to other fibers for the making of cordage, but a binder-twine factory used it at least as late as 1903. There was no longer any demand for hempen cloth.[57]

The making of clothing was a highly sweated industry for which there are no very reliable statistics before 1890, but in that year the factory production amounted to $251,000,-000, whereas twenty years earlier the estimate for both home and shop was $147,650,000. Women's garments remained largely in the hands of the local dressmakers, but in the same twenty years the distaff increment of the total increased from $13,000,000 to $68,000,000. Most of the work in both branches was by hand and foot, but some quite effective power sewing machines, even for buttonholes, had appeared before 1890. Cutting machines and mechanical pressers were displacing scissors and the tailor's goose. By 1885, medium-grade ready-to-wear suits were as good as the hand-tailored ones of a few years before, but memories of the astonishingly fitting garments so often "handed down" from the shelves in earlier days, lingered on into the twentieth century, long after the original meaning of "hand-me-downs" had grown obscure and confused with "secondhand." Woolen hats came from the factories of New York, New Jersey, and Connecticut after the patent on the machine expired in 1874, and Danbury, Connecticut, was becoming famous for the product, as was Gloversville, New York, for the apparel that gave the town its name. Knit goods, mainly hosiery and underwear, increasingly of cotton, came mainly from a domestic-system of management but also to some extent from factories. By 1883, machines were imported for full knitting of stockings. Before this, flatware was cut and then shaped on sewing machines.[58]

The Germans, as prominent in tanning as they were in brewing, gave the leadership to the making of leather in forty states. The bulk of the product went into shoes and other wearing and carrying apparel and the rest was for industrial use. Goatskins for Morocco leather came from India, horsehides for cordovan, as well as kangaroo pelts, from Australia. Enameled and patent leather were becoming popular. New England manufactured about two-thirds of the shoes, the national value rising from $147,000,000 in 1870 to $166,000,000 in 1880 and $220,000,000 in 1890. The processes were about all mechanical by the latter date. There were few pegged soles after 1880, and nails did not flourish long before sewed soles virtually became universal. By 1890, the Goodyear welt was becoming popular, at which time there were factories in thirty-five states. After 1877 there had been mechanical lasting and heel-and-edge trimming. A doubling of sales of footwear in the 1880s brought the income to $18,632,000, or about thirty cents per capita. Though no significant inventions appeared in the rubber industry, consumption increased, mainly in overshoes, boots, and raincoats. These garments, along with hose and belting, consumed the bulk of the raw material before the popularization of rubber tires. The greatest importation of crude rubber was the 16,-400 long tons of 1888.[59]

The volume of housing construction, carried on by craftsmen following whatever design suited the fancy of the owner, is a figure that, then as well as later, must largely be guessed. There has never been a universal requirement of building permits, while hopes of outwitting the tax assessor have generally kept reported building costs below actualities. The better houses of the time, and some of the worst ones as well, will for some time to come be sufficient evidence of the types of structure. But building in the transportation industry was not a matter of conjecture, as the next chapter indicates.

Chapter XV

TRADE AND TRANSPORTATION

DURING the Centennial years, several developments and changes occurred in the business of getting the products of factory and farm into the hands of consumers. Produce exchanges had grown up in Chicago, New York, St. Louis, Philadelphia, Milwaukee, Kansas City, and New Orleans, in that order, between 1848 and 1871, and in the latter year New York added a Cotton Exchange to her list. Then, in 1881 the Minneapolis Chamber of Commerce and in 1882 the New York Coffee Exchange joined the ranks. No others of importance were started until after 1900.[1] The activities of such bodies caused the farmers to protest often and loud. Also, however ill-founded, a feeling prevailed that the stock exchanges meddled enough in financial affairs so as to cause business disturbances.

The New York Stock Exchange, dating back to 1792, handled 117,078,167 shares in 1881 but only 85,821,027 in 1887, just before stock gambling began to pick up after the recession. Seats sold for $25 in 1823, but climbed up to $13,000 in 1879 and $25,000 in 1889. The Consolidated Stock Exchange of New York started with mining securities in 1875 but, in 1885, combined with the Petroleum Exchange begun in 1880. It also dealt in railroad shares, and differed from the New York Stock Exchange mainly in that it handled odd lots of less than a hundred shares. The Curb Market, dating from about 1880, took care of stocks not listed on the organized exchanges and was largely dependent on the New York Stock Exchange.[2] Wholesale dealers of the era were beginning to feel dependence on the trade associations growing up among the manufacturers, such as the American Paper and Pulp Association (founded 1878), the American Dental Trade Association (1882), and the National Paint, Oil, and Varnish Association, Inc. (1890).[3]

Among retail agencies developing significantly were department stores, mail-order houses, and chain stores. Alexander T. Stewart's department store on lower Fourth Avenue in New York, the great pioneer of Civil War days and earlier, was to be taken over in 1896 by John Wanamaker of Philadelphia, renowned in the same business since 1877. Marshall Field, long after amassing a fortune from army contracts in shoddy during the Civil War, established another such store in Chicago in 1881, and came to be known as the greatest wholesale and retail dealer in drygoods in the world, as Wanamaker was the most famous Sunday-school superintendent and Stewart an outstanding early merchant prince. After 1870, such merchandise outlets on a smaller scale became common in the larger cities and received the condemnation of lesser retailers as being monopolistic and unfair to competitors.[4]

Following the successful venture of Montgomery Ward of Chicago in 1872, the Butler Brothers, wholesalers of Boston, issued a mail-order catalog in 1878, and in 1886 Richard W. Sears branched out from the selling of watches to friends, through the mail, into a full-fledged business in Minneapolis. He later moved to Chicago and, with his old associate A. C. Roebuck, founded the establishment of Sears, Roebuck and Co. in 1893. The benevolence of the Post Office Department in allowing low rates on the mailing of catalogs was of assistance in this movement. William L. Douglas, later governor of Massachusetts, and James Means began selling shoes by mail about 1883.[5] The Great Atlantic and Pacific Tea Company grew out of a small start in 1859 when George H. Hartford bought a store founded in the previous year. He opened his hundredth one in 1880, a good start toward his ultimately huge empire. Bernard H. Kroger started at Cincinnati in 1882 and had seven stores in 1891. After several early failures, Frank W. Woolworth succeeded at Lancaster, Pennsylvania, in 1879, and started a new store at Scranton in 1880, thus inaugurating the idea of the five-and-ten-cent store.[6]

Meanwhile, the evils of company stores, with their extortionate prices and the compulsory patronage of employees—whether enforced by bookkeeping, by payment in script redeemable nowhere else, or by threat of discharge—continued in mill towns of the North and South alike as well as on the plantation, despite poorly written adverse legislation in a dozen or more states. The courts voided one such act of 1881, in Pennsylvania, as a violation of contract.[7] In the general retail trade, there was a high rate of casualties, nearly half falling out of the contest during five years in some of the states.[8]

In the 1880s, advertising began to take on the aspect of big business that became so conspicuous in the following decades. In newspapers and periodicals alone, the cost of this medium of selling grew from 26 cents per capita of the population of the country in 1867 to 78 cents in 1880 and $1.13 in 1890. One wonders how much it cost to plaster painted signs on the barns, roofs, sheds, fences, trees, rocks, and poles along the roads the nation over. Then, there were the billboards and the stage curtains in the theaters. Patent-medicine companies set the pace by utilizing hundreds of religious journals to hawk nostrums and frauds among the more gullible wights, and thereby aroused suspicion against all advertising, but not enough to check its growth. "St. Jacob's Oil for Rheumatism" and hundreds of similar, sometimes harmless, specifics and panaceas sustained the business, helped to develop new methods, and demonstrated the power of advertising. A favorite deceit was to set up the copy in the form of unlabeled news items. Although the amount of journalistic advertising tripled in the last decade of the century, only Sapolio, Royal Baking Powder, Pears' Soap, and Ivory Soap, aside from the patent medicines, conducted widespread and continuous campaigns. About seventy-five other products and services made nationwide efforts on a less systematic basis.[9]

The expansion of the insurance business took many forms and directions. Probably the oldest of all, dating back to the Roman Empire, was marine insurance, which in the United States suffered from the decline of the merchant marine during the Civil War and after. But foreign companies began to take hold in New York in 1871; within the next three years seven of them were represented there, and by 1905, fifteen. By that time there were only three American companies in the state, doing about half of the declining business. What really kept them alive was their moving over into fire insurance.[10] The Chicago and Boston fires of 1871 and 1872 wiped out many of the fire-insurance companies that had been springing up and growing for eighty years, after which associations of underwriters began solving rate problems and standardizing policies. The mill mutuals of New England originated the use of safety devices and inspection, on the theory that it was cheaper to prevent fires than to pay for them. The stock companies soon followed the example, providing regular inspection and, in the 1880s, advocating sprinkling systems.[11] Probably it was James G. Batterson of the Travelers Insurance Company of Hartford who made the first contract for accident insurance when, in 1864, he orally insured James Bolter for $5000 in case he were killed by an accident while he took a walk, the cost being two cents. By 1905, this sort of business was extracting premiums of about $15,000,000 annually.[12] Not until 1889 did employer's liability become important enough to attract any attention, after which it had a phenomenal growth, reaching $1,120,000 in premiums in 1890 and $14,700,000 in 1904.[13]

In life insurance, after about 1870, the most conspicuous feature was the tontine policy, a form of gambling on survivor benefits beyond the initial recipient. Between 1860 and 1872, the life-insurance business expanded beyond any reasonable expectation of demand, with the consequence that between 1868 and 1877 there were over one hundred failures. Henry B. Hyde of the Equitable Life Assurance Society of New York saved his company from insolvency by adopting the tontine system for a big selling campaign. After 1870, nearly two-thirds of his business was of this nature, and in the next twenty years about four-fifths of all companies followed the practice. Claims started coming soon after 1880, and it was found that the companies had looted the funds through high salaries, big buildings, large commissions, balm to legislatures, and other devious ways, and could not make full payments. Equitable paid as low as 30 per cent, rarely more than 60, and averaged 50 on the agents' original estimates. Northwestern Mutual was probably the only company doing such business that escaped such a record or a worse one. Between 1878 and 1890, the number of active companies rose from thirty-five to fifty, and their coverage of ordinary life policies from $1,481,000,000 to $3,621,000,000. Industrial policies, with a first recorded coverage of $443,000 in 1876, soared to $428,789,000 in 1890. Starting with Prudential in 1875, Metropolitan, John Hancock, and other companies soon engaged in this specialty of insuring the little fellow for small amounts on weekly or monthly premiums. Assessment insurance by fraternal organizations and cooperatives got its first great impetus in the 1870s when the old-line organizations were failing or being investigated. In 1886 there was a list of 367 associations, with no assurance that it was complete. Many of these were mutuals, selling on a haphazard actuarial basis and maintaining a high mortality rate of their own. The truly fraternal companies fared much better.[14]

The national production handled and insured by many of the agencies so far mentioned rose from an average annual value (measured by the prices of 1919) of $9,340,000,000 in the eighth decade of the century to $17,875,000,000 in the ninth and $24,170,000,000 in the last, while the current valuation of manufactures alone was $5,370,000,000 in 1879 and $9,372,000,000 in 1889.[15] The railroads were taking an expanding part in the transportation of this mass of goods. For example, in the 1880s they increased their percentage of the cotton trade from 19 to 30 while coastwise vessels and the rest declined from 81 to 70. On the other hand, as the center of wheat production shifted westward, Chicago began losing out to Minneapolis and Duluth in the handling and the railroads to the Great Lakes steamers in the hauling, while Southern ports rarely got a tenth of the business and more often less than half that.[16]

In 1877–90, the mileage of railroads operated grew from 79,000 to 166,700 and all track from 97,300 to 208,150. Except for the recession years of 1884 and 1885, passenger and freight revenues increased steadily from $347,705,000 to $734,822,000. Data are lacking for the earlier years, but in 1882–90, passenger-miles mounted from 7,688,469,000 to 12,521,566,000 and freight ton-miles from 39,302,209,000 to 79,192,985,000.[17] Of the 73,000 miles of first line built from 1880 to 1890, about 40,000 comprised the five new transcontinental connections and their networks of branches, as well as other Western roads that did not reach the Pacific coast. The Southern Pacific–Santa Fe, terminated in 1881; the Texas & Pacific–Southern Pacific and the through Southern Pacific, in 1882; and the through Santa Fe and the Northern Pacific, in 1883, were matched by the Canadian Pacific in 1885. With the Union and Central Pacific of 1869, there were now seven routes from coast to coast, six of them in the United States, and the Great Northern, soon to be the eighth, had got a start. The Denver & Rio Grande, in its progress to Salt Lake City, had a contest with the Santa Fe that reached violence and prolonged litigation over the use of the Royal Gorge. The Burlington and the Frisco were among other participants in the scramble for construction.[18]

Under federal legislation passed from 1850 to 1871, the government gave, mainly to the Western lines, 134,000,000 acres of land directly to the companies for building the railroads, and another 49,000,000 acres came from the government through the intermediary of the states or, in Texas, from the state for the same purpose. These 183,000,000 acres, or 286,000 square miles, constituted an area larger than the state of Texas and was nearly a tenth of the whole United States, with a value conservatively estimated at $516,-000,000. The earliest grants were six square miles for each mile of right of way. Then the Union and Central Pacific got twenty miles on the same basis, and finally the gift to the Northern Pacific was forty sections a mile all the way from the western border of Minnesota to Puget Sound, totaling 40,895,000 acres. The directors calculated that, at two dollars an acre, this largesse would build the railroad. Actually, by 1880, land was averaging $0.75 an acre, while the lowest average for any line was $2.14. Consequently, the people of the United States not only donated the railroads, they even paid the companies a bonus for accepting them. The Southern Pacific received 32,514,000 acres, the Union and Central Pacific approximately 30,000,000, and thus down through the Santa Fe, the Missouri Pacific, and the Chicago & Northwestern, to the paltry 3,375,000 acres given to the Burlington.[19]

In the East, construction was less spectacular, the systems having been pretty thoroughly constructed before 1877. Yet some 18,000 miles appeared east of the Mississippi River, two-thirds of it in the East North Central states. The Buffalo-to-Chicago extension of the Nickel Plate, completed in 1882, furnished additional competition with the New York Central.[20] The South had very little more mileage in 1880 than a decade earlier. Then, the addition of 14,396 miles by 1890 brought the total to 27,655. In the West South Central division, mileage tripled. The Cincinnati Southern, built and owned by the municipality and running to Chattanooga, cost $10,000,000. It started operation in 1877, but four years later the city leased it, though continuing to retain ownership.[21] Albert Fink of the Louisville & Nashville has been called the founder of the science of railroad economics.

Nowhere was there much achievement in equipment and mechanical devices. Sleeping and dining cars, the air brake, and block signals all came before 1877, and the automatic coupler appeared in successful design only in 1889. Its adoption was gradual until a federal law of March 2, 1893, made it obligatory in interstate traffic. Achievements in safety appliances were otherwise all in the way of expansion of use.[22] The standard gauge of track never became universal but when, in 1886, the South accepted it, it became nearly so. Lengthened trains, larger cars, and consequently heavier locomotives made the replacement of light iron rails with more hefty steel ones imperative, along with general improvements in the roadbeds. The Santa Fe was one of many railroads that, for this reason, had to rebuild the main lines in the 1880s. So, by 1890, railroading had reached a condition of stability to which only less essential refinements, increases in comfort and aesthetic enjoyment, could be added. The major systems were complete. In 1877, the investment in railroads and

equipment was $4,180,192,000 but the capitalization was
$626,010,000 greater, half of all of it in bonds. In 1890, the
figures were $8,789,222,000 and $1,313,414,000, the bonds
being well over half.[23] Actually, the bonds were the real
capitalization, the stocks and the surplus valuation being
water.

In 1877, all streetcars were horse-drawn, and a few of them
remained so after 1910. Until 1887, when the first fragmentary electric railroads came to Massachusetts, the horse cars
in that state were a greater financial success than the later
electric cars, and the equipment and mileage of track were
constantly improving and increasing. The first installation of
cable cars began in San Francisco in 1879, that form of traction being the most successful on steep hills. In time, the
cables were put underground so that the tracks resembled
those of the central-third-rail trolley system. Though diminishing in number, the San Francisco cable lines have never
ceased to operate. Before 1890, several of the larger cities
had them, there being 55 different companies operating on
488 miles of track. At the same time, 506 horse-car systems
controlled 5661 miles, 126 electric railroads had 1261 miles,
and steam power was in use by 74 enterprises on 711 miles.
Every major section of the country had some of each kind
except for the South Central states, which had no cables.[24]

Interurban lines were to come after 1890, by which time
a few tracks already extended beyond the city limits. Elevated railroads had been in operation in New York since
1868, and by 1877 were collecting 3,000,000 fares annually.
At this time Cyrus W. Field started backing them with all his
wealth. It was he who built a great system. In three years, the
number of passengers grew to well above 60,000,000. After
1880, the movement was on to abolish free and perpetual
franchises for surface and elevated lines, and agitation flourished for municipal ownership and control. In 1888, Mayor
Abram S. Hewitt of New York proposed the public construction of an elevated system to be leased to private operators,
but for another six years the legislature refused to follow his
suggestion.[25] The period of domination of the streetcar com-

panies, and the cities as well, by corrupt bosses had its origins before 1890, but blossomed completely thereafter.

Among the means of transportation, the country roads played a humble but important part. Over these rough highways, when they were not hub-deep in mud, the farmers harried their flocks, droves, and herds, and trudged beside or rode in their wagons, often many miles, to get their livestock and crops to the market places and return with provisions. From the decline of the plank-road movement until nearly 1880, these capillaries of commerce did little but deteriorate. Such few of them as were kept up at all were in the immediate vicinity of the cities. Then the bicycle clubs began agitation for betterment, but achieved little in the next decade. A rough estimate of what was called "surfaced roads" shows about 95,000 miles in 1877 and 106,000 in 1890, but "surfaced" often meant occasional dragging or some sand or gravel thrown on the top. The first few miles of cement and brick roads in the United States were laid in two Ohio counties in 1891. An account of a good-roads convention at Iowa City in 1883[26] calls to mind the fact that the Hawkeye State did not really begin to pull itself out of the mud until after the fall of 1926, when thousands of cars leaving Iowa City following a football game mired down in solid rows for several miles in all directions, froze there, and had to wait until the following spring for excavation.

The oldest and cheapest of all the mediums of transportation were the waterways, but at best they were slow, and in the interior of the country the railroads made incessant and ever more ominous inroads. Steamboating on much of the Mississippi system was declining in glory in the final quarter of the nineteenth century. After the St. Louis World's Fair of 1904, rarely did a steamboat whistle sound below Cairo, Illinois. In 1875, 64.8 per cent of the South's cotton went to the coastal markets by water. The volume rose a third in the next five years, but the percentage fell. By 1890, the number of bales was three-fifths below the figure for 1880 and the rivers carried only 19.8 per cent of the crop. The jetties of 1879 at the mouth of the Mississippi were helpful to the ocean trade of New Orleans, but they could not long foster the river craft. The index of steamboat arrivals (1845–48 = base of 100) stood at 99 in 1876–80 but only 82 in 1886–90. The number of boats remained the same but they carried less. Only on the Ohio and its tributaries was there any gain. Also, the business on the Eastern rivers caused a rise for the whole country. The fact that the Western rivers carried over 28,000,000 tons of freight in 1889 depended mainly on the handling of two-thirds of this in fleets of barges pushed by towboats. Two-thirds of the barge trade (over 12,000,000 tons) was on the Ohio River and its deepest tributaries, the movement of coal to Pittsburgh and down the river being the bulk of it. One tow of thirty-two barges to New Orleans in 1878 moved 22,200 tons at a cost of about 75 cents a ton. Grain and forest products also ranked high, but below coal.[27]

The Mississippi River Commission, authorized by Congress in 1879 after long and persistent lobbying by the rivermen, tried by dredging and other comparatively futile means to maintain a channel of from four and a half to six feet between Minneapolis and St. Louis, but the progress was slow. A Missouri River Commission of 1882 was hardly any more successful. What ultimately became a much more feasible plan was that of building dams and locks along the Ohio River to maintain a minimum depth of six feet. The first set of these was completed in 1885. The dams had movable sections that could be let down to the bed at the deepest part so as to let the boats through unimpeded at high stages of the river, the locks coming into use at other times. The work reached completion late in 1929. Such devices were suited to the Ohio River, because of its high banks and stability of channel. But on the Mississippi and Missouri, the current would simply cut a new channel at flood stage and leave the dams high and dry. Not until about 1930 did a widely different system of control prove successful on the Missouri. Annual bills for river work passed Congress from 1877 to 1882; then they became biennial.[28] The trouble was that too much of the money went for levees, which made floods all the worse when they washed out, and not enough for upstream reservoirs to maintain a year-round channel.

What the government did to the Ohio river system was

actually to make canals for steam navigation of the major parts. New York decided in 1903 to enlarge, alter the course of, and make a barge canal out of the old Erie project.[29] For decades before that time the traffic on the existing one remained virtually static. Freight originating on the Erie in 1877 was 3,254,367 tons. In 1880 the amount was appreciably greater (a little over 4,600,000), but in the other years until 1890 the figure was much closer to the initial one. The whole artificial system of the state kept remarkably close to 5,000,000 tons during all of the fourteen years. In the same period, the ton-miles of the railroads in New York grew threefold, to 9,940,000,000, while the combined river and canal traffic in 1890, 1,310,000,000 ton-miles, was hardly 8 per cent greater than in 1877.[30] For most of the country, this was a period of continually declining use of the canals that had been so prominent for a generation before 1850. By the end of the decade, nearly half the original 4800 canal miles were in total disuse. The anthracite canals of Pennsylvania joined in the general lapse. The Illinois-Michigan canal reached its height of tonnage in 1882 after a cut in rates to offset railroad competition, but thereafter the business fell off steadily.[31] The great exception to the general trend of the 1880s was the interlake canals carrying the ships loaded with the new products of the Great Lakes states. The Soo Canal tonnage of over 9,000,000 in 1890 was ten times that of 1877.[32]

This lake shipping was the one branch of internal-waterway transportation that flourished, and it did so amazingly. The cargoes of iron and copper ores, lumber, and grain going to or from Chicago and other points on Lake Michigan and to Lake Erie, between 1870 and 1890, made the business compare favorably with that of the railroads.[33] The number of vessels engaging in the trade grew from about 3000 in 1877 to 3500 in 1890, but their aggregate tonnage rose from 610,000 to 1,063,000. Sailing vessels initially outnumbered those steam-propelled by more than two thirds, but, at the end of the period, steam was ahead by a quarter and had doubled the tonnage of the "windjammers." Both kinds had increased in average capacity.[34] In 1881, a canal circumventing the falls in the St. Marys River admitted larger ships to

Lake Superior, and in that year some 1,500,000 or more tons of freight came down to Lake Huron.[35]

In 1884, bulk wheat from Canada began arriving and reached the volume of three million bushels two years later.[36] Through the years, the shipments of wheat and flour from Chicago by Great Lakes steamers and by rail were fairly equal, the amount doubling between 1876 and 1890. The ratio in the latter year was 85 to 90 in favor of the railroads, the measure being millions of bushels.[37] A shift from wooden to steel ships accompanied the movement from sails to steam. The first iron steamer, built at Cleveland in 1882, was of three thousand tons capacity. The demands of the ore traffic made holds of great size a necessity.[38] Steel vessels appeared in 1886 and whaleback freighters in 1888 or 1889. Nineteen or twenty of the latter came from the shipyards in two years, but the difficulty of loading and unloading the whalebacks kept them from becoming greatly popular, and down to 1930 less than a hundred had been built. They were by no means as "typical of ships on the Lakes" as the school geographies of around 1900 pictured them. They were just novel. The evolution of derricks and shovel buckets between 1878 and 1890, taking the place of wheelbarrows and Irishmen for loading and unloading, did much to advance Great Lakes shipping.[39]

American ships on the high seas became so few before 1905 as to be mainly of antiquarian interest. In 1860, the domestic fleet carried 66.5 per cent of all exports and imports, but the figure was only 23.9 in 1876–80, 14.1 in 1886–90, an even 10.0 in 1896–1900, and slightly less than that in the next five years before growth began. The value of all exports and imports averaged $1,206,000,000 in 1876–80 and $1,398,000,000 in 1886–90, of which, in the two periods, 20,-000,000 and 58,000,000 came by land from north and south of the borders. The coastwise trade was widely different. By law, this could be carried only in vessels of American ownership. When the imperialism of McKinley's administration resulted in the acquisition of far-flung insular possessions, these islands, by a legal twist reminiscent of the English navigation laws of the seventeenth century, became a part of the "coastline," thus giving a monopoly to the American merchantmen in trading back and forth with them. For this reason, the coastwise ships had a prospering business while those in foreign trade languished.[40]

Reported craft of five tons or more engaged in coastal, intercoastal, and internal (Great Lakes) commerce increased in tonnage from 2,540,322 in 1877 to 3,409,435 in 1890, while those in foreign trade declined from 1,570,600 to 928,062. At the latter date, 86 per cent of the tonnage of all was of wooden construction and 53 per cent used the winds for power.[41] Changes in the coastal business consisted mainly of a growing control by railroad corporations and a tendency in cargoes away from general merchandise and toward bulky freight, such as coal, ice, and lumber. On the Pacific coast, trade kept pace with population, and lumber predominated. This heavy freight furnished a revival of wooden shipbuilding. The wooden schooners, becoming prolific by 1880, were more economical in both construction and operation than iron or steel vessels, at least until 1914. Tows of barges, as on the Mississippi, competed heavily with the schooners.[42] The intercoastal trade, around Cape Horn, waned after the coming of the transcontinental railroads, though there was some revival by way of the Panama portage line after 1890. Whatever went by sea was the amount permitted by the railroad companies, which, through various arrangements, controlled the ships. A pooling arrangement made in 1878 also allowed these companies to fix rates over the Panama route.[43] Interest in this short cut stimulated agitation for an American canal across some part of Central America.

There were 1029 vessels built in the shipyards of the United States in 1877, with a gross tonnage of 176,592. Except for low output in 1880 and during 1885–87, there was not much change in number, and the total in 1890 was 1051. But the average size was creeping up, for in that year the tonnage was 294,123. The construction of sailing craft fluctuated considerably. There were 581 launched in 1877, totaling 106,331 tons; 460 of 59,057 tons in 1880; 721 of 137,-046 tons in 1883; 423 of 48,590 tons in 1888; and 505 of 102,873 tons in 1890. These were the high and low points in the ragged curve.[44] Most of the building of the steel navy occurred in Philadelphia, near to the source of the materials, and in private yards, thus creating facilities for peaceful use as well. Newport News and San Francisco also participated in an important way. The decline of the high-seas merchant fleet was partially offset by sales abroad and by the growth of the coastwise trade. Higher returns for capital in manufactures than in shipping seem to have been an important factor in the shift in control of the foreign traffic, but added to it were the annoyances of the registry law, the competition of low-paid foreign seamen, and the cheaper costs of construction abroad. The building of steel ships at the Great Lakes ports flourished because of the isolation that eliminated the chance of foreign participation. The old yards in Maine kept busy building square-riggers, as at Bath, but they also profited from the demand for schooners by the coastwise shippers.[45]

A consideration of foreign trade in the most important commodities of export and import may be found on pages dealing with their production or demand, and repetition here is needless. Such commerce was a relatively small but very necessary fraction of the American economy.

In 1880, the sea fisheries brought in a catch valued at $32,-822,000 and the amount in 1890 was but infinitesimally greater in the old grounds from Newfoundland to the Gulf of Mexico, but the addition of the Great Lakes and the Pacific coast brought the total to $38,329,000. Losses of a sixth by value in New England were counterbalanced by gains everywhere else, and particularly in the Gulf states. New England still had a strong lead, but the Chesapeake and Middle Atlantic states, second and third, were not remotely behind. Salmon fisheries were largely responsible for giving the Pacific area fourth place in 1890, while the Great Lakes states stood fifth, followed by the Gulf and the South Atlantic states in order. In 1860, there had been 163,000 gross tons of vessels engaged in the cod and mackerel fisheries and 167,000 in whaling. In 1870 the figures were 91,000 and 68,000; in 1880, 78,000 and 38,000; and in 1890, 68,000 and 19,000. Appetites for the old staples of the fishing trade seem to have been changing, while the whale was becoming unimportant. In an age of steel corset stays and coal-oil lamps, American whalers steadily let the Norwegians take over the remnant of the business. By 1947, only a thousand tons of whaling vessels remained under registry of the United States, but the aromatic cod fleets also had declined to only twice that amount.[46]

The telephone was no doubt of some tiny use in the conduct of local trade but, by 1890, its long-distance phase was too rudimentary for consideration except as a possibility and promise. The well-established telegraph and cables, however, were of immense importance. Beginning in 1877, there were all but sanguinary battles between rivals for monopoly of the telegraph business while the lines were following the growing railroad systems. A contest in that year between William H. Vanderbilt's Western Union and Gould's Atlantic and Pacific companies resulted in a compromise. Two years later, Gould expanded his holdings and formed the American Union Telegraph Company capitalized at $10,000,000, made an agreement with the French Cable Company, and extended his wires so rapidly that Vanderbilt surrendered in 1881. The merger took the Western Union name and Gould's management, floating in seas of watered stock. Raids on other major competitors soon made the monopoly almost complete. In 1880, there had been 77 companies, mostly small, whereas in 1902 there were only 25, the few rivals of any size again being relatively small. With the consolidation of 1881, Western Union had four-fifths of the lines, three-quarters of the stations, and nine-tenths of the messages and revenue.[47]

But rivalry was not at an end. In 1881, John W. Mackay, of Virginia City mining fame, founded the Postal Telegraph Company, and two years later James Gordon Bennett of the *New York Herald*, who wanted exclusive service when needed, joined him in forming the Commercial Cable Company. Before this, Western Union possessed one of the four transatlantic cables, all of which charged 50 cents a word. The Mackay-Bennett combination laid two competing cables in 1884 and reduced the charge to 40 cents. A rate war ensued, ending in 1888 with an agreement on 25 cents

for all. Meanwhile, the depression had put the Postal Telegraph Company in receivership, but Mackay rescued it and
kept up his competition with Gould to the best of his means.
Cables to Mexico and other Latin-American countries also
appeared in these years.[48]

Lack of public sympathy either with Vanderbilt or Gould,
in their struggle for dominance, evoked the "Antimonopoly
Song" of 1888, written by some weary victim of extortionate
rates and sung to the tune of "John Brown's Body."[49]

For Vanderbilt and Company, 'tis indeed a gilded age,
But poverty increases, and 'tis thus that tramps are made.
Shall it, will it be continued when the people's votes are
weighed?
> As we go marching on.

No! We'll hang Jay Gould on a sour apple tree,
And bring to grief the plotters of a base monopoly;
From the heartless ghouls of booty we're determined to go
free,
> As we go marching on.

Statements such as this, as well as protests against irregu-
larities in rates, were factors, from 1880 to 1900, in the demand for public ownership and operation of the telegraph.
The battle "raged in the magazines . . . with a ratio of about
ten shots for it to one against." Of nineteen Senate and House
committees expressing opinions on this issue over a period of
years, seventeen were in favor. Wanamaker, with no effect,
used his influence with President Harrison in favor of the idea,
but no later Postmaster General ever made an effort.[50]

Wanamaker, in his official position at the time and not as
a private merchant, was at the head of America's greatest
and most efficient business enterprise, which would also have
been financially prosperous except for favors wrung from it
for corporations and companies. There had been a time when
private capitalists thought they should handle the mails and
coin the money on contract with the government. Failing in
this, they were now determined to hold on to the two greatest rivals of the Post Office in the field of communications—
express and the telegraph. The postal service, run for the

good of the people instead of for profit, operated at a deficit between 1877 and 1890, except for 1882 and 1883, the largest deficit being $7,481,410 in 1885.[51] But this was far less than the losses incurred in the Star Route frauds or through the subsidies paid to transportation agencies in the form of mail contracts. Had it not been for these concessions to private business, there could have been a constant surplus for expansion of services. The annual revenue advanced from $25,531,585 to $60,882,098,[52] and by 1885 the letter postage was down from three cents to two for half an ounce (later a full ounce), and second-class privileges from two cents a pound to one, another deficit-producing subsidy, this time in favor of the newspapers and their advertisers. Postmaster General Vilas defended this gift on grounds of public welfare. In 1885–86, Congress also established special delivery, and in 1890 there was a tentative movement toward rural free delivery, but this reform had to wait for another six years.[53]

The express companies rarely gave information to the census bureaus, and then only scattered bits, but by 1886, Adams, among the largest, was paying the railroads more than $2,000,000 a year for carrying its letters and packages. These agencies gave service to Western mining camps ahead of the arrival of post offices, and for years after the coming of the transcontinental railroads their wagons met the trains to care for distribution at remote points. In 1880 Wells Fargo listed seventy-six offices in five states of the extreme Northwest, some on stagecoach lines and others on railroads. In addition to Wells Fargo and Adams, the American and the United States companies exerted powerful influence on governmental policy toward the business. Senator Thomas C. Platt, president of the United States Company, used his government prestige in a potent manner. Wanamaker credited these four companies with being the great obstacle in the way of the creation of a parcel-post system in the Post Office Department. The Interstate Commerce Commission also felt their power, expressing doubt as to its authority to interfere in a rate war that began in 1886 and lasted three years before the parties returned, by mutual agreement, to the old charges. In 1886, Chief Justice Morrison R. Waite and a ma-

jority of the Supreme Court upheld the right of one company
to exclude all others from a railroad on which it had prior
rights, in order to avoid inconvenience and confusion. Other
court decisions barred railroads from establishing their own
competing express companies.[54]

In 1882, American Express began competing with the Post
Office in the issuance of money orders, and in 1888 Wells
Fargo was able, through connections, to become the first actually coast-to-coast express company. The stories of raids on
the express stages by Indians, professional robbers or "road
agents," and just plain ornery badmen have had their day
in the penny dreadfuls, dime novels, and motion pictures, and
no correction of the impressions made will appear here. It is
more significant to note that patrons' resentment over out-
rageous charges—twenty-five cents for a letter—created sympathy for the robbers, many of the citizens simply laughing
at news that another Wells Fargo express box "had been
looted." Sheriffs and marshals often were unable to extract
any information from witnesses. The opening of the Black
Hills to gold miners in 1876 furnished a golden opportunity,
and the height of banditry in that area came in the next two
years,[55] thus adding to the prosperity of one of the oldest
forms of commerce.

POSTSCRIPT

And cast in some diviner mold,
Let the new cycle shame the old![1]

SO ORDERED John Greenleaf Whittier in the last lines of
his "Centennial Hymn," written for the opening of the International Exhibition in Philadelphia, May 10, 1876.
Whether the subsequent years were cast in a "diviner mold"
is certainly open to question, and yet in some ways the "new
cycle" did shame the old. When Grover Cleveland, in Chicago, pressed the button that opened the World's Columbian
Exposition, May 1, 1893, it started the massive 14,000 horsepower engine in Machinery Hall. The Corliss engine, the wonder of the Philadelphia show seventeen years before, had developed only 5000 horsepower. In the industrial sphere there
had been great progress.

America's prosperity in the Centennial years centered
around its railroads, which by the 1890s claimed twice the
track mileage of 1876. Railroads stimulated industrial growth
both as a giant consumer and as a conveyor to new markets.
They helped Chicago enlarge by better than a half million
in the decade between 1880 and 1890, and in 1893 transported thousands to see the sprawling displays of the Columbian Exposition on the lake front in Jackson Park. But the
railroads also reflected the robber-baron business philosophy
of the time, assisting the growth of monopolies with rebates,
and themselves engaging in monopolistic tactics through
traffic pools. In some areas their competitive methods resulted in rate wars, while in noncompetitive areas they levied
discriminatory, even ruinous, charges to recoup rate war
losses. During the Centennial years there was no significant
letup in these practices, although banker control of the roads
during and following the depression of the 1890s tended to

annul such procedures and substitute more sophisticated devices for them.

Business, plunging headlong into expansion, assisted by tremendous technological advance and mechanized production methods, sought to assure profit margins on the one hand through trusts and on the other through advancing technology, searching for new markets while wresting older ones from competitors. Businessmen spoke about the survival of the fittest, embracing Darwin's biological theories as an economic fact of life. But by 1893 production began to outrun markets, and the World's Fair in the Windy City, opened on a note of optimism, actually heralded a financial panic and depression. The remainder of the gay nineties proved to be not very gay after all. Still, the Centennial years provided a very substantial cornerstone for twentieth-century American industry to build on.

Labor, in its reaction to the pressures and the brutality of the swiftly enlarging industrial revolution, muddled through a new stage of organization. First came the Knights, who dreamily envisioned a revision of the entire economic system, and then the more pragmatic American Federation of Labor, determined to operate within the confines of that system. In 1877 the great railroad labor disturbances served notice to Americans, still primarily rural-oriented, that labor would be heard. The demonstrations continued throughout the Centennial years. By 1893 labor had won no great concessions, and had managed to rouse the ire of much of the public. For its great period of advance it had to await the 1930s. But again, twentieth-century labor owed its beginnings to the Centennial years.

Chronically unhappy, the farmers justly complained that their income kept slipping faster than the general wage-price index did. Mechanization and the expansion of cultivated area had much the same effect on the farmer as industrial mechanization and expansion had on business, except that the farmer felt it more personally. Wheat, which in 1876 sold at about one dollar a bushel, had fallen to less than half that figure by 1893. Farmers turned, as the American debtor-farmer chronically had, to the old panacea of inflation, on the

theory that it would increase prices and allow them to pay
their debts more easily. So they championed first greenbacks,
and later free silver, but inflation continued to elude them.
Ultimately, in the first decade of the new century, the farmer
found the good years he had so long sought. Then the
amount of money in circulation per capita did increase to desired levels, ironically enough due to increased stocks of gold.
The Grange, the Farmers Alliances, and the People's Party
desired other economic ends besides inflation, although free
silver was the magic that first united and then destroyed the
agrarian political alliance that the Populists represented.
Agrarians struck at monopolies that kept their expenses high,
singling out the railroads. For a decade the Granger laws
amended some of their grievances; an antitrust law passed
Congress, only to be nullified in practice by conservative
courts, and worse, to be used subsequently against farmer
and labor combinations. Even so, the legislation provided a
precedent and a platform for twentieth-century controls.

In certain rural and urban areas politics had fallen into the
hands of bosses and their machines. In the same manner that
the machines of industry more and more efficiently produced
goods, the political machines yielded votes. Both Republicans
and Democrats proved good at this sort of manipulation, and
both parties seemed to depend on it and upon other devices
to the exclusion of real issues. Even the tariff question was
not always enough to bring about party line votes in Congress. The Republicans waved the venerable "bloody shirt"
at the Democrats, and each party attempted to exploit the
other's scandals. Certainly neither paid the slightest attention to social justice. In an address delivered in Boston, late
in 1887, James Russell Lowell expressed these sentiments,
and more. "The success of the party," he said, "becomes only
too soon of more importance than that of any principles it
may be supposed to have. . . ." The chief use of the party
platform, Lowell opined, was to erect a "screen . . . of its
planks to hide its principles from every profane eye." The
only real difference between the parties that he could see
was that "one was *in* and wished to stay there, and the other
was *out* and *did n't* wish to stay there." Lowell lamented,

"Have we not more than once seen men nominated for the highest office . . . , men with no opinion that could be found out, but who would serve as well as another . . . to divide the booty?" He decried "the decay of civic courage," and concluded that "our politics call loudly for a broom. There are rubbish-heaps of cant in every corner . . . that should be swept out for the dustman Time to cart away and dump beyond sight or smell of mortal man."[2]

In many other ways, the Centennial years were years of beginnings too. As the period opened, the troops left the last Southern occupation posts, making way for an era of enlarged Jim Crowism and setting back Reconstruction's progress in civil rights for Negroes and poorer whites. In many lines of technology, as was demonstrated at the great fairs, America continued to leap ahead. Its navy and merchant marine grew. Railroad and industrial equipment became larger, heavier, faster, more efficient. Businesses such as advertising and insurance mushroomed into new areas. But, said James Russell Lowell at Harvard's 250th anniversary, "I am saddened when I see our success as a nation measured by the number of acres under tillage or bushels of wheat exported; for the real value of a country must be weighed in scales more delicate than the Balance of Trade." Not that such things can be ignored. "Material success is good," Lowell conceded, "but only as the necessary preliminary of better things."[3]

During the Centennial years, many farmers, labor leaders, and a few intellectuals agreed with Lowell, by pointing out the need for economic, political, and social reform. Yet these groups often worked at cross purposes, and except for a few instances seldom commanded a very large national following. But during the Centennial years industry spawned another group of Americans, an urban middle-class of white-collar workers. Between 1870 and 1910 this new group increased numerically about eight times, while the older middle-class of professional men and small businessmen more than doubled in size, along with the rest of the population. Both middle-class groups felt the economic and political threat of expanding big business on the one side and growing labor organization on the other, and, in the earlier Mugwump tradition, fought to control business in the economic sphere by regaining and then retaining control of the government on all levels, municipal, state, and national. Calling themselves progressives, regardless of their party affiliation, they were able to build on the foundations of reform laid in the Centennial years.

Among other things, they strengthened the Interstate Commerce Act of 1887 with the Hepburn Act of 1906 and the Mann-Elkins Act of 1910. They acknowledged that the Sherman Antitrust Act of 1890 had not been effective, yet in a flurry of antimonopoly activity they bested such behemoths as Standard Oil, the American Sugar Refining Company, and the American Tobacco Company. They passed pure food and drug legislation, a meat inspection act, and, under Theodore Roosevelt, forbade corporations to make campaign contributions. Under William Howard Taft they limited campaign expenditures on the national level and required they be made public. They failed in their first campaign for tariff revision under Taft, but succeeded—if temporarily—with Woodrow Wilson's Underwood Tariff on the eve of World War I. They attended to the financial problems of boom and bust first with the Aldrich-Vreeland Act of 1908, and then more firmly with the Federal Reserve Act of 1913. In 1916, through a rural credits law, they extended to the farmers the credit facilities that manufacturers and merchants had obtained with the Federal Reserve Act. Under Taft, labor received the recognition long overdue it with a cabinet post, and workingmen in the civil service received disability compensation with the Federal Workingmens Compensation Act of 1916. Populists of the 1890s cheered the ratification of the 16th Amendment in 1913, which permitted the levying of a federal income tax, and nineteenth-century critics of the "millionaires club" applauded the ratification of the 17th Amendment later in the same year, providing for the direct election of senators. The progressives swept out state houses sometimes with more energy and effectiveness than they were able to equal in Washington, often (but not always) with help from farmer and labor groups in the Centennial years tradition, and in-

stituted such measures as the initiative, referendum, and re-
call.

The social-justice movement, coming alive in the Centennial years, blossomed in the Progressive Era. Women, already
organized in clubs across the country before 1890, doubled
their club membership thereafter and fought for political and
legal equality and an array of other reforms. The journalistic
literature of exposure that antedated the Centennial years
blossomed on a new scale as the muckrakers probed municipal and corporate corruption and prodded progressives into
action. Yet no one pretends that the progressives solved all of
the problems that arose in the Centennial years, for they did
not. Modified by conditions in the twentieth century, later
generations in their New Deals, Fair Deals, New Frontiers,
and Great Societies continued the struggle. Lowell could take
heart, for in a very real way the Centennial years provided
the necessary preliminary for the better things that Americans in the next century strove to attain.

NOTES

PREFACE

[1] *Agricultural History*, Vol. 37, No. 2 (April, 1963), p. 119.

[2] *Ibid.*, p. 117.

[3] *Ibid.*, p. 119.

[4] Frederick C. Dietz's eulogy, mimeographed, no title, no date.

[5] [Fred A. Shannon,] "The Contributions of History and the Social Sciences to the Curriculum in American Civilization," mimeographed, no date, p. 1. The remainder of the following discussion in this vein is from the same source, pp. 1–12, *passim*.

[6] Fred A. Shannon, "Culture and Agriculture in America," *Mississippi Valley Historical Review*, Vol. XLI, No. 1 (June, 1954), pp. 3–20. The address was before the forty-seventh annual meeting of the society, Madison, Wisconsin, April 22, 1954.

Chapter I: THE NATION'S CENTENNIAL

[1] U.S. *Statutes at Large*, XXVI, 62.

[2] Derived from *Statistical Abstract of the United States*, 1941 (Washington, D.C., 1942), pp. 1–5.

[3] U.S. *Twelfth Census: Population*, Pt. I, pp. xxxvi, xxxvii.

[4] *Historical Statistics of the United States*, 1789–1945 (Washington, D.C., 1949), Series B 12, p. 25.

[5] *Ibid.*, B 31, p. 26.

[6] *Ibid.*, B 72–80, p. 27.

[7] *Ibid.*, C 6–21, p. 45.

[8] *Ibid.*, B 40–47, p. 27.

[9] *Ibid.*, B 194, p. 30.

[10] U.S. *Eleventh Census: Compendium*, Pt. I, *Population*, p. lxxxviii.

[11] *Historical Statistics*, B 279–303, p. 32.

[12] Joseph A. Hill, "Illiteracy," Bureau of the Census (U.S. *Twelfth Census: Supplementary Analysis and Derivative Tables, Special Report*, Washington, D.C., 1906), p. 332; *The Statesman's Yearbook: Statistical and Historical Annual of the States of the World for the Year 1901* (London, 1901), pp. 33, 622.

[13] U.S. Commissioner of Education, *Report*, 1907 (Washington,

D.C., 1908), II, 551; *Statistical Abstract*, 1891, pp. 254–55; Edgar W. Knight, *Public Education in the South* (New York, 1922), pp. 415–16, 419–20.

14 *Statistical Abstract*, 1948, p. 128.

15 See James L. Mursell, *Education for American Democracy* (New York, 1943), pp. 72–73; Ernest Carroll Moore, *Fifty Years of American Education: A Sketch of Education in the United States from 1867 to 1917* (Boston, 1917), pp. 70–74; Edgar Wallace Knight, *Education in the United States* (Boston, 1934), pp. 386–87; U.S. Commissioner of Education, *Report*, 1907, II, 571.

16 U.S. Bureau of Education, *Report of the Commissioner*, 1883–84 (Washington, D.C., 1885), p. xcix; *ibid.* 1893–94 (Washington, D.C., 1896), I, 150.

17 See Burke A. Hinsdale, "Training of Teachers," *Monographs on Education in the United States*, ed. Nicholas Murray Butler (Albany, 1900), I, 12–38; Edwin Grant Dexter, *History of Education in the United States* (New York, 1904), pp. 379–96; J. P. Gordy, *Rise and Growth of the Normal School Idea in the United States* (U.S. Bureau of Education, Circular of Information No. 8, Washington, D.C., 1891), pp. 99, 104–5, 130.

18 Merle Curti, *Social Ideas of American Educators* (New York, 1935), pp. 215–32; U.S. Commissioner of Education, *Report*, 1877, p. lxxxv; National Education Association, *Journal of Proceedings and Addresses*, 1885 (New York, 1886), p. 176.

19 U.S. *Eleventh Census: Statistics of Churches*, pp. xvii, xxiv; H. K. Carroll, in *The American Church History Series*, ed. Philip Schaff and others (New York, 1893), I, xvii, xxxv–xxxvi, 160.

20 Carroll, in *American Church History*, I, xx, xxii, xxiii.

21 William Warren Sweet, *Revivalism in America: Its Growth and Decline* (New York, 1945), pp. 174–75; William Warren Sweet, *The Story of Religion in Modern America* (2d rev. ed., New York, 1950), pp. 352–53.

22 Harvey Wish, *Society and Thought in America* (New York, 1950–52), II, 160–61, 168; Herbert Wallace Schneider, *Religion in 20th Century America* (Cambridge, Mass., 1952), p. 87; Charles W. Ferguson, *The Confusion of Tongues* (Garden City, N.Y., 1928), pp. 22–25, 70, 133, 137, 139.

23 James Freeman Clarke, *Ten Great Religions: An Essay in Comparative Theology* (Boston, 1871; 32d ed., 1892).

24 Charles Robert Darwin, *The Descent of Man and Selection in Relation to Sex* (London, 1871), II, 389.

25 For details see Stow Persons, "Evolution and Theology in America," Chapter XI in *Evolutionary Thought in America*, ed. Stow Persons (New Haven, 1950), especially pp. 426–27, 450–51; Arthur Meier Schlesinger, "A Critical Period in American Religion," Massachusetts Historical Society, *Proceedings*, LXIV (Boston, 1932), 523–29.

[26] Charles Augustus Briggs, *The Bible, the Church and the Reason* (New York, 1892), pp. 120–22, 236–47; 278; Stewart G. Cole, *History of Fundamentalism* (New York, 1931), pp. 34, 46; Andrew Dickson White, *History of the Warfare of Science with Theology in Christendom* (New York, 1903), II, 371–73, 377–78, 386.

[27] Sweet, *Religion in Modern America*, pp. 334, 345–52; William Warren Sweet, *Methodism in American History* (New York, 1933), pp. 350–51.

[28] Schlesinger, "Critical Period in American Religion," pp. 534–35.

[29] See Charles Howard Hopkins, *Rise of the Social Gospel in American Protestantism* (New Haven, 1940); and Henry F. May, *Protestant Churches and Industrial America* (New York, 1949).

[30] Hopkins, *Social Gospel*, pp. 53–117; May, *Protestant Churches*, pp. 170–262.

[31] Arthur Meier Schlesinger, *Rise of the City, 1878–1898* (New York, 1933), pp. 339–40.

[32] Winston Churchill, *The Inside of the Cup* (New York, 1913), *passim*, especially pp. 491–510.

Chapter II: THE UNDOING OF RECONSTRUCTION

[1] "Aids to Railroads," Federal Coordinator of Transportation, Section of Research, *Public Aids to Transportation* (Washington, D.C., 1938), II, Pt. I, 32–33, 52–55; Fred A. Shannon, *The Farmer's Last Frontier: Agriculture, 1860–1897* (New York, 1945), pp. 64–65.

[2] Paul H. Buck, *The Road to Reunion* (Boston, 1937), pp. 102–3, 105–7.

[3] Francis Butler Simkins, *A History of the South* (New York, 1953), pp. 311–12.

[4] Bourbon leaders are considered in relation to their economic connections in Willie D. Halsell, "The Bourbon Period in Mississippi," *Journal of Southern History*, XI (February, 1945), 519–37; Alex Mathews Arnett, *The Populist Movement in Georgia* (New York, 1922), pp. 22, 31, *et circa;* C. Vann Woodward, *Tom Watson, Agrarian Rebel* (New York, 1938), pp. 58–65; *ibid., Origins of the New South, 1877–1913* (Baton Rouge, 1951), pp. 9–14, 19–21; Francis Butler Simkins, *Pitchfork Ben Tillman, South Carolinian* (Baton Rouge, 1944), p. 79.

[5] Paul Lewinson, *Race, Class & Party: A History of Negro Suffrage and White Politics in the South* (New York, 1932), p. 54.

[6] United States v. Crosby, 25 *Federal Cases, Circuit and District Courts, 1789–1880* (St. Paul, 1896), 701–5; United States v. Reese, 92 U.S., 214–56.

7 United States v. Amsden, 6 *Federal Reporter* (St. Paul, 1881), 819–24.

8 United States v. Harris, 106 U.S., 629–44.

9 U.S. *Statutes at Large*, XX, 152.

10 Stephen B. Weeks, "The History of Negro Suffrage in the South," *Political Science Quarterly*, IX (December, 1894), 692; Lewinson, *Race, Class & Party*, pp. 58–59, 65; Woodward, *Origins of the New South*, p. 55.

11 William A. Dunning, "The Undoing of Reconstruction," *Atlantic Monthly*, LXXXVIII (October, 1901), 443; *Laws and Resolutions of the State of North Carolina, 1876–1877* (Raleigh, 1877), pp. 518–19, 521–22; *North Carolina Reports*, February session, 1892 (Raleigh, 1892), p. 240.

12 Weeks, "History of Negro Suffrage," p. 693.

13 Alfred H. Colquitt, "Is the Negro Vote Suppressed?" *The Forum*, IV (November, 1887), 273.

14 Dunning, "Undoing of Reconstruction," p. 444.

15 *The General Statutes of South Carolina*, 1882 (Columbia, 1882), Ch. VIII, sec. 116, p. 43; Weeks, "History of Negro Suffrage," p. 694.

16 Dunning, "Undoing of Reconstruction," p. 444.

17 *Ibid.*, pp. 444–45; Colquitt, "Is the Negro Vote Suppressed?" p. 273; Woodward, *Origins of the New South*, p. 56; Lewinson, *Race, Class & Party*, pp. 65–68.

18 Constitution of Mississippi, Art. XII, sec. 244, in Charles Kettleborough, ed., *The State Constitutions* (Indianapolis, 1918), pp. 763–64.

19 As quoted in Charles A. Beard, *Contemporary American History, 1877–1913* (New York, 1914), p. 8.

20 Colquitt, "Is the Negro Vote Suppressed?" p. 272; Lewinson, *Race, Class & Party*, p. 58; Vernon Lane Wharton, *The Negro in Mississippi, 1865–1890* (Chapel Hill, N.C., 1947), p. 202.

21 109 U.S., 3–63.

22 Woodward, *Origins of the New South*, pp. 210–11.

23 *Ibid.*, pp. 211–12.

24 Personally observed on December 31, 1924.

25 Personally observed in July, 1948.

26 E. Franklin Frazier, *The Negro in the United States* (New York, 1949), p. 159.

27 Woodward, *Origins of the New South*, pp. 158–59.

28 Thomas D. Clark, "The Country Newspaper: A Factor in Southern Opinion, 1865–1930," *Journal of Southern History*, XIV (February, 1945), 23–24; George Allen Hubbell, "Kentucky in the New Nation," *History of the States* (Vol. I of *The South in the Building of the Nation*, ed. J. A. C. Chandler [Richmond, 1919]), pp. 319–20.

29 The main constitutional amendments, laws, and judgments

are recorded in the session laws of Arkansas (1883), 346; Georgia (1877), 24–25; Louisiana (1882), 96–97; North Carolina (1879), 183–88; South Carolina (1879), 104–7; Virginia (1891–92), 533–42; and in 15 Florida, 455–553, especially 491; Ben: Perley Poore, ed., *Federal and State Constitutions* . . . (Washington, D.C., 1877), II, 1096 (for Mississippi); Tennessee, *Senate Journal*, 1885, p. 91; and *Commercial and Financial Chronicle and Hunt's Merchants' Magazine*, January 13, 1877, p. 28 (for Alabama). See also B. U. Ratchford, *American State Debts* (Durham, N.C., 1941), pp. 191–96; Willard A. Scott, *The Repudiation of State Debts* (New York, 1893), *passim*.

30 Woodward, *Origins of the New South*, pp. 89–96.

31 Paul Wallace Gates, "Federal Land Policy in the South, 1866–1888," *Journal of Southern History*, VI (August, 1940), 303, 309, 312–13.

32 *Ibid.*, pp. 304, 313–16, 318, 321, 326–27, 330.

33 Woodward, *Origins of the New South*, pp. 117–18.

34 Holland Thompson, *The New South: A Chronicle of Social and Industrial Evolution* (New Haven, 1919), p. 25.

35 Woodward, *Origins of the New South*, pp. 67–69.

36 *Ibid.*, pp. 68–72.

37 Bernard C. Steiner, "History of Maryland," *The South in the Building of the Nation*, ed. James Curtis Ballagh (Richmond, 1909), I, 221.

38 William O. Scroggs, "Convict and Apprentice Labor in the South," *Economic History, 1865–1909* (Vol. VI of *The South in the Building of the Nation*), p. 48; Woodward, *Origins of the New South*, pp. 212, 215.

39 *Biographical Directory of the American Congress, 1774–1949* (Washington, D.C., 1950), p. 811.

40 Scroggs, "Convict and Apprentice Labor," p. 50.

41 Wharton, *The Negro in Mississippi*, pp. 237–38.

42 Clark, "The Country Newspaper," pp. 21–22.

43 Except as otherwise indicated, this and the following paragraphs are based on Shannon, *The Farmer's Last Frontier*, pp. 80–100.

44 Robert Preston Brooks, *Agrarian Revolution in Georgia* (Madison, Wis., 1914), p. 57. Woodward, *Origins of the New South*, pp. 179–80, 205–6; U.S. *Twelfth Census: Agriculture*, V, Pt. I, lxxi.

45 Shannon, *The Farmer's Last Frontier*, p. 361.

46 *Ibid.*, p. 364.

47 Thomas D. Clark, "The Furnishing and Supply System in Southern Agriculture since 1865," *Journal of Southern History*, XII (February, 1946), 36–37.

48 *Ibid.*, p. 26; Jacqueline P. Bull, "The General Merchant in the

Economic History of the New South," *Journal of Southern History*, XVIII (February, 1952), 51.

[49] T. S. Stribling, *The Store* (London, 1932).

[50] Bull, "The General Merchant," p. 53.

[51] W. J. Cash, *The Mind of the South* (New York, 1941), pp. 163–64.

[52] Arnett, *The Populist Movement in Georgia*, p. 57; M. B. Hammond, *The Cotton Industry: An Essay in American Economic History* (New York, 1897), p. 155; Theodore Saloutos, "The American Society of Equity in Kentucky: A Recent Attempt in Agrarian Reform," *Journal of Southern History*, V (August, 1939), 348–49.

[53] Fred Albert Shannon, *America's Economic Growth* (3d ed., New York, 1951), pp. 345–46; Taylor v. Georgia, 315 U.S., 25–31.

Chapter III: HAYES AND PARTY DISSENSIONS

[1] Munn vs. Illinois, 94 U.S., 113.

[2] Charles Richard Williams, *The Life of Rutherford Birchard Hayes: Nineteenth President of the United States* (2 vols., Boston, 1914), I, 461.

[3] David Saville Mussey, *James G. Blaine: A Political Idol of Other Days* (New York, 1934), p. 133.

[4] George Frederick Howe, *Chester A. Arthur: A Quarter Century of Machine Politics* (New York, 1934), p. 101.

[5] Donald Barr Chidsey, *The Gentleman from New York: A Life of Roscoe Conkling* (New Haven, 1934), p. 278.

[6] Williams, *Life of Hayes*, II, 16–17.

[7] William Dudley Foulke, *Life of Oliver P. Morton* (Indianapolis, 1899), II, 480.

[8] Venila Lovina Shores, *The Hayes-Conkling Controversy, 1877–1879* (Northampton, Mass., 1919), p. 218; Edwin Earle Sparks, *National Development, 1877–1885* (New York, 1907), pp. 105–6; the other cabinet members were John Sherman of Ohio, Treasury; George W. McCrary of Iowa, War; Richard W. Thompson of Indiana, Navy; and Charles Devens of Massachusetts, Attorney General. Of these, only Sherman was an old party wheel horse.

[9] For the repeal of the election laws see Chapter II of this volume.

[10] William Dudley Foulke, *Fighting the Spoilsmen* (New York, 1919), p. 7.

[11] *Ibid.*, p. 10.

[12] Williams, *Life of Hayes*, I, 460–62.

[13] *Ibid.*, II, 72–75; Shores, *Hayes-Conkling Controversy*, pp. 244–45.

[14] Frank Mann Stewart, *The National Civil Service Reform League* (Austin, Tex., 1929), p. 23.

[15] Williams, *Life of Hayes*, II, 76–77; Shores, *Hayes-Conkling*

Controversy, p. 221; "Second Report of the Commission on the New York Custom House, and Instructions Relating Thereto," *House Executive Document* No. 8, 45 Cong., 1 Sess. (1877), pp. 38–40.

16 James D. Richardson, ed., *A Compilation of the Messages and Papers of the Presidents, 1789–1897* (10 vols., Washington, D.C., 1907), VII, 450.

17 *Ibid.*, pp. 450–51.

18 Shores, *Hayes-Conkling Controversy*, pp. 221, 239; Williams, *Life of Hayes*, II, 86.

19 Richardson, *Messages and Papers*, VII, 465–66; Chidsey, *Life of Conkling*, pp. 251–52.

20 Howe, *Chester A. Arthur*, pp. 79–80; Williams, *Life of Hayes*, II, 86–87; Chidsey, *Life of Conkling*, p. 252.

21 Williams, *Life of Hayes*, II, 92; Shores, *Hayes-Conkling Controversy*, p. 253.

22 H. J. Eckenrode, *Rutherford B. Hayes: Statesman of Reunion* (New York, 1930), p. 275.

23 Chidsey, *Life of Conkling*, p. 268.

24 John Sherman, *Recollections of Forty Years* (2 vols., Chicago, 1895), II, 681–85.

25 Lyon N. Richardson and Curtis W. Garrison (eds.), "George William Curtis, Rutherford B. Hayes, and Civil Service Reform," *Mississippi Valley Historical Review*, XXXII (September, 1945), 238.

26 *Harper's Weekly*, XXV (February 26, 1881), 130.

27 Carl Russell Fish, *The Civil Service and the Patronage* (Cambridge, Mass., 1904), p. 217.

28 *Our Government—For Spoils or Service?* (Public Affairs Pamphlet No. 3, Washington, D.C., 1936), p. 5.

29 Dorman B. Eaton, *Civil Service in Great Britain* (New York, 1880).

30 To be discussed in Chapter X.

31 These platforms are in *Appletons' Annual Cyclopaedia*, 1878, see index.

32 See Alexander C. Flick and Gustav S. Lobrano, *Samuel Jones Tilden: A Study in Political Sagacity* (New York, 1939), p. 429 *et seq.*

33 *Appletons' Annual Cyclopaedia*, 1878, pp. 433, 578, 599, 667, 684.

34 *Ibid.*, pp. 9, 222, 815.

35 *Ibid.*, pp. 443, 675, 771.

36 *Ibid.*, pp. 9, 221, 432 for Democrats, pp. 536, 567, 667, 815, 830 for Republicans.

37 C. Vann Woodward, *Reunion and Reaction: The Compromise of 1877 and the End of Reconstruction* (Boston, 1951), pp. 232–33; Alfred R. Conkling, *The Life and Letters of Roscoe Conkling, Orator, Statesman, Advocate* (New York, 1889), p. 569.

38 William E. Chandler, *Letters of Mr. William E. Chandler Relative to the So-Called Southern Policy of President Hayes, Together with a Letter to Mr. William Lloyd Garrison* (Concord, N.H., 1878); *Appletons' Annual Cyclopaedia*, 1878, pp. 623, 684.

39 *Appletons' Annual Cyclopaedia*, 1878, pp. 222, 452, 467, 561, 594, 598, 608–9.

40 *Ibid.*, pp. 9, 630, 783.

41 Ellis B. Usher, *The Greenback Movement of 1875–1884 and Wisconsin's Part in It* (Milwaukee, 1911), pp. 41–42; *Appletons' Annual Cyclopaedia*, 1878, p. 433; Woodward, *Reunion and Reaction*, p. 243.

42 *Appletons' Annual Cyclopaedia*, 1878, pp. 452, 684.

43 *Ibid.*, pp. 9, 433, 468, 534, 783.

44 See *ibid.*, pp. 432, 441, 442, 443, 783, for examples.

45 See *ibid.*, pp. 441, 442, 577, 668.

46 *Ibid.*, pp. 578, 609.

47 *Ibid.*, pp. 220, 236, 534, 598, 675, 668, 683.

48 *Ibid.*, pp. 9, 23, 505, 577, 675.

49 *Ibid.*, p. 566.

50 George F. Warren and Frank A. Pearson, *Gold and Prices* (New York, 1935), pp. 30–31.

51 Alex Mathews Arnett, *The Populist Movement in Georgia* (New York, 1912), p. 65; Max LeRoy Shipley, "The Greenback Issue in the Old Northwest" (Thesis in the University of Illinois Library, Urbana), p. 9.

52 *The National Greenbacker* (Rochelle, Ill.), August 2, 1878, p. 3.

53 See below, p. 168.

54 *Republican Campaign Textbook for 1878* (Washington, D.C., 1878), p. 1.

55 *Appletons' Annual Cyclopaedia*, 1878, p. 808.

56 John R. Commons and others, *History of Labour in the United States* (4 vols., New York, 1918–35), II, 246–47; Usher, *The Greenback Movement*, p. 56; Fred Emory Haynes, *James Baird Weaver* (Iowa City, 1919), p. 103; Max Cortis Kelley, "The Greenback Party in Illinois, 1876–1884" (Thesis in the University of Illinois Library, Urbana), p. 34; Fred E. Haynes, *Third Party Movements since the Civil War, with Special Reference to Iowa: A Study in Social Politics* (Iowa City, 1916), pp. 125, 135.

57 Charles Richard Williams (ed.), *Diary and Letters of Rutherford Birchard Hayes* (5 vols., Columbus, Ohio, 1922–26), III, 508.

58 Edward McPherson, *A Hand-Book of Politics for 1878* (Washington, D.C., 1878), pp. 141–43; *ibid.*, 1880, pp. 95–99. McPherson's totals do not always agree with the actual count from which he compiled them.

59 Dorman B. Eaton, *The Spoils System and Civil Service Reform in the Custom House and Post Office at New York* (New

York, 1881), pp. 27, 38, 70, 75; Stewart, *National Civil Service Reform League,* pp. 23–24; Foulke, *Fighting the Spoilsmen,* pp. 7–8.

Chapter IV: GARFIELD AND CONFUSION

[1] *Congressional Globe,* 39 Cong., 1 Sess., p. 2299.

[2] *New York Herald,* June 3, 1880.

[3] Theodore Clark Smith, *The Life and Letters of James Abram Garfield* (2 vols., New Haven, 1925), II, 963.

[4] *New York Herald,* June 4, 1880.

[5] *Ibid.,* June 5, 1880.

[6] *Ibid.,* June 6, 1880.

[7] *Ibid.,* June 7, 1880; E. E. Brown, *The Life and Public Services of James A. Garfield* (Boston, 1881), pp. 187–88.

[8] Alexander K. McClure, *Our Presidents and How We Make Them* (New York, 1900), pp. 272–73.

[9] Smith, *Life of Garfield,* II, 991.

[10] McClure, *Our Presidents,* p. 274.

[11] McPherson, *Hand-Book of Politics,* 1880, pp. 189–91.

[12] *Ibid.,* pp. 195–96.

[13] *Ibid.,* p. 194; Edward Stanwood, *History of the Presidency* (Boston, 1900), pp. 412–13; Alexander K. McClure, *Recollections of Half a Century* (Salem, Mass., 1902), p. 446.

[14] J. B. McClure, *Life of General Hancock* (Chicago, 1880), pp. 70–71; John W. Forney, *Life and Military Career of Winfield Scott Hancock* (Philadelphia, etc., 1880), pp. 369–70; McPherson, *Hand-Book of Politics,* 1880, p. 194; A. K. McClure, *Our Presidents,* pp. 278–79.

[15] McPherson, *Hand-Book of Politics,* 1880, p. 195.

[16] McClure, *Our Presidents,* pp. 282–83; James Herron Hopkins, *A History of Political Parties in the United States* (New York, 1900), pp. 162–63; Ernest H. Cherrington, *The Evolution of Prohibition in the United States* (Westerville, Ohio, 1920), p. 166.

[17] Smith, *Life of Garfield,* pp. 54, 104, 106–7, 110, 112, 173, 201, 355, 519, 631, 636, 639, 677, 691, 718–36; McClure, *Life of Hancock,* pp. 35, 37, 39–40, 47–48.

[18] Stanwood, *History of the Presidency,* pp. 415–18; *Appletons' Annual Cyclopaedia,* 1880, p. 576; Smith, *Life of Garfield,* II, 1027–30, 1039–41.

[19] McClure, *Our Presidents,* pp. 283–84.

[20] McPherson, *Hand-Book of Politics,* 1884, pp. 1–3.

[21] Smith, *Life of Garfield,* II, 1012–17, 1032–34, 1103–4.

[22] The other cabinet members, chosen without regard to Conkling's wishes, were Wayne MacVeagh of Pennsylvania for Attorney General, Samuel J. Kirkwood of Iowa as Secretary of the Interior,

Robert T. Lincoln of Illinois to be Secretary of War, and William H. Hunt of Louisiana for Secretary of the Navy.

[23] Howe, *Chester A. Arthur*, pp. 128, 132–33, 148; Chidsey, *Life of Roscoe Conkling*, pp. 332–33, 341, 346, 355–56; Smith, *Life of Garfield*, II, 1105–6, 1134–37; *Appletons' Annual Cyclopaedia*, 1881, pp. 644–50.

[24] Smith, *Life of Garfield*, II, 1156–58; Richardson, *Messages and Papers*, VIII, 147.

[25] J. Martin Klotsche, "The Star Route Cases," *Mississippi Valley Historical Review*, XXII (September, 1935), 413–14.

[26] Howe, *Chester A. Arthur*, pp. 180, 183; Klotsche, "Star Route Cases," pp. 407–8; Marshall Cushing, *The Story of Our Post Office: The Greatest Government Department in All Its Phases* (Boston, 1893), p. 32.

[27] Robert Granville Caldwell, *James A. Garfield, Party Chieftain* (New York, 1931), p. 335; Klotsche, "Star Route Cases," pp. 409–11.

[28] Klotsche, "Star Route Cases," pp. 407–9, 413; Smith, *Life of Garfield*, II, 1158–60; Caldwell, *James A. Garfield*, p. 334; Howe, *Chester A. Arthur*, p. 179; *Appletons' Annual Cyclopaedia*, 1882, p. 753.

[29] Howe, *Chester A. Arthur*, pp. 181–85; Klotsche, "Star Route Cases," pp. 414–15. The other new members of Arthur's cabinet were Secretary of State Frederick T. Frelinghuysen of New Jersey, Secretary of the Navy William E. Chandler of New Hampshire, Secretary of the Treasury Charles J. Folger of New York, who was followed in 1884 first by Walter Q. Gresham and then by Hugh McCulloch, both of Indiana, and Secretary of the Interior Henry M. Teller of Colorado. Howe was followed as Postmaster General by Gresham in 1883 and when Gresham moved to the Treasury Department Frank Hatton of Iowa completed the term.

[30] Howe, *Chester A. Arthur*, pp. 184–86, 189–91; *Appletons' Annual Cyclopaedia*, 1882, pp. 753–67.

[31] *New York Herald*, July 3, 1881, p. 7; Smith, *Life of Garfield*, II, 1179.

[32] Charles J. Guiteau, "Autobiography," printed in *New York Herald*, October 6, 1881, pp. 5–6; *New York Herald*, July 3, 1881, pp. 7–8; *New York Times*, July 3, 1881, p. 1 (first quotation); Smith, *Life of Garfield*, II, 1179; Caldwell, *James A. Garfield*, p. 350 (another version of Guiteau's first utterance). See also, Walter Channing, "The Mental Status of Guiteau, the Assassin of President Garfield," *Boston Medical and Surgical Journal*, CVI (March 30, 1882), 295.

[33] Charles F. Folsom, "The Case of Guiteau, Assassin of the President of the United States," *Boston Medical and Surgical Journal*, CVI (February 16, 1882), 145–46; Stewart Mitchell,

"The Man Who Murdered Garfield," *Massachusetts Historical Society, Proceedings,* XLVII (1941–44), 453–89.

³⁴ Folsom, "Case of Guiteau," pp. 147–49; *New York Herald,* October 6, 1881, p. 5.

³⁵ The report of the autopsy is printed in Brown, *James A. Garfield,* pp. 505–19.

³⁶ *Appletons' Annual Cyclopaedia,* 1882, p. 809.

Chapter V: ARTHUR AND HIS KNIGHTS

¹ Howe, *Chester A. Arthur,* pp. 152–55, 158–59; Ruth C. Silva, *Presidential Succession* (Ann Arbor, Mich., 1951), pp. 117–19; Charles Callan Taneill, *The Congressional Career of Thomas Francis Bayard, 1869–1885* (Washington, D.C., 1946), pp. 297–99; Sherman, *Recollections,* II, 831; George F. Hoar, *Autobiography of Seventy Years* (2 vols., New York, 1903), II, 168–69.

² *Senate Report* No. 576, 47 Cong., 1 Sess. (1882); Stewart, *National Civil Service Reform League,* pp. 32–33.

³ *Appletons' Annual Cyclopaedia,* 1882, pp. 693–94.

⁴ *Ibid.,* pp. 614, 693–94; Richardson, *Messages and Papers,* VIII, 145–47; Stewart, *National Civil Service Reform League,* pp. 38–41; United States Civil Service Commission, *Fourth Report* (Washington, D.C., 1888), pp. 542–46. For the Curtis decision see 106 U.S., 371–79; *Supreme Court Reporter,* I, 381.

⁵ A. Bower Sageser, *The First Two Decades of the Pendleton Act: A Study of Civil Service Reform* (Lincoln, Nebr., 1935), pp. 41–48, 51; Fish, *Civil Service and Patronage,* pp. 218–21; Howe, *Chester A. Arthur,* pp. 206–7; Dorothy Ganfield Fowler, *The Cabinet Politician: The Postmasters General, 1829–1909* (New York, 1943), p. 180; United States Civil Service Commission, *History of the Federal Civil Service, 1789 to the Present* (Washington, D.C., 1941), p. 50.

⁶ In the Senate, 23 Republicans, 14 Democrats, and 1 Independent voted for the bill; 5 Democrats against; while 14 Republicans, 18 Democrats, and 1 Readjuster did not vote at all. In the House it was 102 Republicans, 49 Democrats, and 4 Greenbackers for; 7 Republicans, 39 Democrats, and 1 Greenbacker against; 39 Republicans, 41 Democrats, and 7 Greenbackers not voting. McPherson, *Hand-Book of Politics,* 1884, pp. 8–18; Sageser, *The Pendleton Act,* pp. 57–59.

⁷ U.S. *Statutes at Large,* XXII, 403–7.

⁸ Dorman B. Eaton, "Two Years of Civil Service Reform," *North American Review,* CXLI (July, 1885), 21–22; *Senate Report* No. 576, 47 Cong., 1 Sess. (1882), pp. 2–3.

⁹ Foulke, *Fighting the Spoilsmen,* p. 38.

¹⁰ George S. Bernard, *Civil Service Reform versus the Spoils*

System (New York, 1885), App., p. 118; William E. Foster, *The Civil Service Reform Movement* (Boston, 1881), pp. 28–29.

[11] Foulke, *Fighting the Spoilsmen*, pp. 41–45; National Civil Service Reform League, *Proceedings*, 1887, pp. 36–37; Richardson, *Messages and Papers*, VIII, 844–51; Stewart, *National Civil Service Reform League*, p. 52; Indiana Civil Service Reform Association, *Document* No. 2 (Indianapolis, 1886), pp. 5–29.

[12] National Civil Service Reform League, *Proceedings*, 1884, pp. 12–13; *ibid.*, 1885, p. 27; Stewart, *National Civil Service Reform League*, pp. 34–37; Massachusetts, *Revised Laws* (Boston, 1902), pp. 324–31.

[13] U.S. *Statutes at Large*, XII, 501–2; R. N. Baskin, *Reminiscences of Early Utah* (Salt Lake City, 1914), p. 69.

[14] U.S. *Statutes at Large*, XVIII, Pt. 3, pp. 253–56; John Codman, *A Solution of the Mormon Problem* (pamphlet, New York, 1885), p. 4; 98 U.S., 145–69.

[15] Richardson, *Messages and Papers*, VII, 606; *ibid.*, VIII, 11, 57; Dyer Dan Lum, *Utah and Its People* (pamphlet, New York, 1882), p. 13; U.S. *Tenth Census: Population*, pp. 81–82; James H. Snowden, *The Truth about Mormonism* (New York, 1926), pp. 302–3.

[16] *Delegate from Utah* (pamphlet, Salt Lake City, 1881), *passim*; Nels Anderson, *Desert Saints* (Chicago, 1942), pp. 310–11.

[17] U.S. *Statutes at Large*, XXII, 30–32; U.S. *Senate Journal*, 47 Cong., 1 Sess. (1881), p. 92; *Congressional Record*, 47 Cong., 1 Sess., pp. 1157–58, 1195–1201, 1207–9.

[18] Robert Joseph Dwyer, *The Gentile Comes to Utah: A Study in Religious and Social Conflict* (Washington, D.C., 1941), p. 219; *Provo, Pioneer Mormon City* (WPA project, Portland, Ore., 1942), p. 109; Helen Mar Whitney, *Why We Practice Plural Marriage* (Salt Lake City, 1884), pp. 15–18, 63.

[19] 113 U.S., 143–49; Anderson, *Desert Saints*, pp. 313–14, 324; *Utah Statehood, Reasons Why It Should Not Be Granted: Report of the Utah Commission* (pamphlet, Salt Lake City, 1887), Pt. II, pp. 24–25; M. Hamlin Cannon (ed.), "The Prison Diary of a Mormon Apostle," *Pacific Historical Review*, XVI (November, 1947), 393–95.

[20] *Congressional Record*, 48 Cong., 1 Sess., pp. 354–64; Richardson, *Messages and Papers*, VIII, 361–62.

[21] U.S. *Statutes at Large*, XXIV, 635–41.

[22] Snowden, *Truth about Mormonism*, pp. 308–9; 136 U.S., 1–68; Baskin, *Early Utah*, pp. 183–84.

[23] Baskin, *Early Utah*, p. 238.

[24] U.S. *Statutes at Large*, XXII, 5–6.

[25] *The Nation*, XXXV (November 9, 1882), 391; *Harper's Weekly*, XXVI (November 11, 1882), 706; *Appletons' Annual Cyclopaedia*, 1882, p. 678; Richard Grant White, "The Business of

Office-Seeking," *North American Review,* CXXXV (July, 1882), 38.

26 *Appletons' Annual Cyclopaedia,* 1882, pp. 188–89, 421, 498, 555, 594.

27 Sherman, *Recollections,* II, 845; *The Nation,* XXXV (November 9, 1882), 391; *ibid.* (November 16, 1882), 414, 416.

28 *The Nation,* XXXIV (June 8, 1882), 476; *Commercial and Financial Chronicle,* January 6, 1883, p. 7; Commons, *History of Labour,* II, 316.

29 D. Leigh Colvin, *Prohibition in the United States* (New York, 1926), p. 134; *Appletons' Annual Cyclopaedia,* 1882, pp. 79–81, 592, 671–72; Sherman, *Recollections,* II, 846–47; *Congressional Directory,* 1884, pp. 9–11, 54, 73.

30 Haynes, *Third Party Movements,* pp. 144–47, 221.

31 Edward McPherson (ed.), *The Tribune Almanac and Political Register,* 1883, p. 96; McPherson, *Hand-Book of Politics,* 1884, pp. 1–3, 129–31.

32 James Truslow Adams (ed.), *Dictionary of American History* (New York, 1940), V, 412; Donald W. Mitchell, *A History of the Modern American Navy from 1883 through Pearl Harbor* (New York, 1946), p. 10; Frank M. Bennett, *The Steam Navy of the United States* (Pittsburgh, 1896), pp. 772–74.

33 *House Executive Document* No. 1, Pt. 3, 47 Cong., 1 Sess. (1882), pp. 5, 6, 29, 37; Bennett, *Steam Navy,* p. 775; Richardson, *Messages and Papers,* VIII, 51–52; Mitchell, *History of the Modern Navy,* p. 11; *House Report* No. 653, 47 Cong., 1 Sess. (1882), p. vii; U.S. *Statutes at Large,* XXII, 291–93.

34 French E. Chadwick, *The American Navy* (Garden City, 1915), pp. 249–50; *House Executive Document* No. 1, 47 Cong., 1 Sess., p. 180; Mitchell, *History of the Modern Navy,* p. 16; Richardson, *Messages and Papers,* VIII, 140–61; *House Executive Document* No. 1, 47 Cong., 2 Sess. (1883), pp. 21–23.

35 Bennett, *Steam Navy,* p. 77; U.S. *Statutes at Large,* XXII, 474, 476–78.

36 Richardson, *Messages and Papers,* VIII, 180–82, 209–10, 247–48.

37 *House Executive Document* No. 1, Pt. 3, 48 Cong., 2 Sess. (1885), pp. 3–7, 10–13, 15.

38 After consulting with the Attorney General, Augustus H. Garland of Arkansas, the Advisory Board made a new analysis of Roach's contract which resulted in the joint conclusion that there had been no dishonesty on the part of the naval officials who had drawn it up. But the bad publicity growing out of the scandal was probably a cause of Roach's failure in business and the losing of his mind. George F. Parker, "How Cleveland and Whitney Made the New Navy," *Saturday Evening Post,* CXCV (May 19, 1923), 46; *House Executive Document* No. 1, 49 Cong., 1 Sess. (1886), pp.

xix, xx, xxiii, xxv, 319, 322–23; Mitchell, *History of the Modern Navy,* pp. 16–17.

³⁹ Lewis Nixon, "The New American Navy," *Cassier's Magazine,* VII (December, 1894), 101; *Senate Document* No. 117, 58 Cong., 3 Sess. (1905), III, 17; Edward Simpson, "The United States Navy in Transition," *Harper's New Monthly Magazine,* LXXIII (June, 1886), 11, 17; *House Executive Document* No. 1, Pt. 3, 49 Cong., 2 Sess. (1886), VII, 7; George T. Davis, *A Navy Second to None: The Development of Modern American Naval Policy* (New York, 1940), pp. 44–45; *House Executive Document* No. 1, 50 Cong., 2 Sess. (1888), VIII, vi; *ibid.,* 51 Cong., 1 Sess. (1889), I, 15; Robley D. Evans, *A Sailor's Log: Recollections of Forty Years of Naval Life* (New York, 1901), p. 240; *Congressional Record,* 51 Cong., 1 Sess., pp. 5276–98; *Senate Executive Document* No. 43, 51 Cong., 1 Sess. (1890), pp. 13–14.

⁴⁰ Compiled from *The Statesman's Yearbook,* 1882 (London, 1882), p. 585; *Senate Document* No. 117, 58 Cong., 3 Sess. (1904–5), p. 14.

Chapter VI: TARIFF PROTECTION AND POLITICS

¹ Frank W. Taussig, *The Tariff History of the United States* (8th ed., New York, 1931), pp. 164–69, 194–95, 219–29; David R. Dewey, *Financial History of the United States* (10th ed., New York, 1928), pp. 396–98; Ida M. Tarbell, *The Tariff in Our Own Times* (New York, 1911), p. 109, for the name "Mongrel tariff."

² Thomas Hudson McKee, *The National Conventions and Platforms of all Political Parties, 1789–1900* (Baltimore, 1900), p. 165.

³ Edward Stanwood, *American Tariff Controversies in the Nineteenth Century* (2 vols., Boston, 1903), II, 195, 197–98.

⁴ "Samuel J. Randall," in Dumas Malone (ed.), *Dictionary of American Biography* (New York, 1935), XV, 350–51.

⁵ Tansill, *Congressional Career of Bayard,* pp. 103–4; James A. Barnes, *John G. Carlisle: Financial Statesman* (New York, 1931), pp. 45–46.

⁶ Dewey, *Financial History,* pp. 415–17; *Historical Statistics,* Series P 97, p. 296; U.S. *Statutes at Large,* XX, 265; John W. Oliver, *History of the Civil War Pensions, 1861–1885* (Madison, Wis., 1917), p. 70; *House Committee Report* No. 387, 46 Cong., 3 Sess. (1881), pp. 6–13; *House Report* No. 783, 49 Cong., 1 Sess. (1885–86), p. 4; Paul Studenski and Herman Krooss, *Financial History of the United States* (New York, 1952), p. 164.

⁷ Dewey, *Financial History,* pp. 426–29; Edward Campbell Mason, *The Veto Power: Its Origins, Development and Functions in the Government of the U. S., 1789–1889* (Boston, 1890), p. 104; *House Journal,* 47 Cong., 1 Sess. (1881–82), pp. 1788–89; Hoar,

Autobiography, II, 113; *Harper's Weekly*, XXVI (August 12, 1882), 498; *The Nation*, XXXV (August 10, 1882), 101; Albert Bushnell Hart, "Biography of a River and Harbor Bill," American Historical Association, *Papers*, III, No. 1 (New York, 1887), 192; U.S. *Statutes at Large*, XXII, 174, 191–213, 345.

[8] *Historical Statistics*, Series P 89, 97, 132, pp. 296, 306.

[9] Stanwood, *American Tariff Controversies*, II, 202–3; U.S. *Statutes at Large*, XXII, 64; *The Nation*, XXXIV (June 15, 1882), 491.

[10] Taussig, *Tariff History*, p. 231; Stanwood, *American Tariff Controversies*, II, 203–7; Tarbell, *The Tariff*, p. 106; James Ford Rhodes, *History of the United States from Hayes to McKinley, 1877–1896* (New York, 1919), p. 174.

[11] Sherman, *Recollections*, II, 852; Stanwood, *American Tariff Controversies*, II, 208–12, 215–16; William A. Robinson, *Thomas B. Reed, Parliamentarian* (New York, 1930), pp. 94–96.

[12] Taussig, *Tariff History*, pp. 232–33, 249–50; Stanwood, *American Tariff Controversies*, II, 217; Matthew Josephson, *The Politicos, 1865–1896* (New York, 1938), pp. 330–33.

[13] Sherman, *Reminiscences*, II, 852–54; Stanwood, *American Tariff Controversies*, II, 217–18; Henry L. Stoddard, *As I Knew Them* (New York, 1927), p. 214.

[14] U.S. *Statutes at Large*, XXII, 491.

[15] Taussig, *Tariff History*, pp. 233–50.

[16] Barnes, *John G. Carlisle*, pp. 57–58, 61, 67–74; Robinson, *Thomas B. Reed*, pp. 102–4; Festus Paul Summers, *William L. Wilson and Tariff Reform* (New Brunswick, N.J., 1953), pp. 53–54.

[17] Barnes, *John G. Carlisle*, pp. 78–81, 96; Stanwood, *American Tariff Controversies*, II, 220–21; Taussig, *Tariff History*, pp. 251–52.

[18] Robert McElroy, *Grover Cleveland, the Man and the Statesman* (2 vols., New York, 1923), I, 268; McKee, *National Conventions and Platforms*, pp. 204–5, 211–12; Barnes, *John G. Carlisle*, p. 82.

[19] Barnes, *John G. Carlisle*, pp. 99–100, 107–8, 109; Stanwood, *American Tariff Controversies*, II, 225; Taussig, *Tariff History*, p. 252.

[20] Richardson, *Messages and Papers*, VIII, 580–91; McPherson, *Hand-Book of Politics*, 1888, pp. 89–91; *ibid.*, 1890, pp. 1–3.

[21] Sherman, *Recollections*, II, 1009–10; Stanwood, *American Tariff Controversies*, II, 230–32, 234, 236, 239–42; Taussig, *Tariff History*, pp. 254–55; Allan Nevins, *Grover Cleveland: A Study in Courage* (New York, 1932), p. 386.

[22] For the election of 1888, see Chapter IX, below.

[23] Charles Sumner Olcott, *The Life of William McKinley* (2 vols., Boston, 1916), I, 4, 5, 137, 138, 154, 157; *Congressional*

Record, 50 Cong., 1 Sess., pp. 4407, 6658; Taussig, *Tariff History,* p. 258.

[24] McKee, *National Conventions and Platforms,* p. 240.

[25] Richardson, *Messages and Papers,* IX, 32–58.

[26] Robinson, *Thomas B. Reed,* pp. 199–234.

[27] Stanwood, *American Tariff Controversies,* II, 259–63.

[28] Taussig, *Tariff History,* pp. 256–83.

[29] Shannon, *America's Economic Growth,* p. 499.

[30] *Historical Statistics,* Series P 97, p. 296.

[31] Taussig, *Tariff History,* pp. 274, 275, 284; Harry Thurston Peck, *Twenty Years of the Republic, 1885–1905* (New York, 1906), pp. 215–16; Tarbell, *The Tariff,* pp. 210–11; Dewey, *Financial History,* p. 442.

Chapter VII: THE GROWTH OF MONOPOLIES

[1] Thomas C. Cochran and William Miller, *The Age of Enterprise* (New York, 1961), pp. 107–11, 119–53; John F. Stover, *American Railroads* (Chicago, 1961), pp. 74–75.

[2] Walter Adams and Horace M. Gray, *Monopoly in America: The Government as a Promoter* (New York, 1955), *passim.*

[3] Matthew Josephson, *The Robber Barons* (New York, 1934).

[4] *New York Times,* August 6, 1951, p. 23; *Time,* LVIII (August 13, 1951), 50.

[5] Lynn Thorndike, *The History of Medieval Europe* (Boston, 1917), p. 249.

[6] Allan Nevins, *The Emergence of Modern America, 1865–1878* (New York, 1927), pp. 194–202, quoted words on pp. 194, 199. An even more excoriating characterization of Gould is in Harry Thurston Peck, *Twenty Years of the Republic, 1885–1905* (New York, 1906), pp. 47–48.

[7] Rudolf Alexander Clemen, *The American Livestock and Meat Industry* (New York, 1923), pp. 179–80, 201–2.

[8] Rhodes, *Hayes to McKinley,* pp. 17–18; Lee Benson, *Merchants, Farmers, and Railroads, 1850–1877* (Cambridge, Mass., 1955), p. 47.

[9] Ellis Paxson Oberholtzer, *A History of the United States since the Civil War* (5 vols., New York, 1917–37), IV, 387.

[10] Robert Edward Riegel, *The Story of Western Railroads* (New York, 1926), pp. 155–56, 198, 200, 217–19.

[11] *Ibid.,* pp. 158–59, 217; [U.S.] Industrial Commission, *Final Report* (19 vols., Washington, 1900–2), XIX, 333.

[12] Woodward, *Origins of the New South,* pp. 121–22; Industrial Commission, *Report,* XIX, 333, 336; Riegel, *Western Railroads,* pp. 157–58, 200.

[13] George Pierce Baker, *The Formation of the New England*

Railroad Systems: A Study of Railroad Combination in the Nine-teenth Century (Cambridge, Mass., 1937), pp. 245–55; W. F. Gephart, *Transportation and Industrial Development in the Middle West* (New York, 1909), pp. 177–78; Woodward, *Origins of the New South*, p. 121.

14 Riegel, *Western Railroads*, pp. 161, 170–78, 204, 207; Oberholtzer, *History of the United States*, IV, 602–5.

15 George T. Clark, *Leland Stanford: War Governor of California, Railroad Builder, and Founder of Stanford University* (Stanford, 1931), pp. 188–89, 301, 334–39.

16 Thomas C. Cochran and William Miller, *The Age of Enterprise: A Social History of Industrial America* (New York, 1942), p. 132.

17 Josephson, *Robber Barons*, pp. 227–28.

18 Woodward, *Origins of the New South*, pp. 1–7, 31–37, 41–50; Nelson Trottman, *History of the Union Pacific: A Financial and Economic Survey* (New York, 1923), pp. 238, 240–41; A. J. Y. Brown, *The American Economy, 1860–1914* (New York, 1951), pp. 65, 73–74.

19 H. T. Newcomb and Edward G. Ward, "Changes in the Rates of Charge for Railway and Other Transportation Services," U.S. Department of Agriculture, Division of Statistics, *Miscellaneous Series, Bulletin* No. 15, rev. (Washington, D.C., 1901), esp. pp. 21–23, 25–26.

20 Personal observation. See also Eliot Jones, *Principles of Railway Transportation* (New York, 1924), p. 106; Oberholtzer, *History of the United States*, IV, 388–90.

21 Oberholtzer, *History of the United States*, IV, 390–91; Cochran and Miller, *Age of Enterprise*, p. 132; *Kansas City Times*, February 5, 1938, p. 1.

22 94 U.S., 164.

23 Cochran and Miller, *Age of Enterprise*, p. 169; Lewis H. Haney, *A Congressional History of Railways in the United States, 1850–1877* (Madison, Wis., 1910), pp. 288–90.

24 Richardson, *Messages and Papers*, VIII, 185.

25 Oberholtzer, *History of the United States*, IV, 392; 118 U.S., 557.

26 *Senate Report* No. 46, 49 Cong., 1 Sess. (1886), Pt. I, pp. 180–81; U.S. *Statutes at Large*, XXIV, 379–87; Ida M. Tarbell, *The Nationalizing of Business, 1878–1898* (New York, 1936), pp. 92–93, 97–101, gives a good account of the whole situation.

27 Interstate Commerce Commission, *Reports and Decisions* (New York, 1889–), I–IV, *passim;* William Zebina Ripley, *Railroads: Rates and Regulations* (New York, 1912), pp. 463, 469, 474; *ibid.*, ed., *Railway Problems* (Boston, 1907), *passim,* for decisions of the I.C.C. and Supreme Court action on appeals; Chicago, Milwaukee and St. Paul Railway Company v. Minnesota, 134 U.S., 418.

28 Industrial Commission, *Report*, XIX, 334–37; N. S. B. Gras and Henrietta M. Larson, *Casebook in American Business History* (New York, 1939), pp. 552–60; Frederick Lewis Allen, *The Great Pierpont Morgan* (New York, 1949), pp. 59–62; Lewis Corey, *The House of Morgan: A Social Biography of the Masters of Capital* (New York, 1930), pp. 159–60, 165, 167, 174–77.

29 William Wilson Cook, *Trusts* (New York, 1888), pp. 5–6.

30 Richard Theodore Ely, *Problems of Today* (New York, 1888), p. 111. See also George W. Stocking and Myron W. Watkins, *Monopoly and Free Enterprise* (New York, 1951), p. 30.

31 Victor S. Clark, *History of Manufactures in the United States* (2 vols., Washington, D.C., 1916, 1928; 3 vols., New York, 1929), I, 458; William Z. Ripley, ed., *Trusts, Pools and Corporations* (Boston, 1905), pp. xi–xii; Industrial Commission, *Report*, XIX, 596–97.

32 Ida M. Tarbell, *History of the Standard Oil Company* (2 vols., New York, 1904), I, 44–207; Burton J. Hendrick, *The Age of Big Business* (New Haven, 1919), pp. 31–43; Henry Rogers Seager and Charles A. Gulick, *Trust and Corporation Problems* (New York, 1929), pp. 108–10, 116; Henry Demarest Lloyd, "Story of a Great Monopoly," *Atlantic Monthly*, XLVII (March, 1881), 317–34.

33 Allan Nevins, *John D. Rockefeller: The Heroic Age of American Business* (2 vols., New York, 1940); *ibid.*, *Emergence of Modern America*, p. 399.

34 Tarbell, *Standard Oil Company*, I, 190–232; *ibid.*, II, 31–62; Hendrick, *Age of Big Business*, pp. 50–51.

35 Tarbell, *Standard Oil Company*, I, 239–62; *ibid.*, II, 3–30, 120; Hendrick, *Age of Big Business*, pp. 52–53.

36 Tarbell, *Standard Oil Company*, II, 88–128.

37 *Ibid.*, II, 129–141.

38 Ripley, *Trusts, Pools and Corporations*, p. xiii; Clark, *History of Manufactures*, II, 234–35, 237–38, 242–45, 505, 512, 513; Henry Demarest Lloyd, *Wealth against Commonwealth* (New York, 1894), pp. 537–44.

39 Henry George, *Progress and Poverty: An Inquiry into the Cause of Industrial Depressions, and of Increase of Want with Increase of Wealth, the Remedy* (New York, 1879); Edward Bellamy, *Looking Backward, 2000–1887* (Boston, 1888); William Godwin Moody, *Land and Labor in the United States* (New York, 1883). Concerning the accuracy of Lloyd, see Chester M. Destler, "Wealth against Commonwealth, 1894 and 1944," *American Historical Review*, L (October, 1944), 49–72; correspondence regarding the article in *ibid.*, L (April, 1945), 676–89; and Destler's mimeographed continuation of his letter in *ibid.*

40 *House Report* No. 3112, 50 Cong., 1 Sess. (1888); Tarbell, *Nationalizing of Business*, pp. 214–16; U.S. *Statutes at Large*, XXVI, 209–10.

41 Cochran and Miller, *Age of Enterprise*, pp. 171–72.

42 *Ibid.*, pp. 170, 172; Clark, *History of Manufactures*, II, 511–12; Ripley, *Trusts, Pools and Corporations*, p. xiii; Industrial Commission, *Report*, XIX, 598, 601.

43 Industrial Commission, *Report*, XIX, 595, 598, 605; Ripley, *Trusts, Pools and Corporations*, pp. xv, xvi; Hendrick, *Age of Big Business*, p. 139; Herbert B. Dorau, ed., *Materials for the Study of Public Utility Economics* (New York, 1930), pp. 91–95.

44 Hendrick, *Age of Big Business*, pp. 55–56.

Chapter VIII: THE ELECTION OF 1884

1 The platforms and other material on the national conventions are in McPherson, *Hand-Book of Politics*, 1884, pp. 197–222.

2 Morris Hillquit, *History of Socialism in the United States* (5th ed., New York, 1910), pp. 216–19, 221; Richard T. Ely, *The Labor Movement in America* (rev. ed., New York, 1890), pp. 269–70, 275–76; Howard H. Quint, *The Forging of American Socialism: Origins of the Movement* (Columbia, S.C., 1953), pp. 23–24; Nathan Fine, *Labor and Farmer Parties in the United States, 1828–1928* (New York, 1928), pp. 97, 102–3, 106, 116–17, 149.

3 Andrew Dickson White, *Autobiography of Andrew Dickson White* (2 vols., New York, 1905–7), I, 209–10.

4 *Dictionary of American Biography*, XI, 341.

5 McPherson, *Hand-Book of Politics*, 1884, Greenbackers, pp. 215–18; Anti-Monopoly, p. 219; American, p. 220; Prohibition, pp. 220–22.

6 Nicholas Murray Butler, *Across the Busy Years: Recollections and Reflections* (2 vols., New York, 1939–40), I, 216; White, *Autobiography*, I, 204.

7 Butler, *Across the Busy Years*, I, 216–17; Sherman, *Recollections*, II, 868, 886, 889; Joseph Benson Foraker, *Notes of a Busy Life* (2 vols., Cincinnati, 1916), I, 151–67.

8 H. C. Thomas, *The Return of the Democratic Party to Power in 1884* (New York, 1919), pp. 124, 145–47; Howe, *Chester A. Arthur*, pp. 215, 216, 256, 262, 264–65; Shelby Moore Cullom, *Fifty Years of Public Service: Personal Recollections of Shelby M. Cullom, Senior United States Senator from Illinois* (Chicago, 1911), p. 205; McClure, *Recollections*, p. 122; Hugh McCulloch, *Men and Measures of Half a Century* (New York, 1889), p. 484; Fowler, *The Postmasters General*, pp. 183–84, 186–87.

9 Howe, *Chester A. Arthur*, pp. 263–64.

10 Nevins, *Grover Cleveland*, pp. 159–60; Thomas, *Return of the Democrats*, pp. 157, 166, 168; Cullom, *Recollections*, pp. 185–88; McPherson, *Hand-Book of Politics*, 1884, p. 200; Republican National Committee, *Proceedings of the Eighth Republican Con-*

vention Held at Chicago, Illinois, June 3, 4, 5 and 6, 1884 (Chicago, 1884), pp. 141–62.

[11] Clarence Lee Miller, *The States of the Old Northwest and the Tariff, 1865–1888* (Emporia, Kan., 1929), p. 157.

[12] Thurman, McDonald, and Hoadly obtained formal presentation, and the first two had a fair showing with 88 and 56 votes respectively, but Hoadly got only 3. Thomas, *Return of the Democrats*, pp. 169–72; McPherson, in his *Hand-Book of Politics, 1884*, p. 215, gets confused on the second ballot and its amendments. More dependable is *Official Proceedings of the National Democratic Convention Held in Chicago, Ill.; July 8th.; 9th.; 10th.; and 11th.; 1884* (New York, [1884?]), pp. 227, 241, 247.

[13] Thomas, *Return of the Democrats*, pp. 173–74.

[14] *Ibid.*, pp. 72–73, 173–77; Allan Nevins (ed.), *Letters of Grover Cleveland, 1850–1908* (Boston, 1933), p. 14; Nevins, *Grover Cleveland*, pp. 61–62, 153.

[15] Thomas, *Return of the Democrats*, pp. 181–82, 201; White, *Autobiography*, I, 208; Henry Cabot Lodge, *Selections from the Correspondence of Theodore Roosevelt and Henry Cabot Lodge, 1884–1918* (2 vols., New York, 1925), I, 5–12, 26–28; Henry F. Pringle, *Theodore Roosevelt: A Biography* (New York, 1931), pp. 87–88.

[16] Butler, *Across the Busy Years*, I, 305–10; Nevins, *Grover Cleveland*, pp. 147, 150–54; McClure, *Recollections*, p. 126; Thomas, *Return of the Democrats*, pp. 188–94. See note 12, above, on McPherson.

[17] Benjamin F. Butler, *Butler's Book: Autobiography and Personal Reminiscences of Major-General Benj. F. Butler* (Boston, 1892), pp. 981–82; Thomas, *Return of the Democrats*, pp. 183–86.

[18] Thomas, *Return of the Democrats*, pp. 102–5, 141; White, *Autobiography*, I, 209; Nevins, *Grover Cleveland*, pp. 142–43; McPherson, *Hand-Book of Politics*, 1884, pp. 199–206; 213–15.

[19] McPherson, *Hand-Book of Politics*, 1884, pp. 204–5; Thomas, *Return of the Democrats*, pp. 214–15.

[20] George S. Boutwell, *Why I Am a Republican: A History of the Republican Party, a Defense of Its Policy and the Reasons which Justify Its Continuance in Power, with Biographical Sketches of the Republican Candidates* (Hartford, 1884), pp. 95–106; Wirt Armistead Cate, *Lucius Q. C. Lamar: Secession and Reunion* (Chapel Hill, N.C., 1935), pp. 399–404.

[21] Thomas, *Return of the Democrats*, pp. 205–7; Nevins, *Grover Cleveland*, pp. 160–62.

[22] Peck, *Twenty Years of the Republic*, pp. 34–37, first quotations; McClure, *Our Presidents*, p. 312; Thomas, *Return of the Democrats*, pp. 212–13; Nevins, *Letters of Cleveland*, pp. 37–38; Nevins, *Grover Cleveland*, pp. 162–69.

[23] Peck, *Twenty Years of the Republic*, p. 43.

[24] Nevins, *Grover Cleveland*, pp. 148, 170–73; Thomas, *Return of the Democrats*, pp. 210–12; Nevins, *Letters of Cleveland*, pp. 14, 34; *Butler's Book*, p. 983; Peck, *Twenty Years of the Republic*, p. 46.

[25] Thomas, *Return of the Democrats*, pp. 122–23, 197; Nevins, *Letters of Cleveland*, p. 37.

[26] Peck, *Twenty Years of the Republic*, pp. 46–48; Thomas, *Return of the Democrats*, pp. 225–26.

[27] Harold F. Gosnell, *Boss Platt and His New York Machine: A Study of the Political Leadership of Thomas C. Platt, Theodore Roosevelt, and Others* (Chicago, 1924), pp. 20–21, 31–32; Chidsey, *Life of Roscoe Conkling*, p. 374 (quotation from Conkling), 376–77; Thomas, *Return of the Democrats*, p. 202.

[28] Thomas, *Return of the Democrats*, pp. 141–42, 218–19, 221, 227; Nevins, *Grover Cleveland*, pp. 187–88.

[29] Chauncey M. Depew, *My Memories of Eighty Years* (New York, 1922), p. 145; Nevins, *Grover Cleveland*, pp. 181–82; Peck, *Twenty Years of the Republic*, pp. 43–44.

[30] Nevins, *Grover Cleveland*, pp. 182–83; Thomas, *Return of the Democrats*, p. 208; Peck, *Twenty Years of the Republic*, pp. 44–46.

[31] For example, see Sherman, *Recollections*, II, 890; Depew, *Memories*, pp. 139–40; Howe, *Chester A. Arthur*, p. 266; Thomas, *Return of the Democrats*, pp. 226–31; Nevins, *Grover Cleveland*, pp. 169, 186–87.

[32] McPherson, *Hand-Book of Politics*, 1888, pp. 1–3.

Chapter IX: CLEVELAND AND RESPECTABILITY

[1] Richardson, *Messages and Papers*, VIII, 299, 303.

[2] The other members of the cabinet were Secretary of the Treasury Daniel Manning of New York, succeeded in 1887 by Charles S. Fairchild of the same state; Secretary of War William C. Endicott of Massachusetts; and Attorney General Augustus H. Garland of Arkansas.

[3] Peck, *Twenty Years of the Republic*, pp. 57–58, 92–94.

[4] *Ibid.*, pp. 56, 71–78; 83–89.

[5] Charles S. Hamlin, "The Presidential Succession Act of 1886," *Harvard Law Review*, XVIII (January, 1905), 187–90; Silva, *Presidential Succession*, pp. 120–23; Barnes, *John G. Carlisle*, pp. 111–12; Stanwood, *History of the Presidency*, pp. 450–52; Hoar, *Autobiography*, II, 171; U.S. *Statutes at Large*, XXIV, 1–2.

[6] U.S. *Statutes at Large*, XXIV, 373–75.

[7] *Ibid.*, XXIV, 500; Hoar, *Autobiography*, II, 143–44; McPherson, *Hand-Book of Politics*, 1888, p. 46.

[8] Robert E. Riegel, *American Moves West* (rev. ed., New York,

1947), pp. 502–4; Ray Allen Billington, *Westward Expansion: A History of the American Frontier* (New York, 1949), pp. 669–70; Loring Benson Priest, *Uncle Sam's Stepchildren* (New Brunswick, N.J., 1942), pp. 188–97; U.S. *Statutes at Large*, XXIV, 388–91.

9 U.S. *Statutes at Large*, XXIV, 391–92; McPherson, *Hand-Book of Politics*, 1888, pp. 13–15.

10 McPherson, *Hand-Book of Politics*, 1888, pp. 47–48.

11 *Ibid.*, pp. 64–66.

12 D. W. Lusk, *Politics and Politicians of Illinois, 1809–1887* (Springfield, Ill., 3d ed., 1887), p. 670; *Chicago Daily News*, November 4, 1886, p. 5; *Cincinnati Daily Times-Star*, October 5, 1886, p. 4; *Daily Illinois State Journal*, November 3, 1886; *ibid.*, November 6, 1886.

13 *Daily Illinois State Journal*, November 4, 1886.

14 Logan Esarey, *A History of Indiana* (2 vols., Indianapolis, 1915–18), II, 955.

15 *Cincinnati Enquirer*, June 18, 1886, p. 3; *Tribune Almanac*, 1887, p. 76; Miller, *Old Northwest and the Tariff*, pp. 137–40.

16 *Boston Post*, November 6, 1886.

17 *Boston Herald*, November 3, 1886; *Tribune Almanac*, 1887, pp. 86–88. Stanwood, *American Tariff Controversies*, II, 226, seems to think that "there is no evidence of any sort, certainly none in the result of the elections, that the people, the common people, . . . were thinking about the tariff. They voted each man with his party." It could be that Stanwood did not peer far into the evidence.

18 James Gillespie Blaine, *Political Discussions, Legislative, Diplomatic and Popular, 1856–1886* (Norwich, Conn., 1887), p. 488; William Graham Sumner, "Mr. Blaine on the Tariff," *North American Review*, CXLIII (October, 1886), 398–405; Nevins, *Grover Cleveland*, p. 281; David Lindsey, *"Sunset" Cox, Irrepressible Democrat* (Detroit, 1959), p. 244.

19 McPherson, *Hand-Book of Politics*, 1888, pp. 89–91.

20 Hoar, *Autobiography*, II, 145.

21 Nevins, *Grover Cleveland*, pp. 243, 248, 251; Peck, *Twenty Years of the Republic*, pp. 146–48.

22 Robert M. LaFollette, *Autobiography* (Madison, Wis., 1911), pp. 60–62; U.S. *Statutes at Large*, XXIV, 310–35.

23 Hart, "Biography of a River and Harbor Bill," pp. 191–94; McPherson, *Hand-Book of Politics*, 1888, pp. 49–51.

24 Mason, *The Veto Power*, pp. 168, 179; *Senate Journal*, 49 Cong., 1 Sess. (1887), pp. 957–58.

25 Richardson, *Messages and Papers*, VIII, 415–17.

26 George F. Parker (ed.), *The Writings and Speeches of Grover Cleveland* (New York, 1892), p. 377.

27 Oliver, *Civil War Pensions*, pp. 104–12, 115; Nevins, *Grover Cleveland*, pp. 326–27.

[28] A bill passed the House as late as January 2, 1925, for an honorable discharge of a veteran of more than sixty years before, with no votes for or against, Speaker Nicholas Longworth breaking the tie of 0 to 0 and passing the measure after a member had explained that the sole purpose was to get the man on the pension rolls. Personal observation.

[29] Mason, *The Veto Power*, pp. 87–88; Nevins, *Grover Cleveland*, pp. 328–91; Peck, *Twenty Years of the Republic*, pp. 89–92; McPherson, *Hand-Book of Politics*, 1890, p. 26, for number of vetoes. They were 250 by message and 47 pocketed. Another 227 became law by lapse of time, without approval.

[30] U.S. *Statutes at Large*, XXV, 173–74.

[31] *Ibid.*, XXIV, 371–72.

[32] McPherson, *Hand-Book of Politics*, 1888, pp. 17–22, 29.

[33] William H. Glasson, *Federal Military Pensions in the United States* (New York, 1918), pp. 208–10, 212–18; Nevins, *Grover Cleveland*, pp. 330–31.

[34] Glasson, *Military Pensions*, pp. 223–38; U.S. *Statutes at Large*, XXVI, 182–83; *Historical Statistics*, Series P 97, 98, p. 296; Peck, *Twenty Years of the Republic*, pp. 197–98.

[35] McElroy, *Grover Cleveland*, I, 205–8; Nevins, *Grover Cleveland*, pp. 332–34; Richardson, *Messages and Papers*, VIII, 578–79.

[36] Denis Tilden Lynch, *Grover Cleveland: A Man Four-Square* (New York, 1932), p. 338; John and William Tecumseh Sherman, *The Sherman Letters* (New York, 1894), p. 375.

[37] Nevins, *Grover Cleveland*, p. 333; *New York Tribune*, June 15–22, 1887, esp. pp. 1–2 of June 17.

[38] Nevins, *Grover Cleveland*, pp. 333–39; McElroy, *Grover Cleveland*, I, 205–9.

[39] U.S. *Statutes at Large*, XXXIII, Pt. 1, p. 1284.

[40] Alexander D. Noyes, *Forty Years of American Finance: A Short Financial History of the Government and People of the United States since the Civil War, 1865–1907* (New York, 1909), pp. 133–34; E. Benjamin Andrews, *The United States in Our Own Time* (New York, 1903), p. 550; Stanwood, *History of the Presidency*, p. 448; Peck, *Twenty Years of the Republic*, pp. 148–51.

[41] *Appletons' Annual Cyclopaedia*, 1888, pp. 778–80; McKee, *National Conventions and Platforms*, pp. 248–51.

[42] Quint, *Forging of American Socialism*, pp. 54–55.

[43] *Appletons' Annual Cyclopaedia*, 1888, pp. 777–78, 780.

[44] *Ibid.*, pp. 773–74.

[45] *Ibid.*, pp. 775–77.

[46] Gail Hamilton [M. A. Dodge], *Biography of James G. Blaine* (New York, 1895), pp. 604, 606.

[47] *Appletons' Annual Cyclopaedia*, 1888, pp. 774–75.

[48] *Ibid.*, pp. 781–82.

[49] Andrews, *United States in Our Own Time*, pp. 557–58.

[50] Russell H. Conwell, *The Romantic Rise of a Great American*

(New York, 1925), pp. 109–11; Herbert Adams Gibbons, *John Wanamaker* (2 vols., New York, 1926), I, 258–59, tells of a charge made after the election, one that Wanamaker stoutly denied, that he gave Quay this $400,000 to buy votes on Long Island so as to assure a majority in the state of New York.

[51] Donald L. McMurry, "The Political Significance of the Pension Question, 1885–1897," *Mississippi Valley Historical Review*, IX (June, 1922), 30.

[52] Andrews, *United States in Our Own Time*, p. 557; Stanwood, *History of the Presidency*, p. 481.

[53] Andrews, *United States in Our Own Time*, pp. 550, 553; Stanwood, *History of the Presidency*, pp. 482, 484; *New York Tribune*, October 31, 1888, pp. 1–2.

[54] Peck, *Twenty Years of the Republic*, p. 161.

[55] The Prohibitionists received 249,506 votes, Union Labor 146,953, United Labor 2818, American 1591, and others 7006. The Socialists in the city of New York had finally nominated a candidate for President to whom they gave 2068 votes. Stanwood, *History of the Presidency*, pp. 483–85; Andrews, *United States in Our Own Time*, p. 558; *Appletons' Annual Cyclopaedia*, 1888, p. 782; McPherson, *Hand-Book of Politics*, 1890, pp. 245–48.

[56] The other cabinet members were Treasury, William Windom of Minnesota; War, Redfield Proctor of Vermont; Navy, Benjamin F. Tracy of New York; and Interior, John W. Noble of Missouri.

Chapter X: FINANCIAL AND AGRARIAN PROBLEMS

[1] This chapter is based in part on Shannon, *America's Economic Growth,* pp. 397–419; Shannon, *The Farmer's Last Frontier,* pp. 291–328.

[2] For census and midcensus years, *Statistical Abstract*, 1948, p. 408; for other years, population figures in *ibid.*, p. 9, divided into circulating-money figures in *Historical Statistics*, Series P 151, p. 274.

[3] Warren and Pearson, *Gold and Prices*, pp. 30–31.

[4] *Ibid.*; U.S. Department of Agriculture, *Yearbook*, 1899 (Washington, D.C., 1900), pp. 759–64, 818. In addition, consider that the farm value of the nine leading crops and of the six most valuable kinds of animals in 1880 was a little over $5,000,000,000, while that of manufactures was only 7.4 per cent greater, then note that the prices of farm and nonfarm products were averaged together to obtain the composite "all commodities" on the statisticians' charts. It becomes evident that an index for manufactures alone would be as far above the all-commodities curve as farm prices were below, and that the real disadvantage of the agriculturist in selling and buying was twice what the statisticians' curves would, at first glance, seem to indicate.

5 John D. Hicks, *The Populist Revolt* (Minneapolis, 1931), p. 60.

6 Newcomb and Ward, "Changes in Rates," pp. 21, 23, 25.

7 *U. S. Tenth Census: Transportation*, bottom folio, p. 23.

8 Newcomb and Ward, "Changes in Rates," pp. 21–26; Solon Justus Buck, *The Granger Movement: A Study of Agricultural Organization and Its Political, Economic, and Social Manifestations, 1870–1880* (Cambridge, Mass., 1913), pp. 233–37.

9 *Yearbook of Agriculture*, 1899, p. 759.

10 Earl W. Hayter, "An Iowa Farmers' Protective Association: A Barbed Wire Patent Movement," *Iowa Journal of History and Politics*, XXXVII (October, 1939), 339; Hicks, *Populist Revolt*, pp. 6, 15, 18–19.

11 Fred A. Shannon, "A Post Mortem on the Labor-Safety-Valve Theory," *Agricultural History*, XIX (January, 1945), 31–37.

12 Claude L. Benner, *The Federal Intermediate Credit System* (New York, 1926), pp. 18, 20–23; Hicks, *Populist Revolt*, pp. 21–24.

13 Hicks, *Populist Revolt*, pp. 24–29.

14 Personal observation.

15 Hicks, *Populist Revolt*, pp. 30–32, 84.

16 Registries of Deeds in the Wabaunsee County Court House, Alma, Kansas.

17 See W. F. Mappin, "Farm Mortgages and the Small Farmer," *Political Science Quarterly*, IV (September, 1889), 433–51.

18 Hicks, *Populist Revolt*, pp. 32–35, 95, 160.

19 "Inflation and the West," *The Nation*, VI (March 5, 1868), 187–90.

20 "The Debtor Class," *The Nation*, XVIII (April 23, 1874), 262–63.

21 U.S. *Statutes at Large*, XVII, 424–36.

22 J. Laurence Laughlin, *The History of Bimetallism in the United States* (4th ed., New York, 1896), pp. 67, 297.

23 *Historical Statistics*, Series G 120, pp. 151–52.

24 Roy Harrod, *The Dollar* (New York, 1954), pp. 8, 17.

25 Laughlin, *Bimetallism*, pp. 102–5, 256–58; U.S. *Statutes at Large*, XIX, 215.

26 U.S. *Statutes at Large*, XVIII, Pt. I, 296.

27 Dewey, *Financial History*, pp. 372–74.

28 *Historical Statistics*, Series N 165, p. 275; U.S. *Statutes at Large*, XX, 87.

29 Dewey, *Financial History*, p. 375.

30 *Ibid.*, pp. 441–42; U.S. *Statutes at Large*, XXII, 162–66, esp. 165.

31 Dewey, *Financial History*, pp. 389–91.

32 See *ibid.*, pp. 379–81.

33 The whole of Laughlin, *Bimetallism*, is permeated, sometimes caustically, with the gold-standard argument; Dewey, *Finan-*

cial History, pp. 402–13, is more judicious. See also Alonzo B. Hepburn, *History of Currency in the United States* (New York, ed. of 1916), pp. 229–50, 287–304, 342–50, 421–25. The ratio of silver to gold from 1789 to 1945 is in *Historical Statistics,* Series N 184, pp. 277–78.

34 Laughlin, *Bimetallism,* pp. 211–16.

35 U.S. *Statutes at Large,* XX, 25–26.

36 Dewey, *Financial History,* pp. 407–8; Laughlin, *Bimetallism,* pp. 297, 298.

37 Except as otherwise indicated, the paragraphs on the alliances draw from Fred A. Shannon, "C. W. Macune and the Farmers' Alliance," *Current History,* XXVIII (June, 1955), 330–35; and Roy Vernon Scott, "Milton George and the Western Rural" (Thesis in the University of Illinois Library).

38 *Western Rural,* March 6, 1880, p. 76; *ibid.,* November 13, 1880, p. 364; *ibid.,* December 3, 1892, p. 775; *Industrial Struggle* (Chicago, 1893), p. 33; Milton George (ed.), *The Western Rural Year Book* (Chicago, 1886), p. 142. *Industrial Struggle,* like the other two, reflects the voice and control of Milton George.

39 *Chicago Tribune,* October 6, 1881, p. 7.

40 National Farmers' Alliance, *History of the Alliance Movement* (Chicago, 1882), pp. 11–12, another *Western Rural* publication.

41 Hicks, *Populist Revolt,* pp. 96–104.

42 N. B. Ashby, *The Riddle of the Sphinx* (Chicago, 1892), pp. 465–69. See also N. A. Dunning (ed.), *Farmers' Alliance History and Agricultural Digest* (Washington, D.C., 1891), pp. 226–28; *National Economist,* November 16, 1889, p. 134; J. E. Bryan, *The Farmers' Alliance: Its Origin, Progress, and Purposes* (Fayetteville, Ark., 1891), p. 69; Carl C. Taylor, *The Farmers' Movement, 1620–1920* (New York, 1953), p. 219; *Prairie Farmer,* LXII (December 13, 1890), 792.

43 Hicks, *Populist Revolt,* pp. 104–13; Francis Butler Simkins, *The Tillman Movement in South Carolina* (Durham, N.C., 1926), pp. 147–48; H. R. Chamberlain, *The Farmers' Alliance: What It Aims to Accomplish* (New York, 1891), p. 28.

44 Solon Justus Buck, *The Agrarian Crusade* (New Haven, 1921), pp. 111–31; Clarence Herman Nixon, "The Cleavage within the Farmers' Alliance Movement," *Mississippi Valley Historical Review,* XV (June, 1928), 22–33; Hallie Farmer, "The Economic Background of Frontier Populism," *Mississippi Valley Historical Review,* X (March, 1924), 406–27; Hicks, *Populist Revolt,* pp. 114–25.

45 Shannon, "Macune and the Farmers' Alliance," pp. 332–35. The essence of the subtreasury concept went into the United States Warehouse Act of August 11, 1916, and later expanded mightily. If, since 1933, Congress has carried the proposal to extremes, it should be remembered that Macune advocated the storage of *imperishable* goods.

[46] Hicks, *Populist Revolt*, pp. 427–30.

[47] U.S. *Statutes at Large*, XXVI, 289–90.

[48] Dewey, *Financial History*, pp. 436–38.

[49] John Sherman, *Recollections of Forty Years* (Chicago, 1895), II, 1070–71, 1188.

[50] See tables in Laughlin, *Bimetallism*, pp. 297, 298, on which these calculations are based.

Chapter XI: THE FARMERS

[1] Lowden's statement to Midwestern farmers based on personal recollection.

[2] Charles H. Cochrane, "Past, Present and Future of American Meats," *Moody's Magazine*, V (December, 1907), 38–39. The "embalmed beef" scandal did not come until the war with Spain; this prejudice may help explain a sharp decline in meat exports during the following decade: *Statistical Abstract*, 1948, p. 916.

[3] *Statistical Abstract*, 1948, pp. 916–17; *Historical Statistics*, Series M 58, p. 246.

[4] Frank H. Hitchcock, "Agricultural Exports of the United States, 1851–1902," U.S. Department of Agriculture, Division of Foreign Markets, *Bulletin* 34 (Washington, D.C., 1903), p. 9. According to this source, the percentage of farm products shipped abroad to the total of exports was 84.3 in 1880, nine points lower in 1890, and 61.6 in 1900.

[5] Based on figures in P. K. Whelpton, "Occupational Groups in the United States, 1820–1920," American Statistical Association, *Journal*, XXI (September, 1926), 339–40. Before 1920, the census takers did not record farm population as distinguished from nonfarm, but for a century before this they had been listing people according to their occupations. Statisticians have unscrambled these figures for the years following 1860 and have shown that the ratio of farm to entire population was fairly close to that of employment on the farm to the total. See also *Statistical Abstract*, 1948, p. 9; and *Historical Statistics*, Series B 304, pp. 33–34.

[6] *Historical Statistics*, Series F 29, 30, p. 121.

[7] *Ibid.*, Series E 182, 187, 214, 226, 229, pp. 106, 108, 109. The corn crop referred to in the text, from 1877 to 1890, is that for all purposes, including that which meat animals consumed.

[8] *Yearbook of Agriculture*, 1899, p. 818.

[9] *Historical Statistics*, Series E 218, p. 108.

[10] C. Warren Thornthwaite, assisted by Helen I. Slentz, *Internal Migration in the United States* (Philadelphia, 1934), pp. 5–6, and Plate II.

[11] Shannon, "Post Mortem on the Labor–Safety-Valve Theory," pp. 36–37.

[12] Everett N. Dick, *The Sod-House Frontier, 1854–1890* (New York, 1937), p. 186.

[13] *Ibid.*, pp. 188–98.

[14] Carl Wittke, *We Who Built America: The Saga of the Immigrant* (New York, 1939), pp. 149–53.

[15] Marcus Lee Hansen, *The Mingling of the Canadian and American Peoples* (New Haven, 1940), pp. 184–218.

[16] George M. Stephenson, *A History of American Immigration, 1820–1924* (Boston, 1926), pp. 51–52; Wittke, *We Who Built America*, pp. 201–3, 207–10.

[17] Stephenson, *American Immigration*, pp. 30–37; Wittke, *We Who Built America*, pp. 262, 269–71, 286–87, 289, 293–96, 300–38, 405–18.

[18] Shannon, *Farmer's Last Frontier*, pp. 131–47, and Plate facing p. 160.

[19] T. Swann Harding, *Two Blades of Grass: A History of Scientific Development in the U. S. Department of Agriculture* (Norman, Okla., 1947), pp. 30–33, 147–51.

[20] *Ibid.*, pp. 33–34, 173–77.

[21] *Ibid.*, pp. 40, 42, 61–63, 83.

[22] Joseph Cannon Bailey, *Seaman A. Knapp, Schoolmaster of American Agriculture* (New York, 1945), pp. 109–32.

[23] Shannon, *Farmer's Last Frontier*, pp. 156–61.

[24] Moody, *Land and Labor, passim.*

[25] Paul W. Gates, "Recent Land Policies of the Federal Government," *Certain Aspects of Land Problems and Government Land Policies* (Part VII of the Land Planning Committee of the National Resources Board, *Report on Land Planning*, Washington, D.C., 1935), p. 65.

[26] Louis Bernard Schmidt and Earle Dudley Ross, *Readings in the Economic History of American Agriculture* (New York, 1925), pp. 370–80; U.S. *Sixteenth Census: Agriculture*, III (*General Report*), p. 718.

[27] Schmidt and Ross, *Readings*, pp. 381–89.

[28] Fred A. Shannon, "The Status of the Midwestern Farmer in 1900," *Mississippi Valley Historical Review*, XXXVII (December, 1950), pp. 492–95.

[29] U.S. Commissioner of Agriculture, *Report*, 1863 (Washington, D.C., 1863), p. 203.

[30] Alva Wilfred Craver, "Factors Which Tend to Cause Fluctuations in the Price of Live Hogs and Pork Products" (Thesis in the University of Illinois Library), pp. 35–37, 64.

[31] William H. Brewer, "The Past and Future of Connecticut Agriculture," Connecticut Board of Agriculture, *Twenty-Fourth Annual Report*, 1890 (Hartford, 1891), p. 165; Philip Morgan and Alvan F. Sanborn, "The Problems of Rural New England," *Atlantic Monthly*, LXXIX (May, 1897), p. 584.

[32] U.S. *Eighth Census: Agriculture,* pp. 184–87; *Yearbook of Agriculture,* 1899, pp. 765–70, 820–21; Frederick Irving Anderson, *The Farmer of To-morrow* (New York, 1913), p. 18.

[33] U.S. *Eighth Census: Agriculture,* p. vii; U.S. *Twelfth Census: Agriculture,* I, 142; *Statistical Abstract,* 1926, pp. 580–81.

[34] C. N. Hall, "Some Features of Old Connecticut Farming," *New England Magazine,* XXII, N.S. (July, 1900), p. 549.

[35] *Yearbook of Agriculture,* 1899, p. 60.

[36] Clifton Johnson, "The Deserted Homes of New England," *Cosmopolitan,* XV (June, 1893), p. 220.

[37] William Henry Bishop, "Hunting an Abandoned Farm in Connecticut," *Century Magazine,* XLVII, O.S. (April, 1894), pp. 915–24.

[38] Charles C. Nott, "A Good Farm for Nothing," *The Nation,* XLIX (November 21, 1889), 406–8; Brewer, "Connecticut Agriculture," pp. 161–62.

[39] T. S. Gold, *Handbook of Connecticut Agriculture* (Hartford, 1901), pp. 32, 41–88 *passim;* Joseph B. Walker, "The Progress of New England Agriculture during the Last Thirty Years," *New Englander and Yale Review,* XLVII (October, 1887), 233–45.

[40] Henry E. Alvord, "Dairy Development in the United States," *Yearbook of Agriculture,* 1899, pp. 381–402; Milton Whitney and Marcus L. Floyd, "Growth of the Tobacco Industry," *ibid.,* pp. 429–40; Herbert J. Webber and Ernst A. Bessey, "Progress of Plant Breeding in the United States," *ibid.,* pp. 465–90.

[41] George K. Holmes, "Supply of Farm Labor," U.S. Department of Agriculture, Bureau of Statistics, *Bulletin* 94 (Washington, D.C., 1912), pp. 14–16, 19–20, 31–33; Industrial Commission, *Report,* X, 46, 117–18. The percentage of wage laborers and female wage laborers in the total of persons receiving income directly from agriculture dropped to 35.5 and 14.9 by the census of 1890, which omitted some classes. Apparently there was no real decline, for when the earlier method of enumeration was resumed in 1900 the numbers of 43 and 15 were quite close to those of 1880.

[42] George K. Holmes, "Wages of Farm Labor," U.S. Department of Agriculture, Bureau of Statistics, *Bulletin* 99 (Washington, D.C., 1912), pp. 29–30, 32–33.

[43] Shannon, "Status of the Midwest Farmer," pp. 496–99, 501–6.

Chapter XII: THE BIRTH PANGS OF LABOR

[1] For background, see Selig Perlman, *A History of Trade Unionism in the United States* (New York, 1922), pp. 265–84.

[2] A good example is Philip S. Foner, *History of the Labor Movement in the United States, from Colonial Times to the Founding of the American Federation of Labor* (New York, 1947).

[3] Nevins, *Emergence of Modern America*, pp. 319–26.

[4] Clark, *History of Manufactures*, II, 178.

[5] Frank Tracy Carlton, *The History and Problems of Organized Labor* (rev. ed., Boston, 1920), pp. 455–56, 460.

[6] *Ibid.*, pp. 480, 482–83, 485–89.

[7] Figures from *Historical Statistics*, Series B 304, pp. 33–34.

[8] February 26, 1885, U.S. *Statutes at Large*, XXIII, 332–33; February 23, 1888, *ibid.*, XXIV, 414–15; Tarbell, *Nationalizing of Business*, pp. 14–15.

[9] Carlton, *Organized Labor*, pp. 389, 392–95, 401, 419.

[10] U.S. *Statutes at Large*, XXII, 214–15.

[11] Tarbell, *Nationalizing of Business*, pp. 182–84; U.S. *Statutes at Large*, XXIII, 60–61; *ibid.*, XXV, 182–84.

[12] Foner, *History of the Labor Movement*, p. 489.

[13] David A. Shannon, *The Socialist Party of America: A History* (New York, 1955), pp. 49–50.

[14] *Historical Statistics*, Series B 319, pp. 35–36, for immigration; *Statistical Abstract*, 1931, p. 39, for Chinese nationals; *Statistical Abstract*, 1948, p. 19, for all Chinese.

[15] Foner, *History of the Labor Movement*, pp. 489–93; Mary Roberts Coolidge, *Chinese Immigration* (New York, 1919), pp. 113–20; Commons, *History of Labour*, II, 252–61.

[16] Quint, *Forging of American Socialism*, pp. 14–15; Commons, *History of Labour*, II, 264.

[17] Nevins, *Emergence of Modern America*, p. 375.

[18] *Senate Report* No. 689, 44 Cong., 2 Sess. (1877), p. viii; Coolidge, *Chinese Immigration*, p. 97.

[19] Tien-Lu Li, *Congressional Policy of Chinese Immigration* (Nashville, 1916), pp. 26–32; *House Executive Document* No. 1, 47 Cong., 1 Sess. (1882), Pt. I, pp. 171–78; William M. Malloy, ed., *Treaties, Conventions, International Acts, and Protocols between the United States and Other Powers, 1776–1909* (2 vols., Washington, 1910), I, 237–39.

[20] Coolidge, *Chinese Immigration*, pp. 168–78; Elmer Clarence Sandmeyer, *The Anti-Chinese Movement in California* (Urbana, Ill., 1939), pp. 93–94; U.S. *Statutes at Large*, XXII, 58–61.

[21] *House Report* No. 614, 48 Cong., 1 Sess. (1884); U.S. *Statutes at Large*, XXIII, 115–18; Tien-Lu Li, *Congressional Policy of Chinese Immigration*, pp. 47–48.

[22] *House Executive Document* No. 102, 49 Cong., 1 Sess. (1886), pp. 49–64, 71; Arthur H. Smith, *China and America Today* (New York, 1907), p. 164.

[23] *Senate Executive Document* No. 273, 50 Cong., 1 Sess. (1888), pp. 2–5; Sandmeyer, *Anti-Chinese Movement*, p. 101; U.S. *Statutes at Large*, XXV, 504; Tso-Chien Shen, *What Chinese Exclusion Really Means* (New York, 1942), p. 27.

24 *Senate Executive Document* No. 97, 51 Cong., 1 Sess. (1890), Pt. VII, p. 4.

25 Hiram S. Maxim, "The Chinese and the South African Labour Problem," *Fortnightly Review*, LXXIX, O.S. (March, 1903), 507–8, 510–11.

26 Anzia Yerzierska, "How I Found America," in Harry R. Warfel, Ralph H. Gabriel, and Stanley T. Williams (eds.), *The American Mind* (New York, 1937), pp. 1050–56.

27 Carlton, *Organized Labor*, pp. 427–33.

28 Marvin W. Schlegel, *Ruler of the Reading: The Life of Franklin B. Gowen, 1836–1889* (Harrisburg, Pa., 1947), pp. 143–49, 290.

29 Fred Albert Shannon, *The Organization and Administration of the Union Army, 1861–1865* (2 vols., Cleveland, 1928), II, 222–23.

30 Schlegel, *Life of Gowen*, pp. 87–98, 150.

31 Anthony Bimba, *The Molly Maguires* (New York, 1932), *passim*.

32 J. Walter Coleman, *The Molly Maguire Riots: Industrial Conflict in the Pennsylvania Coal Region* (Richmond, Va., 1936), pp. 4, 61.

33 *Ibid.*, pp. 168–69.

34 *Ibid.*, pp. 70–167; Schlegel, *Life of Gowen*, pp. 126–52; Bimba, *Molly Maguires*, pp. 82–121.

35 Schlegel, *Life of Gowen*, pp. 286–87; Coleman, *Molly Maguire Riots*, p. 168.

36 Coleman, *Molly Maguire Riots*, pp. 169–71.

37 Schlegel, *Life of Gowen*, p. 152.

38 Commons, *History of Labour*, II, 45–46, 301–6. The author of the first 191 pages of this volume is John B. Andrews, and of the rest Selig Perlman. Perlman's *History of Trade Unionism* (see note 1 above) is largely a summary of the first two volumes of Commons and associates.

39 Norman J. Ware, *The Labor Movement in the United States, 1860–1895: A Study in Democracy* (New York, 1929), pp. 23, 26–27, 36, 49–50, 53–54, 56, 61; Commons, *History of Labour*, II, 195–202; Nevins, *Emergence of Modern America*, p. 393.

40 Ware, *Labor Movement*, pp. xi–xviii.

41 *Ibid.*, pp. xvi, 41, 62, 89.

42 *Ibid.*, pp. 329–33; Commons, *History of Labour*, II, 431–37.

43 Ware, *Labor Movement*, pp. 66–69.

Chapter XIII: INDUSTRIAL STRIFE, 1877–90

1 Joint Committee of the Pennsylvania General Assembly, *Report of the Committee Appointed to Investigate the Railroad Riots*

in July, 1877 (Harrisburg, Pa., 1878), pp. 2, 37, 42; Commons, *History of Labour,* II, 185, 188–89; Gerald N. Grob, "The Railroad Strikes of 1877," *Midwest Journal of Political Science,* VI (Winter, 1954–55), 16–34.

² Donald L. McMurry, *The Great Burlington Strike of 1888: A Case History in Labor Relations* (Cambridge, Mass., 1956), pp. 29–31, 37; Commons, *History of Labour,* II, 62, 67–68, 186, 313.

³ Commons, *History of Labour,* II, 186–88; Frederick T. Wilson, "Federal Aid in Domestic Disturbances, 1787–1903," *Senate Document* No. 209, 57 Cong., 2 Sess. (1903), pp. 189–94; U.S. Secretary of War, *Report, 1877–78* (*House Executive Document* No. 1, Pt. 2, 45 Cong., 2 Sess. 1879), pp. 92–98.

⁴ Wilson, "Federal Aid in Domestic Disturbances," pp. 189–205, 315–37; Bennett Milton Rich, *The Presidents and Civil Disorder* (Washington, D.C., 1941), pp. 72–86.

⁵ Philip A. Slaner, "The Railroad Strikes of 1877," *Marxist Quarterly,* I (April–June, 1937); Commons, *History of Labour,* II, 188–90.

⁶ Commons, *History of Labour,* II, 190–91; Pennsylvania Adjutant General, *Annual Report, 1877* (Harrisburg, 1878), pp. 45–47, 60, 65–71, 76–85, 94–104, 123–24, 149–52; New York, *Assembly Documents, No. 6, 1878* (Albany, 1878), I, 7–10; Wilson, "Federal Aid in Domestic Disturbances," pp. 194–205.

⁷ Felix Frankfurter and Nathan Greene, *The Labor Injunction* (New York, 1930), p. 3.

⁸ Edwin E. Witte, "Early American Labor Cases," *Yale Law Journal,* XXXV (May, 1926), 835–37.

⁹ United States v. Clark, 25 *Federal Cases,* 443; United States v. Stevens *et al.,* 27 *Federal Cases,* 1312; Secor v. Toledo, Peoria and Warsaw Railway, 21 *Federal Cases,* 968, 971; King *et al.* v. Ohio and Mississippi Railway, 14 *Federal Cases,* 539; Elwin W. Sigmund, "Railroad Strikers in Court: Unreported Contempt Cases in Illinois in 1877," Illinois State Historical Society, *Journal,* XLIV (Summer, 1956), *passim.* See Walter Nelles, "A Strike and Its Legal Consequences—An Examination of the Receivership Precedent for Labor Injunction," *Yale Law Journal,* XL (February, 1931), 507–54, for analysis of opinions.

¹⁰ Ruth A. Allen, *The Great Southwest Strike* (Austin, 1942), pp. 12–14.

¹¹ Ware, *Labor Movement,* pp. 127–28.

¹² Joseph R. Buchanan, *The Story of a Labor Agitator* (New York, 1903), pp. 70–99; Allen, *Southwest Strike,* p. 18; Ware, *Labor Movement,* pp. 134–36; Commons, *History of Labour,* II, 367–68.

¹³ Ware, *Labor Movement,* pp. 139–45; Commons, *History of Labour,* II, 368–70; Buchanan, *Labor Agitator,* pp. 142–63, 215–39, 248.

[14] Allen, *Southwest Strike*, pp. 22–25, 27.

[15] *Ibid.*, pp. 56–60, 96; Commons, *History of Labour*, II, 383. As a part of the settlement of the 1885 coal strikes on the Gould system, Powderly had promised that no future strikes would be called on that system until a conference with officials of the railroads was held. The Texas Pacific was in receivership in 1886, and Irons attempted to contact the receiver, but to no avail, so Irons called the strike. However, in the case of the Missouri Pacific, Irons was apparently forced into calling the men out without the promised consultation. Thus the suspicion that Hoxie was behind this act.

[16] Allen, *Southwest Strike*, pp. 34–43, 54, 137, 143–44; Peck, *Twenty Years of the Republic*, p. 128. See also Martin Irons, "My Experiences in the Labor Movement," *Lippincott's Magazine*, XXXVII (June, 1886), 618–27.

[17] Allen, *Southwest Strike*, pp. 63–153; Ware, *Labor Movement*, pp. 147–48; *Investigation of Labor Troubles in Missouri, Arkansas, Kansas, Texas, and Illinois* (*House Report* No. 4174, 49 Cong., 2 Sess., 1887), pp. i–xxv.

[18] Ware, *Labor Movement*, pp. 148–49.

[19] *In re* Doolittle and another, Strikers, 23 *Federal Reporter*, 544; *In re* Wabash R. Co., 24 *Federal Reporter*, 217; United States v. Berry and others, 24 *Federal Reporter*, 780; United States v. Kane and others, 23 *Federal Reporter*, 748, 756; Frank and others v. Denver & R. G. Ry. Co., 23 *Federal Reporter*, 757.

[20] Buchanan, *Labor Agitator*, pp. 228–30.

[21] *In re* Higgins and others, 27 *Federal Reporter*, 443; Allen, *Southwest Strike*, pp. 71, 81–86, esp. 82; Missouri Bureau of Labor Statistics and Inspection, *The Official History of the Great Strike of 1886 on the Southwestern Railway System* (Jefferson City, Mo., 1886), *passim*.

[22] McMurry, *Burlington Strike*, pp. 31–33, 36, 66, 138–53, 251; Ray Ginger, *The Bending Cross: A Biography of Eugene Victor Debs* (New Brunswick, N.J., 1949), p. 46.

[23] McMurry, *Burlington Strike*, pp. 6–8, 11–16, 20–23, 25, 38, 40, 61, 64.

[24] *Ibid.*, pp. 4–5, 103, 108–9, 130–31, 138, 246, 248, 254; Commons, *History of Labour*, II, 474–75.

[25] McMurry, *Burlington Strike*, p. 273.

[26] *Ibid.*, pp. 108, 174–204, esp. 199.

[27] Terence V. Powderly, *Thirty Years of Labor, 1859–1889* (Columbus, Ohio, 1890), pp. 442–43.

[28] Harry W. Laidler, *Boycotts and the Labor Struggle* (New York, 1914), p. 430.

[29] McMurry, *Burlington Strike*, pp. 113–37, 250.

[30] Ware, *Labor Movement*, pp. 42, 243–98; Commons, *History of Labour*, II, 176–77, 302, 306–9, 314, 318–31, 396–410.

[31] Commons, *History of Labour*, II, 110–11, 319, 322, 327–28, 513; Fine, *Labor and Farmer Parties*, p. 135; Ware, *Labor Movement*, p. 297.

[32] Commons, *History of Labour*, II, 384–85, 414, 479.

[33] *John Swinton's Paper* (New York), May 16, 1886, p. 1.

[34] Quint, *Forging of American Socialism*, pp. 18–21.

[35] Commons, *History of Labour*, II, 296–97.

[36] Peck, *Twenty Years of the Republic*, p. 129; Charles Ramsdell Lingley, *Since the Civil War* (New York, 1920), pp. 316–17.

[37] Ginger, *Bending Cross*, pp. 45, 191.

[38] Henry David, *The History of the Haymarket Affair: A Study in the American Social-Revolutionary and Labor Movements* (New York, 1936), pp. 341–42; Edward L. Sheppard, *The Radical and Labor Periodical Press in Chicago: Its Origin and Development to 1890* (Urbana, Ill., 1949), p. 25.

[39] *The Accused the Accusers: The Famous Speeches of the Eight Anarchists in Court* (Chicago, n.d.), p. 106.

[40] Lucy E. Parsons (ed.), *Life of Albert R. Parsons* (2d ed., Chicago, 1903), pp. 273–74; David, *Haymarket Affair*, pp. 90, 96, 330–31; Sheppard, *Radical and Labor Press*, p. 31.

[41] Parsons, *Life of Parsons*, pp. 280–81; Sheppard, *Radical and Labor Press*, pp. 31–32.

[42] Parsons, *Life of Parsons*, p. 275.

[43] David, *Haymarket Affair*, pp. 334–41.

[44] *Ibid.*, pp. 186–90, 192–94, 198–204; Ware, *Labor Movement*, pp. 314–15.

[45] Ware, *Labor Movement*, p. 315.

[46] *Ibid.*, pp. 315–16; David, *Haymarket Affair*, pp. 111, 221–24, 228, 237–392, 426–78. Gary's version is in Joseph E. Gary, "The Chicago Anarchists of 1886: The Crime, the Trial, and the Punishment," *Century Magazine*, XXIII, N.S. (April, 1893), 803–37.

[47] Peck, *Twenty Years of the Republic*, p. 130.

[48] George A. Schilling was an Illinois Socialist Labor leader, influential in first the Chicago Federation of Labor and the Illinois Federation of Labor, and in 1893 headed the Illinois Bureau of Labor Statistics.

[49] Eugene Staley, *History of the Illinois State Federation of Labor* (Chicago, 1930), pp. 67–69; American Federation of Labor, *Proceedings, 1887* (Bloomington, Ill., 1905), pp. 11–12.

[50] August Spies and Albert R. Parsons, *The Great Anarchist Trial: The Haymarket Speeches* (Chicago, 1886), *passim; Accused the Accusers*, pp. 95, 155.

[51] Edward and Eleanor Marx Aveling, *The Working-Class Movement in America* (2d ed., London, 1891), p. 167.

[52] Quint, *Forging of American Socialism*, pp. 33–35.

[53] Commons, *History of Labour*, II, 474–77.

Chapter XIV: INVENTION AND INDUSTRY

[1] *Statistical Abstract*, 1948, p. 896.

[2] Waldemar Kaempffert, *A Popular History of American Invention* (2 vols., New York, 1924), I, 446–49, 457–59; Francis Arthur Jones, *Thomas Alva Edison: Sixty Years of an Inventor's Life* (New York, 1907), pp. 137–38; Edward W. Byrn, *The Progress of Invention in the Nineteenth Century* (New York, 1900), pp. 276, 280; Frank P. Bachman, *Great Inventors and Their Inventions* (New York, 1918), p. 252.

[3] Abbott Payson Usher, *A History of Mechanical Inventions* (New York, 1929), pp. 366–68; Kaempffert, *History of Invention*, I, 567–68; Mary Childs Nerney, *Thomas A. Edison, A Modern Olympian* (New York, 1934), p. 86; *New York Times*, October 19, 1931, p. 25.

[4] Byrn, *Progress of Invention*, pp. 69, 71; Edison Electric Light Company v. U. S. Lighting Company, 53 *Federal Reporter*, 592–99.

[5] *Specifications and Drawings of Patents Issued from the United States Patent Office* (Washington), May, 1878, No. 203411, p. 181; *ibid.*, February, 1879, No. 212183, p. 422; *ibid.*, September, 1883, No. 285451, p. 1582.

[6] U.S. *Eleventh Census: Manufacturing Industries*, Pt. III, pp. 239–40.

[7] *Specifications of Patents*, March, 1883, No. 274290, p. 1346; *ibid.*, May, 1888, Nos. 381968–381969, pp. 101–7, Nos. 382279–382282, pp. 589–99.

[8] U.S. *Twelfth Census: Manufactures*, Pt. IV, p. 158.

[9] *Ibid.*, p. 164; *New York Times*, October 19, 1931, p. 24; Byrn, *Progress of Invention*, p. 56; Kaempffert, *History of Invention*, I, 124–25.

[10] *Specifications of Patents*, August, 1886, Nos. 347140–347142, pp. 921–24.

[11] U.S. *Eleventh Census: Manufacturing Industries*, Pt. III, p. 269.

[12] Assembly of the State of New York, *Journal*, 111 Sess. (Troy, N.Y., 1888), p. 1871.

[13] "The Telephone," *Scientific American*, XXXVI (March 31, 1877), 191–200; Kaempffert, *History of Invention*, I, 330–35; Dorau, *Public Utility Economics*, p. 44.

[14] Hendrick, *Age of Big Business*, pp. 99–103, 113–16; Dorau, *Public Utility Economics*, pp. 33–35.

[15] Kaempffert, *History of Inventions*, I, 228, 233–34; *Specifications of Patents*, April, 1890, No. 425140, p. 1086; Clark, *History of Manufactures*, II, 829.

[16] Kaempffert, *History of Inventions*, I, 423; Byrn, *Progress of*

Invention, p. 178; W. F. Ogburn, "The Influence of Invention and Discovery," *Recent Social Trends in the United States* (2 vols., New York, 1933), I, 145, 147; Clark, *History of Manufactures*, II, 831.

[17] Clark, *History of Manufactures*, II, 690.

[18] *Ibid.*, II, 692; *Specifications of Patents*, November, 1895, No. 549160, p. 149; Kaempffert, *History of Inventions*, I, 155.

[19] Clark, *History of Manufactures*, II, 150, 151, 159.

[20] *Bradstreet's, A Journal of Trade, Finance and Public Economy*, XLVII, O.S. (New York, October 4, 1879), 2–3.

[21] Clark, *History of Manufactures*, II, 161.

[22] *Bradstreet's*, IX, N.S. (January 12, 1884), 3.

[23] *The Manufacturers' Review and Industrial Record*, XVIII (York, Pa., January 15, 1885), 34.

[24] Clark, *History of Manufactures*, II, 163–64; *Bradstreet's*, XVIII, N.S. (January 11, 1890), 19; *ibid.*, XIX, N.S. (January 3, 1891), 3.

[25] Edwin Frickey, *Production in the United States, 1860–1914* (Cambridge, Mass., 1947), p. 54.

[26] U.S. *Eleventh Census: Manufacturing Industries*, Pt. I, pp. 10, 73–84; Newel Howland Comish, *Marketing of Manufactured Goods* (Boston, 1935), p. 6.

[27] Victor S. Clark, "Modern Manufacturing Development in the South, 1880–1905," *South in the Building of the Nation*, VI, 298.

[28] *Bradstreet's*, XLVII, O.S. (October 15, 1879), 4–5; Worthington C. Ford, "Imports and Exports," *One Hundred Years of American Commerce*, ed. Chauncey M. Depew (2 vols., New York, 1895), I, 24; Clark, *History of Manufactures*, II, 173.

[29] Clark, *History of Manufactures*, II, 171–72.

[30] U. S. *Twelfth Census: Manufactures*, Pt. I, p. clxxv.

Percentage of Total of All Manufactures, by Sections

Section	NUMBER OF ESTABLISHMENTS		CAPITAL		VALUE OF PRODUCT	
	1870	1890	1870	1890	1870	1890
New England	12.8	13.6	23.1	18.0	23.8	16.0
Middle Atlantic	34.7	35.2	42.7	39.2	41.8	38.9
South	15.4	13.1	6.6	7.8	6.6	7.5
Central	33.5	31.8	24.4	29.7	24.9	31.4
Mountain	1.5	3.2	1.0	2.0	1.1	3.0
Pacific	2.1	3.1	2.2	3.3	1.8	3.2

[31] U.S. *Eleventh Census: Manufacturing Industries*, Pt. I, p. 30.

[32] Broadus Mitchell, *The Rise of Cotton Mills in the South* (Baltimore, 1921), pp. 57, 69; Clark, "Manufacturing Development in the South," pp. 264–66; Woodward, *Origins of the New South*, pp. 143–44; T. D. Clark, "The Country Newspaper," pp. 11–12; Melvin T. Copeland, *The Cotton Manufacturing Industry of the United States* (Cambridge, Mass., 1912), p. 39; Clark, *History*

of Manufactures, II, 385; U.S. *Eleventh Census: Manufacturing Industries,* Pt. III, pp. 5, 168, 171–72.

33 William O. Scroggs, "The New Alabama, 1880–1909," *South in the Building of the Nation,* II, 313; U.S. *Eleventh Census: Mineral Industries,* pp. 14, 355, 417; *ibid., Manufacturing Industries,* Pt. III, pp. 386, 447; Clark, "Manufacturing Development in the South," pp. 272, 278; Clark, *History of Manufactures,* II, 219, 240–41.

34 U.S. *Twelfth Census: Manufactures,* Pt. III, p. 812; *Statistical Abstract,* 1948, p. 724.

35 Woodward, *Origins of the New South,* pp. 309–10; Clark, *History of Manufactures,* II, 484.

36 Nannie Mae Tilley, *The Bright-Tobacco Industry, 1860–1929* (Chapel Hill, N.C., 1949), pp. 510, 532, 545–46, 549, 551, 555–57, 559, 563, 570; Joseph C. Robert, *The Story of Tobacco in America* (New York, 1949), p. 145.

37 Clark, *History of Manufactures,* II, 533–34.

38 U.S. Census Bureau, *Special Reports: Mines and Quarries* (Washington, D.C., 1902), pp. 665, 669, 704–5; Howard N. Eavenson, *The First Century and a Quarter of American Coal Industry* (Pittsburgh, 1942), pp. 418, 420.

39 John Fulton, *Coke* (Scranton, 1906), pp. 134–35; T. H. Byrom and J. E. Christopher, *Modern Coking Practice* (New York, 1910), p. 36; Clark, *History of Manufactures,* II, 514–16.

40 U.S. *Twelfth Census: Mines and Quarries,* p. 730; *Eleventh Census: Manufactures,* X, Pt. III, p. 269; Clark, *History of Manufactures,* II, 517–18. A tierce, according to Webster, is a measure that falls between a barrel (U.S. measure, 31.5 gallons) and a hogshead (63 to 140 gallons, but usually 63 U.S. gallons), often containing 42 wine gallons. A wine gallon and a U.S. gallon are the same measure. Therefore, the output of petroleum rose from 13,-350,000 tierces (17,800,000 barrels) in 1877 to 44,824,000 (59,-765,333 barrels) in 1890.

41 Albert Sidney Bolles, *Industrial History of the United States* (Norwich, Conn., 1879), p. 216; Hal Bridges, *Iron Millionaire: Life of Charlemagne Tower* (Philadelphia, 1952), pp. 135–36, 153–71, 223, 283; U.S. *Twelfth Census: Mines and Quarries,* p. 410.

42 *Appletons' Annual Cyclopaedia,* 1891, p. 5; U.S. *Twelfth Census: Mines and Quarries,* pp. 299, 404–5; Clark, *History of Manufactures,* II, 197.

43 U.S. *Eleventh Census: Manufacturing Industries,* III, 396, 400; Clark, *History of Manufactures,* II, 200, 202, 204, 215.

44 Bolles, *Industrial History,* p. 214; J. S. Jeans, *Steel: Its History, Manufacture, Properties, and Uses* (London, 1880), p. 148; Malcolm Keir, *Manufacturing Industries in America* (New York, 1920), pp. 133–34; Clark, *History of Manufactures,* II, 214, 249; U.S. *Eleventh Census: Manufacturing Industries,* Pt. III, p.

400; *Twelfth Census: Manufactures*, Pt. IV, pp. 23–24, 74–75; *ibid.*, *Mines and Quarries*, pp. 437–38.

45 *Manufacturers' Review and Industrial Record*, XXIII (February, 1890), 114; U.S. *Twelfth Census: Manufactures*, Pt. IV, pp. 212, 344; *Bradstreet's*, X, N.S. (August 16, 1884), 103.

46 U.S. *Twelfth Census: Mines and Quarries*, pp. 482, 484–85, 492, 498; Clark, *History of Manufactures*, II, 368–69; *Bradstreet's*, XIX, N.S. (January 10, 1891), 23.

47 U.S. *Eleventh Census: Mineral Industries*, p. 173; Clark, *History of Manufactures*, II, 368, 370–74, 376; J. H. Jones, *The Tinplate Industry* (London, 1914), p. 84.

48 Clark, *History of Manufactures*, II, 129–30, 492–94, 524–26; *Statistical Abstract*, 1931, p. 807; James Gillinder, "American Glass Interests," *One Hundred Years of American Commerce*, I, 279, 281.

49 John W. Blodgett, "The Lumber Industry," *A Century of Industrial Progress* (Garden City, N.Y., 1928), p. 28; B. E. Fernow, "American Lumber," *The Making of America*, ed. Robert M. La-Follette (10 vols., Philadelphia, 1905), III, 361; Clark, "Manufacturing Development in the South," pp. 267, 293; *Bradstreet's*, XVIII, N.S. (January 4, 1890), 6.

50 J. Seymour Currey, *Manufacturing and Wholesale Industries of Chicago* (3 vols., Chicago, 1918), I, 304; *Bradstreet's*, XLVIII, O.S. (September 1, 1880), 6; *ibid.*, XIX, N.S. (April 11, 1891), 231.

51 William C. Edgar, *The Story of a Grain of Wheat* (New York, 1909), pp. 151, 164–65; Charles Byron Kuhlmann, *The Development of the Flour-Milling Industry in the United States* (Boston, 1929), pp. 91, 114, 125, 127, 134–35; *Bradstreet's*, XIII, N.S. (January 30, 1886), 70; Edward Van Dyke Robinson, *Early Economic Conditions and the Development of Agriculture in Minnesota* (Minneapolis, 1915), pp. 76–78.

52 Clark, *History of Manufactures*, II, 505–6, 508; *Bradstreet's*, XIII, N.S. (January 30, 1886), 70.

53 Clark, *History of Manufactures*, II, 508–12; *Bradstreet's*, XVIII, N.S. (March 15, 1890), 170; James Cooke Mills, *Searchlights on Some American Industries* (Chicago, 1911), p. 42.

54 Willis N. Baer, *The Economic Development of the Cigar Industry in the United States* (Lancaster, Pa., 1933), p. 50; Clark, *History of Manufactures*, II, 513; Clark, "Manufacturing Development in the South," pp. 294–95.

55 Copeland, *Cotton Manufacturing*, pp. 27, 34, 238, 268–69; *Bradstreet's*, XLVII, O.S. (October 4, 1879), 5; *Manufacturers' Review*, XXIII (January, 1890), 36; Clark, *History of Manufactures*, II, 408–10.

56 Arthur Harrison Cole, *The American Wool Manufacture* (2 vols., Cambridge, Mass., 1926), II, 70, 89, 284; Paul T. Cherington,

The Wool Industry (Chicago, 1916), I, 82; Clark, *History of Manufactures*, II, 418, 420–22, 431, 433.

57 Frank R. Mason, *The American Silk Industry and the Tariff* (Cambridge, Mass., 1910), pp. 4–5, 20–23, 28, 34, 48–53; Ratan C. Rawlley, *Economics of the Silk Industry* (London, 1919), p. 308; Clark, *History of Manufactures*, II, 126, 456, 549; W. D. Darby, *Rayon and Other Synthetic Fibers* (New York, 1929), pp. 8, 12; Brent Moore, *A Study of the Past, the Present and the Possibilities of the Hemp Industry* (Lexington, Ky., 1905), p. 89.

58 Clark, *History of Manufactures*, II, 443–48, 466.

59 *Ibid.*, II, 463–64, 468–71, 478–79; Frederick J. Allen, *The Shoe Industry* (Boston, 1916), pp. 59–60; Howard and Ralph Wolf, *Rubber: A Story of Glory and Greed* (New York, 1936), p. 402; Leonard E. Carlsmith, *The Economic Characteristics of Rubber Tire Production* (New York, 1935), p. 33.

Chapter XV: TRADE AND TRANSPORTATION

1 Minneapolis Chamber of Commerce, "The Exchanges of Minneapolis, Duluth, Kansas City, Mo., Omaha, Buffalo, Philadelphia, Milwaukee and Toledo," American Academy of Political and Social Science, *Annals*, XXXVIII (1911), 555, 562, 568; Arthur P. Marsh, "Cotton Exchanges and Their Functions," *ibid.*, XXXVIII, 580; S. S. Huebner, "Functions of Produce Exchanges," *ibid.*, XXXVIII, 319–20.

2 George Rutledge Gibson, *The Stock Exchanges of London, Paris, and New York* (New York, 1889), pp. 68, 74, 85, 107–10; Robert Irving Warshow, *The Story of Wall Street* (New York, 1929), pp. 341–42; State of New York, *Report of Governor Hughes' Committee on Speculation in Securities and Commodities* (New York?, 1909), pp. 11, 13–14.

3 Philip P. Gott, "The Trade Associations—Their Growth and Activities," *The Development of American Industries: Their Economic Significance*, ed. John George Glover and William Bouck Cornell (rev. ed., New York, 1941), p. 942.

4 Paul H. Nystrom, *Economics of Retailing* (2 vols., New York, 1915), I, 91, 127, 133, 134, 139, 146; Paul D. Converse and Harvey W. Huegy, *Elements of Marketing* (3d ed., New York, 1947), pp. 45–46.

5 Godfrey M. Lebhar, *Chain Stores in America, 1859–1950* (New York, 1952), pp. 39–40; Frank Presbrey, *The History and Development of Advertising* (Garden City, N.Y., 1929), pp. 256–87.

6 Lebhar, *Chain Stores*, pp. 20, 22–23, 29–31, 37, 43. See also John P. Nichols, *The Chain Store Tells Its Story* (New York, 1940), pp. 57–72.

7 Ole S. Johnson, *The Industrial Store: Its History, Operations, and Economic Significance* (Atlanta, 1952), pp. 21–40.

[8] Theodore Marburg, "Domestic Trade and Marketing," *The Growth of the American Economy,* ed. Harold Francis Williamson (New York, 1951 ed.), pp. 522–23.

[9] Neil H. Borden, *The Economic Effects of Advertising* (Chicago, 1942), pp. 47–48; Presbrey, *History of Advertising,* pp. 294, 300, 338–39, 343, 348, 359–90.

[10] Solomon Huebner, "The Development and Present Status of Marine Insurance in the United States," American Academy of Political and Social Science, *Annals,* XXVI (1905), 423–49.

[11] F. C. Oviatt, "Historical Study of Fire Insurance in the United States," *ibid.,* XXVI, 352–55.

[12] Edson S. Lott, "Accident Insurance," *ibid.,* XXVI, 483–84.

[13] W. F. Moore, "Liability Insurance," *ibid.,* XXVI, 499, 517.

[14] Shepard B. Clough, *A Century of American Life Insurance: A History of the Mutual Life Insurance Company of New York, 1843–1943* (New York, 1946), pp. 128, 130, 370, 372; R. Carlyle Buley, *The American Life Convention: A Study in the History of Life Insurance* (2 vols., New York, 1953), I, 91, 101, 107–10, 114–20; Burton J. Hendrick, *The Story of Insurance* (London, 1907), pp. 127, 133–48, 168, 208–9.

[15] George Soule, *Economic Forces in American History* (New York, 1952), p. 206; John H. Frederick, *The Development of American Commerce* (New York, 1932), p. 157.

[16] Emory R. Johnson, T. W. Van Metre, G. G. Huebner, and D. S. Hanchett, *History of Domestic and Foreign Commerce of the United States* (2 vols., Washington, D.C., 1915), I, 272–75, 281.

[17] *Historical Statistics,* Ser. K 1, 2, 9, 11, 13, 15, p. 200.

[18] Riegel, *America Moves West,* pp. 554–62.

[19] Thomas Donaldson, *The Public Domain* (Washington, D.C., 1884), pp. 269–73; "Aids to Railroads," pp. 32–33, 52–55; Henry George, *Our Land and Land Policy* (New York, 1901 ed.), pp. 20–21, 24, 33; Paul Wallace Gates, "The Homestead Law in an Incongruous Land System," *American Historical Review,* XLI (July, 1936), 657.

[20] A. J. Y. Brown, *The American Economy, 1860–1940* (New York, 1951), p. 59. See also Taylor Hampton, *The Nickel Plate Road* (Cleveland, 1947), pp. 99, 163–64.

[21] Woodward, *Origins of the New South,* p. 120; D. Philip Locklin, *Economics of Transportation* (3d ed., Chicago, 1947), p. 98.

[22] Slason Thompson, *Short History of American Railways* (Chicago, 1925), pp. 204, 208, 211, 236, 238, 268.

[23] Riegel, *Western Railroads,* pp. 265–66, 272–73; Woodward, *Origins of the New South,* pp. 123–24; *Historical Statistics,* Ser. K 18–21, p. 201.

[24] Edward S. Mason, *The Street Railway in Massachusetts: The Rise and Decline of an Industry* (Cambridge, Mass., 1932), pp. 4, 6; George R. Chatburn, *Highways and Highway Transportation*

(New York, 1923), p. 22; U.S. Census Office, *Street and Electric Railways*, Bulletin 3 (Washington, D.C., 1903), pp. 5, 8.

25 James Blaine Walker, *Fifty Years of Rapid Transit, 1864–1917* (New York, 1918), pp. 76, 80–81, 111–14, 122–26, 129–30, 138.

26 James Rood Doolittle (ed.), *The Romance of the Automobile Industry* (New York, 1916), pp. 16–17, 263–64; *Historical Statistics*, Ser. K 174, p. 220; Albert C. Rose, "The Highway from the Railroad to the Automobile," *Highways in Our National Life: A Symposium*, ed. Jean Labatut and Wheaton J. Lane (Princeton, N.J., 1950), pp. 82–83, 85.

27 Stuart Daggett, *Principles of Inland Transportation* (3d ed., New York, 1941), p. 45; Louis C. Hunter, *Steamboats on the Western Rivers: An Economic and Technological History* (Cambridge, Mass., 1941), pp. 563–66, 571–74, 580, 587–90, 622.

28 Hunter, *Steamboats*, pp. 213–14; Archer Butler Hulbert, *Historic Highways of America* (16 vols., Cleveland, 1902–4), IX, 213; Johnson and others, *Domestic and Foreign Commerce*, II, 323.

29 Johnson and others, *Domestic and Foreign Commerce*, I, 318.

30 *Historical Statistics*, Ser. 168–71, pp. 218–19.

31 Chester Lloyd Jones, *The Economic History of the Anthracite-Tidewater Canals* (Philadelphia, 1908), pp. 50, 59, 94, 120, 147, 155, 163, *et passim*; Alvin F. Harlow, *Old Towpaths: The Story of the American Canal Era* (New York, 1926), p. 287.

32 Frickey, *Production in the United States*, pp. 108–9.

33 Johnson and others, *Domestic and Foreign Commerce*, I, 269.

34 H. Gerrish Smith and L. C. Brown, "Shipyard Statistics," *The Shipbuilding Business in the United States of America*, ed. F. G. Fassett (2 vols., New York, 1948), I, 76.

35 Clark, *History of Manufactures*, II, 533; Norman Beasley, *Freighters of Fortune: The Story of the Great Lakes* (New York, 1930), pp. 219–20.

36 Beasley, *Freighters of Fortune*, pp. 224–25.

37 *Inland Water Transportation in the United States*, U.S. Bureau of Foreign and Domestic Commerce, Miscellaneous Series, No. 119 (Washington, D.C., 1923), p. 59.

38 Beasley, *Freighters of Fortune*, p. 183; Walter Havighurst, *The Long Ships Passing: The Story of the Great Lakes* (New York, 1942), p. 222.

39 John G. B. Hutchins, *The American Maritime Industries and Public Policy, 1789–1914: An Economic History* (Cambridge, Mass., 1941), p. 461; James Cooke Mills, *Our Inland Seas: Their Shipping and Commerce for Three Centuries* (Chicago, 1910), p. 219; Beasley, *Freighters of Fortune*, pp. 227, 229–30, 254.

40 *Statistical Abstract*, 1941, p. 517; Hutchins, *American Maritime Industries*, pp. 35, 482.

41 *Historical Statistics*, Ser. 96, 97, 99–102, p. 207.

42 Johnson and others, *Domestic and Foreign Commerce*, I, 351; Hutchins, *American Maritime Industries*, pp. 360, 544–47, 552, 556, 564.

43 Johnson and others, *Domestic and Foreign Commerce*, I, 362; Hutchins, *American Maritime Industries*, p. 573.

44 Smith and Brown, "Shipyard Statistics," p. 68.

45 Johnson and others, *Domestic and Foreign Commerce*, II, 316; Hutchins, *American Maritime Industries*, pp. 426, 438, 540; William Hutchinson Rowe, *The Maritime History of Maine: Three Centuries of Shipbuilding & Seafaring* (New York, 1948), pp. 161–62, 234.

46 *Statistical Abstract*, 1931, pp. 456, 761–62; *ibid.*, 1948, p. 559.

47 James M. Herring and Gerald C. Cross, *Telecommunications: Economics and Regulation* (New York, 1936), pp. 3, 11–12; Alvin F. Harlow, *Old Wires and New Waves: The History of the Telegraph* (New York, 1936), pp. 408–9, 410–12, 414–15, 418.

48 Harlow, *History of the Telegraph*, pp. 424–28; George P. Oslin, "The Telegraph Industry," *American Industries*, eds. Glover and Cornell, pp. 754–55.

49 Harlow, *History of the Telegraph*, p. 405.

50 *Ibid.*, pp. 338–39.

51 *Historical Statistics*, Ser. P 167, p. 309.

52 *Ibid.*, Ser. P 165, p. 309.

53 Clyde Kelly, *United States Postal Policy* (New York, 1931), pp. 76–80; Pao Hsun Chu, *The Post Office of the United States* (2d ed., New York, 1932), pp. 63, 90–91; Daniel C. Roper, *The United States Post Office: Its Past Record, Present Condition, and Potential Relation to the New World Era* (New York, 1917), p. 75.

54 Alvin F. Harlow, *Old Waybills: The Romance of the Express Companies* (New York, 1934), pp. 314–24, 458, 460–61; Oscar Osburn Winther, *The Old Oregon Country: A History of Frontier Trade, Transportation and Travel* (Bloomington, Ind., [1950]), p. 272.

55 Harlow, *Express Companies*, pp. 313–14, 423–31; Agnes Wright Spring, *The Cheyenne and Black Hills Stage and Express Routes* (Glendale, Calif., 1949), pp. 183–84; Alden Hatch, *American Express Company: A Century of Service* (Garden City, N.Y., 1950), p. 86.

POSTSCRIPT

1 *The Poetical Works of John Greenleaf Whittier* (Boston: Houghton, Mifflin and Company, 1892), IV, 205–7.

2 James Russell Lowell, *Literary and Political Addresses* (Boston: Houghton, Mifflin and Company, 1890), pp. 182–86.

3 *Ibid.*, pp. 173–74.

BIBLIOGRAPHY*

GENERAL

Whatever may be said of the *American Nation* series of half a century ago, Edwin Erle Sparks, *National Development, 1877–1885* (New York, 1907) and David Rich Dewey, *National Problems, 1885–1897* (New York, 1907) have not outlived their usefulness. Other works include Ellis Paxson Oberholtzer, *A History of the United States since the Civil War* (5 vols., New York, 1917–37); James Ford Rhodes, *History of the United States from Hayes to McKinley, 1877–1896* (New York, 1919), a conservative interpretation; Harry Thurston Peck, *Twenty Years of the Republic, 1885–1905* (New York, 1906), erratic, but generally sound and well-informed; E. Benjamin Andrews, *The United States in Our Own Time* (New York, 1903), more judicious than Peck; and Charles A. Beard, *Contemporary American History, 1877–1913* (New York, 1914).

Volumes 8–10 of *A History of American Life*, Arthur M. Schlesinger and Dixon Ryan Fox, eds., are purposely light on politics, but have many pertinent suggestions about economic developments. They are Allan Nevins, *The Emergence of Modern America, 1865–1878* (New York, 1927); Ida M. Tarbell, *The Nationalizing of Business, 1878–1898* (New York, 1936); and Arthur Meier Schlesinger, *The Rise of the City, 1878–1898* (New York, 1933). A broader view in a similar vein is Blake McKelvey, *The Urbanization of America* (New Brunswick, N.J., 1963). *The New American Nation* series, still in gestation, does not as yet have any parallels to Sparks and Dewey, but Harold U. Falkner's *Politics, Reform, and Expansion, 1890–1900* (New York, 1959) provides an excellent trailer to this volume.

Also useful are Ray Ginger's *Age of Excess: The United States from 1877 to 1914* (New York, 1965), a recent and individualistic treatment; Samuel P. Hayes, *The Response to Industrialism: 1885–1914* (Chicago, 1957); and Edward C. Kirkland, *Industry Comes of Age: Business, Labor, and Public Policy, 1860–1897* (New York, 1961), the last two volumes primarily

* At no point does this book depend on manuscripts. See the Preface for Shannon's remarks on this point.

economic in approach, in contrast to Ginger. H. Wayne Morgan
(ed.), *The Gilded Age: A Reappraisal* (New York, 1963), is un-
even, while Ray Ginger (ed.), *The Nationalizing of American
Life, 1877–1900* (New York, 1965), though more fragmentary,
has better balance; but both have merit.

The Congressional series of documents comes under so many
differing titles that a separate listing of all seems unnecessary. The
footnotes include all actually used. The *Congressional Record* and
the *Journal* of the *House* and of the *Senate* may also be thus
informally treated, as well as the *Census* of the United States, the
tenth, eleventh, and twelfth being most useful for this study. Of
special publications by the federal government, those used most
often, in descending order, were Bureau of the Census, *Statistical
Abstract of the United States* (77th ed., Washington, D.C., 1956),
and earlier; *ibid., Historical Statistics of the United States,
1789–1945* (Washington, D.C., 1949), for long-range tables;
James D. Richardson (ed.), *A Compilation of the Messages and
Papers of the Presidents, 1789–1897* (10 vols., Washington, D.C.,
1896–99); *Biographical Directory of the American Congress,
1774–1949* (Washington, D.C., 1950), not often cited but incessantly consulted; U.S. *Statutes at Large* (Vols. 19–26, Washington, D.C., 1879–93); *United States Reports* (Vols. 95–141, New
York, 1890–1902); *Industrial Commission, Final Report* (19
vols., Washington, D.C., 1900–2); William M. Malloy (ed.),
*Treaties, Conventions, International Acts, and Protocols between
. . . the United States and Other Powers, 1776–1909* (2 vols.,
Washington, D.C., 1910); and Ben: Perley Poore (ed.), *Federal
and State Constitutions* . . . (Washington, D.C., 1877).

New constitutions and amendments after 1877 are in Charles
Kettleborough (ed.), *The State Constitutions* (Indianapolis, 1918).
Not all cases finally settled in the lower courts of the United States
were reported, but, for those that were, see *Federal Reporter*
(Vols. 1–40, St. Paul, 1880–90). State and territorial laws and
court reports go under at least as many titles each as there were
governmental divisions.

THE NATION'S CENTENNIAL

The vital statistics came from the various *Census* reports and
from the *Statistical Abstract* and *Historical Statistics* listed above.
Of the histories of education, the following proved most helpful:
Ernest Carroll Moore, *Fifty Years of American Education: A
Sketch of Education in the United States from . . . 1867 to 1917*
(Boston, 1917); Edgar Wallace Knight, *Education in the United
States* (Boston, 1934); Edwin Grant Dexter, *History of Education
in the United States* (New York, 1904); James L. Mursell, *Edu-*

cation for American Democracy (New York, 1943); U.S. Bureau of Education, Report of the Commissioner, 1883–1884 (Washington, D.C., 1885); J. P. Gordy, Rise and Growth of the Normal School Idea in the United States, U.S. Bureau of Education, Circular of Information No. 8 (Washington, D.C., 1891); Burke A. Hinsdale, "Training of Teachers," Monographs on Education in the United States, ed. Nicholas Murray Butler, I (Albany, 1900), 12–38; Merle Curti, The Social Ideas of American Educators (New York, 1935); and Harvey Wish, Society and Thought in Modern America (New York, 1952).

There is a great storehouse of information on religious ferment in Philip Schaff, H. C. Potter, and S. M. Jackson (eds.), The American Church History Series (13 vols., New York, 1893–98). Some of the aberrations of the nineteenth century are recorded in Herbert Wallace Schneider, Religion in 20th Century America (Cambridge, Mass., 1952). William Warren Sweet, The Story of Religion in Modern America (2d rev. ed., New York, 1950), is a scholarly summary of the whole movement. Special phases are the themes of William Warren Sweet, Revivalism in America: Its Growth and Decline (New York, 1945), and Methodism in American History (New York, 1933); Arthur Meier Schlesinger, "A Critical Period in American Religion," Massachusetts Historical Society, Proceedings, LXIV (Boston, 1932), 523–29; Charles W. Ferguson, The Confusion of Tongues: A Review of Modern Isms (Garden City, N.Y., 1928); and Henry F. May, Protestant Churches and Industrial America (New York, 1949). Stewart G. Cole, The History of Fundamentalism (New York, 1931), might be read in conjunction with Charles Augustus Briggs, The Bible, the Church and the Reason: The Three Great Fountains of Divine Authority (New York, 1892), an exposition and defense of the higher criticism. James Orval Filbeck, The Christian Evidence Movement . . . (Kansas City, Mo., 1946), is a fundamentalist defense. A survey of revivalism is William G. McLoughlin, Jr., Modern Revivalism: Charles Grandison Finney to Billy Graham (New York, 1959). The movement resulting in the institutionalized church, especially in its theology and social theory, is traced in Charles Howard Hopkins, The Rise of the Social Gospel in American Protestantism (New Haven, 1940). Related matters are found in Andrew Dickson White, A History of the Warfare of Science with Theology in Christendom (2 vols., New York, 1903); Stow Persons (ed.), Evolutionary Thought in America (New Haven, 1950); and Richard Hofstadter, Social Darwinism in American Thought, 1860–1915 (Philadelphia, 1944). Treatments of the temperance and prohibition movement, by its friends, include D. Leigh Colvin, Prohibition in the United States (New York, 1926); and Ernest H. Cherrington, The Evolution of Prohibition in the United States (Westerville, Ohio, 1920).

THE SOUTH

The South in the Building of the Nation (13 vols., Richmond, 1909-13), each volume with a separate editor, is a cooperative work with the usual high and low spots. In Wendell Holmes Stephenson and E. Merton Coulter (eds.), *A History of the South* (10 vols., Baton Rouge, 1947-), C. Vann Woodward's *Origins of the New South, 1877-1913* (1951) is of the highest order interpretively and factually. Francis Butler Simkins, *A History of the South* (New York, 1953), is somewhat in the nature of a textbook, with many valuable features from a conservative viewpoint. Valuable also are William B. Hesseltine, *A History of the South* (New York, 1936), and Emory Q. Hawk, *Economic History of the South* (New York, 1934), the latter being more useful than some of its critics would indicate. Holland Thompson, *The New South: A Chronicle of Social and Industrial Evolution* (New Haven, 1919), is brief, popular, but still enlightening. A typical product of the Southern white gentleman's interpretation is the somewhat statistical Philip A. Bruce, *The Rise of the New South* (Philadelphia, 1905).

William A. Dunning, "The Undoing of Reconstruction," *Atlantic Monthly*, LXXXVIII (October, 1901), 437-49, has been an inspiration to later writers. Among other arresting interpretations are C. Vann Woodward, *Reunion and Reaction: The Compromise of 1877 and the End of Reconstruction* (Boston, 1951); Paul H. Buck's Pulitzer Prize winner, *The Road to Reunion* (Boston, 1937); Willie D. Halsell, "The Bourbon Period in Mississippi Politics," *Journal of Southern History*, XI (November, 1945), 519-37; Willard A. Scott, *The Repudiation of State Debts* (New York, 1893); and B. U. Ratchford, *American State Debts* (Durham, N.C., 1941). On the color line there are Paul Lewinson's analytical *Race, Class & Party: A History of Negro Suffrage and White Politics in the South* (New York, 1932); E. Franklin Frazier, *The Negro in the United States* (New York, 1949), a sociological treatment; Vernon Lane Wharton, *The Negro in Mississippi, 1865-1890* (Chapel Hill, N.C., 1947); and Stephen B. Weeks, "The History of Negro Suffrage in the South," *Political Science Quarterly*, IX (December, 1894), 671-703. Vincent P. De Santis, *Republicans Face the Southern Question—The New Departure Years, 1877-1897* (Baltimore, 1959) and Stanley P. Hirshon, *Farewell to the Bloody Shirt: Northern Republicans and the Southern Negro, 1877-1893* (Bloomington, Ind., 1962) both cover about the same ground. More specialized are Dewey W. Grantham, Jr., *Hoke Smith and the Politics of the New South* (Baton Rouge, 1958); and Olive H. Shadgett, *The Republican Party in Georgia: From Reconstruction Through 1900* (Athens,

Ga., 1964). A contemporary Southern defense of disfranchisement by one who knew what happened is Alfred H. Colquitt, "Is the Negro Vote Suppressed?" *Forum*, IV (November, 1887), 268–78.

Paul Wallace Gates, "Federal Land Policy in the South, 1866–1888," *Journal of Southern History*, VI (August, 1940), 303–30, reviews the Southern extension of Western scandals. Oscar Zeichner, "The Transition from Slave to Free Labor in the Southern States," *Agricultural History*, XIII (January, 1939), 22–23, is a powerful short account. Some deviations from Zeichner's picture appear in Thomas D. Clark, "The Furnishing and Supply System in Southern Agriculture since 1865," *Journal of Southern History*, XII (February, 1946), 24–44; and Jacqueline P. Bull, "The General Merchant in the Economic History of the New South," *ibid.*, XVIII (February, 1952), 37–59. The rural press appears in Thomas D. Clark, "The Country Newspaper: A Factor in Southern Opinion . . . , 1865–1930," *ibid.*, XVI (February, 1948), 3–33. A wider view of the Southern attitudes can be gleaned from W. J. Cash, *The Mind of the South* (New York, 1941); Edgar W. Knight, *Public Education in the South* (New York, 1922); Rayford W. Logan, *The Negro in American Life and Thought: The Nadir, 1877–1901* (New York, 1954); and C. Vann Woodward, *The Strange Career of Jim Crow* (New York, 1955).

POLITICS

Autobiographies, Recollections, and Collected Writings

This paragraph is highly selective, comprising only such works as went into the writing of the book. The items appear in alphabetical order according to the surnames of the participants without comment or evaluation. James G. Blaine, *Twenty Years of Congress: From Lincoln to Garfield* (2 vols., Norwich, Conn., 1884–86); James Gillespie Blaine, *Political Discussions . . . Legislative, Diplomatic and Popular* (Norwich, Conn., 1887); Benjamin F. Butler, *Butler's Book: Autobiography and Personal Reminiscences of Major-General Benj. F. Butler* (Boston, 1892); Nicholas Murray Butler, *Across the Busy Years: Recollections and Reflections* (2 vols., New York, 1939–40); Grover Cleveland, *Presidential Problems* (New York, 1904); Allan Nevins (ed.), *Letters of Grover Cleveland, 1850–1908* (Boston, 1933); George F. Parker (ed.), *The Writings and Speeches of Grover Cleveland* (New York, 1892); Shelby Moore Cullom, *Fifty Years of Public Service: Personal Recollections of Shelby M. Cullom, Senior United States Senator from Illinois* (Chicago, 1911); Chauncey M. Depew, *My Memories of Eighty Years* (New York, 1922); Joseph Benson Foraker, *Notes of a Busy Life* (2 vols., Cincinnati, 1916); Charles Richard Williams (ed.), *Diary and Letters of*

Rutherford Birchard Hayes (5 vols., Columbus, Ohio, 1922–26);
George F. Hoar, *Autobiography of Seventy Years* (2 vols., New
York, 1903); Robert M. LaFollette, *Autobiography* (Madison, Wis.,
1911); Henry Cabot Lodge (ed.), *Selections from the Correspondence of Theodore Roosevelt and Henry Cabot Lodge, 1884–1918*
(2 vols., New York, 1925); Alexander K. McClure, *Recollections
of Half a Century* (Salem, Mass., 1902); Hugh McCulloch, *Men
and Measures of Half a Century* (New York, 1889); John Sherman, *Recollections of Forty Years in the House, Senate and Cabinet*
(2 vols., Chicago, 1895); John and William Tecumseh Sherman,
The Sherman Letters (New York, 1896); Henry L. Stoddard, *As
I Knew Them* (New York, 1927); and Andrew Dickson White,
Autobiography of Andrew Dickson White (2 vols., New York,
1905–7).

Biographies

The form of alphabetical arrangement of the preceding paragraph
applies here also: Leland Sage, *William Boyd Allison: A Study
in Practical Politics* (Iowa City, 1956); George Frederick Howe,
Chester A. Arthur: A Quarter Century of Machine Politics (New
York, 1934); Charles Callan Tansill, *The Congressional Career
of Thomas Francis Bayard, 1869–1885* (Washington, D.C., 1946);
Gail Hamilton [M. A. Dodge], *Biography of James G. Blaine*
(New York, 1895); David Saville Muzzey, *James G. Blaine: A
Political Idol of Other Days* (New York, 1934); James A. Barnes,
John G. Carlisle, Financial Statesman (New York, 1931); Allan
Nevins, *Grover Cleveland: A Study in Courage* (New York,
1932); Robert McNutt McElroy, *Grover Cleveland, the Man and
the Statesman: Authorized Biography* (2 vols., New York, 1923);
Denis Tilden Lynch, *Grover Cleveland: A Man Four-Square* (New
York, 1932); Donald Barr Chidsey, *The Gentleman from New
York: A Life of Roscoe Conkling* (New Haven, 1935); Alfred
R. Conkling, *The Life and Letters of Roscoe Conkling, Orator,
Statesman, Advocate* (New York, 1889); James W. Neilson, *Shelby
M. Cullom: Prairie State Republican* (Urbana, Ill., 1962); E. E.
Brown, *The Life and Public Services of James A. Garfield* (Boston,
1881), useful mainly for excerpts of current events; Theodore
Clark Smith, *The Life and Letters of James Abram Garfield,
Party Chieftain* (New York, 1931).

Perhaps a few items on Charles Julius Guiteau might follow
Garfield. His own story of his life appeared in the *New York Herald*,
October 6, 1881, pp. 5–6. Speculations concerning this strange man
and his state of mental health appear in Stewart Mitchell, "The
Man Who Murdered Garfield," Massachusetts Historical Society,
Proceedings, XLVII (1941–44), 453–89; John D. Lawson
(ed.), "The Trial of Charles J. Guiteau for the Murder of Presi-

dent Garfield, Washington D. C., 1881," *American State Trials* (17 vols., St. Louis, 1914–36), XIV, 1–158; Charles F. Folson, "The Case of Guiteau, Assassin of the President of the United States," *Boston Medical and Surgical Journal,* CVI (February 16, 1882), 145–53; Walter Channing, "The Mental Status of Guiteau, the Assassin of President Garfield," *ibid.,* CVI (March 30, 1882), 290–96, 303–4.

John W. Forney, *Life and Military Career of Winfield Scott Hancock* (Boston, 1880); and J. B. McClure, *Life of General Hancock* (Chicago, 1880), are campaign biographies. Of a more scholarly nature is Francis A. Walker, *General Hancock* (New York, 1894). Harry J. Sievers continues his scrutiny of *Benjamin Harrison, Hoosier Statesman: From the Civil War to the White House, 1865–1888* (New York, 1959). Other biographies include H. J. Eckenrode, *Rutherford B. Hayes, Statesman of Reunion* (New York, 1930); Charles Richard Williams, *The Life of Rutherford Birchard Hayes, Nineteenth President of the United States* (2 vols., Boston, 1914); Herbert J. Bass, *"I Am A Democrat": The Political Career of David Bennett Hill* (Syracuse, N.Y., 1961); Wirt Armistead Cate, *Lucius Q. C. Lamar: Secession and Reunion* (Chapel Hill, N.C., 1935); William Dudley Foulke, *Life of Oliver P. Morton* (2 vols., Indianapolis, 1899); Harold F. Gosnell, *Boss Platt and His New York Machine: A Study of the Political Leadership of Thomas C. Platt, Theodore Roosevelt, and Others* (Chicago, 1924); William A. Robinson, *Thomas B. Reed, Parliamentarian* (New York, 1930); Henry F. Pringle, *Theodore Roosevelt, A Biography* (New York, 1931); Alexander Clarence Flick and Gustav S. Lobrano, *Samuel Jones Tilden: A Study in Political Sagacity* (New York, 1939); Herbert Adams Gibbons, *John Wanamaker* (2 vols., New York, 1926).

Presidential Campaigns and Elections

The standard reference, of a somewhat pedestrian nature, on this subject is Edward Stanwood, *A History of the Presidency* (Boston, 1900). More comprehensive is James Herron Hopkins, *A History of Political Parties in the United States* (New York, 1900). Both become more palatable when seasoned with a little of Matthew Josephson, *The Politicos, 1865–1896* (New York, 1938). Alexander K. McClure, *Our Presidents and How We Make Them* (New York, 1900), almost belongs in the list of reminiscences. Leonard D. White, *The Republican Era, 1869–1901: A Study in Administrative History* (New York, 1958), is strong on executive-legislative relations. A special study of much value is H. C. Thomas, *The Return of the Democratic Party to Power in 1884* (New York, 1919), and another is Venila Lovina Shores, "The Hayes-Conkling Controversy, 1877–1879," *Smith College*

Studies in History, VI (July, 1919), 211–79. The threat of a vacancy in the Presidency in 1881 and again in 1885 inspired Ruth C. Silva, *The Presidential Succession* (Ann Arbor, Mich., 1951), and Charles S. Hamlin, "The Presidential Succession Act of 1886," *Harvard Law Review,* XXVIII (January, 1905), 182–95. State histories often throw needed light on local problems—books such as Logan Esarey, *A History of Indiana* (2 vols., Indianapolis, Ind. 1915–18); M. P. Breen, *Thirty Years of New York Politics* (New York, 1899); and D. W. Lusk, *Politics and Politicians of Illinois, 1809–1887* (3d ed., Springfield, Ill., 1887). An illuminating study of one election is Herbert J. Clancy, *The Presidential Election of 1880* (Chicago, 1958). The standard collection of party platforms is Kirk H. Porter (ed.), *National Party Platforms* (New York, 1924), but Thomas Hudson McKee (ed.), *The National Conventions and Platforms of All Political Parties, 1789–1900* (Baltimore, 1900), also contains much other pertinent material. Still further information may be procured from *Appletons' Annual Cyclopaedia . . . , 1876–1895* (New York, 1884–96), and Edward McPherson (compiler), *A Hand-Book of Politics,* 1878, 1880, 1884, 1888, 1890 (Washington, D.C., same dates). Sometimes one must also check with the proceedings of the conventions and the campaign textbooks of the parties.

Political Issues

The official history of the federal patronage is the United States Civil Service Commission, *History of the Federal Civil Service, 1789 to the Present* (Washington, D.C., 1941). The first significant scholarly study was Carl Russell Fish, *The Civil Service and the Patronage* (Cambridge, Mass., 1904). An extension of this, with much supplementary information, is A. Bower Sageser, *The First Two Decades of the Pendleton Act: A Study of Civil Service Reform* (Lincoln, Nebr., 1935). Dorman B. Eaton, one of the prime movers of the reform, contributed many articles and books on the subject, a few of which are *Civil Service in Great Britain* (New York, 1880); *The Spoils System and Civil Service Reform in the Custom House and Post Office at New York* (New York, 1881); and "Two Years of Civil Service Reform," *North American Review,* CXLI (July, 1885), 15–24. The account of another early agitator is William Dudley Foulke, *Fighting the Spoilsmen* (New York, 1919). Contemporary narratives include William E. Foster, *The Civil Service Reform Movement* (Boston, 1881); Richard Grant White, "The Business of Office-Seeking," *North American Review,* CXXXV (July, 1882), 27–49; and George S. Bernard, *Civil Service Reform* (New York, 1885). The annual reports of the Civil Service Reform League and of the Civil Service Commission supply most of the missing details. Frank

Mann Stewart, *The National Civil Service Reform League* (Austin, 1929), commemorates the early reformers and their successors, while Lyon N. Richardson and Curtis W. Garrison (eds.), "George William Curtis, Rutherford B. Hayes and Civil Service Reform," *Mississippi Valley Historical Review*, XXXII (September, 1945), 235–50, throws light on some of the early participants. Dorothy Ganfield Fowler, *The Cabinet Politician: The Postmasters General, 1819–1909* (New York, 1943), shows how the regulations can be circumvented. Two recent studies are Ari Hoogenboom, *Outlawing the Spoils: A History of the Civil Service Reform Movement, 1865–1883* (Urbana, Ill., 1961), and Paul P. Van Riper, *History of the United States Civil Service* (Evanston, Ill., 1958).

Polygamy in Utah had many contemporary annalists, both friends and foes of the Mormons. Among such writings are R. N. Baskin, *Reminiscences of Early Utah* (Salt Lake City, 1914); *Delegate from Utah* (pamphlet, Salt Lake City, 1881); Dyer Dan Lum, *Utah and Its People* (New York, 1882); Helen Mar Whitney, *Why We Practice Plural Marriage* (Salt Lake City, 1884); John Codman, *A Solution of the Mormon Problem* (pamphlet, New York, 1885); *Utah Statehood, Reasons Why It Should Not Be Granted: Report of the Utah Commission* (pamphlet, Salt Lake City, 1887); and H. Hamlin Cannon (ed.), "The Prison Diary of a Mormon Apostle," *Pacific Historical Review*, XVI (November, 1947), 393–409. Later, secondary accounts are represented here by James H. Snowden, *The Truth about Mormonism* (New York, 1926); Robert Joseph Dwyer, *The Gentile Comes to Utah: A Study in Religious and Social Conflict* (Washington, D.C., 1941); *Provo, Pioneer Mormon City* (WPA project, Portland, Ore., 1942); and Nels Anderson, *Desert Saints* (New York, 1942).

The general histories, autobiographies, reminiscences and collected writings already listed contain many details on the Star Route scandal, the Indian problem, and pork-barrel legislation, but one item on each might be added: Martin J. Klotsche, "The Star Route Cases," *Mississippi Valley Historical Review*, XXII (September, 1935), 407–18; Loring Benson Priest, *Uncle Sam's Stepchildren* (New Brunswick, N.J., 1942); and Albert Bushnell Hart, "Biography of a River and Harbor Bill," *American Historical Association, Papers*, III, No. 1 (New York, 1887), 180–94. The Civil War veteran's place in politics finds historians in John W. Oliver, *History of the Civil War Pensions, 1861–1885* (Madison, Wis., 1917); William H. Glasson, *Federal Military Pensions in the United States* (New York, 1918); and Donald L. McMurry, "The Political Significance of the Pension Question, 1885–1897," *Mississippi Valley Historical Review*, XI (June, 1922), 19–36. Cleveland's treatment of private-pension bills makes this an appropriate place to list Edward Campbell Mason,

The Veto Power: Its Origins, Development and Functions in the Government of the U. S. . . . , 1789–1889 (Boston, 1890).

The problem of modernizing the navy is most thoroughly discussed in recent literature in Donald W. Mitchell, *A History of the Modern American Navy from 1883 through Pearl Harbor* . . . (New York, 1946). Receding backward in date of publication, there are George T. Davis, *A Navy Second to None: The Development of Modern American Naval Policy* (New York, 1940); George F. Parker, "How Cleveland and Whitney Made the New Navy," *Saturday Evening Post,* CXCV (May 19, 1923), 42–54, the loyal contribution of Cleveland's close friend; French E. Chadwick, *The American Navy* (Garden City, N.Y., 1915), by a former high officer in the navy; Robley D. Evans, *A Sailor's Log: Recollections of Forty Years of Naval Life* (New York, 1901); Frank M. Bennett, *The Steam Navy of the United States* (Pittsburgh, 1896); Lewis Nixon, "The New American Navy," *Cassier's Magazine,* VII (December, 1894), 100–16; and Edward Simpson, "The United States Navy in Transition," *Harper's New Monthly Magazine,* LXXIII (June, 1886), 3–26.

Edward Stanwood, *American Tariff Controversies in the Nineteenth Century* (2 vols., Boston, 1903), is a thorough, protectionist, and sometimes unperceptive treatise on this much-belabored question. A thorough economic discussion is Frank W. Taussig, *The Tariff History of the United States* (8th ed., New York, 1931). Ida M. Tarbell, *The Tariff in Our Times* (New York, 1911), is a sprightly account of the legislation of the post-Civil War years. Sectional influence is the theme of Clarence Lee Miller, *The States of the Old Northwest and the Tariff, 1865–1888* (Emporia, Kans., 1929). Proof that a social Darwinist could in some aspects also be a nineteenth-century economic liberal is seen in William Graham Sumner, "Mr. Blaine and the Tariff," *North American Review,* CXLIII (October, 1886), 398–405. A recent special study is Festus Paul Summers, *William L. Wilson and Tariff Reform* (New Brunswick, N.J., 1953).

TRUSTS AND MONOPOLIES

The latest and a most admirable book on this subject is Walter Adams and Horace M. Gray, *Monopoly in America: The Government as a Promoter* (New York, 1955). Unfortunately for the present purpose, it deals mostly with recent developments. The same is true of George W. Stocking and Myron W. Watkins, *Monopoly and Free Enterprise* (New York, 1951). A stimulating but brief general survey is Burton J. Hendrick, *The Age of Big Business* (New Haven, 1919). Thomas C. Cochran and William Miller, *The Age of Enterprise: A Social History of Industrial*

America (New York, 1942), is penetrating in analysis. Louis M. Hacker, *The Triumph of American Capitalism: The Development of Forces in American History to the End of the Nineteenth Century* (New York, 1940), in spite of an ambitious subtitle, actually ends with Reconstruction, thus playing it safe. Written with more insight than documentation, and with more fairness than some recent critics have granted it, is Matthew Josephson, *The Robber Barons* (New York, 1934). The old stand-bys on railroad problems, not withered by age, are William Zebina Ripley (ed.), *Railway Problems* (Boston, 1907) and *Railroads: Rates and Regulation* (New York, 1912). For the region of most rapid expansion after 1877, Robert Edward Riegel, *The Story of Western Railroads* (New York, 1926), is thorough and adequate for a general survey. In summarized form, the material is also in Robert E. Riegel, *America Moves West* (rev. ed., New York, 1947). Some other aspects can be found in Ray Allen Billington, *Westward Expansion: A History of the American Frontier* (New York, 1949). For individual systems and builders, see George T. Clark, *Leland Stanford: War Governor of California, Railroad Builder, and Founder of Stanford University* (Stanford, 1931), no more filial than is to be expected; Nelson Trottman, *History of the Union Pacific: A Financial and Economic Survey* (New York, 1923); and George Pierce Baker, *The Formation of the New England Railroad Systems: A Study of Railroad Combination in the Nineteenth Century* (Cambridge, Mass., 1937). On financial control of the systems, there is Frederick Lewis Allen, *The Great Pierpont Morgan* (New York, 1949). Not quite as admiring of Pierpontifex Maximus as Allen, is Lewis Corey, *The House of Morgan: A Social Biography of the Masters of Capital* (New York, 1930).

On industrial monopolies, William Z. Ripley (ed.), *Trusts, Pools and Corporations* (Boston, 1905), is still standard reading. Henry Rogers Seager and Charles A. Gulick, *Trust and Corporation Problems* (New York, 1929), though primarily concerned with current issues, also has a historical background. N. S. B. Gras and Henrietta M. Larson (eds.), *Casebook in American Business History* (New York, 1939), supplements Ripley as a source book. A treatise published when the controversy of the 1880s was at its height is William Wilson Cook, *Trusts* (New York, 1888). An early blast at the Standard Oil Company was Henry Demarest Lloyd, "The Story of a Great Monopoly," *Atlantic Monthly*, XLVII (March, 1881), 317–34. Years later, Lloyd expanded this theme to cover the whole monopoly growth in *Wealth against Commonwealth* (New York, 1894). A more benign but not always approving treatment is Allan Nevins, *John D. Rockefeller: The Heroic Age of American Business* (2 vols., New York, 1940). A later and more favorable view of Lloyd is Chester M. Destler, "Wealth against Commonwealth, 1894 and 1944," *American His-*

torical Review, L (October, 1944), 49–72, the "Correspondence" in *ibid.,* L (April, 1945), 676–89, and in Destler's mimeographed follow-up. Ida M. Tarbell, *History of the Standard Oil Company* (2 vols., New York, 1904), springs largely from the various governmental investigations of the trust. Many of the books listed later in the bibliography under Inventions and Industry and Trade and Transportation tell about combination, often in restraint of trade, in the various businesses. The mention of protest literature, aside from Lloyd, should at least include Henry George, *Progress and Poverty: An Inquiry into the Cause of Industrial Depressions, and of Increase of Want with Increase of Wealth, the Remedy* (New York, 1879); William Godwin Moody, *Land and Labor in the United States* (New York, 1883); and Edward Bellamy, *Looking Backward, 2000–1887* (Boston, 1888). Some treatment of the budding utilities monopolies is given in Herbert B. Dorau (ed.), *Materials for the Study of Public Utility Economics* (New York, 1930).

MONETARY AND AGRARIAN PROBLEMS

For a good, concise general history of monetary and other fiscal matters Davis Rich Dewey, *Financial History of the United States* (12th ed., New York, 1934), is still unsurpassed. Paul Studenski and Herman E. Krooss, *Financial History of the United States* (New York, 1952), is a little fuller on some matters, but is somewhat confusing on the elasticity of the national-bank notes. Alexander D. Noyes, *Forty Years of American Finance: A Short Financial History of the Government and People of the United States since the Civil War . . . , 1865–1907* (New York, 1909), is more complete than the two preceding items. Alonzo B. Hepburn, *History of Currency in the United States* (New York, ed. of 1915), is, like the rest, a little hard on the free silverites. A much-needed new look at the currency problems of the last hundred years is Milton Friedman and Anna Jacobsen Schwartz, *A Monetary History of the United States, 1867–1960* (Princeton, N.J., 1963). Special phases are the subjects of Horace White, *Money and Banking* (new ed., Boston, 1935); Wesley Clair Mitchell, *History of the Greenbacks* (Chicago, 1903); Don Carlos Barrett, *The Greenback and Resumption of Specie Payment* (Cambridge, Mass., 1931); and J. Laurence Laughlin, *The History of Bimetallism in the United States* (4th ed., New York, 1896). Roy Harrod, *The Dollar* (New York, 1954), except for some haziness on historical details, is a refreshing relief from the savage hostility of Laughlin toward the silver men. Sidney Ratner, *American Taxation: Its History as a Force in Democracy* (New York, 1942), should make some of the farmers' objections sound reasonable.

Carl C. Taylor, *The Farmers' Movement, 1620–1920* (New York, 1953), is the first comprehensive survey of this subject. Two editorials by Edwin Lawrence Godkin, "Inflation and the West," *The Nation*, VI (March 5, 1868), 187–90, and "The Debtor Class," *The Nation*, XVIII (April 23, 1874), 262–63, exemplify what the farmers resented in Easterners' analysis of the problem. Claude L. Benner, *The Federal Intermediate Credit System* (New York, 1926), though barely touching on the period before 1890, shows what the rural class most lacked in credit at that time. W. F. Mappin, "Farm Mortgages and the Small Farmer," *Political Science Quarterly*, IV (September, 1889), 433–51, touches another sore spot. H. T. Newcomb and Edward G. Ward, "Changes in the Rates of Charge for Railway and Other Transportation Services," U.S. Department of Agriculture, Division of Statistics, Miscellaneous Series, *Bulletin* No. 15, rev. (Washington, D.C., 1901), justifies many accusations of discrimination. Lee Benson, *Merchants, Farmers, and Railroads, 1850–1877* (Cambridge, Mass., 1955), described conditions that persisted long after the terminal date. Earl W. Hayter, "An Iowa Farmers' Protective Association: A Barbed Wire Patent Protest Movement," *Iowa Journal of History and Politics*, XXXVII (October, 1939), 331–62, exposes another sort of farmers' grievance. Paul W. Gates, "Recent Land Policies of the Federal Government," *Certain Aspects of Land Problems and Government Land Policies* (Part VII of the Land Planning Committee of the National Resources Board, *Report on Land Planning*, Washington, D.C., 1935), 60–85, illustrates the evils of land monopoly.

The political and economic activities of the Grangers were on the decline before 1877, so Solon J. Buck, *The Granger Movement: A Study of Agricultural Organization and Its Political, Economic, and Social Manifestations . . . , 1870–1880* (Cambridge, Mass., 1913), is sufficient for that subject. The greenback issue has had several historians, but the party suffered from neglect until Irwin Unger published his Pulitzer Prize-winning work, *The Greenback Era: A Social and Political History of American Finance* (Princeton, N.J., 1964). Earlier efforts included Fred Emory Haynes, *James Baird Weaver* (Iowa City, 1919) and *Third Party Movements since the Civil War* (Iowa City, 1916); and Ellis B. Usher, *The Greenback Movement of 1875–1884 and Wisconsin's Part in It* (Milwaukee, 1911).

John D. Hicks, *The Populist Revolt* (Minneapolis, 1931), has long since supplanted Frank L. McVey, *The Populist Movement* (New York, 1896), as a history of the People's party. Walter T. K. Nugent has brought out an excellent grass-roots study, *The Tolerant Populists: Kansas Populism and Nativism* (Chicago, 1963), while Norman Pollack assessed their ideas in *The Populist Response to Industrial America: Midwestern Populist Thought*

(Cambridge, Mass., 1962). There are numerous official and semi-
official accounts of the Farmers' Alliances, including National
Farmers' Alliance, *History of the Alliance Movement* (Chicago,
1882); H. R. Chamberlain, *The Farmers' Alliance: What It Aims
to Accomplish* (New York, 1891); J. E. Bryan, *The Farmers'
Alliance: Its Origin, Progress, and Purposes* (Fayetteville, Ark.,
1891); N. A. Dunning (ed.), *Farmers' Alliance History and Agricultural Digest* (Washington, D.C., 1891); N. B. Ashby, *The Riddle of the Sphinx* (Chicago, 1892); and Milton George (ed.),
The Western Rural Year Book (Chicago, 1886). Among sectional,
state, and related movements are the following works: Hallie
Farmer, "The Economic Background of Frontier Populism," *Mississippi Valley Historical Review*, X (March, 1924), 406-27; Herman Clarence Nixon, "The Cleavage within the Farmers' Alliance
Movement," *Mississippi Valley Historical Review*, XV (June,
1928), 22-33; Alex Mathews Arnett, *The Populist Movement in
Georgia* (New York, 1922); Robert Preston Brooks, *Agrarian
Revolution in Georgia* (Madison, Wis., 1914); Roy V. Scott, *The
Agrarian Movement in Illinois, 1880–1896* (Urbana, Ill., 1962),
a competent study of farmer organizations; Martin Ridge, *Ignatius
Donnelly: The Portrait of a Politician* (Chicago, 1962) is an ex-
cellent biography of Minnesota's foremost Populist; C. Vann Wood-
ward, *Tom Watson, Agrarian Rebel* (New York, 1938); Francis
Butler Simkins, *The Tillman Movement in South Carolina* (Dur-
ham, N.C., 1926) and *Pitchfork Ben Tillman, South Carolinian*
(Baton Rouge, 1944); and Theodore Saloutos, "The American
Society of Equity in Kentucky . . . A Recent Attempt in Agrarian
Reform," *Journal of Southern History*, V (August, 1939),
347-63.

THE FARMERS

The best guide to the literature of this subject is Everett E. Edwards, *Bibliography of the History of Agriculture in the United
States* (Washington, D.C., 1930). Also by Edwards, "American
Agriculture—the First 300 Years," *Yearbook of Agriculture, 1940*
(Washington, D.C., 1940), pp. 171–276, is indeed brief but it is
the only history of the subject with so long a range, except for a
few painfully elementary treatments. However, Louis B. Schmidt
and Earle Dudley Ross (eds.), *Readings in the Economic History
of American Agriculture* (New York, 1925), is a fairly good substitute for a history. Fred A. Shannon, *The Farmer's Last Frontier:
Agriculture, 1860–1897* (New York, 1945), is the only general
history of the late part of the nineteenth century. U.S. Department
of Agriculture, *Yearbook, 1899* (Washington, D.C., 1900), is 880
pages of reports, statistical data, and historical articles covering

many phases of farming and research, from the establishing of a Bureau of Agriculture in the Patent Office in 1839 until the end of the century. The articles cover pp. 71–663.

General farming problems are covered by the list above. Some special side lines include Allan G. Bogue, *From Prairie to Corn Belt: Farming on the Illinois and Iowa Prairies in the Nineteenth Century* (Chicago, 1963), well-balanced and cautious; Theodore Salutos, *Farmer Movements in the South, 1865–1933* (Berkeley, 1960), a perceptive study; Frank H. Hitchcock, "Agricultural Exports of the United States, 1851–1902," U.S. Department of Agriculture, Division of Foreign Markets, *Bulletin* 34 (Washington, D.C., 1903); C. Warren Thornthwaite and Helen I. Slentz, *Internal Migration in the United States* (Philadelphia, 1934); Fred A. Shannon, "A Post Mortem on the Labor-Safety-Valve Theory," *Agricultural History*, XIX (January, 1945), 31–37, and "The Status of the Midwestern Farmer in 1900," *Mississippi Valley Historical Review*, XXXVII (December, 1950), 491–510; Everett N. Dick, *The Sod-House Frontier, 1854–1890* (New York, 1937); George K. Holmes, "Supply of Farm Labor," U.S. Department of Agriculture, Bureau of Statistics, *Bulletin* 94 (Washington, D.C., 1912), and "Wages of Farm Labor," *ibid., Bulletin* 99 (Washington, D.C., 1912); P. K. Whelpton, "Occupational Groups in the United States, 1820–1920," American Statistical Association, *Journal*, XXI (September, 1926), 335–43; T. Swann Harding, *Two Blades of Grass: A History of Scientific Development in the U. S. Department of Agriculture* (Norman, Okla., 1947); and Joseph Cannon Bailey, *Seaman A. Knapp, Schoolmaster of American Agriculture* (New York, 1945).

The adaptations of New England farming to meet or cope with Western competition receive consideration in William H. Brewer, "The Past and Future of Connecticut Agriculture," Secretary of the Connecticut Board of Agriculture, *Twenty-Fourth Annual Report, 1890* (Hartford, 1891), pp. 153–75; Philip Morgan and Alvan F. Sanborn, "The Problems of Rural New England," *Atlantic Monthly*, LXXIX (May, 1897), 577–98; Frederick Irving Anderson, *The Farmer of To-Morrow* (New York, 1913); C. N. Hall, "Some Features of Old Connecticut Farming," *New England Magazine*, XXII, N.S. (July, 1900), 549–57; Clifton Johnson, "The Deserted Homes of New England," *Cosmopolitan*, XV (June, 1893), 215–22; William Henry Bishop, "Hunting an Abandoned Farm in Connecticut," *Century Magazine*, XLVII, O.S. (April, 1894), 915–24; Charles C. Nott, "A Good Farm for Nothing," *The Nation*, XLIX (November 21, 1889), 406–8; T. S. Gold, *Handbook of Connecticut Agriculture* (Hartford, 1901); Joseph B. Walker, "The Progress of New England Agriculture . . . during the Last Thirty Years," *New Englander and Yale Review*, XLVII (October, 1887), 233–45; Harold Fisher Wilson, *The Hill Coun-*

try of Northern New England (New York, 1936); and William H. Brewer, *The Brighter Side of New England Agriculture* (Manchester, N.H., 1890).

LABOR

The classic in the field of labor history is John R. Commons (ed.), *History of Labour in the United States* (4 vols., New York, 1918–35). Volume II, after 1877, is almost wholly by Selig Perlman, who also condensed and extended the work in *A History of Trade Unionism in the United States* (New York, 1922). Philip S. Foner, *History of the Labor Movement in the United States, . . . from Colonial Times to the Founding of the American Federation of Labor* (New York, 1947), is a careful and accurate piece of writing, but omits things that do not suit the author's thesis. Of a general nature also is Joseph G. Rayback, *A History of American Labor* (New York, 1959). Contemporary scholarly works were Richard Theodore Ely, *The Labor Movement in America* (rev. ed., New York, 1890) and *Problems of Today* (New York, 1888). The old labor leader George E. McNeill also had noted academic aid in editing *The Labor Movement: The Problem of Today* (New York, 1887). Frank Tracy Carlton, in *The History and Problems of Organized Labor* (rev. ed., Boston, 1920), is at his best on the problems.

The standard history of the Knights of Labor is Norman J. Ware, *The Labor Movement in the United States, 1860–1895; A Study in Democracy* (New York, 1929). Terence V. Powderly, *Thirty Years of Labor, 1859–1889* (Columbus, Ohio, 1890), is the Grand Master's defense of his own activities. Henry J. Browne, *The Catholic Church and the Knights of Labor* (Washington, D.C., 1949), presents the point of view of Powderly's church. The earliest official account of the A. F. of L. is Peter J. McGuire, *The Amercian Federation of Labor: Its History and Aims* (New York, 1893). For more complete works, see Lewis L. Lorwin, *The American Federation of Labor* (Washington, 1933); Samuel Gompers, *Seventy Years of Life and Labor: An Autobiography* (2 vols., New York, 1925); Bernard Mandel, *Samuel Gompers: A Biography* (Yellow Springs, Ohio, 1963); Philip Taft, *The A. F. of L. in the Time of Gompers* (New York, 1957); and Leo Wolman, *The Growth of Trade Unions* (New York, 1924). Eugene Staley, *History of the Illinois State Federation of Labor* (Chicago, 1930), deals with an affiliate of the international body, at the center of disturbances in the 1880s. A leading labor weekly at the same time was *John Swinton's Paper* (New York, 1883–87). Excellent on the struggle between the Knights of Labor and the A. F. of L. is Gerald N. Grob, *Workers and Utopia: A*

Study of Ideological Conflict in the American Labor Movement, 1865–1900 (Evanston, Ill., 1961).

The background for the immigrant in labor history is in Carl Wittke, *We Who Built America: The Saga of the Immigrant* (New York, 1939); George M. Stephenson, *A History of American Immigration, 1820–1924* (Boston, 1926); and Marcus Lee Hansen, *The Mingling of the Canadian and American Peoples* (New Haven, 1940), completed by John Bartlett Brebner. An account of one of the immigrant's experiences in American sweatshops is Anzia Yerzierska, "How I Found America," *The American Mind*, Harry R. Warfel, Ralph H. Gabriel, and Stanley T. Williams, eds. (New York, 1937), pp. 1050–56. The Oriental phase has many expositions, important among them being Mary Roberts Coolidge, *Chinese Immigration* (New York, 1909); Elmer Clarence Sandmeyer, *The Anti-Chinese Movement in California* (Urbana, Ill., 1939); Hiram S. Maxim, "The Chinese and the South African Labor Question," *Fortnightly Review*, LXXIX (March, 1903), 506–11, drawing illustrations from the American scene; Tso-Chien Shen, *What Chinese Exclusion Really Means* (New York, 1942); Tien-Lu Li, *Congressional Policy of Chinese Immigration* (Nashville, 1916); and Arthur H. Smith, *China and America Today* (New York, 1907).

Responsibility for violence in labor-management disputes is dispassionately assessed in Louis Adamic, *Dynamite* (New York, 1931). See also Robert Hunter, *Violence and the Labor Movement* (New York, 1914). Anthony Bimba, *The Molly Maguires* (New York, 1932), tries too hard to prove that the victims of Gowen and the Pinkertons were all doctrinaire strivers for a classless society. Much more reasonable, yet doing full justice to the Mollies, if there was such an organized group, are Walter J. Coleman, *The Molly Maguire Riots: Industrial Conflict in the Pennsylvania Coal Region* (Richmond, 1936); then, in some respects still better, Marvin W. Schlegel, *Ruler of The Reading: The Life of Franklin B. Gowen, 1836–1889* (Harrisburg, Pa., 1947); and perhaps the best, Wayne G. Broehl, Jr., *The Molly Maguires* (Cambridge, Mass., 1964). One may look in vain in Richard Wilmer Rowan, *The Pinkertons: A Detective Dynasty* (Boston, 1931), for any disreputable activity of that agency; it bears all the earmarks of a company-inspired document. The use of federal troops to help the employers suppress strikes is expounded in Frederick T. Wilson, "Federal Aid in Domestic Disturbances, 1787–1903," *Senate Document* No. 209, 57 Cong., 2 Sess. (1903); and Bennett Milton Rich, *The Presidents and Civil Disorder* (Washington, D.C., 1941). The emergency first causing governors to call for such aid is covered in Gerald N. Grob, "The Railroad Strikes of 1877," *Midwest Journal of Political Science*, VI (Winter, 1954–55), 16–34; Pennsylvania General

Assembly, *Report of the Committee Appointed to Investigate the Railroad Riots in July, 1877* (Harrisburg, 1878); Adjutant General of Pennsylvania, *Annual Report, 1877* (Harrisburg, 1878); Philip A. Slaner, "The Railroad Strikes of 1877," *Marxist Quarterly*, I (April–June, 1937), 214–36; and the vivid book by Robert V. Bruce, *1877: Year of Violence* (Indianapolis, 1959).

Accounts of the railroad strikes of 1884–88 are Joseph R. Buchanan, *The Story of a Labor Agitator* (New York, 1903); Ruth A. Allen, *The Great Southwest Strike* (Austin, 1942); Missouri Bureau of Labor Statistics and Inspection, *The Official History of the Great Strike of 1886 on the Southwestern Railway System* (Jefferson City, Mo., 1887); and Donald L. McMurry, *The Great Burlington Strike of 1888: A Case History in Labor Relations* (Cambridge, Mass., 1956). The use of boycotts and injunctions in such periods of turmoil is presented in Harry W. Laidler, *Boycotts and the Labor Struggle* (New York, 1913); Felix Frankfurter and Nathan Greene, *The Labor Injunction* (New York, 1930); John Philip Frey, *The Labor Injunction* (Cincinnati, n.d.); Edwin E. Witte, "Early American Labor Cases," *Yale Law Journal*, XXXV (May, 1926), 825–37; Walter Nelles, "A Strike and Its Legal Consequences . . . ," *ibid.*, XL (February, 1931), 507–54; and Elwin W. Sigmund, "Railroad Strikers in Court . . . Unreported Contempt Cases in Illinois in 1877," Illinois State Historical Society, *Journal*, XLIV (Summer, 1956), 190–209.

On the anarchist trial of 1886, by far the most competent work is Henry David, *The History of the Haymarket Affair: A Study in the American Social-Revolutionary and Labor Movements* (New York, 1936). The presiding judge's view of his own participation is in Joseph E. Gary, "The Chicago Anarchists of 1886 . . . the Crime, the Trial, and the Punishment," *Century Magazine*, XXIII (April, 1893), 803–37. Alan Calmer, *Labor Agitator: The Story of Albert R. Parsons* (New York, 1937), regardless of its slant, is worth cautious attention. For reliable information on John P. Altgeld the reader had better consult Waldo R. Browne, *Altgeld of Illinois: A Record of His Life and Work* (New York, 1924), and Harry Barnard, *"Eagle Forgotten": The Life of John Peter Altgeld* (Indianapolis, 1938). The case for the anarchists is best told by themselves, their families, and their friends, including Lucy E. Parsons (ed.), *Life of Albert R. Parsons* (2d ed., Chicago, 1903); August Spies and Albert R. Parsons, *The Great Anarchist Trial: The Haymarket Speeches* (Chicago, 1886); August V. T. Spies, *August Spies' Autobiography* (Chicago, 1887); and *The Accused the Accusers: The Famous Speeches of the Eight Anarchists in Court* (Chicago, n.d.). Emma Goldman, *Living My Life* (2 vols., New York, 1931), contains some reflections on the subject, while Emma herself is the subject of Richard Drinnon's

Rebel in Paradise: A Biography of Emma Goldman (Chicago, 1961). Charles Carroll Bonney, *The Present Conflict of Labor and Capital* (Chicago, 1886), covers a broader canvas. Edward L. Sheppard, *The Radical and Labor Periodical Press in Chicago: Its Origin and Development . . . to 1890* (Urbana, Ill., 1949), covers the anarchist papers, such as *The Alarm* and *Arbeiter Zeitung*. George Zacher, *The Red International* (London, 1885), considers the more pacific wing of the anarchists.

Nathan Fine, *Labor and Farmer Parties in the United States, 1828–1928* (New York, 1928), though poorly organized, contains much valuable data on the subject. For the socialist movement, the old classic by Morris Hillquit, *History of Socialism in the United States* (5th ed., New York, 1910), is no longer the final work; older works are largely supplanted by Howard H. Quint, *The Forging of American Socialism: Origins of the Modern Movement* (Columbia, S.C., 1953), and its companion volume, David A. Shannon, *Socialist Party of America: A History* (New York, 1955). Ray Ginger, *The Bending Cross: A Biography of Eugene Victor Debs* (New Brunswick, N.J., 1949), though lacking footnotes and bibliography, comes carefully from the best of sources. A European view of the American socialist and labor activities is Edward and Eleanor Marx Aveling, *The Working-Class Movement in America* (2d ed., London, 1891).

A statistical analysis of the cost of living without much interpretation is Clarence D. Long's *Wages and Earnings in the United States, 1860–1890* (Princeton, N.J., 1960).

INVENTIONS AND INDUSTRY

The monumental work on this subject is Victor S. Clark, *History of Manufactures in the United States* (2 vols., Washington, D.C., 1916, 1928; another ed., 3 vols., New York, 1929). Others of less magnificent scope are Malcolm Keir, *Manufacturing Industries in America* (New York, 1920); John George Glover and William Bouch Cornell (eds.), *The Development of American Industries: Their Economic Significance* (rev. ed., New York, 1941); and Alfred D. Chandler, *Strategy and Structure: Chapters in the History of Industrial Enterprise* (Cambridge, Mass., 1962). Albert Sidney Bolles, *Industrial History of the United States* (Norwich, Conn., 1879), comes a little too early to be of much help. Additional information appears in James Cooke Mills, *Searchlights on Some American Industries* (Chicago, 1911); Edwin Frickey, *Production in the United States, 1860–1914* (Cambridge, Mass., 1947); J. Seymour Currey, Manufacturing and Wholesale Industries of Chicago (3 vols., Chicago, 1918); *The Manufacturers' Review and Industrial Record* (Vols. XVIII–XXIII, New York, 1885–

90); and *Bradstreet's, A Journal of Trade, Finance and Public Economy* (Vols. XLVII–XLVIII, O.S., II–XIX, N.S., New York, 1879–91).

The final authority on patents is *Specifications and Drawings of Patents Issued from the United States Patent Office* (Washington, D.C., 1876–95). Among the secondary publications, Waldemar B. Kaempffert (ed.), *Popular History of American Invention* (2 vols., New York, 1924), is the one most indispensable. Other valuable ones are Edward W. Byrn, *The Progress of Invention in the Nineteenth Century* (New York, 1900); George Iles, *Leading American Inventors* (New York, 1912); Abbott Payson Usher, *A History of Mechanical Inventions* (New York, 1929); and Frank P. Bachman, *Great Inventors and Their Inventions* (New York, 1918). As examples of accounts of individual inventors and of specialties, there are Francis Arthur Jones, *Thomas Alva Edison: Sixty Years of an Inventor's Life* (New York, 1907); Mary Childs Nerney, *Thomas A. Edison, A Modern Olympian* (New York, 1934); Matthew Josephson's top-notch study, *Edison: A Biography* (New York, 1959); "The Telephone," *Scientific American*, XXXVI (March 31, 1877), 191–200; and James Rood Doolittle (ed.), *The Romance of the Automobile Industry* (New York, 1916).

Accounts of individual industries are numerous, the following ones being representative. There are many books and articles just as good as, and maybe some better than, those in the following list, but the reading of them all in order to write one chapter was too appalling a task. Howard N. Eavenson, *The First Century and a Quarter of American Coal Industry* (Pittsburgh, 1942), is quite exhaustive to 1885. For a continuation, there is Glenn Lawhon Parker, *The Coal Industry: A Study in Social Control* (Washington, D.C., 1940). T. A. Rickard in *A History of American Mining* (New York, 1932), confines himself largely to the metallic ores. The processing of coal, largely for use in the iron trade, is the subject of John Fulton, *Coke* (Scranton, 1906), and T. H. Byrom and J. E. Christopher, *Modern Coking Practice* (New York, 1910). The very general James M. Swank, *History of the Manufacture of Iron in All Ages . . . , to 1891* (2d ed., Philadelphia, 1891), and the early J. S. Jeans, *Steel: Its History, Manufacture, Properties, and Uses* (London, 1880), need supplementation from Stephen L. Goodale (compiler), *Chronology of Iron and Steel* (Pittsburgh, 1920); Herbert N. Casson, *The Romance of Steel* (New York, 1907); and Joseph G. Butler, *Fifty Years of Iron and Steel* (7th ed., Cleveland, 1923). Hal Bridges, *Iron Millionaire: Life of Charlemagne Tower* (Philadelphia, 1952), deals with the ore industry of Minnesota. Other basic industries receive treatment in J. H. Jones, *The Tinplate Industry* (London, 1914); Henry G. Tyrrell, *History of Bridge Engineering* (Chicago,

1911); Lester T. Sunderland, *Fifty Years of Portland Cement* (Chicago, 1923); Williams Haynes and Edward L. Gordy (eds.), *Chemical Industry's Contribution to the Nation, 1635–1935* (New York, 1935); James E. Defebaugh, *History of the Lumber Industry of America* (2 vols., Chicago, 1906–7); Harold C. Passer, *The Electrical Manufactures, 1875–1900* (Cambridge, Mass., 1953); and various articles in Chauncey M. Depew (ed.), *One Hundred Years of American Commerce* (2 vols., New York, 1895); Robert M. LaFollette (ed.), *The Making of America* (10 vols., Philadelphia, 1905); and *A Century of Industrial Progress* (Garden City, N.Y., 1928).

Among the histories of major industries for the preparation of foods are Rudolf Alexander Clemen, *The American Livestock and Meat Industry* (New York, 1923); Institute of American Meat Packers, *The Packing Industry* (Chicago, 1924); Charles H. Cochrane, "Past, Present and Future of American Meats," *Moody's Magazine*, V (December, 1907), 37–39; Charles Byrom Kuhlmann, *The Development of the Flour-Milling Industry in the United States* (Boston, 1929); William C. Edgar, *The Story of a Grain of Wheat* (New York, 1911); Paul L. Vogt, *Sugar Refining Industry in the United States* (Philadelphia, 1908); and James H. Collins, *The Story of Canned Foods* (New York, 1924). For fisheries, see the next section. Another industry with an agricultural basis is presented in Thomas C. Cochran, *The Pabst Brewing Company* (New York, 1946). Various forms of tobacco manufactures are covered in Meyer Jacobstein, *The Tobacco Industry in the United States* (New York, 1907); Joseph C. Robert, *The Story of Tobacco in America* (New York, 1949); Nannie Mae Tilley, *The Bright-Tobacco Industry, 1860–1929* (Chapel Hill, N.C., 1948); and Willie N. Baer, *The Economic Development of the Cigar Industry* in the United States (Lancaster, Pa., 1933).

Histories of textiles, mostly for clothing, are Broadus Mitchell, *The Rise of Cotton Mills in the South* (Baltimore, 1921); M. B. Hammond, *The Cotton Industry: An Essay in American Economic History* (New York, 1897); Melvin T. Copeland, *The Cotton Manufacturing Industry of the United States* (Cambridge, Mass., 1912); Arthur Harrison Cole, *The American Wool Manufacture* (2 vols., Cambridge, Mass., 1926); Paul T. Cherington, *The Wool Industry* (Chicago, 1916); Arthur H. Cole and H. F. Williamson, *The American Carpet Manufacture* (Cambridge, Mass., 1941); Frank R. Mason, *The American Silk Industry and the Tariff* (Cambridge, Mass., 1910); Ratan C. Rawlley, *Economics of the Silk Industry* (London, 1919); Brent Moore, *A Study . . . of the Past, the Present and the Future Possibilities of the Hemp Industry* (Lexington, Ky., 1905); and W. D. Darby, *The Rayon and Other Synthetic Fibers* (New York, 1929). Frederick J. Allen, *The Shoe Industry* (Boston, 1916), and Howard and Ralph Wolf, *Rubber: A Story of Glory and Greed* (New York, 1936), as well, for the period under review, pertain mainly to the clothing industry. A selected few other manufactures are treated in Leonard E. Carlsmith, *The Economic Characteristics of Rubber Tire Production* (New York, 1935); Edward Orton, *Progress of the Ceramic Industry* (Madison, Wis., 1903); Lyman H. Weeks, *A History of Paper Manufacturing in the United States, 1690–1916* (New York, 1916); and Charles W. Moore, *Timing a Century: History of the Waltham Watch Company* (Cambridge, Mass., 1945).

TRADE AND TRANSPORTATION

The starting point for this subject is Emory R. Johnson, T. W. Van Metre, G. G. Huebner, and D. S. Hanchett, *History of Domestic and Foreign Commerce of the United States* (2 vols., Washington, 1915). Depew, *One Hundred Years of American Commerce*, LaFollette, *The Making of America*, and *A Century of Industrial Progress*, listed in the previous section, also have a place here. A sufficient basis for an understanding of the exchanges is in Robert Irving Warshow, *The Story of Wall Street* (New York, 1929); George Rutledge Gibson, *The Stock Exchanges of London, Paris, and New York* (New York, 1889); Minneapolis Chamber of Commerce, "The Exchanges of Minneapolis, Duluth, Kansas City, Mo., Omaha, Buffalo, Philadelphia, Milwaukee, and Toledo," American Academy of Political and Social Science, *Annals*, XXXVIII (1911), 545–70; and State of New York, *Report of Governor Hughes' Committee on Speculation in Securities and Commodities* (New York, 1919).

The wholesale and retail trades appear in Newel Howland Comish, *Marketing of Manufactured Goods* (Boston, 1935); Paul D. Converse and Harvey W. Huegy, *Elements of Marketing* (3d ed., New York, 1947); Paul H. Nystrom, *Economics of Retailing* (2 vols., New York, 1915); John P. Nichols, *The Chain Store Tells Its Story* (New York, 1940); Godfrey M. Lebhar, *Chain Stores in America, 1859–1950* (New York, 1952); Ole S. Johnson, *The Industrial Store: Its History, Operations, and Economic Significance* (Atlanta, 1952); Ralph M. Hower, *History of Macy's of New York, 1858–1919* (Cambridge, Mass., 1946); Boris Emmet and John E. Jeuck, *Catalogues and Counters: The History of Sears, Roebuck and Company* (Chicago, 1950); and in certain articles in Harold Francis Williamson (ed.), *The Growth of the American Economy* (New York, ed. of 1951). For the goods handled by merchants, see John H. Frederick, *The Development of American Commerce* (New York, 1932), and George Soule, *Economic Forces in American History* (New York, 1952). Advertising is covered in a capable manner in Frank Presbrey, *The History and Development of Advertising* (Garden City, N.Y., 1929); and Neil H. Borden, *The Economic Effects of Advertising* (Chicago, 1942).

Most forms of insurance are considered in Burton J. Hendrick, *The Story of Insurance* (London, 1907); Solomon Huebner, "The Development and Present Status of Marine Insurance in the United States," American Academy of Political and Social Science, *Annals*, XXVI (1905), 421–52; F. C. Oviatt, "Historical Study of Fire Insurance in the United States," *ibid.*, XXVI, 335–58; Edson S. Lott, "Accident Insurance," *ibid.*, XXVI, 483–98; W. F. Moore, "Liability Insurance," *ibid.*, XXVI, 499–519; Shepard B. Clough, *A Century of American Life Insurance: A History of the Mutual Life Insurance Company of New York, 1843–1943* (New York, 1946); and R. Carlyle Buley, *The American Life Convention: A Study in the History of Life Insurance* (2 vols., New York, 1953).

There is enough on the surrender of public lands for railroad building in Thomas Donaldson, *The Public Domain* (Washington, D.C., 1884); "Aids to Railroads," Federal Coordinator of Transportation, Section of Research, *Public Aids to Transportation* (Washington, D.C., 1938), II, Pt. I; Henry George, *Our Land and Land Policy* (New York, ed. of 1901); and Paul Wallace Gates, "The Homestead Law in an Incongruous Land System," *American Historical Review*, XLI (July, 1936), 652–81. Riegel, *Story of Western Railroads*, previously listed, is largely devoted to construction, and A. J. Y. Brown, *The American Economy, 1860–1940* (New York, 1951), contains further information. Western railroading during the Centennial years is thoroughly treated by Oscar O. Winther in *The Transportation Frontier: Trans-Mississippi West, 1865–1890* (New York, 1964). Supplementing these are Taylor Hampton, *The Nickel Plate Road* (Cleveland, 1947); James B. Hedges, *Henry Villard and the Railways of the Northwest* (New York, 1930); James L. Marshall, *Santa Fe: The Railroad that Built an Empire* (New York, 1945); Robert J. Casey and W. A. S. Douglas, *Pioneer Railroad: The Story of the Chicago and Northwestern System* (New York, 1948), journalistic but containing some facts; and Richard C. Overton, *Burlington West: A Colonization History of the Burlington Railroad* (Cambridge, Mass., 1941). Julius Grodinsky defends Jay Gould in the not very readable but nevertheless remarkable volume *Transcontinental Railway Strategy, 1869–1893: A Study of Businessmen* (Philadelphia, 1962). None of the crop of centennial histories of railroading that came out in the 1920s is of much importance except for isolated facts, and sometimes for illustrations. William Z. Ripley, *Railroads: Finance and Organization* (New York, 1915); Eliot Jones, *Principles of Railway Transportation* (New York, 1924); and D. Philip Locklin, *Economics of Transportation* (3d ed., Chicago, 1947), deal with management.

Streetcar lines are considered in George R. Chatburn, *Highways and Highway Transportation* (New York, 1923); Edward S. Mason, *The Street Railway in Massachusetts: The Rise and Decline of an Industry* (Cambridge, Mass., 1932); U.S. Census Office, *Street and Electric Railways, Bulletin* No. 3 (Washington, D.C., 1903); James Blaine Walker, *Fifty Years of Rapid Transit, 1864–1917* (New York, 1918); and W. F. Gephart, *Transportation and Industrial Development in the Middle West* (New York, 1909). Jean Labatut and Wheaton J. Lane (eds.), *Highways in Our National Life: A Symposium* (Princeton, N.J., 1950), and Stuart Daggett, *Principles of Inland Transportation* (3d ed., New York, 1941), both contain material on the old dirt road.

Louis C. Hunter, *Steamboats on the Western Rivers: An Economic and Technological History* (Cambridge, Mass., 1941); William E. Lass, *A History of Steamboating on the Upper Missouri River* (Lincoln, Neb., 1962); Charles H. Ambler, *History of Transportation in the Ohio Valley* (Glendale, Calif., 1932); and William J. Petersen, *Steamboating on the Upper Mississippi* (Iowa City, 1937), cover river traffic adequately. Canals are the subject of some of the volumes in Archer B. Hulbert, *Historic Highways of America* (16 vols., Cleveland, 1902–4); of Alvin F. Harlow, *Old Towpaths: The Story of the American Canal Era* (New York, 1926); and of Chester Lloyd Jones, *The Economic History of the Anthracite-Tidewater Canals* (Philadelphia, 1908).

Shipbuilding and the merchant marine on the Great Lakes, in the coastwise trade, and on the high seas are encompassed by F. G. Fassett (ed.), *The Shipbuilding Business in the United States of America* (2 vols., New York, 1948); William Hutchinson Rowe, *The Maritime History of Maine: Three Centuries of Shipbuilding & Seafaring* (New York, 1948); Norman Beasley, *Freighters of Fortune: The Story of the Great Lakes* (New York, 1930); *Inland Water Transportation in the United States*, U.S. Bureau of Commerce, Miscellaneous Series No. 119 (Washington, D.C., 1923); Walter Havighurst, *The Long Ships Passing: The Story of the Great Lakes* (New York, 1942); James Cooke Mills, *Our Inland Seas: Their Shipping and Commerce for Three Centuries* (Chicago, 1910); and John G. B. Hutchins, *The American Maritime Industries and Public Policy, 1789–1914; An Economic History* (Cambridge, Mass., 1941). The titles of Raymond McFarland, *A History of the New England Fisheries* (New York, 1911); Harold A. Innis, *The Cod Fisheries* (New Haven, 1940); and Homer E. Gregory and Kathleen Barnes, *North Pacific Fisheries . . . with Special Reference to Alaska Salmon* (New York, 1939), round out the maritime theme.

Alvin F. Harlow, *Old Wires and New Waves: The History of the Telegraph* (New York, 1936), and James M. Herring and Gerald C. Cross, *Telecommunications Economics and Regulation*

(New York, 1936), will have to serve for that subject, as will Marshall Cushing, *The Story of Our Post Office: The Greatest Government Department in All Its Phases* (Boston, 1893); Clyde Kelly, *United States Postal Policy* (New York, 1931); Pao Hsun Chu, *The Post Office of the United States* (2d ed., New York, 1932); and Daniel C. Roper, *The United States Post Office: Its Past Record, Present Condition, and Potential Relation to the New World Era* (New York, 1917), for the greatest medium of distant communication. The private competitor of the post office is considered in Oscar Osburn Winther, *The Old Oregon Country: A History of Frontier Trade, Transportation and Travel* (Bloomington, Ind., [1950]), and is the central theme of Alden Hatch, *American Express Company: A Century of Service* (Garden City, N.Y., 1950); Agnes Wright Spring, *The Cheyenne and Black Hills Stage and Express Routes* (Glendale, Calif., 1949); and Alvin F. Harlow, *Old Waybills: The Romance of the Express Companies* (New York, 1934).

INDEX

Adding machine, invention of, 243
Advertising industry: exploited by railroads, 163–64; beginnings of, 262, 281; by newspapers, 276
Agricultural Wheel, 154, 175
Agriculture, 28, 34; Secretary of, 140; and tariffs, 181; scientific advancements of, 184, 186, 188, 190, 196, 198; Department of, 189–90, 255; colleges for, 190, 195–96. *See also* Farming
Alarm, The, 236
Aldrich, Nelson W., 71, 100
Aldrich-Vreeland Act of 1908, 282
Alger, Russell A., 156–57
Allison, William B., 71, 118, 156
Amalgamated Association of Iron and Steel Workers, 234, 240
Amendments to Constitution: 5th, 103; 14th, 13, 19, 22, 57, 76, 103; 15th, 15, 19; 16th, 282; 17th, 282; 20th, 142; prohibition, 124
American Bell Telephone Company, 122, 242
American Dental Trade Association, 260–61
American Express Company, 277
American Federation of Labor, 216, 227, 279; and farmers, 176; and Gompers, 206; organized, 234–36; growth of, 240
American Paper and Pulp Association, 260
American party, 61
American Prohibition party, 123
American Protective Association, 205
American Sabbath Union, 11
American Sugar Refining Company, 282
American Telephone and Telegraph Company, 243
American Tin Plate Company, 103, 145
American Tobacco Company: a monopoly, 103, 248; and trusts, 118, 282
American Union Telegraph Company, 274
Ames, Oakes, 103
Ammon, Robert H., 221–22
Anaconda mines, 251
Anarchist, The, 237
Anarchists: and Socialist Labor party, 124; Haymarket Affair, 235–39; "judicial murder" of, 240
Ancient Order of Hibernians, 213–14
Andrews, Samuel, 115
Angell, James B., 208

Animal Industry, Bureau of, 189
Anti-Alien-Contract-Labor Act, 227
Antialienism, 204
Antimonopoly party, 81, 282; in 1884 election, 120, 123, 125, 128, 130
Antipolygamy Act, 75–76
Antitrust Law, 104, 120, 280
Appleby, John F., 188
Appropriations Bill, 150
Arbeiter Zeitung, 236–37
Archbold, John D., and Standard Oil Company, 115, 117, 122
Armament race, 83
Armour, Herman Ossian, 138
Army. *See* Federal troops
Arrears Act of 1879, The, 149–50
Arthur, President Chester A.: collector, New York Customhouse, 42–44; vice presidential nomination, 56; a Stalwart, 68; civil service reform, 69, 155; spoils system, 70; messages to Congress, 73, 90; appointments of, 74; and Mormons, 76–77; recommendations for Navy, 82–83, 85; on tariff, 86, 93; on public works, 89; on interstate traffic, 111; popularity of, 126; characteristics of, 140; on immigration, 208
Arthur, Peter M., 220, 230–31
Assassinations, 44, 69
Associated Press, 65, 146
Associations, trade, 260. *See also* specific name of association
Astruc, Jean, 11
Atkinson, Edward, 247
Atlanta, 83
Authoritarian religion, 10
Automobile industry, 244

Babcock, Stephen M., 188
Baker, Jehu, 145–46
Balance of trade, 281
Balloting. *See* Voting
Baltimore and Maryland Railroad, strikes against, 221
Baltimore and Ohio Railroad: and rate wars, 108; reorganization of, 113; and petroleum industry, 116; strikes against, 219
Bankhead, John H., 27
Banks: notes, 50–51; and farmers, 162, 177; interest rates of, 164, 166; national, 175, 180
Baptists, 8, 12
Batterson, James G., 263
Bayard, Thomas F.: senator, 60, 128, 130, 140; President pro tem, 71; on tariff, 80; presidential